Varieties of Realism

To the memory of my father, who imbued me
with a passion for the physical sciences
and introduced me to their metaphysical
profundity and moral seriousness

ROM HARRÉ

Varieties of Realism

A Rationale for the Natural Sciences

Basil Blackwell

© Rom Harré 1986

First published 1986

Basil Blackwell Ltd
108 Cowley Road, Oxford OX4 1JF, UK

Basil Blackwell Inc.
432 Park Avenue South, Suite 1503,
New York, NY 10016, USA

British Library Cataloguing in Publication Data

Harré, Rom
    Varieties of realism.
    1. Science – Philosophy
    I. Title
    501   Q175
    ISBN 0-631-12592-2

Library of Congress Cataloging in Publication Data

Harré, Rom.
    Varieties of realism.
    Bibliography: p.
    Includes index.
    1. Science – Philosophy.   2. Experience.   3. Realism.
    I. Title.
    Q175.H32735   1986   501   86-11748
    ISBN 0-631-12592-2

Typeset by Joshua Associates Ltd
Printed in Great Britain by
Butler & Tanner Ltd, Frome and London

Contents

Contents

Foreword

This work has grown out of a constellation of different attempts to repair the ramparts of scientific realism recently broached by new attacks from philosophers and by an assault from an unexpected quarter, the sociology of science. The defence of a generally realist position in the philosophy of science has often been called for. Each new wave of antirealist arguments has sharpened our understanding of what realism is. It is unlikely that the human delight in scepticism will ever be appeased. For these reasons I have called this study 'Varieties of realism'. In response to very diverse criticisms realism has taken many forms. Who can say what is yet in store? An early version of the ideas expressed herein has been about in typescript under the title 'The representation of nature'. Occasional references to that work have appeared, but it has been wholly absorbed into this one.

I have been helped most generously by many friends. Part one has benefited from discussions with Nicholas Maxwell, Bill Newton-Smith, David Miller and Kathy Wilkes. For part two I have had the help of Larry Roberts, David Bostock, Graham Nerlich, Robert Weingard, Harvey Brown and Malcolm Musa. Part three was greatly strengthened by discussions with Ed Reed and Marjorie Grene. Part four began as a talk to the Philosophy of Science colloquium at Pittsburgh and I am grateful to Nicholas Rescher and others for a lively and constructive session. However, as those ideas developed this section has turned into a virtual collaboration with Jerry Aronson. Part five draws on much contemporary physics, and partly grew out of physics and philosophy classes given jointly with Ian Aitchison. I am particularly grateful for the immense amount of trouble which he has taken with my education in these matters. I have also had the pleasure of sharing in seven years of instruction by Michael Redhead in the same Oxford school. John Roche has given me invaluable advice on the problems surrounding the basic concepts of electromagnetism. The views I have developed on necessity and probability in part six owe a good deal to discussions with Ed Madden and Simon Blackburn. I hoped to pass off my mistakes in physics to my friends and to keep my errors in philosophy to myself, but however willing the pupil and unstinting and expert the instruction, confusion is bound to creep in. I can only hope that the philosophical insights survive it. A few notes have been added in last minute corrections to one or two passages which are misleading as they stand or are in need of amplification.

I must also express my thanks to the General Board of the Faculties of Oxford University and to the Principal and Fellows of my college for a sabbatical leave during which the most part of this work was written; and to the State University of New York at Binghamton for the opportunity to try out much of this study on several groups of lively graduate students.

Linacre College
Oxford, 1986.

Part One

Locating Realism

Didn't the discoveries of Copernicus, or even of Columbus appear at first
sight useless and ridiculous, while some trifling rubbish written by a crank
seemed to be truth itself?

Anton Chekhov, *Three Sisters*

Introduction

The scientific enterprise has always attracted criticism. Its claims to provide
trustworthy knowledge have been attacked by sceptics and its claims to
moral hegemony have never gone undisputed. Yet if the achievements of the
scientific community are set against those of any other moiety of Western
civilization, one can hardly fail to be impressed both by the vast store of
knowledge that has been accumulated on almost every conceivable aspect of
the natural world and by the extraordinary stability and rigid implementation of the scientific morality. In my view science is not just an epistemological but also a moral achievement. In defending the scientific
community's just claims to knowledge I am also defending the moral
superiority of that community relative to any other human association.

I believe that the scientific community exhibits a model or ideal of
rational co-operation set within a strict moral order, the whole having no
parallel in any other human activity. And this despite the all-too-human
characteristics of the actual members of that community seen as just another
social order. Notoriously the rewards of place, power and prestige are often
not commensurate with the quality of individual scientific achievements
when these are looked at from a historical perspective. Yet that very
community enforces standards of honesty, trustworthiness and good work
against which the moral quality of say Christian civilization stands
condemned.

Recent attacks on the rationality of science are therefore doubly
disturbing. Not only do they threaten the trustworthiness of the knowledge

produced by the practices of the scientific community but they undermine its standing as a moral exemplar. There seem to be two lines of attack which interact with one another. The knowledge practices of the scientific community seem to be in thrall to a kind of paradox, sharply perceived nearly a century ago by C. S. Peirce (1931). On the one hand 'practically speaking many things are substantially certain' (vol. 1, sect. 152) but on the other any enquirer 'must be ready at all times to dump his whole cartload of beliefs, the moment experience is set against them' (vol. 1, sect. 55). In response to classical scepticism Peirce insists that there can only be real doubt when a person doubts 'because he has positive reason for it . . .' (vol. 5, sect. 265). In short 'even though we tell ourselves we are not sure, we cannot clearly see how we fail of being so' (vol. 4, sect. 62). Cheryl Misak (1986), to whom I owe notice of this aspect of Peirce's thought, sums it up nicely as follows: '[According to Peirce] "Absolute truth" is the settled belief of the community of enquirers, and "indubitable propositions are the settled opinions of individual enquirers". But no individual can be absolutely certain without "the verdict of the final scientific community" [and that we, as historically situated human beings, can never have].' Any simplistic claim to a monopoly of unrevisable and hence absolutely trustworthy knowledge on the part of the members of the scientific community must be discounted.

The more recent but complementary attack has come from sociologists interested in the structure and dynamics of scientific communities. Their works emphasize the 'discovery' that individual scientists are 'all-too-human' and that the life of the scientific community can be portrayed as a career oriented power struggle. Scientific research is not the be-all and end-all of the community's practices but is *used* by the members as a main tool in their ruthless self-promotion and careerism. A scientific reputation is a kind of symbolic capital asset which can be cashed in for various other appealing goods. This denigratory view of the moral standards of the community of scientists is itself partly supported by conclusions drawn from the sceptical attack. If scientific practices are basically irrational, mere problem-solving and if what passes for scientific knowledge is but a historically conditioned consensus, then the moral claims of the community to be the guardians of a kind of purity of practice against the blandishments of careerism and the temptations of wishful thinking are spurious. How did the philosophy of science get into this predicament?

The ebb and flow of the tide of scepticism has continued since the very birth of what we now recognize as science. The most persistent source of scepticism has been the perennial difficulty of sustaining a claim to have a reliable method for the discovery of truth and for the infallible elimination of falsehood, with respect to a corpus of beliefs about the natural world. In recent times the attack on science seems to me to have grown out of a largely unformulated intuition that much contemporary philosophy of science has been based on an untenable logical essentialism. Critics have seen that the concepts and standards of traditional logic cannot capture the characteristic features of scientific practices, and cannot explain how they could generate reliable knowledge. Most critics seem also to have assumed that any defence of scientific realism, the idea that theorizing is about the real world, is tied up with logical essentialism and with the natural concomitant of that dogma, that science is the search for truth. Furthermore logical essentialism has also encouraged the barely acknowledged assumption of most traditional philosophers of science that there is one philosophy of science, which, if only we could formulate it, would give an account of all those practices that are characteristic of the scientific community.

The upshot of these observations has been a loose cluster of ideas that mark off contemporary antirealism from older forms of scepticism. Since truth and falsity are unattainable, the community must actually be undertaking nothing but the solving of interest-relative problems. What is to count as a problem and what is acceptable as a solution are both relative to the current beliefs and practices of the community. Since the actual ways by which scientific theories are persuasively recommended are not rational in the sense of logically irresistible, any technique of persuasion can be used to try to promote the acceptance of a favoured scientific theory and the rejection of its rivals. Closely connected with this idea is the claim that there is no way of ranking scientific beliefs in any progressive order. In each epoch there is a reigning cluster of practices, metaphysical presuppositions and exemplars of good work, relative to which each scientific community judges its productions. There can be no justification for assessing the achievements of the scientific communities of other ages according to our standards. In short, the idea of a cumulative body of well-attested scientific knowledge is a myth. The more extreme among the sceptics are inclined to say we know no more about the physical world than did our predecessors of, say, 1580.

David Stove (1982) has pointed out, in an amusing commentary upon contemporary scepticism, that this conclusion is absurd. Could anyone seriously doubt that the blood in the human body circulates? Could anyone but an eccentric hold that our knowledge of the inferior planets, say that they are lumps of rock, is no better than the view of those who thought they were intelligences? Does it make any sense at all to doubt that water is predominantly H_2O? Or that electromagnetic fields 'obey' Maxwell's Laws? Contemporary sceptics must mean something other than their words seem to convey.

One way of getting at the 'real message' is to see these ideas as a reaction to an overblown form of realism. Many realists have based their defences of scientific realism on the doctrine (one might almost say the dogma) of bivalence, the principle that most theoretical statements of a scientific discourse are true or false by virtue of the way the world is, whether or not we, as limited human investigators, can know it. Other realists have persisted with the idea that the essence of scientific discourses and material practices, such as experimentation, is some abstract logical framework. Sceptics have had little difficulty in demonstrating that no real scientific research programme could come anywhere near realizing the bivalence principle in practice, nor have they had much trouble in showing that real scientific thinking could make little use of logical schemata if its cognitive and material practices were made explicit. It looks as if the work of a scientific community can be rational only at the cost of being impossible, while, on the other hand, the extreme sceptical reaction offers nothing but a caricature of what we know the scientific achievement to have been. What has gone wrong?

Each party to the dispute has, in my judgement, fallen into error. Contemporary sceptics have slipped into the commission of the 'philosophers' fallacy', the fallacy of high redefinition. By their defining, even only tacitly, such cognitive phenomena as scientific knowledge in terms of truth and falsity, the demands placed on a community which has the task of accumulating some of 'it' are set in such a way that 'it' can never be achieved. 'Look,' shouts the triumphant sceptic, 'you haven't given us what we want by way of knowledge, so scientists haven't made any progress at all!' Similarly Miller's important (1985) argument, to be discussed further in chapter 2, to the effect that there could never be good reasons for a scientific belief does not show that there aren't any good reasons. It does show that the concept of 'good reason', as it is used by the scientific and to an extent by the lay community, does not yield to an explicatory analysis in logicist terms. So to the fallacy of high redefinition, the 'philosophers' fallacy', we must add the fallacy of logical essentialism. The theory of science to be expounded in parts three, four and five is set firmly against logical essentialism. The giving of primacy to logical structures as the inner essence of discourse has had a disastrous effect in philosophy of science, vividly illustrated by the implausibility of Hempel's (1965) account of scientific explanation. The same doctrine appears again in Popper's (1959) early form of fallibilism. The endless difficulties these philosophical theories encounter are best taken as *reductiones ad absurdum* of logical essentialism, rather than local difficulties to be smoothed away by a yet more ingenious exploitation of the basic idea. Ironically many realists are not innocent of responsibility for their own downfall. By adopting the principle of bivalence and accepting, often implicitly, a logicist account of scientific rationality, they have helped to dig the pit into which they have fallen and to sharpen the stake on which they have been therein impaled. Logic does have a place in the creation of scientific discourse, but not at its core. That is formed by semantic structures, and relations of likeness and difference. A clear-eyed look at the cognitive and material practices of the scientific community will reveal that logic is a socially motivated addition, a rhetorical contribution to persuasive power.

Logic and with it the principle of bivalence migrate from the epistemology of science to the persuasive rhetorics of scientific communities, and to a place among the moral concepts that guide proper behaviour in that community. Some questions that have troubled philosophers of science can be quickly settled if this change of locality can be made to stick. For instance, the question whether logic is empirical is neatly settled in the negative if it is rhetorical. The problem of bad fit among the component concepts of a theoretical matrix cannot be tidied up by the use of the principle that forbids inconsistency in a discourse with a logical structure at its core. The usual objection to permitting an inconsistency to lie and fester in a theory is that it allows the inference of any consequence whatever, thus making a mockery of the idea of a theory as having sharply demarcated domains of acceptable and unacceptable consequences. But that kind of permissive inference is licensed only by reference to the principles of a rather narrow propositional logic. If they are not the principles that give a rigid skeleton to scientific discourses consistency may not be so obviously desirable a desideratum after all.[1] Of course, if one becomes vulnerable to certain communally supported critical attacks on the grounds of inconsistency, common prudence suggests that one's discourse should be made to display admirable logical properties. But that says nothing about its quality as a contribution to science (Knorr-Cetina, 1981).

None of the foregoing entails that logic is not a central and ineliminable tool of the metascientist. Later in this part I shall be trying to show that David Miller (1985) has fallen into into the philosophers' fallacy. My fond hope that he will suddenly see the error of his ways rests on our joint acceptance of certain elementary logical principles. Were he to spot – unlikely though it might be – an inconsistency in my discussion, I would be obliged to put the matter right, by restoring consistency. It is just because logic is a proper part of metascience that it is, within the practices of the scientific community, a part of rhetoric.

If my diagnosis is right that contemporary antirealism has been born out of commissions of the philosophers' fallacy of high redefinition, realism cannot be defended within any framework that explicitly or tacitly involves bivalence, or logicism. The project of a modest realism can only be to try to create a form of realism that is close to scientific practice and that lacks the fatal features. The argument will in the end be directed to trying to establish that existence is prior to theory, and that while no ontology for science could be absolute, nevertheless ontologies (realized in referential practices) are always, at any moment, less revisable than their associated belief-systems. As I have already remarked, and now reiterate, on this view truth and falsity migrate from the epistemology of science to the morality of its human community. The account of science to be set out in what follows is based on the thought that 'science' is not a logically coherent body of knowledge in the strict, unforgiving sense of the philosophers' high redefinition, but a cluster of material and cognitive *practices*, carried on within a distinctive moral order, whose main characteristic is the trust that obtains among its members and should obtain between that community and the larger lay community with which it is interdependent. Each kind of practice makes possible a research field; for instance, cytoskeleton research emerged out of and displaced cell boundary research, not because some ideal of knowledge had been fulfilled, but because new material practices became available. It is part of my purpose to hammer home that point, a project I began with my study of the multiple roles of experimentation in science (Harré, 1984). Science is an activity: it is something people *do*. Some, but not all of that doing is thinking, and a yet more minor part of it is producing discourses in which the results of making those material manipulations and doing that thinking are recorded. Perhaps a second 'philosophers' fallacy', ancestor of the fallacy of high redefinition, is to mistake the discourse and its properties for the practice of which it is a partial and rhetorically distorted representation. I take the problem of *scientific* knowledge to be tackled by the work of philosophers making explicit the tacit skills, both conceptual and practical, of the scientific community.

The idea of a philosophical study of the moral order that obtains in the scientific community is not new. But the significance of admitting it to the centre of our interest has rarely been acknowledged. I hope to show that science has a special status, not because it is a sure way of producing truths and avoiding falsehood, but because it is a communal practice of a community with a remarkable and rigid morality – a morality at the heart of which is a commitment that the products of this community shall be trustworthy. A first task for a moralist of science will be the analysis of the concept of trust. Science is not just a cluster of material and cognitive practices but is a moral achievement as well. I believe it to have been the most remarkable moral achievement of mankind, and that antirealism, which, like it or not, seeps out into the lay world as antiscience, is not only false but morally obnoxious as a denigration of that amazing moral phenomenon. Alongside the moral order of the scientific community our social and commercial moralities look pretty squalid. I confess to approaching the defence of modest realism not only with an intellectual interest in an intriguing philosophical problem, but with a moral fervour in defence of the unique qualities of a community the downfall of which would be an irretrievable moral loss.

My aim in this study is to show that it is far more illuminating to assume that the essences of human cognitive processes and structures are semantic networks, webs of meaning held together by ordered sequences of analogies. Metaphor and simile are the characteristic tropes of scientific thought, not formal validity of argument. We can defend the rationality of the scientific enterprise and so win back moral respect for it as a disinterested institution for the garnering of trustworthy knowledge, which the scientific community is in danger of losing, if we tackle the problem of understanding scientific practices, both material and cognitive, without the assumption of logical essentialism.

1

Science as a Communal Practice

The sociological stance

The most remarkable advance in our understanding of the cluster of diverse practices we call 'science' has come about through the realization that scientific work is done by a socially structured community of men and women. The science we consume, so to speak, is the final product of the complex interplay of social forces and cognitive and material practices. For those whose philosophy of science is but the result of the analysis of printed scientific texts, the illusionist trick of the scientific community in concealing the scaffolding behind a rhetoric of superior rationality has been almost wholly successful. The fact that people grub around in laboratories trying to make things work, that they busy themselves in the search for specimens and so on, is concealed in such concepts as 'basic statements' and 'observation languages'. In the course of this work I shall try to disentangle the various strands that go towards the creation of a discourse that presents publicly trustworthy knowledge. The discourses of scientists will not be taken for granted as the given objects of study, but rather as objects of interest in themselves, whose provenance is a matter for philosophical investigation. At the same time, as I have suggested, science is not only the major intellectual achievement of mankind but also its most remarkable moral order. The fact that science is marked with its human origin will turn out to be no good ground for the current wave of scepticism.

The first impulse imparted to the philosophy of science by the realization that science was the work of a community of persons, rather than the clean-cut product of the working of an abstract and perfectible 'logic engine', was a shift towards relativism. What was to count as an established fact was seen to be relative to the established meaning of the terms in which it was expressed, which was itself historically conditioned by the beliefs of the community. It was further claimed that the transition from one system of beliefs to another was accomplished by social rather than by rational processes. For some authors it seemed to be assumed that a transition to a new system of belief could not be rational if powered by social forces. It is precisely this assumption that I shall be challenging in this work. Sociologists were familiar with these ideas since Mannheim's (1960) proposal for a sociology of knowledge. Philosophers were first acquainted with them through the writings of T. S. Kuhn (1962), though these were largely a reworking of the insights of Ludwig Fleck (1935), against a renovated background of dramatic historical examples. In what follows I shall eschew Kuhn's loose terminology of 'paradigms', revolutionary and normal science', etc. , and return to the concepts of Fleck.

Recently a still more profound insight into the relationship between the scientific community and its product 'scientific knowledge' has come from the application of an analogue of Marxist political analysis to the activities of the community. We start with the banal idea that a community exists for the manufacture of a certain class of products. The deep insight comes from applying the principle that the social organization of the community derives from the nature of the product and the consequential necessities of the process of its manufacture. The social motor that drives the system of production is not the desire to fill the world with these products, but the urge to accumulate something analogous to capital. Just as the 'logic of capital' drives the economic production system, so the 'logic of something-analogous-to-capital' will be seen to drive the scientific production system.

What does the scientific community produce? The naïve answer is 'Truth'. But at least since the days of David Hume we know that answer will not do, unless the notion of 'truth' is radically downgraded. Scientific method cannot produce 'Truth'. But turn an innocent eye on the doings of the science tribe and the answer is obvious. The community exists to produce *writings*. Libraries, studies, bookshops and the like are filled with the products of the scientific community. This document you have in your hand is just such another. As products these writings have a certain form. They are ordered in accordance with certain public standards of rationality. They are decorated with 'data', and they are signed. The class structure and interclass dialectic of the scientific community must be such as will enable the production of documents in this form. The middle classes of the tribe work to import 'logic' into the writings. The lower classes, those we see as laboratory technicians, graduate students, explorers, and the like work to produce the inscriptions we call 'experimental (or observational) data', while the upper classes exist primarily as repositories of social prestige, and are needed to put their names to the writings. These features of the work of the scientific community can be discussed without paying any attention to the content of the writing it produces.

But what fuels this engine? The 'symbolic capital' of the science tribe is 'reputation'. The 'logic' of reputation is similar to that of the monetary capital that powers the engine of material production. If the product of a subgroup of the community is acceptable to the community at large, then the manufacturer's reputation is enhanced. That enlarged reputation can be used to improve facilities, to acquire the grants necessary to hire more staff and so on. And this leads to increased production of high-quality goods, yet further enhancing reputation. Just as in the case of monetary capital the logic of scientific reputation is to feed on itself to produce more of itself. The product is a kind of incidental spin-off of the real core of the process. Now the explanation of the class dialectic and the division of labour becomes clear. The upper classes already have capital (reputation) which is invested in new products when the research director puts his name to a piece of work. The other names on the published paper identify members of the middle classes, who begin to accumulate capital for themselves if the product is successful, that is if the paper is widely cited. Eventually they may be able to set up their own firms, say as professors in provincial universities. The laboratory technicians who contribute the 'data' are as anonymous as the production-line workers of a great car plant.

The analysis of social microstructure I have just outlined runs somewhat counter to the sociology of knowledge as it is practised by adherents of the 'Edinburgh strong programme' (cf. Barnes, 1977). That programme is based on the idea that aspects, perhaps all aspects of knowledge-garnering by a scientific community, including what knowledge itself is taken to be, can be explained by reference to social causes and influences. But in the writings of the 'Paris' school (cf. Latour and Woolgar, 1979) the causal relationship is reversed. The social microstructure of science is induced by properties of the scientific product. By 'induced' I mean brought about by a very complex interplay of causal processes and semantic influences. Latour's researches demonstrate how the social structure of the scientific community is what it is, so as to produce texts of a certain form. The direction of influence is from text to microstructure. This does not preclude the possibility of there being a further sociological explanation for the forms taken by scientific texts.

The sociological explanation of the form of the texts which itself influences the social structure of the community that exists to produce such writings, turns on the study of tasks typical of the middle classes of that community. Their task is the insertion of the logical properties of the text. According to the 'Paris' school, logic is added to a text to prepare for and to deal with those public debates through which the community determines the fate of the text. Among the conventions of the debate are rights to make accusations of illogic. But according to this way of looking at the matter the logical properties of a scientific discourse are rhetorical and do not contribute, except marginally, to its epistemic value as science, in so far as that value can be divorced from community evaluations within the context of the conventions of debate. I find myself in substantial agreement with this position. Throughout this book I shall be returning to a critical assessment of logical essentialism, the idea that the essences of scientific discourses and practices are logical structures. The transposition of logic from epistemically significant inner essence to socially motivated rhetorical device is very much in keeping with my general theme of anti-essentialism. In so far as this little work itself is logically coherent it is the result of a fear of accusations of illogic, rather than the effect of any conviction that logic can reveal that which informed intuition cannot.

Looked at from the point of view of rhetoric methodology includes not only the doing of experiments to swell one's repertoire of anecdotes to display one's own ingenuity and to denigrate the cleverness or skill of one's rivals, but also the provision of 'rational' arguments for use in those communities where that literary style is valued. (Perhaps a difference in the rhetorical conventions is part of the barrier that is alleged to separate politicians and scientists.) But methodology must also include the ways by which a power-base can be secured in the expressive order of the community, from which one can speak and write with the authority of reputation. This has been well described by Bourdieu as the accumulation of symbolic capital. Contrary to the views of the Edinburgh school the anthropological stance to the understanding of science shows that it is not so much that there are social influences on the beliefs that are shared by moieties of the community, but that the securing of belief is a social activity, conducted within the rhetorical conventions of one's community and with whatever social power one can accumulate.

There is now a considerable literature in this style, some of it of great subtlety (cf. the overviews by Overington, 1979, and Manicus and Rosenberg, 1985). But even within this framework there remains an unanswered question. Why are the products of the scientific community marketable? Until this question is answered we cannot begin to understand why the production of scientific writings enhances reputation. We must raise the issue of quality. Why are some writings worthless and others valued? An obvious answer could be: some writings express false or ill-founded beliefs and others true or well-founded beliefs. But we know already from the tradition, that we can never know whether a belief about the behaviour and nature of natural objects is really true or really false. Many beliefs which have seemed to be true have come to be thought false, and some which have been thought to be obviously false have come to seem to be true. There *is* quality control in the manufactories of the science tribe but it cannot be summed up in such a naïve principle as 'Accept the true and reject the false'.

The scientific community exercises quality control over its products, not by the analogue of market forces, but by the informal yet rigorous maintenance of a moral order. To make a claim to knowledge on what the community takes to be inadequate grounds is a venial sin. But to make up data without basing it on experimental or observational procedures, as Sir Cyril Burt is alleged to have done, or to ignore or suppress whole clusters of experiments that 'went wrong', as Millikan seems to have done (Holton, 1981), is a mortal sin. Conceived in the moral order, these failings are as fatal to scientific reputation as the disclosure of embezzlement is fatal to a man's financial credit. A certain kind of trust has been broken.

To trust someone is to be able to rely on them in the matter in question. If the scientific moral order is to be analysed in terms of trust, apropos of what is reliability in question? It can be nothing but the quality of the goods. The moral order obtaining in the science tribe sees to it that quality is maintained. People do not produce shoddy or dishonest work, not just because of the social power of the community to withdraw its respect and cancel a reputation, but because as members of that community they subscribe to its moral order. I shall be proposing that quality is defined *for the moral order* in terms of the unattainable virtues of the achievement of truth and the avoidance of falsity. The community's practices involve weaker but more subtle standards of value.

These actual standards of value are closely tied up with the idea of mutual trust. They invoke a certain measure of public reliability. Scientists believe that things personally unknown to them are as *another scientist* says they are. And this trust is itself based upon shared standards of work and adherence to the common moral order. 'Seek truth and eschew falsehood' is not a methodological principle but a moral injunction. It has to do with the conditions under which trust is maintained. Trust is not maintained by telling each other only literal truths. Under that constraint the members of the community would perforce remain forever silent. It is enough that they tell each other what they honestly believe to be the truth.

For there to be public reliability something must exist independently of whomsoever first found it. And the language in which discoveries, insights, judgements and so on are mutually communicated must, by the same token, be meaningful independently of the particular individual who uses it. Whether there could be a scientific language which was meaningful independently of any community and its beliefs is a large speculation. The version of realism to be defended in this work does not depend upon it. The fact that scientific descriptions and explanations are not free of influences from the values and interests of the community in which they are promulgated does not make them untrustworthy. At most it warns us that any view is liable to that partiality that comes from conscious or unconscious selection from the myriad of matters upon which an opinion depends. Recent work in the sociology of science has shown with a wealth of detail that the standards of the assessment of the worth of scientific products are located in and peculiar to quite specific communities. This is the phenomenon of 'indexicality'. Science is a communal practice with communal standards of good work. But, as I have argued, these practical standards – what is to count as a pure sample, for instance – are embodied in a strict moral code, which is enforced over *all* the communities which lay claim to be part of the larger social world of science.

Why do these communities have just this moral code or some variant of it? The answer can be found in the fact that the product of these communities, scientific knowledge, is itself defined in moral terms. It is that knowledge upon which one can rely. That reliance might be existential, concerning what there is or might be, or it might be practical, concerning what can and cannot be done, or both. The moral quality of the product comes through clearly in the kind of outrage felt by the community at the disclosure of scientific fraud. It is not just that unreliable information has been promulgated, but that the trustworthiness of the scientific community has been called into question, even if only momentarily. The Burt scandal was morally double-edged. On the one hand there was the damage done to innocent children by an education system based on inaccurate psychological premises. On the other was the damage done to the moral standing of the scientific community by the disclosure that one of its prominent members was probably dishonest, relative to the community's own standards. The practical reliability of scientific knowledge is required to sustain its moral quality. So the way is open for a *non-sociological explanation* of why adherence to the moral code of scientific practice generally results in communal products which possess the moral quality, trustworthiness, upon which the further existence of the community depends. Trustworthiness is not just a moral quality. It is also an epistemic standard. The task of the philosophy of science is now defined. Those who suppose that the sociology of science pre-empts all philosophical questions concerning the methodology of science have simply misunderstood the significance of the indexicality of communal standards, and this includes some sociologists of science (cf. again the excellent summary by Overington, 1979). Other communities, for instance religious orders, do not enforce *that* moral order because they are not in the business of producing practically reliable scientific knowledge.

Given the massive amount of research on these matters, it would be unwise to dispute that there are social influences on what people take themselves to know. There are two questions, on the answers to which the fate of scientific realism hangs.

1   Can it be demonstrated that what we believe is produced by social influences alone? It seems clear from the summary of the strong programme by Manicus and Rosenberg that no one seriously subscribes to that view now. Manicus and Rosenberg seem to be saying that 'belief is the causal product of a variety of mechanisms, physical, psychological and sociological' (p. 85).

2   Can social influences be distinguished from influences that stem from the state of the physical or other relevant world? If we cannot make the distinction the only possible outcome is scepticism. If there are real-world influences we cannot pick them out and so can make no empirical assessment of beliefs, however imperfect. If we can make the distinction then scientific realism is possible and the strong programme ceases to be a threat to a suitably updated version of the traditional account of science. It is impossible to tell on which side Manicus and Rosenberg take their stand, but it easy to see to which of these positions the proponents of the strong programme are committed. Barnes (1977) and Bloor (1976), in trying to prove the strong programme empirically offer historical examples in which they claim to identify the social influences on scientific beliefs and their assessment. Presumably *they* can make the distinction! If they can, so can we lesser mortals, and scientific realism is restored. If the distinction cannot be made the strong programme cannot be proved; but if the distinction can be made the strong programme is weakened so that it fails to sociologize the philosophy of science.

Can we delete the social influences on belief one by one, leaving behind a proportionately richer but never wholly pure set of influences deriving, even if obscurely, from the physical world? Paradoxically this is just what the study of the sociology of knowledge can do for us. A successful exercise of that discipline does not lead to pessimistic relativism, but it supports an optimistic yet modest realism. It may be that one must concede some restrictions on the extent to which the programme of recognizing and purging social influences on science can be achieved. A philosopher of science is also a member of a culture-circle (or a 'thought-collective', to use Fleck's felicitous phrase). Such a person has an ideological basis to all their thought, and perhaps no one is capable of making the roots of their beliefs wholly explicit. There may even be an indefinite regress of presuppositions to be revealed, and who is to say that a recognizable Collingwoodian absolute presupposition will always be revealed after a finite number of steps? But retrospectively, once the ideology of the thinkers no longer provides the underpinnings of their thought and material practices, the programme might be realized. Yet how can we say that, detached from those underpinnings, we, their successors, are really reproducing *their* thought and practices? Nevertheless it does remain true to say that the more skilled one is in the sociology of knowledge the more one is capable of deleting just those influences that traditional philosophy of science overlooked. But that programme can never be fully carried out, or at least no one could know that it had been.

A defence even of the modest realism to be advocated in this work requires that the sociological reduction of epistemology is halted somewhere short of an 'absolute' relativism. To defend modest realism one does not have to be able to eliminate social influences once for all and globally from one's account of the practice of science. All one needs is a cluster of concepts and a methodology for eliminating them case by case. For example, one can see how to dismantle radical behaviourism by eliminating the ideological and philosophical (positivist) elements from the total doctrine, leaving a tiny core of phenomena, the artefacts generated by the Skinner box. Nor does one need a technique which is guaranteed to eliminate all reference to non-real-world influences from any one case. All that is needed is that some should be recognizable and eliminable. As in any other field of human endeavour one can look to progress to eliminate more. Indeed, once the metaphysical and political background of the community has changed, that which is recognized as 'genuine' from the science of the past, that is belief whose ground does seem to be worldly phenomena, while involving one's own ideology, is at least partially disinfected of that of the past.

A nice example of research through which social and political influences can be disentangled from the traditional scientific-empirical reasons for belief is to be found in Gereon Walters's (1985) recent unveiling of the story of Mach's alleged rejection of relativity. It turns out that Ernst Mach did not reject relativity theory. His son, Ludwig, however, did, passing off the preface to the posthumous edition of the second volume of Mach's *Optics* as his father's own. Walters (1985) has shown, in detail, how Ludwig Mach slid into a rejection of relativity theory to resolve his financial problems. A certain Herr Pfaff offered to finance the posthumous publication of the latter part of the *Optics*. Pfaff, probably animated by anti-Semitism, was strongly opposed to relativity theory. It seems beyond reasonable doubt that Ludwig Mach's 'conversion' and subsequent forging of the anti-relativistic preface of the second volume was animated by the chance of financial gain. Seeing this against the background of the disturbances in German society during and immediately after the First World War puts the story within a broader sociological framework. The influences cited in this story stand out sharply against the kind of reasons put forward by Einstein in his letter of 13 June 1913. He tells Mach that 'Next year, at the solar eclipse, it should turn out whether the light rays are bent by the sun, whether, in other words, the basic and fundamental assumption of the equivalence of accelerated reference frames and the gravitational field really holds.'

In considering the value of sociological analyses of the conditions under which scientific beliefs are formed and communally accepted or rejected, one must admit that there are real-world influences on belief. One could hardly claim that states of the world caused correct beliefs since those states are also implicated in false beliefs too. Moreover it is surely equally necessary to admit that there are cognitive influences on the way one reads instruments, assesses what one has seen, heard, and so on. The modern descendants of Ludwig Fleck have done a service in reminding the scientific community that there are also social influences on what members believe and how they assess the beliefs and proposals of others. But the *point* of scientific research is to minimize the latter. The community reckons, over the years, to distinguish and separate off those influences which the commonsense conception of science would regard as extraneous.

Under the blue flag

Polanyi (1962) was one of the first to promote the idea of science as the practice of a community of scientists, a collective whose daily activities were dominated by a moral order. By virtue of adherence to that moral order the community produces 'science', that is trustworthy beliefs about nature presented in an esoteric but public language. If we look at Polanyi's conception of that moral order in the light of the usual distinctions of politics it emerges as a theory of the right. It recommends respect for an elite and it celebrates the conservation of tradition. But unlike some forms of rightist politics it is not an individualist doctrine. On the one hand society exists to provide support for those individual passions the indulgence of which leads to science. But on the other those passions are productive only when they arise within a framework of shared tacit assumptions which create a community of scientists.

Bacon too thought of the scientific community as defined by adherence to a common moral order, but it was not independent of the moral and political aspirations of society at large. The moral value of the pursuit of scientific knowledge came from the value of the general social utility promoted by its achievement. So far as I know Polanyi's idea that the scientific community was built around an autonomous moral order was something new – though the idea has become a commonplace of the discussion of scientific communities since his time, often without acknowledgement of his priority.

Furthermore, in somewhat the way that the current 'Paris' school of the sociology of science derives the social structure of the scientific community and its moral order from the necessities for the production of scientific texts, Polanyi sets out to derive the moral order of the scientific community as he sees it from his conception of the nature of scientific knowledge. In the next section we shall see how Feyerabend derives a morality for scientific achievement which is the antithesis of Polanyi's, from his (Feyerabend's) conception of scientific method. In recent years, then we have the nature of scientific texts, the alleged steps in scientific method and the supposed character of scientific knowledge on offer as bases for the deduction of a morality.

Polanyi's first step is the elimination of the strict concepts of 'truth' and 'falsity' from our account of the practice of science. Traditional scepticism and more subtle difficulties are presented by Polanyi as showing that the attempt to define science as the pursuit of truth is unworkable, while the idea of the elimination of falsity is no better. 'The application of . . . theory to experience is open to the hazards of empirical refutation only in the same sense as a marching song played by the band at the head of a marching column. If it is not found apposite it will not be found popular' (p. 42).

The moral order of science lies in the practice of science itself. As I see it there are six elements or root ideas in Polanyi's conception of the moral order of scientific communities, and I read his enterprise as the attempt to deduce these ideas from the exigencies of the path to what he takes scientific knowledge to be. In his *Personal knowledge* we are taken through the derivation of the scientific moral order at the same time as we are shown the analysis of the products of that order as knowledge. I take these root ideas in turn.

1   The scientific community is structured by respect for an elite. A body of masters *must* exist and be respected by their apprentices because the practice of scientific research is a skill, for which the rules cannot be completely specified. It can be passed on 'only by example from master to apprentice' (p. 53) and hence the range of diffusion of this skill is limited to personal contacts. Again (p. 183) apropos of the valuation of scientific work, Polanyi says 'these conditions and criteria can be discovered only by taking a purely scientific interest in the matter, which can exist only in minds educated in the appreciation of scientific value.'

2   The scientific community is maintained by respect for tradition. 'To learn by example is to submit to authority' (p. 53). And again 'a society which wants to preserve a fund of personal knowledge must submit to tradition' (p. 53). On p. 207 Polanyi comes close to an idea of Goffman's when he says that 'adults . . . place exceptional confidence in the intellectual leaders

of a community', with the implication that 'exceptional trust' entails as its moral correlative 'exceptional probity'.

3   Tradition and the idea of an elite come together in the third component, connoisseurship. 'The large amount of time spent by students of chemistry, biology and medicine in their practical courses shows how greatly these sciences rely on the transmission of skills and connoisseurship from master to apprentice' (p. 55).

4   Those who are masters in the community and those who aspire to that status must, as we noticed under (2) above, accept responsibility. Polanyi calls this 'commitment'. 'It is the act of commitment in its full structure that saves personal knowledge from being merely subjective. Intellectual commitment is a responsible decision, in submission to the compelling claims of which in good conscience I conceive to be true. It is an act of hope, striving to fulfil an obligation within a personal situation for which I am not responsible and which therefore determines my calling' (p. 65).

5   Responsibility is a communal matter, and as such appears in a feature of the community Polanyi calls 'conviviality'. This aspect of the moral order is required partly because we must have 'shared tacit knowledge' for communication to be possible and partly because the motivation of the responsible scientist is not a matter of the imperatives of the logic of scientific discovery, but of the 'intellectual passions' (pp. 134–5). 'The function which I attribute here to scientific passion', he says, 'is that of distinguishing between demonstrable facts which are of scientific interest and those which are not' (p. 135). The 'excitement of a scientist making a discovery is an *intellectual* passion, telling that something is *intellectually* precious, and more particularly that it is *precious to science*' (p. 134). This is the motivational system that sustains the moral activity of scientific work. But what of the obligation which thus motivated we are inclined to fulfil? From the necessity of the tacit component in Polanyi's gestaltist conception of knowledge-garnering we deduce the need for consensus. 'I express what I think the consensus ought to be in respect to whatever I speak of' (p. 209). 'The sentiments of trust and the persuasive passions by which the transmission of our articulate heritage is kept flowing, bring us back to the primitive sentiments of fellowship that exist previous to articulation among all groups of men' (p. 209). At this point it looks as if Polanyi is resting his account on the commonplace that only through some primitive measure of trust is any community possible.

But the consensus that animates scientific societies as moral orders is a joint appraisal of an intellectual domain, of which each consenting participant can properly understand only a small fraction: 'this . . . [forms] a continuous network . . . of critics, whose scrutiny upholds the same minimum level of scientific value' (p. 217). But so would a consensus of knaves and fools, since the nature of consensus is as a self-sustaining commitment. Polanyi's attempt to resolve this difficulty takes us to the sixth root idea in the moral order of the scientific community.

6 Personal responsibility appears through Polanyi's claim that in understanding scientists' statements we must make the 'fiduciary transposition'. Assertions of fact must be transposed into the 'fiduciary mode'. They are to be read not as 'This is true' but as 'Trust me when I say that . . .' On p. 256 the paradoxical character of this step is finally acknowledged. 'The criteria of reasonableness, to which I subject my own beliefs, are ultimately upheld by my confidence in them.' To adopt the fiduciary mode is itself a fiduciary act. But faith in what? Presumably in the ways I have gone about garnering those 'facts' about which I, as a member of the scientific community, demand your (layperson's) trust. My sense of calling is my moral commitment to take what we would now call the indexical features of knowledge claims into account. It is the only way in which we can responsibly answer the question: 'how can we claim to arrive at responsible judgements with universal intent, if the conceptual framework in which we operate is borrowed from a local culture and our motives are mixed up with the forces holding on to social privilege?'

The limitations of Polanyi's views can be pointed out in very short compass. Without some resort to epistemology there could be no way in which the indexicality of claims to knowledge could be eliminated from science. Merely promising faithfully to take them into account goes nowhere to show that the techniques by which the moral responsibility of the community to produce trustworthy knowledge is concretely realized will achieve anything but illusion. We know that the practical utility of a technique may be based on quite faulty beliefs about the physical basis of its manner of working. I too shall, in the end, adopt the fiduciary mode. But the enterprise of this study is to try to show that adopting that attitude with respect to the three methodologies upon which science has now come almost to rest is itself rational – that is, it is a policy adjusted to what we communally take the aims of science to be. However, we do owe to Polanyi one of the first clear statements of the position from which all epistemology must from henceforth take its start: there are no sure foundations for knowledge to be discerned in some basis of final and incorrigible truths; nor can the project of building towards a terminal truth upon the basis of local falsehood possibly succeed. Neither falsehood nor truth is an attainable epistemic ideal. They are proper only for the moral exhortation and castigation of a community of seekers after trustworthy knowledge.

But something further must said about the concept of trust, which is destined to play a large part in the overall argument of this work. Trust appears in both symmetrical (friendship) and asymmetrical (child-parent) relationships. These relationships may be between people or they may be between people and things. For instance one may trust the rope one is using to climb the wall, but neither the rotten wooden ladder nor one's inexperienced fellow climber. Then there is the rather special case of people trusting their eyes, their hunches and so on.

Trust, then, is a characteristic, not of the relation, but of one or both of its members. I suggest that trust belongs to the same category of personal attributes as beliefs, though, as Judith Baker (1985) points out, trust is usually implicit. It is what is taken for granted in a relationship, whether between people or between people and things. It is usually called into question only when it is violated.

Trust is future directed. If trust is spelled out as an explicit belief it amounts to something like the conviction that the person or thing trusted will not let one down, or fail one in certain respects. How can a person fail another person? One way, characteristic of the trust in friendship, is not to offer help or support when the other is in need. Another way, germane to this context, is when the trusted one gives misleading or inaccurate information. A failure of trust is a violation of expectation, that expectation implicit in the moral order of the social moiety in which the relationship is conceived. This is why I want to treat 'I know . . .' and similar propositional operators, as performatives of trust. Particularly in the trust relations in which the moral order of the scientific community is mostly realized, such performatives, though usually only contextually indicated, are the reciprocal acts of trusting relationships.

Trust, though not itself the outcome of an act of commitment by the one who trusts, nevertheless induces an obligation or commitment on the one who is trusted. The reproach 'But I *trusted* you!' expresses the moral condemnation due to those who fail to answer to their commitments or obligations. In symmetrical trust relationships like friendship or common membership of a scientific profession, the reciprocal acts of commitment of the other member by the one who trusts are themselves symmetrical. So, by virtue of the fact that each trusts the other, each is committed. But in asymmetrical trust relationships, like that between student and teacher, the student's trust in the teacher induces an obligation on the teacher not to mislead or otherwise incorrectly inform the student, but notoriously the relationship is not symmetrical. There may be other trust-obligation-inducing relationships between teacher and pupil, of course.

Trust does not develop as the result of an empirical induction on past performances of the one in whom one trusts. It is very often role-related. It is because the trusted one is in the role of parent, guardian, policeman, research supervisor and so on that the trust is there until something happens to upset it. It is the role as much as and in most cases much more than the trusting 'look' of the other (say, one's dog) that induces the reciprocal obligation. This is why there is little room for an empirical induction in the development of trust, and why trust is often immediate and implicit. Introduced to their respective research supervisors, graduate students don't usually put them to the test to see if they are likely to plagiarize their pupils' research efforts. The role of supervisor carries obligations to care for and promote the welfare of the students.

Under the black flag

The moral order of the scientific community is or appears to be elitist, at least in one sense of that term. The valuation of an opinion concerning some matter taken to be scientific is determined by resort to expertise, which is itself guaranteed by a combination of certification and demonstrations of mastery. Philosophers of science undertook to abstract a coherent set of rules of method from successful and unsuccessful practices as these are judged by the community itself. This style of philosophy of science reached its apotheosis in the beautiful studies by Whewell in the first half of the nineteenth century. The rules of method, which developed as the dimensions and depth of scientific research increased, were treated not only as moral imperatives by the community, but also as a theory which could account for the successes and failures of the enterprise as it was defined by the consensus of acknowledged scientists. Despite the protests of philosophers such as Hume, the aim seems to have been well understood as the improving of an imaginative representation of the natures of things as they existed independently of the limited resources of human perception and manipulation.

   Progress in the philosophy of science, as thus conceived, came to an abrupt halt in the twentieth century, with the rise to dominance in the academic community of a corrupting and deeply immoral doctrine, logical positivism. It was positivistic in that it restricted the content, source and test of scientific knowledge to the immediate deliverances of the senses. It was logicist in that it confined the task of philosophers to the laying bare of the logical form of finished scientific discourse. The immoral character of this viewpoint hardly needs spelling out these days. It is highlighted, for example, in Habermas's protest against the importation into human management of those favourite concepts of the positivist point of view, 'prediction' and 'control'. It is the animating philosophy of the morally dubious authoritarianism of Skinnerian psychology.

The perception of the inadequacy of the logicist philosophy of science, as a laying down of the rules of scientific method a priori, seems to have led P. K. Feyerabend to his notorious and violently expressed rejection of the possibility of any general rules of scientific method. His point of view has developed over the years, and in what I take to be something like its definitive form, is summarized in two recent numbers of *New ideas in psychology*. Feyerabend's (1984) argument runs as follows. Certain limits, both methodological and metaphysical, were once thought to define and to protect the domain of scientific enquiry. According to Feyerabend these limits were 'introduced' by philosophers. Modern scientific thought transcends these limits. Hence Feyerabend concludes that 'a philosophy which is adapted to this situation' must have the following features:

1   It *can* comment only on 'what happens in a certain area at a certain time'.
2   It *cannot* define 'general and lasting boundary conditions for research'.

Should there still be someone imbued with the ancient ambitions of philosophy who wished to enunciate a principle applicable to all of science at all times, that principle would have to be 'Anything goes'. This argument is the springboard for an attack on the existing moral order of scientific communities. In its place Feyerabend offers his own. The attack on the moral order of contemporary science is combined with an analysis of the role of what is taken to be scientific rationality in the general ordering of human life. The moral argument appears in its most detailed form in part two of Feyerabend's (1978) *Science in a free society*. I shall set out the course of the argument as it slides from the general to the particular and back again. Since it depends heavily on Feyerabend's general arguments against the possibility of a finite and normative methodology, I shall try to highlight the use of these arguments, in order to deal with them in the latter part of this section.

Feyerabend distinguishes between the factual/normative question 'What is science?' and the question 'What's so great about science?' (to use his own words). The second question is glossed in such a way that an answer, if we could get one, would enable us to show why and in what way modern science was 'preferable to the science of Aristotle, or to the cosmology of the Hopi' (p. 73). As Feyerabend's argument unfolds it becomes clear that the preferability, if any, is to be understood along both a technical and a moral dimension. The weight of the discussion shifts continually towards the latter. It is for this reason that I include Feyerabend among the moralists of science.

Feyerabend's moral dimension seems to involve two quite different kinds of consideration. One has to do with the moral hegemony of scientists in the community at large, in that they claim to be specially worthy of our trust.

The other concerns the moral order of the scientific community. It is elitist in its preference for expert and skilled opinion over lay judgement and democratic consensus. In a later part of his argument Feyerabend extends the issue about expertise into a discussion of the relation of the scientific community to society at large. Though these considerations are very different they are closely linked. The allegedly superior methods that the scientific community has developed to ensure that its claims are trustworthy are maintained by the strictness of the moral order that obtains within the scientific community itself. Feyerabend denies the existence of such methods and ridicules the community's claims to moral hegemony.

His objections to the tacit claim to moral hegemony for the scientific community amount to these:

1   'Scientific rationality' may be no better, indeed it may even be worse, as a general ideology for regulating the relations of people one to another and to the natural world than lay rationality.
2   The claim to a special expertise made by and on behalf of the scientific community is fraudulent.

I do not wish to dispute the first point, except to remark that it is a vulgarized and crass empiricism that passes for scientific rationality in those 'sciences' that are closest to ordinary human concerns, namely psychology and sociology. Objection 2 is another matter.

Feyerabend offers two arguments for his second objection. The first is brusque, simple and absurd. According to Feyerabend there is no scientific method, so there can be no expertise with respect to it. The premise rests on Feyerabend's confidence that he has eliminated the claims of all methodological practices to stand as principles of scientific method by the use of a few historical counter-examples. But the methodological principles whose claims he demolishes are those of crude logicist empiricism, inductivism and fallibilism – but mainly the latter. The basis for the argument is to be found in the pair of 'conclusions' above: that the philosophy of science can comment only on what happens in a certain area and at a certain time, and that philosophers cannot define general and lasting boundary conditions for research.

Consider conclusion 1. One can easily raise doubts as to the force of Feyerabend's case studies. His point of view is nicely summed up in the following passage: 'there *are* methods, there *are* valuable procedures, we don't find them by epistemological theorizing, we don't find them by generalizing from historical instances, we do find them by inspecting such instances one by one, like artists, and using the new imagination created by the inspection to treat new instances in new ways.' This will not do as an argument. For a start the analogy with the work of artists is misleading.

Artists borrow 'solutions' one from another. They use their new imagination to treat new instances in only marginally new ways. The retrospective history of art tends to show up development and evolution rather than radical discontinuities. Be that as it may, the main issue must be what kind of novelty we find *in science*. There is the novelty of new equipment and its effect not only on the empirical range of experimentation but on the imagination of scientists. The Stern–Gerlach apparatus is a case in point. Then there are new effects, for instance the attenuation of viruses accidentally discovered by the prepared mind of Pasteur. Then there are new methodologies, for instance the rapid rise to prominence of the criterion of covariance under a specified co-ordinate transformation, as a necessary condition for a general statement to be a law of nature. In part five of this work I undertake to show that, novel though covariance may seem, it belongs within a general methodology through which a substantialist metaphysics controls the formulation of new hypotheses. Novelties of each kind may occur in interaction one with another or they may appear independently and have to be woven into the mesh of scientific practice. Nothing in Feyerabend's case histories shows that methods may not escalate into methodologies 'by generalizing from historical instances'. In universalist claims for fallibilism and inductivism Feyerabend has taken on some pretty easy targets.

The second conclusion seems to depend on an assumption that the putative methodologies to which Feyerabend believes he has discovered exceptions are all the methodologies there could be. But he has done nothing to show that there could not be more carefully thought-out principles which define a scientific enquiry in general than those which the successive scientific epochs have severally transcended. The discovery of such principles might be accomplished in either of two ways, neither of which has been ruled out by Feyerabend's argument.

1　There are principles that are more general than those mentioned by Feyerabend. His targets are narrowly confined to the logicisms of the alleged inductive method and the fallibilism of Popper. I cannot recall Feyerabend's having discussed *any* other methodological principles seriously. There may be principles even more general than those of the philosophers Feyerabend does not bother to discuss, but they must not be so general as to be devoid of all content. For example, there may be a way of setting up a requirement for a discourse to be a causal explanation that transcends and encompasses both deterministic and indeterministic generative processes.[1] Such a principle would realize the methodological requirement that science should seek causal explanations.

2　There may be more than one but not indefinitely many contexts of

enquiry, in each of which different methodological and metaphysical principles, each cluster of which could be taken as defining a scientific enquiry,
could be rationally defended. So far as one can judge, Feyerabend seems to
think that each research episode is an independent context of enquiry, but
he nowhere offers any criterion by the use of which an instance of a context
of enquiry is to be bounded.

I must confess to some scepticism about the likelihood of achieving 1. But if
a case could be made out for 2 then there might be a third way of doing
science in general that is neither logicist nor anarchistic. It would be
different from the only alternative Feyerabend considers. He treats logicism
and anarchism as if these were exhaustive and exclusive alternatives. But I
know of no argument in his published works which would sustain that view.
The third way would be more context-sensitive than 'frozen' science, and
yet capable of a rational defence in a way that 'open' science, which is
defined only relative to those practices which actually exist, is not.

Another argument, occasionally invoked by Feyerabend, concerns the
content of theories rather than the method of science. For example on p. 105
of *Science in a free society* he says: 'there is not a single important scientific idea
that was not stolen from elsewhere.' This extravagant assertion is used to
bolster the idea that myths and other 'non-scientific ideologies ... can
become powerful rivals to science' (p. 103). Even if acupuncture (a traditional practice which briefly, in China, stood alongside scientific medicine),
and *Naturphilosophie* (a non-scientific metaphysics that boosted the growth
of energetics in physics) are ignored at our peril, that goes nowhere to show
that the methodologies and morality of the scientific community, developed
through a long dialectic of theory and practice (and still developing), are not
the touchstone with which rational people judge the realm of the exotic.

Feyerabend's second argument is equally unsatisfactory and involves the
same trick of claiming to have established startling and sweeping general
conclusions on the basis of a few highly selected examples. On pp. 91–6 of
the work I have been discussing, Feyerabend critically analyses an in-
judicious and historically inept 'refutation' of astrology. This folly is said to
be an example of scientific rationality at work. Then Feyerabend offers us
this wildly disproportionate conclusion: 'These examples, which are not at
all atypical, show that it would not only be foolish *but downright irresponsible*
to accept the judgement of scientists and physicians without further
examination.' For Feyerabend it is not by stricter application of the methodological and moral standards of the scientific community that this 'further
examination' is to be carried out. It is to be conducted by laymen. But from
any single week's issue of *Science news* I could pick out twenty or more
examples of good, clear, morally responsible exercises of scientific

rationality. If Feyerabend's argument is supposed to be inductive then it is vulnerable to a competitive accumulation of examples. I have no doubt I can match each of his examples of shoddy reasoning with a multitude of pieces of 'good work'. But more seriously an examination of pp. 91–6 of Feyerabend's book shows that his criticism of the intellectual follies of the authors and signatories of the quoted attack on astrology beautifully exemplifies the very canons of 'scientific rationality' he purports to be deriding. It is one thing to prove that scientists are sinners – who cares? – but quite another thing to prove that their moral order is seriously defective by some more universal and humane standard. This Feyerabend has quite failed to do. In fleshing out the argument in a long footnote to p. 97 Feyerabend makes a number of further unsubstantiated remarks about what he pleases to call 'scientific medicine'. Interestingly, at the end of the footnote, layfolk are advised to 'use experts . . . but never to rely upon them entirely.' No doubt a canon of good sense, but it goes no way to support the original claim.

By way of summary we might distinguish two issues. Is scientific method (and by that I do not mean some form of logicism and/or empiricism) and scientific morality, the fiduciary act of committing oneself to make one's scientific utterances fiduciary acts, the best way to discipline a community which exists to find out about the natural world? The second issue concerns the generalization of scientific method to other fields of human interest. Would the making of everyday decisions for the general guidance of life be best achieved by adopting and adapting the methods and morality of the scientific community? To the former this book is a prolonged and affirmative answer. I leave the latter as an open question, but confess that my own answer would be a qualified no.

'A banner with a strange device'

It may be possible to agree on the nature of the moral order actually maintained by the scientific community, and yet to dispute its claim to an absolute moral hegemony in the light of some larger notion of moral worth, derived from general considerations concerning the quality of life. Nicholas Maxwell (1984) begins his argument for an amplification of the moral order of the scientific community by describing a philosophy which, he claims, is actually operative within that community. He calls this the 'philosophy of knowledge'. The nineteen theses which he uses to define the philosophy of knowledge include the telling assumption that 'at the paradigmatic core of that position is an uncritical empiricism'. Maxwell calls it 'standard empiricism'.

According to the philosophy of knowledge the basic aim of science is to produce 'reliable, objective, factual knowledge' (p. 16). Most scientists seem to believe that this can be achieved only if that aim is pursued independently of 'psychological, sociological, economic, political, moral and ideological factors and pressures' (p. 16). 'Standard empiricism' is the doctrine that 'the assessment of the results in science ... must be ... with respect to ... observational and experimental evidence' (p. 21). As a moral system for the ordering of life in the community of scientists the philosophy of knowledge justifies the authoritative character of the scientific judgements made by the community, and disqualifies the comments of lay persons (p. 25). But Maxwell believes that many members of the scientific community see the internal moral order in relation to a larger humanitarian enterprise, the general betterment of the quality of human life. On this, the standard humanitarian or Baconian view, the connection is simple: by providing mankind with objective truths, in so far as these can be attained, and thus preserving it from the pursuit of illusions and from the basing of practical policies on erroneous beliefs, the scientific community contributes, in the best possible way, to the general humanitarian aim. This can be illustrated in medicine, agricultural science, geology, engineering and so forth. Misapplications of scientific knowledge, relative to the general humanitarian aim, are failures of the moral order of the body politic, not of the moral sensibility of the scientific community.

Maxwell argues that the philosophy of knowledge is not so much an evil as an invitation to settle for a more impoverished science than might be achieved. This impoverishment can be detected at two levels in the work of the scientific community. Within the existing moral order a simplistic adherence to 'standard empiricism' actually frustrates the growth of scientific knowledge, that is, trustworthy belief. By inhibiting the speculative and imaginative extension of scientific thought characteristic of the work of the great innovators under the impulse towards a wider understanding of nature, the impulse towards natural philosophy, the broader programme of science is frustrated. This is particularly clear in those human studies which aspire to the honorific status of 'behavioural sciences', such as social psychology (Harré, 1983; Gergen, 1983). However, the impoverishment is also evident in the most advanced physical sciences. As Maxwell remarks (p. 99) 'those few scientists who prize the search for understanding above all else, and who protest [at the hegemony of simplistic empiricism] will tend to be dismissed as unscientific metaphysicians or philosophers.' Even physicists are sometimes guilty of adopting an attitude that the history of their own discipline has demonstrated, only too frequently, is counterproductive. However, Maxwell tries to subsume under the one 'philosophy of wisdom' both the morality of a science directed to the resolution of human problems, and the attitude to science as a road to a deep understanding of the world, displayed by such philosopher-scientists as Faraday and Einstein. (See particularly pp. 181–9). His argument depends on a generalization of the concept of 'love', from a supervening moral attitude to interpersonal relations, to a general attitude of reverence for the physical universe as such. This fundamental premise of Maxwell's reasoning seems to me not well established.

Apropos the philosophy of science Maxwell (pp. 32 ff.) makes the point that the standard 'problems' in the philosophy of science, such as the problem of induction, are consequences of adopting standard empiricism, not inevitable paradoxes of the search for a knowledge of nature. Though he does not put the matter quite like this, one could treat these 'problems' as *reductiones ad absurdum* of that doctrine. The failure of standard empiricism does not show that a better account of the knowledge-garnering ways of science cannot be formulated within the *moral* position Maxwell calls the 'philosophy of knowledge'. Maxwell seems to me to slip into the same error of reasoning that I have claimed undermines Feyerabend's position. Because some particular philosophy of science is objectionable – say, 'standard empiricism' – no other can be found which could guide scientists towards their moral ambition of obtaining trustworthy knowledge of the natural world. This led Feyerabend to the dramatic conclusion that the task of the philosophy of science can be no more than the cataloguing of particular and unique cases of success and failure in science, with respect to that aim. It leads Maxwell to suggest, despite his occasional comments to the contrary, that only by adopting a new moral order, the philosophy of wisdom, will the creative aspect of scientific thought be freed from the shackles of crude empiricism. But in the existing moral order, seen aright, standard empiricism is a discipline, a 'Rule', not an epistemology. In subserving the establishment of trust it need not subvert the growth of science. Maxwell is surely right to say that sometimes it *has*, but that does not entail that it must. So far the absolute need for a new moral order to hold hegemony over the old has not been established.

At the back of Maxwell's moral criticism of the philosophy of knowledge is his belief that the larger problems of human life could be solved, or at least steps towards solving them be more readily taken, if we could 'develop socially influential traditions of enquiry and education devoted to the promotion of co-operative, rational problem-solving in life'. The larger problems come down, according to Maxwell, to the difficulties people have in finding out what they value and how to live to achieve that value. But these problems appear in the foreground, so to speak, as the apparent impossibility of achieving nuclear disarmament and of alleviating famine in the Third World. Again the question is whether we need a new moral order for science, for the scientific community, as such, to promote these causes. The achievement of co-operative, rational problem-solving has been the chief glory of the scientific community's way of life. The 'political scientism' which had its origins in the Enlightenment had its high point in the Edwardian period. It can be found running through the political novels of H. G. Wells, and much of the socialist thought of the time. It was based on the idea that the way the scientific community went about its daily business, its moral order, which involved the achievement of co-operative, rational problem-solving despite the greed, vanity and variety of its individual members, made it the best possible exemplar for a new moral order for the community at large.

Maxwell's criticism of the hegemonic position of the philosophy of knowledge (chapter 3) depends on a fundamental premise, that 'intellectual priority [should be] given to the task of articulating problems of living, proposing and criticizing possible solutions – problems of knowledge and technology being tackled as rationally related, subordinate, secondary problems.' Judged with respect to this principle science departments of schools and universities are defective according to Maxwell, because they pursue the subordinate rather than the superordinate end. But Maxwell nowhere shows that the Edwardian counsel of perfection for politicians could not be referred to the scientific elite, who, were they to adopt the traditional moral order of their own community, *impartial, co-operative problem-solving* would begin to move towards ways of solving the problems of living. Maxwell has done nothing to establish that a *new* philosophy of wisdom is called for. Indeed, the current criticisms of the human sciences, that they are pseudo-sciences, arises from within the very framework of the existing epistemology and morality of science. Psychologists, particularly social psychologists, have bought a positivist myth, Maxwell's standard empiricism, and have modelled their studies on it. They have thus missed the inwardness of the methodology and metaphysics that has carried the physical sciences forward. How little physics would have advanced had physicists from Bradwardine onwards eschewed philosophical analysis of concepts or refrained from ontological speculation!The real community of scientists does not work within the myth, though it often uses it as a rhetoric. Just the same point can be made about Maxwell's claims that the lay community has failed to manage the uses of scientific knowledge and to avoid the undesirable consequences and dangerous side-effects of ill-judged applications of scientific discoveries.

Maxwell's second line of criticism has to do with the effect of the tacit acceptance of the rule of the philosophy of knowledge on the conduct of scientific research. The argument runs something like this: without co-operative rationality the 'aims and priorities' of research 'will come to reflect merely the special interest of the scientific/academic community itself' and not be 'intelligently chosen so as to help relieve human suffering' (p. 53). What would be needed to make an intelligent choice? According to Maxwell it would mean that scientists should turn from 'high energy physics, of little conceivable potential relevance or interest to the world's poor', towards agricultural, medical and social psychological research. For example (p. 185), 'according to the philosophy of wisdom [Maxwell's name for his preferred moral order] a central and fundamental task of enquiry is to promote the development of good person-to-person understanding between people in the world.' But if such research is to be promoted we had better not give up the philosophy of knowledge as the moral order of the scientific community! We know very well what happens when it is abandoned under the impulse of the philosophy of wisdom, as witnessed in the Lysenko affair, the groundnuts scandal, Skinnerian behaviourism, and many other premature pseudo-scientific or pseudo-technological follies. Of course Maxwell does not suppose that the adoption of the philosophy of wisdom must be at the expense of abandoning the philosophy of knowledge. The issue is always one of hegemony. But he nowhere addresses the source of the corruptions of science which have occurred when the philosophy of wisdom has been untempered by the traditional scientific morality. Maxwell seems to make less of the distinction between the long- and the short-term effects of the accumulation of scientific knowledge of the old fashioned sort than I believe he should. I would venture the historical induction that the long-term effects of deep (esoteric) discoveries have proved more potent in improving the quality of life of mankind at large than the short-term effects of bespoke research. The adoption of the Maxwell reform would, I believe, have a deleterious effect on the chances for the very advances in the quality of life that he (and nearly everyone else) is anxious to promote.

I turn now to look more closely at Maxwell's alternative moral order, the philosophy of wisdom. It depends on the idea that 'all branches of enquiry in the end owe their *intellectual* value to their capacity to enable people to realize what is of *personal* value in life' (p. 58). Wisdom is 'the desire, the active endeavour, and the capacity to discover and achieve what is desirable and of value in life, both for oneself and for others' (p. 66). This is said to be promoted by giving absolute priority to two 'rules of reason'. We must try to improve the articulation of the problems to be solved, and we must 'imaginatively propose and critically assess possible solutions' (p. 67). But these are just the rules which are most characteristic of the technique of traditional scientific methodology! Maxwell's 'philosophy of wisdom' is not a rival to the scientific morality; it is a case of it. It seems to be concerned with *what* research to pursue rather than with *how* to pursue it. The alternative scheme for hegemony in the management of the activities of the scientific community, the philosophy of knowledge, is no rival at all, provided we realize that it can be formulated without recourse to the vulgar doctrines of standard empiricism, doctrines which Maxwell rightly sees are morally obnoxious. The view that standard empiricism is a gross distortion of scientific method is widely held, particularly by the leaders of the 'new psychology' such as Shotter (1985) and Gergen (1983). It is very far from true that 'those concerned to develop academic psychology along rather more philosophy-of-wisdom lines are perhaps unaware of similar efforts being made in sociology, economics, philosophy and education' (p. 276).

There is a proper realm of enquiry into the basic values of human life, into what is worth pursuing and what turns out in the end to be dross. We used to call it 'philosophy'. I do not see that Maxwell has convincingly demonstrated that scientific research must wait upon direction from the philosophy of wisdom. He seems to have run together two rather different matters. We should indeed be vigilant to assess the value in human terms of the research we undertake. Rational judgement in this area is bedevilled by the impossibility of predicting long term costs and benefits. Maxwell's plea for the promotion of a different kind of enquiry is another matter. He calls for efforts to elucidate value in life, and seems to be saying that matters other than 'truth' and 'fact' should be part of what constitutes 'knowledge' (p. 201). According to Maxwell, sensitivity to what one might call 'poetic value' is diminished by the pursuit of science in the traditional way. But his argument modulates into a recital of fairly standard objections, widely shared among philosophers of science, to logicist empiricism. For example Maxwell objects quite correctly to Popper's claim to have identified the concept of simplicity with a measure of theory-content, the latter defined in logicist terms (pp. 211–13). The upshot is a plea for a more explicit attention to metaphysics in the development of physics itself. Well and good. But as I hope to show in part five, like it or not, metaphysics plays a central role in the kind of reasoning popular among theoretical physicists now as always.

However the connection that Maxwell sees between a more sophisticated attitude to research in physics and the philosophy of wisdom eludes me. Physicists in particular have, more often than not, been animated by a cosmic vision. It is as obvious in the style of contemporary physicists like Penrose as it was in the work of Einstein, Faraday or Gilbert. But this poetic vision is worked out within the traditional scientific moral order in which logical consistency and empirical support conspire to create discourses worthy of belief. Neither Feyerabend nor Maxwell has convincingly demonstrated that the moral order of the community whose life is scientific research should be revised to conform to a political ideal of a universal, non-hierarchical social order. (For a more detailed critique of Maxwell's programme for the moral reform of the scientific community, see Kekes (1985) and Maxwell's (1986) reply.)

The epistemologizing of truth

I began this part with Peirce's formulation of the situation that any defender of the traditional conception of the scientific enterprise must face. On the one hand we want to say that scientific statements are true or false by virtue of the way the world is, whether we know it or not, and that the existence of a state of affairs corresponding to the content of the statement in question is just what its being true *is* and the absence of one is what it is to be false. Yet we could never be in a position to know that a scientific statement was true. In recent philosophy this difficulty has been revived through the distinction between the truth-conditions and the conditions for the warrantable assertion of a statement. It is sometimes argued that while it is the truth-conditions which give a statement meaning (perhaps they *are* what the statement means) it is the conditions of warrantable assertability that are germane to the question of what we know.

Since Hume it has been possible to claim that there are no truth-conditions. Indeed I shall be sketching general Humean grounds for just that view below. There are no truth-*conditions*, nor for that matter are there any falsity-*conditions* (Baker and Hacker, 1983), for the kinds of statements which are typical of theories, nor are there any such conditions for general statements, whether theoretical or not. (I take for granted that, though there is no absolute distinction between theoretical and observational statements, at any moment in the development of a science some such distinction can be made.) But such statements are meaningful. It follows that their meaning cannot be identified with their truth-conditions since they do not have any. However, there are conditions for the warranted assertibility and reject-ibility of such statements. I shall be proposing a quite full account of these conditions under the names 'plausibility' and 'implausibility'. However, no combination of these conditions could replace the idea of truth exhaustively, since no epistemic property or combination of properties could be the equivalent of a semantic (ontological) property. There are states of affairs, existing independently of human activities, which are denoted by theoretical and general statements. These states of affairs, however, can be neither the source of the meaning of such statements nor the grounds for our acceptance or rejection of such statements. But could the conditions of warrantable assertability be enough for meaning? Not if their referents are confined to the states and relations among beings of the realm of actual experience, because that would lead straight to a positivistic reduction, contrary to realism. However when we do come to look closely at the conditions for warrantable assertability or of rejection idealized from scientific practice, we shall find that these have just the kind of complexity that permits meaning to enlarge beyond the deliverances of perception to include concepts of beings which are not able to be perceived by any human observer.

Some theoretical statements do refer to states of affairs we shall never perceive. Our grounds for believing them involve the results of experimental manipulations. If both of these principles must be accepted then theoretical statements must mean less than those unreachable states of affairs, but more than the empirical grounds of belief. There is a popular view, expressed in the principle of bivalence, canvassed recently by L. J. Cohen (1985), in a review. (I owe notice of this important review to E. J. Bond.) Cohen remarks that what makes 'There is a polar bear at the North Pole now' true, if it is, is that there is a polar bear at the North Pole, whether anyone knows it or not. This is the truth-condition for the statement. But this will not suffice as a general account for the truth of scientific statements. We already know what it would be like to drop in and spot the bear, nosing around the scraps left behind by the last expedition. For many scientific concepts we have only the sketchiest idea what it would be like to make such an observation of the referent. Most 'scientific' objects are specified in terms of their dispositions, not their occurrent properties. Furthermore there is a good case to be made for the ontology of Neils Bohr, for deep physics. The universal ur-stuff manifests itself in this way or that depending on the kind of equipment that physicists choose to build. The idea that there is an electron at the North Pole now is not at all the same sort of idea as that there is a polar bear there. The ur-stuff at the North Pole no doubt currently has the disposition to be shaped up by a suitable piece of apparatus but until such a one is set up there aren't any electrons, only electron propensities, and we have no idea what occurrent properties they are grounded in.

The way in which theory serves as a guide for the rational exploration of the material world shows that neither of the slogans 'Sense determines reference' and 'Reference determines sense' will do as a unique grounding for a theory of meaning. Sense determines the possibility of reference – that is, it directs a programme of search – while reference, when achieved, brings about the refinement of sense. There is, over time, a dynamic, dialectic interaction between these two aspects of meaning. It follows that only a meaning theory of the Saussurean type will do for a semantics of science. Kind terms must have their meaning partially determined by intralinguistic relations to other meaningful items (*valeur*), and partially determined by extralinguistic relations, that is by their referents (*signifiés*).

2

Realism and Antirealism

Some varieties of realism

Realism: a first approximation

In the practice of the physical sciences we assume, before critical philosophical discussion has affected our attitudes, that our experience stands over against an independent, largely unobservable real world. The problem, for realism, is often thought to be epistemological. Could any of our techniques for studying the world as it is manifested in experience provide us with reliable knowledge of the unobservable reaches of a reality existing independently of ourselves? The problem is made acute because *our* knowledge and *the* real world are different kinds of beings. Knowledge and states of the world are not related in the way that photographs are related to their subjects. But the problem is made insoluble if we are willing to accept as knowledge only that level of belief that is incorrigible.

In the social sciences our individual experience of social activities stands over against a public-collective cognitive object which is the independent social world. But it is independent only in the sense that it is not a product of the activities of any one human being. It is not independent of the collective of persons. Knowledge and the object known are metaphysically of a piece – they are both composed of meanings. The problem for realism in the social sciences arises because the independent collective social world is partially concealed from each individual knower by a screen of ideology, scale and time lapse. But the problem is not philosophically acute, precisely because our social scientific knowledge and the social world which is partially known by social scientists are beings of the same kind.

The project of trying to define and argue for a defensible realism for the physical sciences would be hopeless if there were a successful argument to the effect that our ontology – our categories of existents – must be confined to those categories of beings which we can perceive in the ordinary way of things. For instance, van Fraasen's recent revival of a form of Berkeley's antirealism is based on an argument that if valid would defeat any attempt to defend scientific realism. At this stage of the discussion I leave the notion of 'observing' in a rough state. Distinctions between 'observing', 'seeing', 'perceiving' and the like will be more finely drawn below.

However, any argument which purports to restrict our ontology to those beings we can currently observe by pointing to the continuous revisions of that which we take to exist unobserved is refuted by the observation that *every* empirical claim, regardless of the observability of the category of beings involved, is defeasible, that is, awareness of special conditions or other disconcerting revelations may occur which force us to withdraw it. Captain Ahab's persistent claims to have seen a great white whale, and young Nick's call to Captain Cook that he had seen a distant land, are no more immune from defeat by virtue of the great size of the referents of their assertions than are J. J. Thomson's claims about having 'found' the atom of electricity. The fact that theoretical statements are defeasible does not show that they are not empirical because we can always imagine conditions under which *any* empirical claim would be withdrawn.

I turn now to examine four versions of scientific realism. All four share the assumption that for realists the goal of scientific practice must be defined in terms of truth and falsity, the bivalence principle. Each 'variety' arises by conjoining the bivalence principle with a subsidiary argument.

Bivalence and the argument to the best explanation

The current debate about the proper way to interpret the efforts of scientists to describe and comprehend the world has taken a form which has been determined by the way the defenders of 'realism' and their critics have taken the 'realist' point of view. Scientific realism has been defined in terms of truth and falsity, in particular in terms of the truth and falsity of statements appearing in theories. Newton-Smith (1981a) calls this the minimal form of realism. I would prefer to call this position 'maximal realism', since accepting it would commit one to an epistemological ideal that incorporates the strongest possible relationship between discourses and the world, namely truth and falsity. Since this ideal is unattainable setting one's sights upon it can only be described as quixotic. It opens the way for crypto-sceptics (such as van Fraasen, 1980) and neo-pragmatists (such as Laudan, 1977). The principle of bivalence runs as follows: 'The theoretical statements of a science are true or false by virtue of the way the world is.'

The argument for scientific realism follows the pattern of inference to the best explanation. Consider some theory with well-attested empirical consequences such as the Newtonian theory of the oceanic tides. Scientific realists of the bivalence school would argue that the best explanation for the superior predictive power of that theory (over against the Galilean theory of tides) is that the Newtonian theory is true. And the best explanation of the relative failure of the Galilean theory is that it is false. Now shift this argument form to a meta-level. The best explanation of the pragmatic success of science in general is that scientific realism is true.

This position is vulnerable to attack from several directions. First of all there is the principle of bivalence itself. It is much too strong. Statements that are accepted as expressions of well-attested beliefs may have to be abandoned or revised according to the theory one holds as much as with respect to the experiences one has (in contexts of well-founded experimental or observational programmes). For example, whether the atomic weight of a chemical element is to be taken as an integral multiple of the atomic weight of hydrogen (in which case all the results arrived at by careful measurement of relative masses must be wrong) or whether the relative weights of the chemical elements are non-integral multiples of the weight of the hydrogen atom depends on whether we believe or do not believe Prout's hypothesis. Take the case too of the cuddly dinosaurs. Tradition, both scientific and popular, has encouraged us to imagine dinosaurs, when their skeletal remains are fully fleshed out, as a race of scaly, cold-blooded lizards, swept from the earth by some mysterious fatality. But another view of dinosaurs has gained some currency recently. Calculations based on the depth and interval between sets of fossil footprints have suggested that dinosaurs might have been a good deal more cuddly than tradition admits. They might have been warm-blooded, as are the birds, their only living descendants. And they might have been furry. With this novel conception in mind some palaeontologists have been able selectively to reperceive features of the structure of dinosaur bones. This interesting cognitive act was reported by a newspaper as follows: 'Dinosaur bones have large blood channels and no growth rings: they are the bones of a warm-blooded creature.' Palaeontologists of the older school must have seen all there was to see of the structure of dinosaur bones, but they 'selectively noticed' different features, perhaps the saurian articulation of the skeleton. If that was the most important feature of the fossil remains for them it is not surprising that they did not pause to puzzle over the inner structure of the bones themselves.

Another instructive example worth quoting in some detail is the case of the Meers fault (Weisburd, 1985).

The Meers fault, a 26-kilometer line cutting brazenly through farms and prairie land in southwestern Oklahoma, is spawning something of a legend in geologic circles. For the last 40 years scores of geologists have tramped all over the fault, thinking it was old and inactive. Even Charles Mankin, Oklahoma's state geologist, recalls spreading out his geologic maps on the fault trace one day 20 years ago without ever noticing just how unusual the Meers fault is. Until recently, no one saw the telltale signs of relatively new movement, perhaps within the last few thousand years, making the Meers fault essentially the only young, surface-breaking rupture east of the Rocky Mountains. Geologists now know that not only is the fault young, but it could produce a magnitude 7 earthquake in the future.

'Sometimes people just don't see what they don't expect to find' said one seismologist on his way to the first symposium on the Meers fault.

Since, in the end, all our current theories are likely to be abandoned or modified there can be no place in science for a sure catalogue of facts of the matter fixed for ever by *the* way the world is. However, as a daily working category the truth or falsity of factual statements is a normal part of the common discourse of scientists. Empirical studies of scientific talk and writing show that the scientific community shares with motor mechanics, housewives and other practical persons an unsophisticated concept of empirical truth. This concept does not find employment for the broader and deeper theories of science whose verisimilitude realists are keen to defend. I shall be returning to discuss this point in more detail. The relation of theory to fact can be enunciated at different levels of strength. A strong neo-Kantian interpretation – that conceptual systems determine what we take the world to be, at least in so far as it appears to us as physical things and substances interacting causally – leads to relativism. No defence of realism can be constructed if one's acknowledgement of the role of theory in the creation of facts goes so far. I shall be setting out a weaker thesis that is compatible with admitting the priority of concepts to facts, but does not slip into the kind of relativism that denies the representational power of human cognition.

But the 'argument to the best explanation' argument is also shaky. As Peter Lipton (1985) has pointed out, there are always at least two ways of evaluating a theory relative to pragmatic success. A theory may be the best theory because it is the most economical, or the simplest or the most elegant. This is the sort of property that Osiander credited the pragmatically successful Copernican theory with in his famous 'preface'. A perfectly good explanation of the pragmatic success of a theory, say in engendering lots of correct predictions and few inaccurate ones, is that it is an elegant summary of the phenomena, though we may imagine all its higher-level statements are false. It is simply restating an important philosophical commonplace to point out that citing the truth of a theory as an explanation of its pragmatic success may be quite correct, but it cannot be the best explanation of that success while there is no general way of disposing of the rival explanations of pragmatic success. But to have a general way of disposing of them is already to have an argument for scientific realism. So the 'argument to the best explanation' argument depends itself on the very principle it is supposed to support.

We can now set out the reasons for abandoning this way of explicating what is meant by scientific realism.

1   It presupposes that the assessment of all forms of cognitive objects in which knowledge might be expressed, including both singular statements and theories, should be expressible in terms of truth and falsity. This allows in the (mild) scepticism of those like Laudan or Nancy Cartwright (1983) who have little difficulty in showing that many interesting kinds of theories cannot be assessed for truth and falsity. Some go on to take that fact as a ground for some form of antirealism. But our strategy should not be to try to defeat Laudan and Cartwright, but to redefine scientific realism in a weaker and more defensible form. By so doing I shall be in a position to accuse them of the fallacy of high redefinition. This is the move by which some established metascientific concept like 'empirical support', which has a well-understood use in scientific discourse, is redefined in such a way that there are no conditions under which it could reasonably be applied.

2   The principle of bivalence is not sensitive to 'ontological depth'. It would still be true, if it were defensible, of antirealist phenomenological reductions or something similar, such as van Fraasen's revival of what amounts to a kind of Berkleyan position. In short it does not draw a sharp enough distinction between realism and antirealism.

3   Truth and falsity are appropriate assessments for universal statements only if the appropriate existential presuppositions are satisfied. But these presuppositions are satisfied by securing reference, and that is a material practice. In short, realism as defined via the bivalence principle is dependent on something more fundamental, the establishment of referential relations to physical beings.

4   Even if I were to concede a use for the concepts of truth and falsehood to designate some ultimate but practically unattainable classification of beliefs about the world of nature, this would not permit the use of the argument to the best explanation. That argument, without an independent proof of scientific realism, is vulnerable to the charge of equivocation with respect to the notion of what is to count as the best explanation of a theory's practical success.

These arguments seem to be enough to show that the defence of truth realism is hopeless.

Bivalence and a conservation of existence condition

It is not so easy to resist the lure of defining realism in terms of the concepts of truth and falsity. After making a promising beginning with the query 'What, in the light of science, can we say about the real furniture of the world?' Mary Hesse (1974) glides over into truth realism, basing her exegesis of realism on these theses (p. 290):

1 Theoretical statements have truth-value.
2 It is presupposed that the material world does not change at the behest of our theories.
3 The realist character of scientific knowledge consists in some sense in the permanent and cumulative capture of true propositions corresponding to the world.

None of these theses is uncontroversial. Her position is not protected against the objections to a standard realism based entirely on the bivalence principle merely by being conjoined with some other conditions. But the interest of her position lies in the way her defensive arguments slide over into another variety of realism, the referential realism being defended in this book.

Hesse offers a number of apparently attractive arguments in support of her 'tepid' realism. According to the 'translation' argument, the antirealist force of the relativity of observations to theory can be deflected by introducing a special criterion. If a translation can be made from a discourse in one theory-system to that in another, *salva veritate*, then that which those discourses are about cannot be theory-relative. 'The entities and systems of entities referred to in both S1 and S2 can be taken to exist, and indeed to be the *same* system of entities, differently described.' This is more or less Putnam's 'Principle of Charity' and has been defended by reference to a commonsensical exposition of the history of science. But this looks like a shift from truth realism to referential realism. What makes the inter-translatable truths not mere notational variants of one another is the idea that they are different descriptions of the same referents. Her actual defence is, then, supportive of a position different from that she sets out to defend. Furthermore she argues that 'existence' is not just a matter of the way a theory is formalized. To exist is not just to be the value of a variable: 'The question of what exists is determined by which set of analogies and expectations is adopted *prior* to formalization.' And one might add by which kinds of beings one rubs shoulders with in making one's way, sometimes with sensory aids, about the physical world.

Without a clear statement of the criteria by which existence claims are to be settled empirically, 'existence' is still theory-relative; only in Hesse's

treatment 'theory' is a good deal more realistic and sophisticated a notion
than the predicate calculus deductive structures of logicist philosophy of
science. Further, the translation argument needs a metaphysical under-
pinning. To establish whether the intertranslatable descriptions 'pick out'
the same entities requires some further specification of what is to be meant
by 'same entity'. Is collocation in space–time enough or should that be
supplemented by some criterion based on similarity of causal powers?
Certainly 'satisfaction of the same description' is not available to Hesse,
since by hypothesis there is no 'same description'. (An extreme extensionalist account of meaning could perhaps be invoked to prove that the
apparently different but intertranslatable descriptions really *meant* the same
however different their associated belief systems would be.) Hesse offers
another attractive argument based on the principle that 'real theoretical
entities' are robust as 'parts of real non-theoretical entities'. 'Theoretical
entities are real entities, and may replace observable entities as primary
individuals, but only in the sense that observable entities may be interpreted
as classes or systems of theoretical entities' (p. 301). Unfortunately the argument leaves out of account the relations between the properties of theoretical and observable entities. To put this another way, the part–whole relation
is useless unless we can also invoke the cause–effect relation to link the
properties of parts with those of wholes (and of course vice versa). Sometimes the parts will be unobservable and their causal powers will be manifested in effects which are properties of observable entities. Sometimes the
wholes will be unobservable and their causal powers manifested in the
properties of observable parts.

More recently Hesse has proposed a position she calls 'practicalism'
(Hesse, 1980). But the argument that would link a realist interpretation to
practical success is vulnerable to the most obvious counter-examples. Take
Lister's proposal of the practice of antisepsis. It was a successful practice,
but Lister, it should be remembered, did not subscribe to the bacterial
theory of disease. The success of the practice would support the bacterial
theory only if a referential–existential relation to bacteria had already been
established. Only then could the practice of antisepsis be redescribed as 'the
practice of killing bacteria' and so its success be able to be cited in support
of bacterial theory. Lister thought that streptococci and some other malign
microorganisms were detached human cells.

A subtly distinctive variant on this account of scientific realism is due to
B. Ellis (1979). He says: 'I understand scientific realism to be the view that
the theoretical statements of science are, or purport to be, true generalized
descriptions of reality.' Ellis notices, correctly, that scientific realism
conceived in terms of truth and falsity, does not require that any theoretical
statements actually be true, much less be known to be true. All that is

required is that we should have some argument to support the view that in principle they could be true or false. It is not part of scientific realism to claim that we could presently know whether theoretical statements in a certain domain are true or false. This outflanks a form of scepticism that appears in the writings of L. Laudan. According to him we should not adopt scientific realism as a working philosophy of science because nearly everything believed by theoretical physicists at some time to be true has had to be given up. Actually Laudan's position is vulnerable to a more modest argument, namely that, while physicists perhaps have not been able to keep their stock of deep and fundamental theories unscathed by later developments, there has been a continual refinement and growing repertoire of very plausible items of information about many kinds of beings whose existence can no longer seriously be called into doubt. But this takes us prematurely into referential realism.

Fiduciary realism: bivalence with faith

Popper's fiduciary realism takes a slightly different form in that the 'truth demand' is not placed on any actual historically situated theory (though all must be susceptible to falsification). The concept of 'truth' defines the terminus towards which successive stages of scientific progress tend while the concept of 'falsity' defines the direction towards that terminus. Thus Popper (1972, p. 57) says: 'While we can never have sufficiently good arguments in the empirical sciences for claiming that we have actually reached the truth, we can have strong and reasonably good arguments for claiming that we have made progress towards the truth.' The concept of 'verisimilitude' and the basic theorem of Tarski's 'theory of truth' are supposed to provide respectively the vector by which the direction of scientific progress is determined and the terminus to which scientific progress is directed. Popper's failure to find a way of defining scientific progress in terms of increasing verisimilitude of successive theories in a domain is notorious, and so is his failure to give an account of in-principle truth-as-correspondence. The former failure stems from his logicism, since he tries to provide a measure of progressiveness in terms of the deductivist notion of truth content and falsity content. The latter disappointment comes from relying on Tarski's formal analysis of the role of the concept 'truth'.

I call Popper's realism fiduciary, a matter of faith, since there is no way in which his methodology of conjectures and refutations could deliver a theory (or even a hypothesis of any degree of generality) that could be known to be true. To define the terminus of enquiry in terms of truth is an act of faith. Popper's philosophical programme in defence of realism is shaped by the need to find some way of damping the oscillations of ever new conjectures as they are refuted and rejected one after the other. Such a damping could be achieved if there was some reason for supposing that a theory could be true of the world, and a criterion could be established for telling which of two theories was nearer the truth. Popper thought he had met both of these conditions, the former by espousing Tarski's 'theory' of truth, and the latter with his own concept of verisimilitude.

Tarski was able to show that in a suitably structured formal system a predicate ' . . . is T' could be defined so that

'p' is T if and only if p

is a provable schema in the system. 'p' is a representation of p in some suitable metalanguage, and the predicate T is interpreted as 'true'. It seems to be generally agreed that Tarski's work disposes of the *formal* difficulty that besets systems of logic through the paradoxes of sentential self-reference, such as 'This sentence is false.' Has this anything to contribute to the philosophical problem of truth? In particular does it go any way at all to establishing the correspondence theory of truth – that what we mean by saying that a certain statement is true is that there is a material state of affairs which corresponds to it?

An obvious difficulty for treating this formal analysis as relevant to the philosophical problem of truth was pointed out by Black (1949). Nothing in Tarski's analysis enables us to tell how the predicate letter T should be interpreted. All we can say is that it refers to some property of the *names* of sentences. This seems to rule out 'true' as a possible interpretation. Names are related to their referents by arbitrary conventions but sentences are not arbitrary in that way. The issue at the heart of the philosophical problem of truth is why 'The horse is black' is the right thing to say in the presence of a black horse, given the existing conventions of English. In the Tarskian context the issue becomes that of finding a reason why '"p" is true' is the right thing to say in the presence of an assertion that p. But the formal answer to that question does not help at all with the question of when p should properly be asserted. If p is the right thing to say then Tarski's 'theory' shows that '"p" is true' can be systematically and consistently sub-stituted for that assertion. Just try a truth-function test on the exemplary sentence above.

Field (1972) has made the most general objection to taking Tarski's formal theory as having any bearing on the philosophical problem of truth. Tarski's proof proffers only a list of descriptions of particular word–world relations. But listing descriptions of cases of correspondence or 'primitive reference' does not explicate that relation. Tarski's 'theory' throws no light on how it is possible for a particular string of words to be a proper statement about some state of affairs and most other strings of words not. Neither the meaning of 'true' nor the criteria for its proper use can be found in the 'theory'. As Field remarks (p. 347) 'Tarski succeeded in reducing the notion of truth *to certain other semantic notions.*' These are 'what it is for a name to denote something', 'what it is for a predicate to apply to something' and 'what it is for a function symbol to be fulfilled by some pair of things'. (See also Field (1972) p. 360.) Ironically the first two are the very conditions which Austin (1961) discerned as the primitive components of the concept of empirical truth.

The reason for the irrelevance of Tarski's 'theory' can be seen if we look more closely at the proposed descriptive language of the basic sentence form of the Tarskian discussion, namely

'p' is true if and only if p

Substitute any particular sentence 'p' for the sentence variable P and we get an assertion like

'The horse is black' is true if and only if the horse is black

This assertion is itself true if and only if the truth values of the statements on either side of the biconditional match. It follows that the second occurrence of the sentence is an assertion. The Tarskian statement simply links one *assertion* with another by a truth-functional connective. As philosophers of science we wanted to hear a theory about the grounds of assertion; that is about

The horse *is* black if and only if

It should now be obvious that the Tarskian 'theory' presupposes that there are such grounds.

A more elaborate philosophical apparatus is needed to site Tarski's 'theory' more accurately. The italicizing of the copula in the above assertion is a representation of the illocutionary force of the statement, namely as an assertion. Tarski could be said to have shown that there is a systematic equivalence between statements with the illocutionary force of assertions of fact and corresponding meta-statements which describe first-order statements as true. This would justify Ramsey's (1931) proposal that we should treat the act of assertion as equivalent to an explicit meta-statement which makes use of the predicate '. . . is true'. It seems clear that Popper cannot find the support he needs from Tarski's formal exercise.

Unfortunately the concept of verisimilitude fares no better. According to Popper, a theory T2 is of greater verisimilitude than a rival theory T1 if the following conditions obtain:

1   The truth content of T2 is greater than that of T1.
2   The falsity content of T1 is greater than that of T2.

In appendix 3 of his 1963 *Conjectures and refutations* Popper offers a quasi-definition for measures of these 'contents'.

The truth content of a theory T is the intersection of the set of statements which follow from T with the set of all true statements, Tau. The relative truth content of two theories, Ta and Tb is the set of true statements which follow from the conjunction of Ta and Tb, excluding those which follow from Tb alone. The falsity-content of a theory T is the relative truth-content of T and the intersection of all the consequences of T with the set of all true statements, Tau. The structure of these definitions can be seen more clearly when represented in Euler circles: see figure 2. 1.

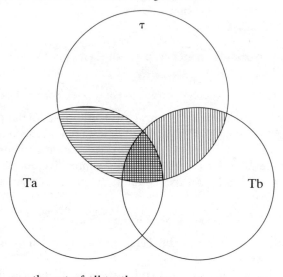

τ = the set of all truths
Ta = the true consequences of theory Ta ≣
Tb = the true consequences of theory Tb ⦀

Figure 2.1   The relative truth content of Ta and Tb

Now consider two theories Ta and Tb. Tb is more verisimilitudinous than Ta:

1 If Tb has greater truth content than Ta, that is if the set of statements, S1, which is the intersection of the statements that follow from Tb with Tau is larger than the set of statements, S2, which is the intersection of the statements which follow from Ta with Tau. (See figure 2. 2.)

2 If the falsity content of Tb is less than or equal to the falsity content of Ta. This condition could be expanded in a manner comparable to the expansion of 1 above.

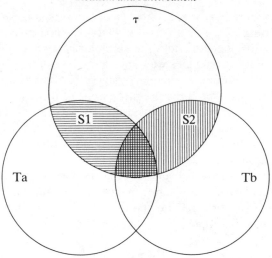

Figure 2.2 Absolute truth content

To put these conditions to use in a practical decision between two rival theories would require that there be some measure of the relative size of the sets S1 and S2, and the corresponding sets required for condition 2. However, if such a measure were conceivable it would require that we have access to Tau, the set of all truths, but according to Popperian methodology we can have no such access.

Any other procedure, such as ordering hypotheses according to the plausibility of the theories from which they are drawn, is also ruled out for Popper, since there is no reference to real content, that is to what the rival theories say about the world, within this purely formal framework. Fiduciary realism at least in logicist form, is inadequate.

The general case against truth realisms

All three 'realisms' depend on a content-free conception of the cognitive operations involved in scientific reasoning. Argument to the best explanation, for instance, is set up in such a way that 'best' has to do with the capacity of a theory to engender consequences, presumably by deductive reasoning. All three share the assumption that the goals of science are the discovery of truth and the exclusion of falsehood, and that these are, in principle, attainable ends. In short all three depend on the implicit assumption that there can be *reasons* for holding that this belief is true while that is false. At this point I draw on a recent paper by David Miller (1985), intended to show that there can be no good reasons, at least in the matter of scientific belief.

Miller presumes that for a reason to be a good reason there must be some formal procedure by which it is tied to that for which it is claimed to be a reason. Deductive logic provides the exemplar of such a tie. He considers three cases. Drawing on Mill's well-known observation, he points out that, since the conclusion of a deductive argument in effect is a restatement of some part of the content of the premises, none of those premises can be a good reason for accepting the conclusion. At least a reason, good or indifferent, must say something different from that which it is supposed to support. The second case is introduced by the following remark: 'just as conclusive reasons, were they to exist, would be sustained by the relation of logical implication or logical consequence, so partially conclusive reasons need a relation of partial implication or partial consequence.' In true logicist style Miller spells out the relation in probabilistic terms, in fact the familiar idea of probabilistic support:

$$s\,(h, e) = p\,(h, e) - p\,(h)$$

where e is evidence, h is a hypothesis and s (h, e) expresses the relation of empirical support of e for h. Miller denies that e is a good reason for believing h (is true?), even if, according to this schema, e supports h (highly). His reason is that e can only be a reason for h if there is some reason for e. 'How', he asks 'are such chains of good reasons ever to get started?' Within a logicist framework no answer could be forthcoming, since it would have to be given in terms of a propositional relation, and that requires always yet another proposition as its second term. To the defensive reply that believing e begs a different question from that begged in believing h Miller replies by adopting an extensional account of 'content', in keeping with his logicist account of good reasons. Thus the fact that e supports h is 'entirely to be explained by the fact that e and h overlap in content'. Or to put the matter another way that part of the content of h which is identical with e is supported trivially by e, while that part which is not is not supported by e at all.

The third argument concerns the application of the complaint, canvassed in the discussion of premises as logically conclusive reasons, to the case of negative evidence. By parity of reasoning any claim that not-e is a good reason for disbelieving h, i. e. believing not-h, must fail. By exploiting a trick of the propositional calculus Miller shows that one could claim that the 'dialectic of criticism' escapes the triviality of the 'monologue of justification' because it leads to different questions being addressed. But he rightly rejects this game as casuistry. There are no negative reasons either.

But then he falls from grace. Committed to a position he calls 'critical rationalism' he slips into the following sophism: we do not need reasons against a hypothesis, he says, to classify it as false. 'All we need is a false consequence of it; not I stress, a reason to suppose that we have identified a false consequence, just a false consequence.' Whatever can this mean? Surely unless you have a reason for supposing that a consequence is false rather than true, you could not tell that you indeed had a false consequence. In a further gloss on this puzzling assertion Miller adverts to the idea of finding 'consequences that contradict other statements that are classified as true'. But they will not supply us with a reason for rejecting the hypothesis under test. Some must be rejected, and by some miracle it is the one with the consequences that all but Miller would say they had reason to think were false that meets that fate.

What has gone wrong? Clearly we have yet another example of the 'philosophers' fallacy', the high redefinition of a commonplace notion, motivated in this case by adherence to logicism, with the consequential and apparently remarkable discovery that we never have good reasons after all. Miller's arguments show that if it had been truth and falsity that the scientific community was trying to establish then there is no possible way within a logicist framework that good reasons could be found for supposing we have either of them. Miller himself introduces a new term, 'disadvantages', for the kind of consideration that scientists or engineers could cite in giving their reasons why it would be a mistake were some hypothesis not thought to be true or some course of action not followed. Once the concept of 'disadvantage' has been introduced it is hard to see how the concept of 'advantage' could be excluded from our metascientific vocabulary. It could be used perhaps to refer to those considerations cited in favour of a theory.

To see how the logicist high redefinition of 'good reason' contrasts with the sort of thing a working scientist might cite as a reason one might try the grounds Harvey offered in support of the hypothesis that the blood in human beings circulated. Broadly considered these fall into two groups: metaphysical considerations based on the Aristotelian idea of the perfection of the circle; and empirical considerations based on quantitative measures of blood volume. The latter turned out to have just the order of magnitude one would expect were the heart to be thought of as an organic pump and the blood vessels a closed hydraulic circuit. Commonsense would say, I suppose, that the metaphysical reasons were not good ones, while the empirical reasons were. We can now see why Miller's depreciation of good reasons is a high redefinition. For him 'good reasons' must be coextensive with that proposition for which they are reasons. This makes sense only if we think of reasons in the logicist sense of instantiations, the white swan which is an instantiation of the propositional function 'something is a swan and is white'. But the fact that the human body contains seven pints of blood is not an instantiation of the circulation hypothesis. Rather it is the sort of thing one would expect if the blood did indeed circulate. It is to be thought of not as a logical consequence of some assembly of propositions, but as a material consequence of the nature of pumps and hydraulic networks.

Miller's high redefinition can, however, be turned to disputatious advantage. It seems to show that studying scientific discourse with the tools of logic provides nothing of use to philosophers interested in how we have managed to acquire better and better knowledge of the physical world. Nor will it help in the search for an account of that improvement. If logicism were our only recourse for understanding we would have no alternative but to accept the sceptic's conclusion that we know no more now than we did in 1580. So let us turn to the study of what scientists take to be the advantages and disadvantages of adopting this or that belief. And since the ideals of truth and falsity seem to be a *fata Morgana* tempting the traveller into the fallacies Miller has identified let us drop them too, at least as putative classifications for cognitive objects of any degree of generality, such as hypotheses and theories.

The failure of logicism would not matter very much if it were not for the fact that there is a short road from the realization that it provides no account of science to the pathological scepticism of those like Feyerabend and Laudan.

Bivalence and the principle of determinateness: Einstein's later philosophy

Einstein's realism, despite the Machean notions that are so prominent in his formulation of special relativity, is to be found already well articulated in the famous paper of 1905. We are asked to compare the underlying physics of the two forms of electromagnetic induction: 'Maxwell's electrodynamics . . . when applied to moving bodies leads to asymmetries, which do not appear to be inherent in the phenomena.' When the magnet is in motion and the conductor at rest there is an electric field in the neighbourhood of the magnet, but when the magnet is at rest and the conductor is in motion 'no electric field arises in the neighbourhood of the magnet.' But the relative motion and the induced currents are the same in both cases. If the magnet was moving relative to the ether in the first case but not in the second then it would follow from the Lorentz law ($F = e (D + v/c \cdot H)$, where D is the electric field and H the magnetic field) that there was an asymmetry in the underlying physical conditions of each case. Why should there be an ether asymmetry when the phenomena are quite symmetrical? I believe that this is not only an argument against the ether as a physical bearer of causality, but also the first appearance of something like the 'hermetic' principle 'As above so below' that so dominated Einstein's later thought.

The occasion for the final formulation of Einstein's realism was the culmination of his long debate with Bohr concerning the status of quantum mechanics. The question had finally crystallized into the issue of completeness. As Einstein put it in the English summary to his brief paper of 1948,

If, in quantum mechanics, we consider the psi-function as (in principle) a complete description of a real physical situation we thereby imply the hypothesis of action-at-distance, an hypothesis which is hardly acceptable [given the firm position of special relativity]. If, on the other hand, we consider the psi-function as an incomplete description of a real physical situation, then it is hardly to be believed that, for this incomplete description, strict laws of temporal dependence hold.

And this dilemma is forced on us, as Einstein reiterated, if we try to apply the quantum mechanical formalism to individual systems. Quantum mechanics can be a complete description only of an ensemble of systems.

At the heart of Einstein's discontent was his dislike of Bohr's ontology, which placed the 'phenomenon', in Bohr's special sense of an indissoluble union of apparatus, its reactions and reality, at the centre of physical science as the basic object of description. Already, as we have seen, in 1905 he had at least tacitly adopted the view summed up by Pais (1982, p. 455) as 'one should seek a deeper-lying theoretical framework which permits the description of phenomena independently of the [experimental] . . . conditions.' The full statement of his conception of physical reality appears in the paper with Podolsky and Rosen (1935). There are two principles for completeness of physical theory:

1 'Every element of physical reality must have a counterpart in physical theory', a statement which should perhaps better be described as a desideratum than a principle.

One should notice that this is a realist principle, since it is not a desideratum tying theory to sense experience. It ties theory to whatever causes sense experience, and of that we can have only an imaginative grasp. It is that which is created freely. As he says in Schilpp (1949–51, vol. II, p. 673), 'we represent the sense-impressions as conditioned by an "objective" and a "subjective" factor.'

2 'If, without in any way disturbing a system, we can predict with accuracy (i. e. with probability equal to unity) the value of a physical quality, then there exists an element of physical reality corresponding to this physical quantity.'

The practical restrictions imposed by the conjugation of physical variables, appearing as complementarity and as the non-commutivity of operators, are bypassed by this principle. If it were accepted, it would severally justify the claims of position, momentum, temporal moment and energy, etc. to be physically real. It is just an accident which of these quantities we chose to measure on a particular occasion, an accident which cuts us off from its conjugate partner. The argument for incompleteness and the acceptance of this account of scientific realism depend heavily upon each other. But this principle is surely mistaken. The value of the diameter of a Ptolemaic epicycle can be determined with probability equal to unity, but that is clearly no ground for accepting epicycles as real. Einstein's variety of realism will not do.

A shift to practice: Grene's 'comprehensive realism'

In her 1983 paper Marjorie Grene mounts an attack on the hegemony of the Cartesian–Lockean framework within which most philosophy of science of the modern era has been worked out. She argues that the impasse of perpetual scepticism is inevitable if there is 'only the subjective flow of alleged bits of mentality and the one-level collisions of least bits of stuff that are allowed to count' (p. 92). Mind and knowledge on the one hand *confront* matter and its organization on the other. Within the Cartesian way of making this distinction (a way we have perpetuated in different forms) there can be no resolution which would establish the possibility of knowledge of the world. It is not that the problem is terribly difficult and awaits a solution. The terms of its presentation are awry.

The notion of 'comprehensive realism' is intended to capture the idea (p. 93) 'that human beings like other animals are comprehended within a real living environment, and within . . . a family of human social worlds'. The point of this idea, as an alternative groundwork to the Cartesian dichotomy, is that it allows us to consider our relation to the physical world in terms of what I would like to call 'practices'. Grene works out this thought in the idea of 'being-in-the-world', drawn from those sinister 'Continental' figures, Merleau-Ponty and Heidegger. It includes 'lived bodiliness', in which 'perception, thought, passion . . . [and] all resonances of our bodily being [are contained].' A good deal is tucked away in the concept of 'resonance' that would have to be brought to light to establish the point of view of comprehensive realism in the way that would shift the entrenched Cartesianism of current philosophy of science. Nevertheless it provides a powerful corrective to the blinkered cognitivism of much contemporary thought. There is little attention in the writings of van Fraasen, for instance, to the fact that scientists do experiments by skilfully shaping and manipulating material stuff.

Adopting a tactic to which I shall later turn myself, Grene, conceding the Humean insights that there are intellectual habits and that induction could not yield truth, turns to the psychology of perception to support, in a general way, the idea that people come to their knowledge of the world by an active manipulation and exploration of it in which 'bodily and mental powers are [inextricably entwined]' (p. 101). Support for the primacy of practice comes from the psychology of J. J. Gibson, to the exposition and defence of which I shall be devoting considerable attention. Grene's ideas, though not fully worked out, will provide a kind of stepping-off point for the kind of modest realism to be defended in this work, and for the basic role that material practices will play in it.

Grene's realism had been anticipated in a way by Robert Boyle in his *Origins of forms and qualities*, in which he argues for realism on the basis of the possibility of certain kinds of mechanical manipulations of matter. Boyle says: 'in the production of . . . effects there intervenes a [hidden] local motion and change of texture by these [mechanical] operations' (p. 112). If a mechanical intervention in nature is effective that tells us the kind of latent process with which we have interfered. Hacking (1983, chapter 16) develops a case which goes beyond Grene's comprehensive realism in a way with which I am in substantial agreement. Like Boyle, Hacking thinks in terms of projects which involve *doing* something with clusters of entities, the effect of which is 'to intefere in other more hypothetical parts of nature.' A hypothetical entity becomes real to us when we use it to investigate something else.

Some varieties of antirealism

Traditional challenges to scientific realism

Most attacks on scientific realism have been mounted on the basis of the assumption that by scientific realism we mean truth realism. Three ways of challenging truth realism have persisted, at least since the astronomical debates of the sixteenth century. The 'epistemic' challenge is based on arguments designed to show that no *human* enterprise could decide whether the typical statements of scientific theories were true or false. This challenge appears sometimes as inductive or 'scope' scepticism, and sometimes as 'depth' scepticism. The latter is nowadays referred to as the problem of the underdetermination of theories by data. The 'metaphysical' challenge calls in question the right of scientists to assume the existence of beings, their states and relations, which cannot be perceived. The 'semantic' challenge depends on a positivistic theory of meaning, which reduces the meaning of any substantive scientific term to the observational criteria we would use to decide whether it was correct to apply it or to refuse to apply it. A scientific realist may be under the illusion that a substantive term in a theory refers to an unobservable being. However, if we attend to the 'empirical' meaning of that term we can see that it must mean something observable. It cannot mean what a scientific realist thinks it does.

The defender of scientific realism seems to face a dilemma:

If theoretical discourse is about what it seems to be about, namely unobserved beings and processes, empirical scepticism entails that no human being can tell whether the discourse is true or false.

If scientific discourse is subject to the bivalence principle then it cannot be about what it seems to be about. It can only be about something that can be observed. It must be the kind of discourse which a human observer can assess for truth and falsity.

If we insist on the literal reading of scientific discourse it seems that it cannot be tested in any way relevant to the putative realist status of its assertions; while if we insist on its empirical testability it seems that theory must be reinterpreted in a non-realist fashion, that is positivistically or conventionalistically. Popper's bold attempt to save scientific realism by insisting on the asymmetry between the possibility of discovering the truth and falsity of theories, abandoning the one in favour of the other under the force of Hume's sceptical arguments, also fails. Duhem (1914) pointed out that even when a strict deductive consequence of a theory is demonstrated to be false, supposing experimentation could achieve such a clear-cut result, *modus tollens* cannot be used to transfer that falsity back to any specific site in the theory or its ancillary assumptions. It has also been pointed out that the methodological principle 'Reject that which has been refuted' can be used categorically only under the inductive assumption that the world will not change so that what was not true today is true tomorrow and for evermore. This version of the principle of the uniformity of nature is no more acceptable than the traditional uniformitarian assumption that would support positive inductive reasoning from the truth of a prediction to the acceptance of the hypothesis from which it was derived.

Hume's (1739) attempts to define the limits of the powers of reason have often been read as an antirealist scepticism. I think this is a misunderstanding of Hume's point of view, which is better treated as an attack on the sovereignty of a logicist conception of reason. But it is worth noticing that his sceptical doubts about the employment of the understanding are based on two distinct sets of considerations. The famous argument that reason cannot justify an induction from particular observation to general law leads to scope scepticism, that is to the conclusion that we cannot demonstrably prove that the laws of nature known to be instantiated in some observation or experiment here and now are true at all places and all times. An equally important Humean argument concerns the empirical standing of the concepts of 'power', 'efficacy' and 'natural necessity'. Hume's contention that these 'ideas' cannot have real-world referents has its full significance only if one knows that the most favoured theoretical entity in eighteenth-century science was the causal power, the precursor of the modern concepts of potential, charge and kinetic energy. The dynamicist philosophy of physics was sandwiched between the corpuscularianism of the seventeenth century and the atomism of the nineteenth. The claim that 'power' concepts have no empirical referents leads to depth scepticism, a blow against the realist interpretation of physical theory, for instance as developed by R. J. Boscovich (1763). Hume's doubts about induction are 'epistemic'. But he turns to a 'semantic' principle, that the meaning of an idea is the impression from which it derives, to induce a 'metaphysical' scepticism about the claims to reality of causal powers. They are reduced to psychological residues precipitated from sequences of like pairs of impressions.

One might be tempted to try to escape the force of Hume's arguments by adopting an inductive strategy to establish the principle of truth realism from incidents in the history of science. Truth-realism would cease to be an absolute guaranteed by some demonstrative argument from incontrovertible premises. It would be offered as a modest inductive generalization. This is the strategy adopted by Lenin (1908). In its current incarnation the argument is often expressed as follows: 'the best explanation for the pragmatic success of a theory (its empirical adequacy) is that it is true.' But there are good reasons for thinking that there are equally attractive alternative explanations for the success of a theory in 'accounting for' the facts in its domain, particularly if 'accounting for' is conceived in the logicist way, a way that generally goes along with the epistemic attitudes of truth realism. Clavius's (1603) paradox shows that pragmatic success can be accounted for by the deductive power of theories which are almost certainly false. Indeed if pragmatic success is understood as the power of a theory to entail those data we take to be observationally or experimentally verified, and not to entail any putative data which experiment or observation shows to be false, then the paradox demonstrates that this condition is satisfied by infinitely many theories, only one of which is true. One's chances of hitting on that theory if one is restricted to an empiricist attitude to science is nearly nil.

Semantic antirealism

Some recent discussions of realism have centred on a generalization of the epistemology of intuitionist interpretations of mathematics to the theory of scientific discourse. This suggestion comes ultimately from M. Dummett (1978). I shall discuss semantic antirealism as it appears in a recent discussion by M. Luntley (1982). Luntley's argument proceeds in two steps. In the first the analogy between intuitionist mathematics and philosophy of science is set out. In the second he tries to show that the resulting 'semantic antirealismn' is, at least with respect to problems of the existential status of 'theoretical entities', a doctrine quite distinct from instrumentalist positivism.

According to intuitionism, proofs in mathematics should be 'constructive'. Consider a statement of the form (Ex) [A (x)]. A constructive proof of a theorem of this logical form requires that the proof provides a definite instance of A (*a*) (where *a* is some natural number) or 'yields an effective means, at least in principle, for finding a proof of such an instance'. The principle of bivalence applies only to those statements for which these conditions are satisfied. If one is prepared to accept the equivalence of scientific realism with a ubiquitous demand for the applicability of the principle of bivalence the analogy is very plain. Only for those entities for which there is an effective proof of their existence does the principle of bivalence come into force as a constraint on statements which denote them. For many important cases there are no 'effective proofs' of the existence of the relevant entities. The bivalence condition cannot then be applied to any discourse which purports to denote them. Hence nothing determinate can be said about their status.

It is in developing the scientific analogue of the mathematical notion of 'effective proof' that Luntley makes the all-important distinction between his view and instrumentalist positivism. He uses an argument first proposed in my *Theories and things* of 1961, and later by G. Maxwell. This argument is to the effect that the result of perceiving something with the help of instruments is as much perception as the kind of awareness of things we can achieve with unaided sight, hearing or touch. The fact that a theory is needed to explain how a microscope works is irrelevant to the issue of the status of those beings which are revealed by the use of such an instrument. An existential continuity can be established which runs from naked-eye vision to microscope-aided perception. Each increase in magnification reveals a feature previously not seen, but the increases that make up the chain are such that at each increment a feature revealed in the immediately prior view is still recognizable. So long as this condition is met for every incremental step, existential family continuity is established. The number of intermediate causal processes that intervene between a micro-organism, say, and the information uptake by the visual system of the beholder is irrelevant to the question of whether or not something real has been perceived. 'Effective proofs' then include the use of instruments to detect beings which first appear on the scientific scene as unobservables, the putative referents of terms whose meaning is created internally in the discourse of theorizing.

So far, so good. But now the antirealism emerges. If there is no 'effective procedure' for detecting the being in question (and sometimes *the* being simply means any specimen of the type of being in question), the above analogy suggests that we should not apply the bivalence principle to statements about such an alleged being. The connection between bivalence and reality does not require that the putative being be declared 'not real' but that investigators accept that the question of its reality is, in the circumstances, indeterminate. The basic realist principle that scientific practice can support claims that there *now* exist or do not exist kinds of things, instances of which are yet to be found, must go. More alarming still, the argument seems to suggest that even when we have found instances of kinds of beings, those members which have not yet been disclosed by an 'effective procedure' cannot be *said* to exist, even if the conditions for their production have been satisfied.

These strange conclusions come about because of a separation between the assertability conditions for some statement referring to hypothetical entities and the conditions for claims about the reality (existence) of such entities. The antirealist restricts the latter to those for which there is an 'effective decision procedure'. Thus if a source of alpha-particles is continuously activated in a laboratory, only those alpha-particles which have actually been detected by a counter can be said to be real. When the counter is switched off and the source is still activated, though we can say meaningfully 'if there were a counter now switched on it would react in a way appropriate to the detection of alpha-particles' we are not entitled to say that there are any alpha-particles in the laboratory at that time. According to Luntley semantic antirealism separates the determining of truth values from the fixing of meaning. Couple this with the bivalence principle and we reach the heart of Luntley's position. In cases where truth value is indeterminate though meaning remains robust, we can make no reality claims.

A curious feature of this view is that only particulars can be shown to exist (and perhaps also not to exist). Were Luntley to concede that the proof of the existence of a veritable alpha-particle demonstrated that there were beings of that kind, the above argument would be less attractive. We would have reason to believe that an apparatus of that sort produced beings of that kind, indeed a stream of them, only a sample of which we have bothered to pick out and study. But we could have chosen a sample different from that which we did select. Does this human act of choice annihilate those we might have studied and bring into being those we now decide to test? Since Luntley's position is that in default of an 'effective procedure' there is no determinate answer to the question of whether a being or beings of a certain kind exist, the impropriety of existence claims in these cases does not entail the propriety of non-existence claims. Nothing one way or the other can be said about that which the activated alpha-source is producing.

The fatal flaw in the whole argument is that it depends on the close tie that is supposed to obtain between bivalence and realism. It is just because bivalence can be imposed only on 'effectively decidable' statements that determinate claims to reality are restricted to those beings which have actually been revealed. Referential realism makes a distinction between 'reasons for believing that there are some of these sorts of beings at this place in the referential grid of space–time' and demonstrations of existence. If the apparatus has been switched on, the fact that some alpha-particles have been detected is enough to count as a good reason for taking the above subjunctive conditional seriously. If that subjunctive conditional is plausible we have good reason for believing in the existence of unobserved alpha-particles. Failure to make this distinction has some quite bizarre consequences. I fall victim to malaria in a place where laboratory facilities are available and the technicians find plasmodia in some of my red corpuscles. I move upcountry and suffer another attack. Is it even remotely plausible to say, as I think Luntley must, that while the meaning of the statement 'There are plasmodia in my blood cells' is the same as it was when uttered in Dar es Salaam it follows from the lack of microscopes upcountry that nothing determinate as to the existence of the hypothetical plasmodia corresponding to the referring expression 'plasmodia' as uttered upcountry can be said? Treating malaria with paludrine would then have to be just an irrational hit-or-miss bit of witchcraft! Symptoms are 'reasons for believing in the existence of instances of well-established causal mechanisms', defeasible reasons no doubt, but then so in the end are microscopical observations and even the results of careful scrutiny with the naked eye. Once Luntley has liberalized the notion of 'observing so and so' to include instruments, it is hard to see how he can find a principled way of stopping the reintroduction of other standard reasons for believing or disbelieving in the existence of kinds of beings, hallowed by past successful practice. If there are such reasons then something determinate, though defeasible, can be said about existence. It is his (dogmatic) adherence to the bivalence principle as the only way of defining the conditions under which scientific, that is determinate, claims to reality or unreality can be made that leads him astray.

A neo-Berkeleyan ontology

Recently van Fraasen (1980) has tried to make a case for an ontology even stricter than Berkeley's (see Moked, 1971). No argument for a modest referential realism could succeed if the interpretation of scientific discourse could be shown to be constrained by an ontology of a Berkeleyan sort. If *percipi* is confined to *esse*, *percipere* is not a ground for an existence claim. The usual menagerie of referents with which scientists have always imaginatively extended their ontologies to anticipate new experience would have to be reduced to members of those kinds with which we have already had sensible acquaintance. We must not, he says, treat unobservables as putative observables. To do so would be to make a mistake of the same kind as someone who thinks that the Empire State Building is portable because King Kong could lift it. This strikes me as a particularly feeble analogical argument on which to hang so radical a revision of scientific ontology. But it is worth examining closely. It makes use of a suppressed premise, something like a principle of linguistic essentialism, a doctrine rightly abominated by Popper and Wittgenstein among others. The underlying logic of van Fraasen's argument must go something like this: 'portable' means 'able to be carried by an unaided human being'. By parity of reasoning, 'observable' means 'able to be observed by an unaided human being'. To argue that something unobservable may come to be observable (and so to speak have been the same thing all along) is to violate the rules of language. So the scientific ontology must be tied to current human capacities for observation. *Percipi est esse*! Van Fraasen generously allows physicists and other simpletons to think in terms of a spurious ontology, that is the realist interpretation of their theories, provided they drop it when they are called upon to say something about the furniture of the world. So the back of the moon did not exist before the Apollo fly-pasts, nor did bacteria before the invention of the microscope. Henry VIII is now thought to have died of syphilis. What can we make of the statement that Henry VIII and Al Capone died of the same disease? It must be nonsense, since for us Renaissance syphilis is an unobservable. Medical historians' accounts of the probable microbial causes of death of Renaissance figures, unless of course it was by execution, drowning and the like observable ends, must be playing games with a spurious ontology.

But the opponents of linguistic essentialism, particularly Wittgenstein, have pointed out that the rules for the use of any conceptual opposition, including that between 'observable' and 'unobservable' things and events, cannot be laid down in advance. Were the Mayor of New York smart enough to hire King Kong there might be thought to be a marked advance in the technology of garbage disposal. No doubt there would then be a shift in the rules for the use of the distinction between the portable and the non-portable. The same argument can be used in the case where a new technique of observation is developed perhaps with the help of more sophisticated instrumentation. The rules for the use of the distinction between observable and unobservable things and events would be expected to change. Not only is the polar distinction between observable and unobservable technically relative but it is also relative to contingent facts about the human senses. The argument that we must take the existence of magnetic fields seriously because there could be creatures with magnetic sensibility is not refuted by arguing that there are in fact no such creatures.

Musgrave (1984) has identified a second fallacy in the way van Fraasen puts his case. According to van Fraasen the nature of human beings entails that the observable/unobservable distinction be drawn where it is currently drawn, with the currently unobservable ruled out of the ontology of science. But the nature of the human senses, which finally fixes this line and defines the scientific ontology for all time, is supposed to be derived from a very sophisticated theory of the physiology of perception. But as Musgrave points out a theory must mention both observable and unobservable states and processes. Therefore, according to the very criterion which van Fraasen proposes as to whether we should accept a theory as true or false, namely the observability of its putative referents, a theory which purports to refer to the unobserved cannot be taken to be true. Hence, by transitivity of inference, neither can its consequences be taken to be true, in particular that the observable/unobservable distinction is an ontological absolute. Of course van Fraasen also commits the formal fallacy of *ignoratio elenchi*, by claiming to draw ontological conclusions from epistemological premises. (For a very thorough critical examination of van Fraasen's project, see Worral, 1984.)

Science as problem-solving

Problem-solving or banausic relativism is a doctrine whose advocates have noticed that belief in theories determines to a large extent what is to count as a problem and what an acceptable solution should be like. Laudan, for example, seems to suppose that by adopting the 'problem-solving' position he can give an account of scientific progress that avoids the difficulties of those who, like Popper, see the advancement of science as a movement towards truth. Like Popper Laudan seems to accept the force of traditional sceptical doubts about the possibility of attaining truth by empirical methods. Unlike Popper he also seems to believe that this makes the movement towards truth not only impossible to consummate, but perhaps even undetectable in principle. Since science cannot therefore be accumulating truth it must be content to see itself as accumulating theory-relative solutions to problems. Laudan's inability to formulate the problem-solving view without drawing on the idea of empirical truth and attainable truth at that has been nicely demonstrated by Newton-Smith (1981b).

Modest scientific realism

The first step in building an array of arguments against antirealism will be to show that global antirealism is unacceptable. Global antirealism has been espoused by such authors as Laudan and van Fraasen largely because they have taken scientific realism to be the global doctrine I have called 'truth realism'. If that is what scientific realism is supposed to be then it is an easy target for sceptical arguments. To defeat global antirealism the doctrines of scientific realism must be so chosen that they do not depend in any essential way on the over-demanding principle of bivalence. I hope to show that the referential realism which I am defending in this study is indeed not dependent in any essential way on the principle of bivalence. So if my project is successful it will escape the traditional arguments against scientific realism. Referential realism leads to a conception of scientific activity as a cunning blend of material and cognitive practices performed within a rigorous moral order which defines 'truth' and 'falsity' as concepts central to the morality with which the scientific community carries on its unique practices. The truth that scientists seek and the falsity they eschew is not the truth and the falsity about which no human being could satisfy themselves. It is a morally qualified knowledge, shaped for a community built upon trust. The defeat of traditional scepticism will not be achieved by the demonstration that the arguments of the sceptics are fallacious. I do not think that they are. Rather it will be achieved by the demonstration that these arguments home in on the wrong targets. The bulk of this study is, then, given over to the construction of a form of scientific realism that needs only a weak system of epistemic concepts, but a strong notion of reference. I offer now an outline sketch of the argument for referential realism.

Most of the leading concepts in the following sketch are terms of art though based upon commonsense meanings, and they will be introduced in a detailed way in the chapters to come. The argument requires a distinction between three epistemic realms, the realm of common perception, the realm of beings which could be observed given certain historical and technical contingencies, and the realm of beings which for a variety of reasons are beyond all human observational capacity. The claim that many of the substantive terms of ordinary language refer to beings, their states and relations which exist independently of human sensibility will be defended by an excursion into the psychology of perception with an exposition of the theories of J. J. Gibson. An inductive argument will be developed to justify the policy of treating the substantive terms of those theories which purport to describe beings which are of the same natural kinds as those we can perceive, and which we have reason to think are currently unobservable by reason of technical inadequacies of our culture, as possibly having real referents. Taken in a policy way, referential realism amounts to the advice 'If a substantive term seems to denote a being of a certain natural kind (and some special conditions are satisfied by the theory in which that term functions) it is worth setting up a search for that being.'

Terra australis was proposed as a hypothetical being within the framework of medieval geophysics. It was of the same natural kind as known land masses, but it was unobservable at the time it was first proposed, by reason of the technical inadequacy of shipping. Eventually ships improved and finally Abel Janzoon Tasman landed in Van Diemen's Land. The back of the moon had the same status until very recently. Policy realism suggests that technical advances should be sought which would make the observing of these putative beings a practical possibility. The development of shipping technology and of space exploration equipment permitted both beings to be found, that is to be added to the catalogue of beings which, if we can perceive the world at all, are part of it. Most of the propositions that theoreticians had believed about Australia and many they had held about the back of the moon turned out to be false, or at best in need of more or less drastic revision. But Australia is not rendered any the less real by the revision of much that was once thought to be true of it. Now we extend the argument to cases where the technical advances required have involved the development of sense-extending instruments like microscopes, X-ray machines, telescopes, and so on. We can refine policy realism to include explorations to decide whether there is a lost continent of Atlantis, whether diseases are caused by micro-organisms, whether there is cavitation in the vicinity of a spinning propeller, whether whales can sing, and so on.

The inductive argument to a general policy realism for theoretical terms for theories whose putative referents are possible existents is based upon a comparative exploration of the significant features of theories of this kind. I shall be building up a concept of 'plausibility' which will capture those features of theories which historical experience shows are good bets for having anticipated experience with the inclusion in their working vocabulary of a robust referring expression. Policy realism then says, 'All future theories possessing the property of plausibility with putative referents in the realm of possible experience should be taken to be within the scope of the methodology of policy realism.' According to the referential realist, science advances by accumulating and sometimes deleting specimens from its collections, which have been gathered by forays into space–time or some other referential grid, guided by theory. At the same time a body of anecdotes is built up concerning unsuccessful hunting expeditions and why they failed. These hunts are *material practices*. Looking for the free quark is something like looking for the okapi, though finding the free quark is not just like finding the okapi. The real world of science is the momentary station on the long trail of explorations which are themselves the intersections of material and cognitive practices.

The above inductive argument is meant to defeat global antirealism. It depends on the claim that the unobservability of the referents of some plausible theories can be remedied by historically conditioned technical advances. This should lead to a distinction between accidental and in-principle unobservability of beings as the putative denotation of theoretical terms. The inductive argument depends on the premise that some unobservables can become observables, so the policy of taking their existence seriously enough to undertake a search is vindicated. It is as well to be cautious about large claims as to the empirical decidability of existence hypotheses. While a communally confirmed claim of the discovery of a yeti uttered by keen observers in the presence of a hairy Himalayan hominid would prove the existence of abominable snowmen, the oft-repeated judgement '*That's* not a yeti' does not disprove the existence of such creatures.

But there are theories which purport to describe states and relations of beings which could never be objects of common experience, even with extensions of the senses. These are the theories of deep physics, of macro-sociology, and some branches of psychology. I hope to show that physicists have created an analogue of the constraint on natural kinds which guaranteed the plausibility of theories like the micro-organic theory of disease. The mathematical properties of deep physical laws, particularly the property of covariance, will be shown to be analogous to the natural-kind constraint on the content of theories whose referents are possible objects of experience. Referential realism can be tentatively extended along the dimensions justified by the analogies upon which I hope to show the mathematical epistemology of deep physics is based.

We need only one example of a theory-led real-world search with a determinate outcome to defeat global antirealism. If that point of view means anything it must entail that no theory-led search could be successful except by accident, that is quite independently of the fact that it had been theory-led. All that is needed is a determinate outcome. A search which fails is as good support for policy realism as a search which succeeds. This simple point takes away much of the antirealist force of Laudan's (1977) catalogue of unsuccessful physical theories. Only by giving such theories a policy realist reading did it become possible to undertake a project which would show that their putative referents did not exist.

Against scepticism in general

Miller's (1985) arguments summarize the reasons one might have for turning away from the endless struggle to impose the strict system of meta-concepts, such as truth and falsity, logical deducibility, etc., on science to a more modest endeavour. One might want to try to understand the conceptual structure and material practices of the scientific community, and, to borrow a term from Miller, to analyse the nature of the 'disadvantages' and advantages that adopting this or that belief or practice might have. This, I believe, was the route taken by Hume. But even modest scientific realism is challenged by true scepticism. To put the matter in a currently fashionable rhetoric, how could Abel Janzoon Tasman know that he was really seeing the coast of *terra australis*? Perhaps all along he was just a brain-in-a-vat hitched to a computer which fed the approriate stimuli to the stubs of his optic nerves. Generalize this speculation to any intellect, including your own, and general scepticism is born. Even the most modest variety of scientific realism would have to be abandoned.

Two sceptical claims must be clearly distinguished. First-order scepticism is expressed in the claim that no human being can know anything. This level of scepticism could be advocated by analysing the concept of knowledge and showing that none of the conditions necessary for the proper application of that concept could be met. Second-order or Cartesian scepticism is expressed in the claim that no human being could know that they knew anything. This level of scepticism is nourished by such fables as the philosopher in the oven, the brain-in-a-vat and the perfect clone. These tales are used to illustrate the point that no human being could tell whether any of their beliefs were genuine.

Dealing with first-order scepticism is the project of this book. One proceeds by identifying the conditions under which scientists claim to know something, and demonstrates that those conditions can be met by a well-trained human being. All sceptical doubts expressed at the first level must fall to an analysis of what certainty *actually* amounts to, grounding a general accusation of the kind I made above against Miller, that of committing the 'philosophers' fallacy' of high redefinition. The point has been made at length by Klein (1981): 'The sceptic has conflated the logical possibility of error with the real chance of being wrong.' All Klein has to do is to show that there are cases where there is no real chance of being wrong. 'A justification', he says (p. 174), 'would be sufficient to provide certainty if it *is* absolutely reliable in the actual situation in which it is employed [that is every consideration which would defeat it is actually misleading]; it cannot be further required that it be able to withstand all possible defeators. What is required is that there be (actually) no significant counterevidence available.' Such an account does not eliminate the logical possibility of 'unknowable defeators'. It shows that to abandon all claims to know because of the logical possibility that such exist is absurd.

The arguments for second-order or Cartesian scepticism are sometimes illegitimately offered in support of first-order scepticism. Clones and brains-in-vats are the hi-tec versions of the philosopher dreaming that he is philosophizing. Clones and other monsters are rolled on not only in support of general scepticism, for instance against the irreducibility of *de re* beliefs, that is against the claim that beliefs about things must be caused by things, but also in defence of individualism in psychology (against collectivist or social-constructionist theories of mind). The clone argument goes like this. A person, say Robert, has a set of beliefs about the world, which we may suppose, for the sake of argument, to have been caused by certain relevant states of the world. Robert thinks he knows that this is so. He is, by virtue of that second-order belief, a scientific realist. Some clever biochemists make a clone of Robert, by exactly copying every one of Robert's molecular structures, including those in which both his first- and second-order beliefs are materially realized. Their private nickname for the clone is 'Hilary' but the clone of course is certain that its name is Robert. Hilary is as sure of both orders of belief as is Robert, but Hilary's first-order beliefs were not produced by things, so his second-order beliefs are wrong. Unless the scientists let on, Hilary can never know that he is not really Robert. For all any one us can think we know we might be like Hilary. So no second-order claim to know that one knows anything about the world can be sustained.

Clone arguments are vulnerable to a rather simple objection. In order to get general scepticism going we must each speculate that we are perhaps clones. But to entertain that suspicion we must also suppose that there is someone, the 'Robert' to our 'Hilary', who does really have empirical knowledge, that is *de re* beliefs. A similar objection can be raised to the use of a clone argument in support of psychological individualism. It confuses the conditions under which a concept could exist in a social order so that it would be available to an individual, with the conditions under which that individual could apply it. For instance Robert's anger might be based on a fancied transgression, and all Hilary's emotional states will be intentionally false, but that goes nowhere to prove the illegitimacy of the claim that the concept of anger can exist only in a society that recognizes transgressions against the person. For similar reasons the brain-in-a-vat speculation will not work as an antirealist argument. To speculate that one might be such a being, one must suppose that somebody is technically competent enough successfully to practise the deception. And that person (or fiend) must know that they know by virtue of their technical competence enough to fool their victim. There cannot be an endless chain of brains-in-vats each engaged in deceptive practices on the next in line.

A final objection turns on the point that the possibility of the situation envisaged in the anecdote depends on conditions which undermine its force. What are the necessary conditions for the brain to formulate the thought 'Perhaps I am really a brain-in-a-vat?' It must have a language with resources enough to make acts of self-reference and predication. But for there to be a language of such a level of sophistication there must be the possibility for the use of public criteria of correctness for such practices. Furthermore, for the brain to have acquired these practices it must once have been an embodied being with legitimate beliefs about a public world. If it can formulate the self-referential speculation it may not be able to be sure that it is not the victim of a hi-tec prank, but it can soon go through the above moves to satisfy itself that not every sentient being could be in such a predicament.

First-order scepticism will fall to the demonstration that there is a working system of concepts and practices which deliver what the community means by scientific knowledge. Second-order scepticism falls to the objection that among the conditions under which it can be formulated are some that entail that it is false.

3

Realism Revised

Referential realism

Distinguished from truth realism

The variety of realism to be elucidated and defended in this work expresses, one hopes, the spirit of scientific realism but escapes the traditional criticisms. It does not depend, in any essential way, on the strict concepts of truth and falsity. I shall call this 'referential realism'. Ellis has called this view 'entity realism'. In the second chapter of van Fraasen's (1980) *Scientific image* we find formulations of truth realism and referential realism carelessly run together. Putnam is perhaps ultimately to blame for a general failure to distinguish these rather different realisms, and this is partly due to his theory of reference, to be tackled in a later chapter. For the moment we simply notice that he offers what he appears to think are equivalent formulations. Van Fraasen follows Putnam when he says:

a realist (with respect to a given theory or discourse) holds that (1) the sentences [*sic*] of the theory are true or false; and (2) that what makes them true or false is something external – that is to say, it is not (in general) our sense data, actual or potential, or the structure of our minds, or our language etc.

Leaving aside the troubles that must surely arise if we try to make sense of the metaphor of 'external', where perhaps van Fraasen means 'independent', we have an account that makes the truth or falsity of the statements of a theory the touchstone of the realist position. But van Fraasen then goes on to say 'That terms in a mature science typically refer [meaning perhaps 'denote'].' He adds, as a gloss, 'that the theories accepted in a mature science are typically approximately true'. And finally he returns to the referential theme to say 'that the same term can refer to the same thing even when it occurs in different theories.' Here are two very different specifications of scientific realism. In his final formulation Van Fraasen drops denotation (reference) and returns to truth: 'Science aims to give us, in its theories, a literally true story of what the world is like; and acceptance of a scientific theory involves the belief that it is true' (p. 8). Van Fraasen blithely recommends his version in the assertion 'This is the correct statement of scientific realism'! But this again elides two very different ideas. The first part ties realism to a true account of what the world is *like*, not of what it is. I suppose this must mean true to some model or analogue. The second part, though vague, suggests realism of a more traditional cast.

The idea of referential realism is not new. St Thomas Aquinas in discussing natural science identifies scientific propositions as those which 'have their term in natural matter'. An obvious objection to the claim that reference can be secured independently of belief in the truth or falsity of certain propositions is that reference is always secured under a description. This is certainly true. However, reference to a referent, once secured, can be maintained through massive deletions from and additions to the corpus of beliefs we hold to be true of that referent. The demonstration of the existence of an exemplar is at once a cognitive and a material practice. A being is located in the grid of space–time, encouraged to display its causal powers and so on. These are not tied strictly to the description under which the being was first looked for, found and identified. We must routinely distinguish the business of establishing that something exists from the ever open possibilities for further research into what it is that exists. A referent can persist as the focus of empirical research and as the subject of predication even through recategorizations of a rather drastic sort. We can maintain our focus on an existent while our researches into its nature lead us to abandon every statement we once thought true of it, except that it exists and that its nature is such as to secure it a place in some referential grid. These matters will be explored in more detail in part two.

The duality between existence and description emerges again in the way existence claims, like much else in science, are based upon both material and cognitive practices. There is the material act of physically demonstrating the presence of a being by drawing our attention to a location in some referential grid, such as the space–time manifold, and so establishing a physical relation between embodied observer and observed being. Then there is the cognitive act of deciding whether we can recognize the occupant of that location as a specimen of the kind in question. Part of my purpose in this study is to highlight the way contemporary philosophy of science has systematically neglected the material practices upon which the whole enterprise of science is ultimately based in favour of cognition.

The defence of referential realism turns in the end on successfully explaining reference without falling back on some implicit recourse to the bivalence principle. We can begin by looking at a classical formulation of the referential position due to Sellars, who expresses it thus: 'to have good reason for holding a theory is *eo ipso* to have good reason for holding that the entities postulated by the theory exist.' 'Truth or falsity' of statements is replaced by 'existence or non-existence' of entities at the heart of a specification of scientific realism. The former depends upon various cognitive practices, the latter upon material practices. The trick is to shift from cognition to practice, in such a way that the act of establishing the existence or non-existence of putative entities will be shown to depend on a material practice for which only some weak alethic notion like 'more or less adequate description' is needed, something falling far short of the rigours of the bivalence principle. Referential realism requires that some of the substantive terms in a discourse denote or purport to denote beings of various metaphysical categories such as substance, quality and relation, that exist independently of that discourse. This will do for the physical sciences, and replaces such question-begging characterizations of reality as van Fraasen's 'external'. But it will need to be qualified in fundamental ways for the social and psychological sciences for which the discourse of mankind is the ultimate reality.

A sketch of policy realism

Plumping for referential realism has some immediate consequences for the practice of science.

1 The existential implications of the referential terms of a theoretical discourse must be taken seriously; in particular, research should be directed to determining whether there are referents for such terms. Under conditions yet to be specified it will be reasonable to set out on an exploration of the physical world to try to find out whether the putative referents exist, that is whether something *roughly* fulfilling the descriptive criteria for beings of the kind in question is to be located in the space–time grid.

2 I do not believe that there is any property of a theoretical discourse that can guarantee, a priori, that its substantive terms will have demonstrative grounding in real denotata. But I hope to show in part four that there is a property of a historically situated scientific discourse which makes it rational to undertake the project of looking for beings which could be the denotata of the referring expressions that appear in a discourse. The favouring property will be called 'plausibility'. An inductive argument will be developed to defend the view that both finding and failing to find referents is inductive support for referential realism. It will emerge that this form of realism must be thought of as a *policy*, the policy of looking for beings sufficiently like the putative referents whose characteristics are prescribed in the theory. This is as much as to say that referential realists take the referential potential of their

discourse seriously. Referential realism would be absurd if it required that realists should believe that they can tell merely from the properties of a theory whether its terms do actually denote something.

Denotation and its demonstrative grounding in independently existing beings in human acts of referring then becomes the focus of our enquiry, in so far as philosophical logic is concerned. In part two I shall try to show how we can add exhibits to our museum of specimens and how we can distinguish spurious from genuine claims to independent existence, without invoking the concepts of truth and falsity as they appear in the strict system. To defend the view that referential realism and truth realism are distinct philosophical theories we need an account of reference that does not depend in any essential way on the strict notions of truth and falsity. Already on offer is Putnam's (1978) and Kripke's (1980) theory of reference, in which the referring relation is essentially a causal residue. In their 'causal theory of reference' the denotation of a term is determined by a causal connection between the referent and the actual uses of that term. This connection has two parts.

1   The link between the referent and the experience by which reference was originally fixed; the experience may be partly social, including a reference-fixing ceremony.
2   The link between the inaugural occasion and subsequent uses.

Apart from the implausibility of treating the history of the referring uses of an expression in terms of causal relations, the theory is of limited utility for science since it requires the experiential manifestation of the entity in question (as a sample perhaps) to be prior to the securing of reference. Causality and hence existential priority flow from referent to referring expression. Of course it is Putnam and Kripke's covert adherence to a form of extensionalism as a general theory of meaning that traps them into this implausible position. Their theory of reference is very similar to Austin's (1961) 'cap-fitting': 'Here's a head, let's find a cap to fit it.' But in science theory usually anticipates experience. We need a bill-filling theory: 'Here's a list of goods, let's fulfil it.' It must be possible for the vocabulary of a scientific discourse to be meaningful without there yet having been found experienceable samples of some of the referential terms. We shall need to build a theory of reference of this second kind. But it will share a basic theme with the views of Putnam and Kripke. Reference is established by achieving a *physical* tie between embodied scientist and the being in question. Its existence is thus tied to that of the scientist. As Hacking correctly notes Putnam's later worries about systematically mismatched referential beliefs are banished once one notices that referring is a material practice (cf. Hacking, 1983, pp. 101–8). In so far as the distinction can be sustained I have tried to keep the term 'denote' for what words do, and 'refer' for the acts of human beings. A referring expression, then, is a denoting term which someone has used to perform an act of reference, as recognized by the community.

The basis of the modest realist claim is that theory can and does anticipate reality. Put thus baldly the claim needs qualification. The argument in favour of referential realism will take different forms depending on whether the putative referents in question are or could be possible objects of manipulation and experience or objects of possible experience and manipulation, or whether they never could be experienced, though they might be indirectly manipulated. There is thus a historically conditioned middle ground between the existents of naïve realism and the hypothetical entities of basic science. The inductive argument to be developed below is to be applied only to theories which purport to describe representations of beings which, though currently unobservable, are of the same natural kinds as beings we can or could observe. A different argument, based on an analogy between the role of natural kind terms in theories whose referents are objects of possible experience and the role of principles of symmetry and conservation in theories whose referents are states of the world beyond all possible experience, will be developed in part five.

For the inductive argument 'securing reference' requires the material practice of locating a specimen that meets certain requirements prescribed in the relevant theory. The material practice of hunting and finding or failing to find needs a grid through which locations likely to harbour specimens can be securely located. For modest referential realism the existence of space–time is an essential condition at least for adopting a policy-realist attitude to theories of the middle sort. But the location-securing grids for social and psychological sciences, and indeed for fundamental physics, may turn out to be rather different from space–time. The study of reference will then include a study of the ontological status of the spatio-temporal manifold.

The modest realism to the defence of which this work is directed is to be understood in terms of material practices rather than logical relations. It amounts to this: the appearance of a substantive term which seems to denote some extra-observational being (distinguished relative to the current state of the experimental arts) should be taken as the ground for a material project, a search of the real world for a being which could serve as its referent. Just what the notion of 'real world' encompasses will be explored in part three. For the moment commonsense understanding must suffice, but this goodwill borrowing will be paid back. New technology may have to be devised to prosecute the search. A great many philosophical problems will have to be dealt with *en route* to a successful defence of this position. The

theory of reference will have to be examined and the theory of meaning
tidied up. The nature of theories will have to be unravelled, and the
concepts of experience, observation and experiment clarified. An important
result of these endeavours will be the discovery that science is grounded not
in an epistemology, but in a moral order.

A triadic theory of science

The argument so far throws into doubt the idea that philosophical analysis
and speculation can lead to the discovery of one ubiquitous schema upon
which to base our discussion of all that commonsense is ready to claim
about the scientific enterprise. The arguments for antirealism generally take
the form of identifying scientific realism with one particular schema, treating it as if it were being offered as a universal theory of science, and then
finding cases which it plainly does not fit.

I hope to show that science does not have one and only one method. But I
am prepared to commit myself to the hypothesis that the bouquet of
methods I shall describe has some claim to be exhaustive. So I shall also be
disputing the Feyerabendian notion that anyone committed to a finite
methodology is entitled only to 'Anything goes'. I believe that science
disposes of three different methodologies, each appropriate to the study of a
specific domain of beings, both natural and cultural. By developing this
intuition together with the idea that scientific activity is set within a moral
order of a quite specific kind, whose lineaments I have sketched in chapter
one, I hope to show just what level of realism can be sustained, in the after-
math of the abandonment of that defined by the bivalence principle. It will
turn out to be a modest but substantial doctrine sufficient to justify the
confidence commonsense has in the ability of the scientific community to
'penetrate the secrets of nature', but without an absurd optimism in
inevitable and indefinite progress. When the triadic methodology of science
is seen clearly, the limits to our acquisition of reliable knowledge will
become apparent. I introduce my trio of methodologies with a classification
of theories according to their cognitive status. I use, for the moment, the
generic concept of 'cognitive object' to postpone the question of the mode of
realization of a theory, whether as a discourse, a diagram, a model or a
mathematical structure.

Type 1 theories: these are cognitive objects with pragmatic properties.
Theories of this type enable the constitution, classification and prediction of
observable phenomena. A typical type 1 theory is Newtonian kinematics.
Different kinds of motion can be differentiated by reference to very precise

definitions of the concepts of velocity, acceleration and so on, in terms of differential coefficients. The history of kinematics between the *De proportionibus* of Bradwardine and the *Principia* of Isaac Newton shows the interplay between the growing sophistication of definitions and the clarification of what kinematic phenomena there are.

Type 2 theories: these are cognitive objects with iconic properties. Theories of this type enable the representation (including sometimes the simple picturing) of a certain class of unobservable beings. Typical type 2 theories are the bacterial theory of disease; the Burges vector theory of crystal fracture, in which dislocations behave like Newtonian particles; plate tectonics; Hales' theory of the motion of the sap; and so on. All such theories involve a *representation*, in some medium or other, of a physical system and its modes of behaviour, which, at the time of the formulation of the theory, had not yet been observed. There are type 2 theories in psychology and sociology, and even in history, but of course the kind of unobserved system they represent will be different from those typical of physical theory. *The vast majority of scientific theories are of type 2.*

Type 3 theories: these are cognitive objects with mathematical properties. Theories of this type enable the representation of non-picturable systems of beings and of their behaviour, interrelations and so on. Such systems form a distinct class of unobservables, since by virtue of their unpicturability they could never be observed by human beings. The ontology behind such theories is embodied in certain mathematical or quasi-mathematical properties of the theoretical discourse, particularly in the trio covariance, symmetry and conservation. Special relativity, in its Einsteinian form, is a theory of this type, as are the theories of quantum field theory. In the special theory of relativity the mathematical property of covariance under the Lorentz transformation, a property already possessed by Maxwell's laws, is extended to the laws of mechanics by a change in the concept of mass. The implicit ontologies of this and other such theories will be discussed in some detail in part five.

Corresponding distinctions among theories in the social and psychological sciences can be set up. A different ontology serves as a foundation, one involving meanings, cognitive processes etc. , as realities. For example ethnomethodology yields type 1 theories of social interaction by looking for patterns among the observable actions, including verbal actions, of a group of actors, picked by reference to the folk meanings given to the events of interest by those actors themselves. Von Cranach's theory of action control involving representations of unobservable hierarchies of means–end pairs, each consisting of a definition of desired outcome and a rule of action to realize it, is a type 2 theory. It is an important implication of his methodology that people can become aware of the means–end pairs that they implicitly draw on when acting. Finally logic-based theories of modular information-processing, such as the approach to the understanding of mind suggested by Fodor, are theories of type 3. The 'machine language' of the processor can never manifest itself to the thinker, except as clothed in one of its products, a natural language. A similar round of examples can be found in sociology.

The defence of scientific realism will take different forms for each type of theory, and be accomplished to a different degree.

I have introduced the triadic theory of science with its trio of methodologies by trading on a commonsense understanding of 'theory'. But 'theory' is altogether too static and rigid a conception. In the detailed discussions of the methodology and metaphysics at work relative to the task of building and testing instances of each theory type, I shall introduce a more dynamic and flexible concept, that of the evolving 'theory-family'. This dynamic cognitive object crystallizes into a single theory only during certain historic moments of equilibrium.

On a literal reading of typical examples from each type we find three levels of existential commitment. With each level we must acknowledge an increasing degree of ontological conditionality and with that a decreasing claim to an unqualified realist reading. For type 1 theories, we, the users, are committed to the existence of phenomena which are or could be available to an unaided observer. (The concept of 'phenomenon' refers to a moment of equilibrium in the dialectic development of a pair of practices, one material and the other cognitive. I shall approach the concept of the phenomenon from many sides as the discussion develops.) I exempt from the 'no-instrument' qualification those devices which serve merely to make more precise and repeatable judgements which can be made without their aid. I have in mind such devices as clocks, rulers, squares etc. There are some subtleties which I am at present ignoring, such as the influences on our concepts of space and time of the way these instruments are constructed and graduated, for instance the difference between analogue and digital clocks. The referents of type 1 theories belong in Realm 1, the realm of actual and possible objects of experience. The moon and Pluto, the Grand Canyon and the Atlantic trench, the tongue and the renal portal vein belong in Realm 1.

For type 2 theories, we, the users, are committed, not only to the ontology of Realm 1 but also to beings which, if real, would be available to and thus phenomena for the amplified human senses. These are objects of possible experience and their certification as part of the real furniture of the world depends on the availability of the necessary technology. Micro-organisms, capillaries and X-ray stars belong in Realm 2.

For type 3 theories we, the users, are committed, not only to the ontologies of Realms 1 and 2 but also to beings which, if real, could not become phenomena for human observers, however well equipped with devices to amplify and extend the senses. Realm 3 is a domain of beings beyond all possible experience. Quantum states, naked singularities, social structure and Freudian complexes are amongst the typical denizens of Realm 3. I choose an odd expression like 'denizen' to alert us to the importance of continual vigilance against the importing of inappropriate ontological assumptions which are embedded in the logical grammar of such apparently innocent expressions as 'entity' and 'state'. Though the characteristics of these realms will be explored in detail some qualifying notes need to be entered here.

1 The boundaries between realms are historically variable for a variety of reasons.

2 Causal assumptions play a role in the methodology of all three realms. I note, for the moment, only the role of causal theories in the realist interpretation of the experiences provided by the instruments of Realm 2 science, in perceiving the coloured patches in the field of a microscope as a micro-organism.

3 Realm 3 is a heterogeneous domain. Beings may be beyond all possible experience because we lack the senses to observe them. The world would appear very differently to a being with magnetic sensibility. They may be beyond all possible experience because they belong to a natural kind of whose mode of manifestation we could form no clear idea, for instance social structure (an abstract system of human relations), or energy states, the most important of which are to be described in the dispositional language of potentials. For example the Lagrangean, '$T - V$', depends on the difference between field energy, described in terms of potential or possible actions, and kinetic energy, described in terms of the actual motion of the physical constituents of a system.

Complex ontological commitments

I have introduced the distinction between Realms 1, 2 and 3 in terms of conceptual distinctions around the notions of 'possibility', 'actuality' and 'experience'. 'Possible', 'actual' and 'experience' were permuted to create epistemic categories, classifying beings by reference to a human scientist's capacities to become acquainted with them. I owe to E. Scheibe (personal communication) the important observation that a full account of Realm 1, the realm of things actually experienced, requires the introduction of possibility as an ontological category. The spatio-temporal relations that obtain among the actual beings of Realm 1 must be supplemented by possible locations and moments to create a manifold rich enough to contain the elementary facts of kinematics. A tidy resolution of this apparent conceptual hiccough would be to treat kinematics as a Realm 2 science, on the grounds that an indispensable subset of the spatio-temporal relations which it describes are objects only of possible experience. And one might go further. Traditionally the laws of kinematics are taken to hold in a space–time manifold which is both dense and continuous. This implies the reality of infinitesimal transitions of location and epoch, which are beyond all possible human experience. Kinematics, on this showing, is at least in part, a Realm 3 science.

The case of kinematics shows that while, in general, the above distinctions between theory types map nicely on to the distinctions between epistemic realms, the fit is not perfect. In the case of kinematics, while the actual values in any case of the variables that appear in the laws are all reducible to functions of spatial, temporal or spatio-temporal relations between observable intervals, the ontology of the theory is much richer. The differential calculus, in terms of which the theory is formulated, requires a spatio-temporal manifold most of the relational properties of which are in Realm 3.

Underdetermination reconsidered

A further consequence of logicism can now be highlighted. This is the myth of the underdetermination of theories by data. For instance the empirical adequacy criterion offered by van Fraasen as a ground for accepting a theory only seems to be the last resort for deciding on the acceptability or unacceptability of theories if we have already bought the underdetermination thesis. Much hinges on what are taken to be relevant data. In the logicist framework these are usually taken to be results of experiments or observations, their relevance to a theory and hence their role as data being determined by whether or not they are deductive consequences of the theory considered only as a set of sentences, coupled with some descriptions of initial conditions. Of course if *these* are the only relevant data, and that is what the empirical adequacy criterion forces on one, then by the paradox of Clavius theories *are* underdetermined by data. However, if one looks at the way theories are actually 'determined', without any prior philosophical commitments, theories seem to stand at the intersection of two streams of influence. There is that which stems from experiment and observation, the influence of data. And there is that which has its source in the ontology of theory-families of which the one in question is a member. I shall show, in part four, how such families are the products of traditions of past scientific and philosophical work. Taking into account all these factors, it is usually the case that the range of alternative theories available to the community as possible explanations of some class of phenomena is very narrow indeed.

I have suggested that there are three kinds of theories, those whose content is exhausted by 'data' in the naïve sense of humanly observable matters of fact; those whose content includes not only data but also putative matters of fact imagined within the constraints of an ontology which is related to that currently embedded in modern, everyday experience; thirdly there are those whose content includes all this but also a speculative component that is 'deeper', in the sense that the ontology within which it is conceived is so far removed from that of everyday experience that the beings proposed by the theory could not become objects of human experience. The importance of the middle kind of theory for the philosophy of science is inestimable, since it is just this kind of theory that provides within the constraints and possibilities of available technology, a speculative, ontology-controlled component that is eventually testable.

All this has a bearing on the argument to the best explanation which I discussed briefly in the last chapter. By analogy we can accept Realm 3 theories by virtue of their being at the intersection of the influences of data and ontology, just like Realm 2 theories. The argument to the best explanation goes like this: the best explanation for the empirical adequacy of a theory is that it is true. But we have seen in chapter two that this way of explaining 'best' will not do. Suppose instead of 'true', and 'false' for the complementary condition, we introduced a notion of plausibility with its complement 'implausibility'. A theory is plausible if it is both empirically adequate and framed within the constraints of the current communally approved ontology. Usually only one theory as a moment in the development of a theory-family meets both constraints. I shall also show how real theory-families, developing in the research traditions of scientific communities, have system properties that ensure that they remain more or less 'on target' as they grow under the two main influences adumbrated above. Argument to the best explanation, *in this sense* and only in this sense, is supported by the induction on the utility of policy realism.

The growth of meaning

With the triadic theory of scientific method goes a triadic theory of meaning. We shall see that meaning arises in scientific cognition both extra and intralinguistically. Quite elementary considerations rule out the possibility of a theory of meaning for science based wholly on extralinguistic relations. Even to pick out a sample with which to fix the meaning of a descriptive term requires the use of concepts. To be able to use a colour patch to teach the meaning of 'cerise' the instructor must be able to indicate somehow to the learner that the hue of the sample is relevant and not its shape or size. How could the acquisition of meanings ever then get underway? One attractive resolution is the hypothesis that words were first used to perform actions and only later came to be used to describe things and processes. Action concepts are first acquired non-linguistically through performances such as those that developmental psycholinguists call 'deixis', intentional pointing, itself developing out of the natural interest in and skill of grasping. A commonsense conceptual scheme must already exist for members of the scientific community before ever they begin the development of the means for scientific discourse. Relative to that conceptual scheme, which essentially embodies the Kantian categories, extralinguistic beings can be picked out and used as samples. Through its role in the conditions for the acquisition of linguistic meaning the Kantian categorial scheme is deeply embedded in scientific discourse.

But discourses referring to the beings of Realm 2 and 3 cannot depend wholly on samples. There must also be intralinguistic meaning creation. For Realm 2 discourse the process of meaning creation will be typically simile. In Realm 2 discourse the natural kinds of Realm 1 must still serve as an ontology. New meanings can arise by emphasizing similarities and deleting differences, for instance in Darwin's creation of the meaning of the neologism 'natural selection'. As we shall see, the Kantian categories linger on in the ontology of Realm 3, through the conservative character of the metaphysical schemes actually invoked in using symmetry, conservation and covariance as prime criteria for assessing claims to the acceptability of putative theoretical descriptions. Energy is in some respects a typical substance, but not in others. In the light of the differences between, say, energy and water it might be wise to make a weaker claim. Perhaps one should say rather that energy is, though not exactly a substance, substantial. Given the important fact that samples of energy are not available in Realm 1 for point-by-point comparison with samples of typical substances such as water, the similarity between the deep grammar of the term 'energy' and that of the term 'water' should not be explained by simile. The trope is metaphor.

The nature of metaphor as a linguistic (semantic) phenomenon has been the subject of a good deal of debate. In this study I shall follow the recent attempt by Janet Martin Soskice (1985) to create a theory of metaphor that avoids a 'two subjects' treatment, and so the danger of collapse into simile, and yet does justice to the source of metaphor in existing linguistic practices. The view that metaphor is merely an ornamental figure replaceable without loss of meaning by a literal transcription has been thoroughly discredited. The least sophisticated of the remaining views is the 'comparison' theory. A metaphor is taken as a collapsed or condensed simile. Metaphors, it seems, can be 'unpacked' into explicit comparisons. 'Electric current' is explained perhaps by this gloss: 'In this and that respect but not these and those electricity is like a fluid'. The truth is that we usually have no basis for a comparison when we resort to metaphor to make our meaning clear. The 'current' image terms are the very terms in which the scientific community describes the phenomenon of electricity. There is no literal vocabulary in which the second member of the comparison could be described (see Schon, 1968)

The same difficulty besets a more sophisticated theory proposed by Max Black (1962). Metaphor is supposed to involve two subjects, each with its 'system of associated commonplaces'. These associated systems interact with one another, in that the secondary subject 'organizes' our thoughts about the primary subject in new ways. In subsequent discussion Black has had great difficulty in preventing his theory from collapsing into a comparison view. Nevertheless the basic intuition, reflecting I. A. Richards' classical distinction between 'tenor', the primary referent of the metaphorical attribution, and 'vehicle', the modifying term which 'carries' the metaphor, seems to be right (Richards, 1936).

The conception of metaphor due to Janet Martin Soskice (1985) is close to that of I. A. Richards. I shall call it 'the displacement theory' following Schon (1968). Metaphor is a trope through which new vocabulary is created. By means of it our conceptual grasp of a subject matter (referent) is enhanced by the use of a term with a well established context of use, and thus an existing deep grammar and set of associated commonplaces. A term used metaphorically is a term used in a new context to express a belief for which there is no existing vocabulary. In using a metaphor we are not comparing the subjects of the attribution of the term in the old and the new contexts, that is looking for similarities and differences between the old and the new extensions of the term. We are not acquainted with the referent of the term in the new context. But perhaps from theory we know some of the things we want to say about it. We are illuminating the new subject by virtue of the existing intension of the displaced term. In the new context that intension will be modified through the exigencies of the new conditions for its use. In this way, through metaphor, new vocabulary can be created within the existing structure of language, so securing the intelligibility of the term in its new context of use. Only the displacement theory of metaphor could explain how the use of terms metaphorically could open up the epistemic access which Boyd (1979) has rightly seen to be their creative function.

Intimations of ontology

There is a close relation between one's account of the modalities of scientific discourse, possibility and necessity, and the principles which govern one's general theory of the nature of the referents of that discourse. Another step along the middle way will be the development of an ontology that is neither wholly materialist nor wholly idealist. I believe that it is another characteristic mistake of philosophers to try to force the ontology of the physical sciences into one or the other mould. At various points throughout this study we shall come across contexts which point to a dual ontology. By 'adoption of a dual ontology' I mean that a general account of the beings to which we can make reference by the use of a discourse requires that the conditions for the empirical application of many important types of concepts involve a material grounding *and a cognitive (or ideal) extension*. The modalities of scientific discourse provide such a context. By 'necessity' I mean the modality which *excludes* some ideal or imagined alternatives to what is. By 'possibility' I mean the modality which *includes* some ideal or imagined alternatives to what is. Logical necessity excludes all ideal alternatives to what is, while logical possibility includes them. By 'excluded' I mean excluded from the concept or state or whatever it is that is modally qualified. The kinds of grounds that are offered for such an exclusion will depend on the kind of being that is modally qualified. The same remark applies to the grounds for inclusion in the case of beings qualified by possibility. Both modalities must be based in a dual ontology in the above sense. In a later section I shall be arguing for a dual ontology treatment of time, the totality of moments. On this view the temporal concepts 'Past' and 'future' are modal concepts. The former has the structure of necessity (the past is determinate and so excludes alternative or possible states of affairs) while the future, as a concept, has the structure of possibility, that is includes alternative or possible states of affairs. To qualify an event as past is to exclude any imagined alternative to that event at that point in the world series. To qualify any event as future is to leave open some set of imagined alternatives. Under the eye of God, but not of Man, future alternatives must be conceptual, since only one of the set of possibilities will occur, at that moment in the universal and actual sequence. Time is materially grounded, I shall argue, only in the indexical act marked by the utterance of 'now'. Similar 'dual ontology' treatments will be offered for concepts like 'law of nature', 'disposition', and so on.

The displacement of truth

The strict system and its limitations for the philosophy of science

It is now time to make good my oft-repeated reservations about the proper location of the concepts of 'truth' and 'falsity'. Philosophers of science have, for the most part, taken the task of the analyst of the knowledge garnering activities of science to be explicable in terms of the concepts of truth and falsity. The way these concepts have been understood has been determined by their behaviour in two rather different contexts. One such context is that created by an interest in the logical structure of scientific discourse. In this context the behaviour of the concepts 'truth' and 'falsity' is controlled by powerful principles such as the principle of non-contradiction. Included among the principles that dominate this context are the truth-preserving transformations of logical entailment, institutionalized in the traditional truth-tables. In this context the syntax of the concepts is determined. The other context is that of the assessment of the descriptive or representational adequacy of statements which purport to refer to all kinds of extralinguistic matters, such as the state of the natural environment, and even the moral hegemony of the Divine order. In this context the meaning of the concepts is determined.

For the purposes of traditional philosophy of science the concept of truth has usually been taken strictly, marking a (perhaps unattainable) perfect match between the sense of the statement and the corresponding state of the world, which, having that sense, it is somehow guaranteed to denote. In the 'strict' system any degree of imperfection in that match is enough to merit the judgement 'false'. This is the sort of assessment scheme typical of those philosophies which take the problem of truth to be concerned with how it is possible for something symbolic (linguistic) to match and/or represent any non-symbolic state of the world. A referential theory of meaning and truth tries to manage with the relation of matching, which, being at root arbitrary, escapes the problem of how words can represent states of the world. The coherence theory of truth, which takes thought and world ultimately to be of the same nature, has not been popular with realists, since its way with truth depends on a background idealism. If 'truth' and 'falsity' are used to mark different degrees of 'fit' of propositions one with another and with meaningful manifestations of the world, of a propositional sort, the mutability and potential variety of meaningful manifestations seem to clash with the idea that there is only one world and the task of science is to describe it. (For a defence of a revised coherentist position, see Rescher, 1973a).

In recent times the analysis of scientific thought has proceeded as if it was obvious that scientific knowledge was built up by creating and refining a *discourse*. But discourse is only one of many modes for the public display of cognition. I believe we need to make use of a wider class of informative entities which I shall call 'cognitive objects'. When knowledge is expressed in the iconic mode as a diagram or model, representational accuracy and inaccuracy (faithfulness, etc.) replace 'truth' and 'falsity' as the main ways of expressing and assessing epistemic worth. A notion like 'representational quality' is obviously better adapted to a less strict dichotomizing of assessments than are 'truth' and 'falsity'. Likenesses can be more or less faithful, drawings and diagrams more or less accurate portrayals of their subject matter. The qualified judgement 'more or less accurate' is certainly easier to analyse than the puzzling idea of degrees of truth. (See Miller A. I. , 1985, on the role of visualisability as a constraint on theory formation in physics.) Truth and falsity seem to be polar or terminal concepts which do not easily admit of degrees. I shall call the assessment system which is based on a polar reading of 'truth' and 'falsity' and which is controlled by the above principles the 'strict' system. Within that system we can find a place for deduction as truth-preserving entailment, and for logical necessity and possibility.

It is ironical that a philosophy of science based on studies of the workings of the strict system has revealed apparently insoluble problems in trying to understand, in terms of that system, how science could be carried on. The problem of induction is the best known, but the paradox of the ravens is at least as disturbing. The former seems to forbid our sustaining truth claims for general empirical statements, while the latter seems to show that not all logically sanctioned transformations of propositions preserve their original epistemic value. These problems emerge as clashes between the basic properties of the strict system and well-founded intuitions of how the assessment concepts of the epistemology of science actually behave. I propose to treat these problems as *reductiones ad absurdum* of the strict system. They are reasons for rejecting it as a basis for a philosophical analysis of scientific activity. I do not think that they are intellectual puzzles to be resolved in the interests of maintaining the hegemony of the strict system.

In part six I shall develop an alternative analysis of the formal structure of law statements that does not draw on the logicist apparatus, the use of which is, I believe, largely responsible for the appearance of these difficulties. The strict system seems to be the progenitor of scepticism. How can any reliable knowledge of the natural world arise out of limited human experience, if the concept of reliable knowledge is spelled out in terms of the strict system?

Scope and depth scepticism

The truth or falsity of statements which 'go beyond experience' can never be determined. For instance we can never be sure of the truth of universal statements such as 'All past, present and future electrons will be negatively charged' unless these statements are being used to inform the reader of a defining or criterial property of the natural kind in question. Similarly we can never be sure of the falsity of existential claims such as 'There are creatures with eyes in their chests' unless the space–time region for the search is strictly bounded. The possibility that universal statements can be shown to be false, through the experimental demonstration of the falsity of a logical consequence of the statement in question, remains open. So does the possibility of showing general existential claims to be true by the discovery of an instance of the kind in question. We still owe to Hume (1739) the most thorough and most influential investigation of the possibility of using the strict system as a basis for the assessment of human claims to possess scientific knowledge, that is as a real working system. As I have argued in chapter two Hume's famous arguments can usefully be separated into two groups. In the one he examines the scope of claims to have general knowledge. He concludes that experience aided by reason cannot give us certain knowledge of future states of affairs. This becomes the 'problem of induction' if we still hanker after that kind of knowledge. In the other he dismisses the conceptual basis of the physics of his day, in which claims to knowledge of the unobservable causes of the observed patterns of events invoked the concept of 'causal power'. The dismissal of the latter is closely linked with an attack on natural necessity. The only modality of which scientific belief admits is pure contingency.

Any claim to have proved by the use of reason the truth of a law of nature on the basis of the kind of evidence that could be turned up by any human project is spurious. To reach from particular items of evidence to laws whose scope is supposed to be universal by the exercise of reason would require some general and incontrovertible principle. The 'uniformity of nature' might serve but its empirical standing is no better than the generalizations it was called in to support. This argument, be it noted, does nothing to show that it is pointless to accommodate our beliefs to the results of our experiments and systematic observations. We can never have logically conclusive grounds for the kinds of beliefs that are the substance of scientific knowledge. These considerations do not require a radical scepticism. Rather they show that the strict system of assessment cannot justly be used in scientific contexts. And thus far I am with Hume. This admission does not rule out the possibility of developing some weaker but more defensible scheme by which a scientific community can distinguish general principles, theoretical prescriptions of so far unobserved entities, etc., which, in the light of their studies, should be thought worthy of belief, from those that are merely useful or from those that should be abandoned. Nor need we be driven to an exclusively psychological or sociological account of why one hypothesis is accepted and another rejected.

Hume's arguments against the use of concepts like 'substance', 'power' and 'causal efficacy' in scientific discourse other than to express psychological states like expectation depend on the same metaphysical scheme as do his arguments against the possibility of induction, namely an atomistic, phenomenalist analysis of experience. If there are no real relations between events, *a fortiori*, there can be no productive relations between events. Locke had already expressed a similar worry about depth in his discussion of real essences. Material things must have real essences. Their behaviour and observable properties stem from their atomic constitutions. According to the corpuscularian philosophy the real essences of particulars are arrangements of particles. These are the physical properties which endow real things with powers to produce the effects they do on sensitive creatures like ourselves, and to engender consequential physical changes in other material beings. But the human perceptual system is so constituted that we cannot observe the fine structures of things. Among other sensory deficits we lack microscopical eyes. There can be no place in our *science* for real essences. This does not make it wrong that Newton and Boyle made vigorous attempts to describe the 'arrangements of parts in the superficies of bodies', but it does mean that one can have no more than opinion concerning them.

Strict assessment assessed

Could we not finally ground the truth and falsity of science in the results of competently used experimental and observational techniques? Studying scientists at work soon makes it clear that experimental results are made germane to the assessment of laws and theories by decisions as to which part of the complex of metaphysics, auxiliary theories and conceptual relations involved in treating any experiment or observation as a test should be taken to be vulnerable to its outcome. There is ultimately no non-arbitrary way of making that decision, I believe. How it is made in particular cases will be determined not only by technical considerations but also by power-relations in the thought-collective, the social order obtaining among this or that group of scientists. Hence any claim to have established the truth of an existential hypothesis or the falsity of a universal claim by reference to the result of experiments or observations is defeasible. This point is sometimes thought to be a modern discovery, but it can be traced back at least as far as Kepler's remarks on the epistemological status of astronomical hypotheses. In the introduction to Darwin's *Origin of species* the author cites a variety of evidence which throws into doubt the utility and plausibility of the traditional conceptual distinction between varieties and species. Darwin lets the evidence speak against the then current metaphysics. But the defenders of *infima species* could and did use the same evidence to demonstrate (to speak for) the rich proliferation of varieties. By adjusting the concept pair 'species/variety' any 'fact' can be accommodated to either grand point of view. Darwin seems to be arguing that if we take a great many facts into consideration only one way of making the distinction is reasonable.

Experimental results are not data in search of a hypothesis. By virtue of our willingness to entertain this or that hypothesis or theory an observation becomes fraught with significance. Only then does it become germane to the question of whether we should accept or reject a hypothesis. We find this most beautifully exemplified in the reasonings of Galileo. By the conceptual transformation of the idea of motion from a 'process of change requiring a sustaining cause', the Aristotelian conception, to a continuous, self-maintaining state, Galileo *provided himself* with an enormous range of diverse evidential anecdotes. Taken within his new framework, certain phenomena with which everyone was capable of becoming acquainted, but which had scarcely been noticed as significant, became potent items of evidence for Galilean physics. For example, once one has in mind the idea of the uncaused persistence of motion, then the hitherto unemphasized fact that a rider can throw up his spear and catch it again, while at the gallop, takes on a strong evidential quality.

From an exhaustive catalogue of the multiplicity and diversity of motions to be observed in the world nothing of unqualified generality could have been induced. An Aristotelian could advance the fact that a rolling ball soon comes to rest, that a coasting ship soon stops moving, and so on, as facts evidential for the principle that without a sustaining cause motion soon ceases. This is why Koyré's epigram 'For it is thought, pure unadulterated thought, and not experience or sense-perception, as until then, that gives the basis for the "new science" of Galileo Galilei' (Koyré, 1968) fails to capture the true beauty of Galileo's method. It is not that Galileo makes 'no appeal to experience' (Koyré, *loc cit.*) in discussing how a ball will fall when dropped from the mast of a ship. His procedure is to demonstrate the power of his physical hypotheses *to provide themselves with evidence culled from experience*. Theory becomes a device for focussing our attention. Theory precedes fact, not because *necesse* determines *esse* as Koyré would have it, but because a theory determines where, in the multiplicity of natural phenomena, we should seek for *its* evidence. Science is empirical because we may fail to find what we want. The task of reconstructing what were the perfectly correct observations which had served as evidence for the Aristotelian point of view, when that was how we looked at the world, can be postponed. Once we have been led to attend to the horseman and his spear, and to see that as the significant fact, our attention is, so to speak, distracted from such matters as that other horse which was needed to keep the exemplary cart in motion. The fact that carts soon stop without horses to pull them ceases to be a fact of any significance. Accommodating the 'old facts' is not then achieved by finding a cunning way of deducing them from the new theory, as the deductivists would have it. We don't bother with them.

In fairness to Koyré it is worth remarking that in a later chapter in the work cited above he comes much closer to the position just sketched. He sees quite clearly that experiments are not, indeed could not be, the inductive grounds for hypotheses, but that it is hypotheses which endow certain experiments with significance and thus tranform their results into 'evidence'. 'Experimentation', he says, is an 'interrogation which pre-supposes and implies a *language* in which to formulate the questions, and a dictionary which enables us to read and to interpret the answers' (p. 19).

Modality

Hume's famous argument against causal necessity – that there is no contradiction in conjoining a description of a cause with the negation of a description of its usual effect – is surely valid. But what does it show? At best it shows that causal or natural necessity is not logical necessity. Indeed that was how Hume seems to have taken the argument, since he went on to give an account of causal necessity in terms of the psycho-logical phenomenon of a habit of expectation formed through exposure to repeated instances of a concomitance of similar pairs of events of the same types. The argument certainly does not show that a statement like 'An unsuspended body in a gravitational field *must* fall if released, *ceteris paribus*' is incoherent. Despite Hume's argument there are all sorts of other possible accounts of the concept of causal or natural necessity that is expressed in the modal vocabulary of scientific discourse than the psycho-logical interpretation he proposes. The actual system of assessment involves a repertoire of modal words which are used to mark certain quite important distinctions. Hume's argument is important to me because it shows that these uses are not explicable in terms of the concepts of the strict system.

It is worth noticing that general existential claims can be shown to be unfalsifiable within the system of strict concepts. And yet the scientific community becomes convinced, and rightly, that certain particular entities and certain kinds of beings do not exist. After the debate is over the community will accept no further claims concerning them. The actual system, then, cannot be isomorphic with the real system, nor can its uses be illuminatingly analysed in terms of the concepts of that system.

A sketch of the actual system

To find accounts of the actual system of assessment in use in science one must bypass the study of printed scientific texts. These texts are written within the conventions of a certain rhetoric, the latest in a sequence of rhetorics, each of which 'secretes' its own philosophy of science. Failing one's own research corpus gleaned by recording the conversations of every-day life in laboratory and common-room, and grubbing round for the remnants of early drafts of scientific papers, one must turn to the literature of the microsociology of science in which the actual system is described. This literature is frequently enlivened with quotations in *oratio recta*. I shall illustrate something of the way the actual system works with descriptions of two main processes: the use of judgements of personal character in deciding on the reliability of the results of research, and the asymmetry in the way data are treated when they are used to support one's own ideas and when they have been quoted in support of the ideas of a rival.

'Who did it?'

Personal character is often quoted as an epistemic warrant. The most striking feature of the actual system is the extent to which assessment of a great variety of factual claims is rooted in judgements of persons rather than in the quality of the experimental researches. These include choices as to which claims should be accorded the status of observational/experimental *results* (and this includes even quantitative data), and the deeper theoretical interpretation of results, for example what molecular structures such and such results indicate. 'Results' do not stand freely, so to speak, as the bench-mark against which reliability is routinely assessed, but are themselves judged for reliability pretty much on the basis of the character of the person who produced them. As Latour and Woolgar (1979) show, 'results' and 'interpretations' are not neutral decontextualized propositions, but come qualified by the name and so by the reputation of the person who obtained them (or under whose aegis they were obtained). Instead of true and false results, we are presented with Green's and Brown's results. In a way the qualification by name is a kind of 'epistemic equivalent' of assessments of truth and falsity, since citing some results as Green's means they can safely be accepted while citing some other results as Brown's means they should be treated with caution. To illustrate, Collins (1981) quotes the following: '[Quest and his group] are so obnoxious, and so firm in their belief that their approach is the right one and that everyone else is wrong, that I immediately discount their veracity on the basis of self-delusion.' The moral status of persons determines the epistemic status of their results. As Latour and Woolgar put it, 'this kind of reference to human agency involved in the production of statements is very common. Indeed it was clear from the participants' discussions that *who* made the claim was as important as the claim itself.'

But is this any more than a specialized form of traditional inductive reasoning? Is the 'who' important as a ground for the assessment of these data as worthy of belief because that person's results have, in the past, turned out to be, in some traditional way, better than the results of others? In their discussion of these points Latour and Woolgar do seem to confuse the question of whether one would wish to collaborate with someone ('No – she's super-competitive!') with whether results, labelled as that person's, should be counted as reliable and thus be incorporated into the discourse as facts. The only non-inductive element in their discussion (pp. 162–5) is their reference to unfavourable assessments based on the principle that if people are too pushy and anxious they will tend to accept sloppy results or indulge in wishful thinking. This is a principle not very different from the one implicit in the quote from Collins above. But the concept of 'sloppiness' seems to make sense only against the background of a quite traditional epistemic concept like 'accuracy'. Nevertheless it is striking that trust-worthiness of colleagues and coworkers has displaced the truth of assertions as the touchstone of acceptance of something as worthy to be believed.

The strict system is forced to try to treat an inductive process from true (or false) singular statements to confirmed (or disconfirmed) hypotheses of greater generality as if it existed as an impersonal schema, the value of which was independent of the person who used it or of their social position in the community of scientists. The actual system has no place for non-inductive singular true statements. The indexicality of the reliability of singular statements to the person who made them, or to the laboratory in which they are represented as a discovery, or to the apparatus one or more of whose states such a statement describes, only makes sense as inductions from past performances of that person, laboratory or apparatus. But these are *inductions from prior inductions*, for example that Green was a pupil of Black and Black's results were always trustworthy. There is no point in this regress at which the naked fact reveals itself to provide a foundation in terms that would be recognized within the strict system. I will call this 'inductive indexicality'.

But more can be said about the grounds for the personal reputations upon which 'inductive indexicality' depends. It is clear from the detailed studies made by Latour and Woolgar, and others, that in the realm of fact-stating discourse, certain kinds of raising of the standards of experimentation were important in the grounding of reputations. This goes back at least as far as the work of Berzelius in developing standards of experimental work that transformed the accuracy of quantitative chemistry (see Harré, 1984). This is quite a complex matter. Standards of experimentation are task dependent. Set a new task and new, sometimes more but sometimes less stringent standards are called for. Latour and Woolgar (1979) note that one effect of adopting a new task definition from a field and of raising the standards, whether by changing some intrinsic attribute of research such as the accuracy demanded of some physical measure or by proposing a research programme that will cost large sums of money, is to eliminate some of the competition. But the idea of 'raising the standards of experimental research' would be in need of explication even if there were no other workers in the field. Compare 'We have found a substance which does what is expected, that is it is biologically active' with 'We have discovered the structure of the substance which exhibits this level of biological activity.' According to Latour and Woolgar the shift from a research task defined in terms of attempts to substantiate the first claim to one intended to substantiate the second transformed the conditions under which the claims of the pro-ponents of different points of view were readable as 'stating the facts'. They quote the following statement (p. 121): 'Everybody knowing the field could make deductions as to what TRF was . . . their conclusions were correct but it took ten years to prove it. . . . To this day I do not believe they had ever seen what they talked about. . . . There is no way you can postulate the amino-acid composition of an unknown substance.' (Quoted as a remark by Guillemin.) For the latter much more stringently controlled chemical tech-niques are required and a much greater investment of time and money. The successful scientists in Latour and Woolgar's moral tale certainly seem to have thought that both the practical and the moral consequences of the shift of the task definition were relevant to their claim for hegemony.

Looking a little more closely at the actual discourse in which these claims are made, the moral element becomes very clear. The exertion of effort is claimed as a mark of moral virtue. For instance a Dr Schally is quoted by Latour and Woolgar (p. 118) as saying 'the only way is to extract these compounds, isolate them. . . . Somebody had to have the guts. . . . now we have tons of it.' Of a colleague Schally remarks with a notable lack of charity, 'of course, he missed the boat, he never dared putting in what was required, brute force' (p. 119). Further studies of the social construction of 'reliability' and 'credibility', particularly in these curious personalized moral terms, can be found in Collins (1981) and in Pickering (1981)

'*Us and them*'

In the actual system there is a marked asymmetry in the criteria by which one judges one's own hypotheses and those which are used to undermine the credibility of those of a rival. Gilbert and Mulkay (1982) show how 'experimental results' are used in a creatively equivocal way in discussions of the belief-worthiness of putative claims to knowledge. In supporting one's own ideas experimental results are cited as robust data, and a traditional inductive schema is invoked as the rationale of the claim. But when a scientist is discussing the ideas of an opponent 'experimental results' are treated as labile, and their supporting role as seen by the opposition appears as mere self-deception. Critics find little difficulty in coming up with an alternative interpretation of the results of their rivals. In this new guise the data no longer support and perhaps even undermine the rival's claim to knowledge. Critics shows no inclination to do similar work on their own results and treat them as if they were 'picked directly from nature'. They are presented as capable of only one interpretation, that under which they support the claim. In the critical phase an epistemological doctrine rather like that of Whewell (1847) or Hanson (1958) is emphasized. Considerable weight is put on the way pre-existing beliefs and theories are involved in the creation of 'data' out of mere 'results'. In neither of the cognitive practices I have described, that is inductive indexicality or the 'us and them' asymmetry, do the traditional concepts of 'truth' or 'falsity' seem to play any part. Instead we get phrases like 'confirmed as being correct over the entire range' (Gilbert and Mulkay, 1982, p. 390); 'S did beautiful experiments which were convincing to me mostly' (p. 391); 'It is very hard to get your hands on these things you are working on' (p. 393); 'these experiments demonstrate that . . . is real' (p. 397); 'see what certain molecular chains are doing' (p. 398); 'N's numbers agree with what S wants' (p. 399), and so on.

Strict assessment and the moral order

The work of Knorr-Cetina (1981), Latour and others has shown that there is a rhetorical use of the terminology of the strict system in the debates through which epistemic assessment of scientific claims are decided, pro tem. The 'logical' properties of discourse such as entailment or consistency (as the avoidance of contradiction) are used as part of the criteria by which scientific productions are assessed in the community's system of credit. They appear as essentially moral properties of an agonistic scientific discourse or debate. We can look upon it as one of the many language games that make up this form of life. I propose in the light of these observations that we should re-interpret the activities of traditional philosophy of science. When philosophers carry on their discussions of science in terms of the strict system they are not describing either the cognitive or the material practices of the scientific community, even in ideal form. They are touching on its moral order.

If we read the realist manifesto 'Scientific statements should be taken as true or false by virtue of the way the world is' as a moral principle it would run something like this: 'As scientists, that is members of a certain community, we should apportion our willingness or reluctance to accept a claim as worthy to be included in the corpus of scientific knowledge to the extent that we sincerely think it somehow reflects the way the world is.' Put this way the manifesto has *conduct-guiding force*. It encourages the good and the worthy to manifest their virtue in trying to find out how the world is. Seeking truth is a hopeless epistemic project, but trying to live a life of virtue is a possible moral ambition. Those who promulgate their ungrounded opinions as if they were proper contributions to the corpus of scientific knowledge are roundly condemned as immoral. Moral principles are those maxims which would guide our conduct were we people of unimpeachable virtue. The moral version of the manifesto cited above would enjoin the carrying out of careful experiments, the avoidance of that kind of wishful thinking which leads to the fudging of results, and so on. The moral force of this kind of principle comes through very strongly in the discussions reported by Latour and Woolgar (1979) concerning the early work on TFH. The practice of science is what it is because the morality of the scientific community is strict. Looked at this way the study of the epistemology of science must begin with philosophical reflection on the actual practices of the community if as philosophers we wish to know what scientific knowledge *is*. Failing to follow this ordinance can lead us to confuse the demands of the moral order of the scientific community, the thought-collective, with the possibilities of the achievement of some ideal form of knowledge given the existing practices. Anthropologists have learned that, when they ask a member of a community for an account of the local kinship system, they are as likely as not to receive an account of the moral order rather than a description of the vagaries of actual practices. Between the stringency of the moral order and the laxity of real life lies an idealization of the latter, made with an eye on the former. It is this third middle way, that is usually the guiding system for the decisions of everyday life. The concepts of the moral system appear in the rhetorical glosses on that life.

The effect of translating the work of a philosopher out of epistemology into morality can be illustrated with the case of Popper's 'fallibilism'. It can comfortably be reinterpreted as a cluster of moral principles, a 'Rule' for the conduct of daily life in a community, a scientific community. As epistemology Popper's ideas have proved rather easy to criticize. For example there is no way conclusively to falsify a universal hypothesis or the theory of which it forms a part. Even if there were, the rejection of a hypothesis just because it has been falsified by an instance would be irrational without some version of the principle of the uniformity of nature as support. But fallibilism can be a guide to 'good conduct'. The morality of the scientific community appears in principles such as 'However much personal investment one has in a theory one should not ignore contrary evidence' or 'One should seek harder for evidence that would count against a theory than for that which would support it', and so on.

Adherence to these and similar principles will help one to resist temptations, such as self-deception. But why is self-deception counted a vice in the moral order of the community of scientists? In the general morality of everyday life self-deception is perhaps a failing but hardly a sin. For an explanation we must return to the idea of a moral order based on trust, which I outlined in chapter 1. Scientific knowledge is a public resource for action and for belief. To publish abroad a discovery couched in the rhetoric of science is to let it be known that the presumed fact can safely be used in debate, in practical projects, and so on. Knowledge claims are tacitly prefixed with a performative of trust. Interpreted within the moral order of the scientific community 'I know . . .' means something like 'You can trust me that . . .', 'You have my word for it'. If what one claims to know turns out to be spurious then on this reading one has committed a moral fault. One has let down those who trusted one. As an ethnomethodologist might put it trustworthy knowledge is what is 'true for all practical purposes'. But that is not the kind of truth epistemology seeks to ground.

This is connected with another moral distinction, that between pretending to have a good reason for stating something when one has not and being genuinely mistaken. Epistemologically they are on the same footing, but morally they could hardly be more distinct. Popperian fallibilism, if interpreted as a moral position, a kind of 'Rule', would differentiate them clearly. In the first case I do not have contrary evidence because I have not bothered to look for it, or have not heeded it, while in the second I have just not happened to come upon it despite genuinely trying to find it. The trust that scientists claim from laypersons entails a commitment to intellectual honesty, to having made attempts to substantiate claims in the way that claims are substantiated in the community. It cannot possibly be based on a naïve claim to have the truth. The same argument which transforms epistemology into the communal 'Rule' would apply to any intellectual community whatever, for instance the community of theologians. What, then, should be the major concern of such studies as the philosophy of science or the philosophy of religion? From the considerations advanced in this chapter it seems that a description of the moral orders of such communities must play an essential part in the philosophical project. But one can go further. If one could develop an idealized version of the actual system of assessment of candidates for belief, one might be able to explain why the use of the actual system does produce material that is valued in those moral orders, and why the strict system is an expression of that morality. We should be able not only to show why the claims of magicians should be taken as less trustworthy than those of engineers, but also why the moral order of the scientific community makes this kind of moral distinction. To accomplish the latter we would need to discuss the morality of science against the background of an idealized version of the cognitive and material practices of that community. There is no need to struggle with the impossible task of trying to prove that the actual practice of science truly realizes an epistemic state of affairs deemed desirable within the scientific community. So the attempt to *define* scientific realism in terms of the principle of bivalence is a mistake, confusing an ethical thesis about honesty of endeavour with an epistemological thesis about how to achieve the highest standards of representational quality for scientific cognition. Scientific practice could never produce cognitive objects to which the strict dichotomy 'true or false by virtue of the way the world is' could be applied in the epistemic mode.

In the philosophy of science we want to be able to explain how imperfect representations can be the basis of trustworthy belief and practice that is 'good enough'. The practices of mankind are very diverse and what is to count as 'good enough' can hardly be given a universal definition. At best we can say what is good enough for a test of a drug, good enough for the design of a bridge, and good enough for the tuning of a symphony orchestra. I have already mentioned the discussion by Latour and Woolgar of the way that standards of assaying can be changed and of the moral advantage of redefining them 'upwards'. For example we could try to show how fulfilling the conditions for 'plausibility of a theory' makes the material practice of looking for exemplars of theoretically prescribed classes of unknown beings a sensible policy. It is worth reminding ourselves that the scorn that has been poured on the naïvety of the D-N 'model' of explanation was justified only in the context of the actual assessment system, that is in the context of what scientists actually did. If this was what scientific explanation had to be then no scientist had ever given one nor ever would. But is it so absurd as a moral ideal?

To my mind the importance of the strict system lies not in epistemology, but in the fact that it represents the most perfect and generally sustained moral order ever created by mankind. Alongside the history of the moral force of the order within the scientific community the minimal success of 'Love thy neighbour' makes a regrettably ironic contrast. Philosophers of science who chose to follow the spirit of the above remarks would be setting out to construct an idealized and abstract version of scientific cognition and its actual assessment modes. But would such a version be normative? Well, it would not be the whole story. It would bring out that part of the normative

background of science that regulates it as a material practice – what someone who joins this community ought to do (just as the 'Rule of St Benedict'
enjoined on Benedictines certain daily observances). One should classify
the beings presented by nature and try to establish their natural kinds. One
should seek for exemplars of the beings whose description has been adumbrated in theory. One should be willing to accept only those laws which are
covariant under the Lorentz transformation, and so on. But the total normative background also involves that which I have called the strict system, the
moral maxims that masqueraded as epistemological categories in traditional
philosophy of science. As an epistemological doctrine 'Seek the truth and
reject falsehood' is worthless, but as a moral maxim it figures a good deal in
one way or another in the occasional sermons that scientists preach.

There is another kind of discourse, the theological, where terms from the
strict system are cheerfully bandied about, and meet much the same fate, the
encouragement of scepticism. No theological statement of which 'God' is
the putative referent could be known to be true or to be false. But there is an
obvious reading of the strict system in this context too as a cluster of moral
maxims, part of the 'Rule' that regulates the theological community.

Simple truth

But, it might be said, surely you cannot be claiming that the commonsense
notions of 'truth' and 'falsity' have no place in the epistemology of natural
science? Indeed not. (See Stove, 1982.) In the sense that what you is say is
true if I, now occupying your standpoint, and sharing with you the bulk of a
conceptual scheme relevant to the matter in question, were to give a similar
account of what can be experienced from that standpoint, then what you
said was true, otherwise not. The comparison is between your discourse and
mine, apropos a common referent. It cannot be between the relation my
discourse has to the common referent and the relation that yours does, since
those relations could not become objects of comparison within a single field
of knowledge. The comparison of discourses has the flavour of the old
coherence theory of truth, while the mention of a common referent reminds
one of the correspondence theory.

From a philosophical point of view this account of the role of true and
false in the discourse of science leaves at least two questions unanswered:

1   How do I know we are noticing something about a common referent?
The material practice of locating referents in space–time relative to other
referents is not enough. Perhaps I can know we are noticing the same thing
only if our discourses are similar.

2 How do I know that our discourses are similar? Clearly there can be no case-by-case comparison to decide the question. It may be that we can do no better than to notice that as members of the same community we manage to coexist and co-ordinate our practical activities in a common form of life, including common rights and duties and a morality in which sincerity of reporting is a common good.

In general I think we have to admit that there are no clear-cut procedures for determining that what you see I see, what you mean I understand, and so on. Only our long-term participation in a common form of life shows that for all practical purposes we inhabit a common world of material things and conversational practices. The use of the concepts of the strict system in their literal acceptation would require a vantage point outside our community and its practices from which aspects of nature could be compared with fragments of discourse as if they were mutually independent of one another. There is no such vantage point, nor could there be. But there are co-operative practices and longstanding communities with their moral orders. It is to these that we must look if anywhere for the foundations of knowledge. However these foundations are not factual but moral.

Despite the arguments for relocating the strict sense of 'true' and 'false' and the tough sense of 'knowledge' it would be absurd to deny that there is a sense of the pair 'truth/falsity' by which scientists, like everyone else, comment upon their observations. It is also obvious that that sense does not extend to the unobservable or the general, that is theories and laws. Discussions of usage (for instance the classical paper by Strawson, 1956) seem to lead to the view that the *words* 'truth' and 'falsity' and their cognates as used for acts of confirmation and disconfirmation of the trustworthiness of an expressed belief or opinion. Their use is part of the machinery for the maintenance of a social network through which an epistemic *moral order* is sustained.

Under what conditions is an expressed belief or opinion about material states of affairs trustworthy? Traditional epistemology transformed the question into a psychological query concerning the perceptual experiences or cognitive states of some other person – and so ran into scepticism. But expressed beliefs are in the public domain, and presented in some common semiotic system, language, diagrams or even within the conventions of an iconography. I shall look at two accounts of the commonsense notion that some of the things we say are true and others false. If you feel you can trust me then you can accept my assurance that this text was produced on an Apricot Portable Computer. And you can pass it on. 'Did you know . . .', etc. Within the social network of trustworthy people and institutions we can reliably inform a confused visitor that it is false that Linacre College is in

Cambridge. But these everyday assurances could not form the basis of an incorrigible foundation for scientific knowledge.

Popper's (1959) account of this kind of statement is designed to put it at the base of some sort of epistemic structure without committing himself to the extence of an incorrigible foundation. To make fallibilism work he needs an empirical anchorage for at least some descriptive statements (to be 'basic statements'). They are to be the ground for the falsification and (under appropriate circumstances) the rejection of hypotheses. But the anchorage does not come from correspondence between a sentence with pre-existing meaning and a datum-like state of affairs. It is created by convention. 'Basic statements', he says, 'are accepted as a result of a decision or agreement in accordance with a procedure governed by rules. . . . Agreement is reached on the occasion of applying a theory.' What could the agreement be about? We are trying to apply the one-fluid theory of electricity. We elect to say 'the e.m.f. is 1 volt is true' when the needle of the voltmeter is at *this* position on the scale. What is fixed by this election? Clearly the meaning of the *term* 'volt', in just the way that the meanings of the terms 'newton', 'metre', and so on are fixed in other contexts. Could we fix the truth of basic statements by a new convention each time we did an electrical experiment? Clearly not. The next use must be in accordance with the standard, and cannot be the fixing of another convention. If every basic statement had its meaning and truth fixed by convention there would be the kind of linguistic chaos envisaged by Wittgenstein, when he tried to imagine an attempt to fix meanings by reference to individual private experiences.

There is an ambiguity in the expression '*the* occasion of applying a theory'. It certainly cannot mean 'each occasion of applying a theory'. It must mean something like 'the first or exemplary occasion of applying a theory'. But this leaves Popper with the same problem as every other philosopher who has addressed these issues has had. How do we know that the term, with that meaning, has been correctly applied in the next and each subsequent occasion? Only if we can know this do we know whether all basic statements using the word 'volt', other than the first one in which the convention was fixed, are true. But to know whether the word has been correctly applied we have to know whether the statement using it is true in some everyday sense. Ellis (1982) has elaborated a novel and attractive version of the traditional account. We use 'true' and 'false' to express epistemic approval. The correspondence theory of truth treats these expressions as assignments of a property ('truth') to the expression of belief. But, according to Ellis, there is no such property. Rather the conditions of social co-ordination of action require a drive towards achieving the maximum of intersubjectivity among belief-systems. Assessments of truth and accusations of falsity are useful for refining belief-systems, but their use creates the illusion of the existence of a pair of properties of propositions, which would be independent of anybody's attitudes.

Epistemic value is a belief-selecting mechanism. These values are themselves selected by reference to the rightness of actions. As Ellis puts it:

$$\frac{Truth}{\text{Belief}} \quad \text{as} \quad \frac{Rightness}{\text{Action}}$$

The only 'unknown' in the equation is 'truth'. Simple truth is, all things considered, what it is most rational to believe, in the contexts of right action. A certain procedure will tell me whether I have just enough eggs to fill the egg box. My belief that there are six eggs will be true just as long as I do not have any over, nor any unfilled spaces. These conditions invoke modes of action rather than modes of cognition. But I believe that Ellis's account of simple truth and falsity must be completed by tying the philosophical analysis into a psychological theory, one which breaks through the 'veil' which any representationalist psychology would still hang between belief and reality, no matter how pragmatically successful our belief-guided practices were to be. A false theory, one must often remind oneself, can produce true predictions. The defence of simple truth will be rounded out in part three with an exposition of Gibson's psychology of perception, which, I believe, provides just what is needed to complete the defence.[1]

I conclude this part with an aphorism from Pascal (for notice of which I am indebted to Frank Grande). It expresses the very same predicament as did Peirce's statement with which I began. 'We have an incapacity for proof, invincible to all dogmatism; we have an idea of truth invincible to all scepticism.'

Part Two

Referring, Searching and Finding

A picture held us captive. And we could not get outside it, for it lay in our language and language seemed to repeat it to us inexorably.

Wittgenstein

Introduction

A truth realism based on propositions has proved vulnerable to sceptical assaults. I hope to create a referential realism based on things. Instead of asking 'Are the statements of this theory true or false?' and doings one's best within human limitations to answer, I believe scientists actually ask 'Do things, properties processes of this sort exist?' and do their best within human limitations to find exemplars. Realism is grounded in a material practice. But there is an obvious objection to this idea. Surely, it will be said, to know that an exemplar of some theory-based prescription exists not only must one have picked out something, but one must believe that it has the requisite properties, location, and so on. Isn't this to believe that certain things are true of the being in question? So in the end referential realism is just truth realism under another name.

However, recent discussions of the theory of reference have made it plain that it is possible successfully to refer to something by the use of a descriptive phrase which is not actually appropriate to the being in question. The point is illustrated in examples of this sort: one can pick out someone at a party with the phrase 'the man drinking gin and tonic', even though on closer inspection it turns out that it would have been more accurate to say 'the woman drinking vodka on the rocks'. This kind of simple example shows that the act of referring cannot be explicated in terms of the truth or falsity of describing. Referring is a human deictic practice, by which, with any means to hand, one person tries to draw the attention of another person to a being in their common public space. It is this thought which animates the discussions of this part, since it is this fact which makes a realist reading of theoretical science possible.

Thinking the matter through further one notices that a temporal dimension must be put on the activities of a scientific community. Of course, searching for a referent involves trying to satisfy a certain cluster of descriptions. Thinking one has found an exemplar involves believing that certain propositions are true. Let us call these 'Eureka! beliefs'. But as a scientific field develops none of those beliefs may survive into later views on the nature and properties of the beings originally disclosed. Successful acts of reference give the community 'epistemic access' (to use Boyd's (1979) felicitous phrase), that is make possible a research programme through which the task of finding out more about the properties of the beings in question is to be tackled. But, once these beings have been disclosed in some material practice, *they* will not go away as our beliefs about them change. There are 'loose cells' in a suppurating wound, whether with Lord Lister we think of them as detached human cells run wild, or with Pasteur as the agents of the infection.

Even so, it may still be objected, there remain some beliefs, the truth of which is required if an existential disclosure is to have any relevance to a scientific research programme. For instance if it could be shown that the wild cells were not things at all, but visual illusions produced by the microscope, wouldn't the conservative basis of a research programme founded on the thinghood of such cells collapse? And couldn't sceptics make the same kind of difficulties about being sure about existence as have traditionally been cited against truth realism? But referential realism is epistemically modest. It makes no assertions about the possibility of there being any absolutely incorrigible existential claims. All that needs to be shown to make this kind of realism viable is that the ontology of a scientific field is more stable than any cluster of other beliefs about it, such as what natural kinds there are and what has or will happen. In part three I shall try to show that there is one 'absolute' qualification on existence. It arises from the reasonable supposition that the human perceptual systems have evolved in such a way that the basic categories of perception must be universal for people. Obviously this is not an absolute absolute, since sentient beings which may have evolved in other environments (Cf. the beings on Larry Niven's *Neutron star*) will be the possessors of perceptual systems that pick up other invariants in the same physical cosmos. The argument is directed to showing only that there is reason to accept our perceptual categories as genuine, not that ours are all that there could be. Again I reiterate that the modest realist does not have to show that there is an incorrigible foundation of knowledge claims concerning an independent physical world grounded in a permanent base of material disclosures – only that an order of revisability exists in which existential displays, created by the use of certain material practices, are the most resistant to revision.

Existential displays and demonstrations must therefore be thought of in a hierarchy of relative revisability, running from categories to kinds to individuals. A claim to have located a thing is more resistant to disproof than is the claim to have located an okapi, and that claim is more resistant than the claim to have located the chief' s favourite okapi, 'Jake'. From the point of view of natural science, kind identifications are surely central. Is the cause of AIDS a virus? Is this the jet of tracks that only a gluon emission could have caused? Is *terra australis* a continent? Discussions of the referential acts that provide the basic groundings of scientific knowledge must include a defence of natural kinds. Again antirealist attacks on natural kinds have been based on the philosophers' fallacy. Kinds need essences. Essences are some sort of absolute. There are no absolutes in the field of natural science. So there can be no point in trying to build a theory of kinds on the basis of the concept of 'essence'. Without that concept kinds are merely convenient human disarticulations of the seamless web of nature. So the idea of 'natural kind' is a fancy. Dispose of the idea that essences must be absolutes and the sceptical argument collapses. I shall try to show that human decisions to classify natural beings are fixed by fiat in contexts of practice. However, it is a prime aim of natural science to try to find out whether the constitution or nature of those beings, as disclosed by work in a theoretical context, justifies making the divisions into practical kinds where practice has drawn them. 'Natural kind' is a concept which can be explicated only within the double framework of practice and theory. Every natural kind is located in both contexts, and cannot be understood by reference to either one alone.

Our theory of reference must not make the achieving of a referential relation between person and thing so fragile a link that every change in the meaning of the vocabulary with which we denote the things we believe to exist requires us to revise our ontology. Nor must it make that link, once achieved, so robust, that we are obliged to hold on to it no matter how much the meaning of our descriptive vocabulary has changed.

4

Referring as a
Material Practice

The meaning of sortal terms

The distinction between prescribing a cluster of characteristics followed by a search for something that more or less adequately exemplifies them, and picking a being, choosing it as an exemplar, and then providing a word for it by some kind of socially recognized baptismal act, has been involved in most of the contemporary discussion of reference. One important application of the distinction is to the problem of explicating the meaning of sortal terms. On one view sortal terms acquire meaning through the existence or formation of an intension, a conceptual cluster. The question of whether there is anything which they can be used correctly to describe is a secondary matter. On this view the meaning of both 'unicorn' and 'horse' is to be accounted for in the same way. It is a scientific, not a semantic, fact that horses exist and unicorns do not. According to the other point of view sortal terms acquire meaning in some kind of dubbing ceremony in which a *chosen* exemplar is named. The act of naming has consequences that control further uses of the word or expression in question. The meaning of the term 'horse' is fixed by the properties that the exemplary being happens to possess, and applies to other beings because they are like it. 'Unicorn' too must get its meaning from an exemplar, say a picture in a book. It could not be based on the image conjured up by an imaginative description unless each term in that description has its own proper history of an origin in the establishment of a relation with an exemplar. In the one theory concepts are prior to existents, and in the other existents, of one sort or another, are prior to concepts. In preferring the former account of the way natural-kind terms are used I opt for an intensionalist account of their meaning. I must defend the possibility of intra- as well as extralinguistic ways of achieving meaning.

It has become very clear in recent discussions that the theory of reference that one adopts is intimately bound up with one's views on the meaning of sortal terms (cf. Evans, 1982). To complement this account of sortal terms I shall be developing a theory of reference that is heavily in debt to the writings of Roberts (1985) and Katz (1979).

DC and IP referential modes

According to Roberts referring is a material practice. It is intimately related to the act of picking a figure from a ground. The two modes recognized by Roberts have a direct application to the understanding of science. Roberts develops his account as a part of the debate around Donellan's (1966) views on reference. There are *DC attributions*, which involve the use of a demonstrative 'D' and a complement 'C' and which are exemplified in statements like 'This grey powder is a sample of gallium.' And there are *IP attributions*, which involve an indefinite pronoun 'I' and an individuating predicate 'P'. The second kind of attribution is exemplified in statements like 'Whatever is the cause of these bubbles is a neutrino.' According to Roberts anyone who wishes to find out whether or not a certain putative referent exists, on the basis of a DC attribution, must be capable of the material practice of picking out a figure from a ground. But in the IP case 'picking out' is not only a material practice. It involves the cognitive act of conceiving and accepting a theoretical account of the possible causes of strings of bubbles. IP attribution involves two steps. In the first, water, as a material being, forms a background against which the string of bubbles appears as a figure. The second step is a cognitive practice, an act of thought. In a great many cases in science theorizing about possible causes precedes empirical picking out of putative referents. In Roberts's terms we could say that the community strives to transform an IP attribution relative to some category of putative referents into a DC attribution. Detailed discussions of cases of this transformation are to be found in chapters 10, 11 and 12. However, in both modes, a physical relationship is established between the embodied *person* who makes the act of reference and some being or other. The physical link is direct or unmediated in the DC mode, but indirect or mediated in the IP mode.

DC reference is typical of those contexts in which the material practice of picking out a figure of the appropriate ontological category is possible, for example picking out a continent or island from the ocean. The 'figure' may remain in focus, so to speak, during an extended sequence of revisions of the 'C' component. Almost all that Abel Janzoon Tasman believed to be true of Australia, except its ontological category and large size, is now thought to be false, but Australia remains.

IP reference involves two contexts, practical and theoretical. DC reference is typical of the discourse appropriate to that aspect of the world I have

called Realm 1, the realm of beings of actual human experience. IP reference is the mode necessary if there are to be referential acts with regard to
beings which we cannot currently experience. But these beings may be
remote from our experience through some contingency of our human size
and location, that is, at least in theory, remediable. But they may, so far as we
now believe, be beyond all possible human experience. In the former case an
IP attribution is transformed into a DC attribution by any suitable technical
advance which would extend the field of the human perceptual systems. In
this way an observer, as materially embodied, is brought into a physical
relationship with another material being. In the latter, as will emerge in the
discussions of ontologies for Realm 3, there will always remain some cases
for which that transformation is impossible.

The next step will be to try to connect these distinctions in modes of
referential discourse with the intensionalist theory of the meaning of sortal
terms. To do this a distinction must be marked out between those predicates
which are currently being taken as part of the defining intension of the kind
term in question, and those which are merely contingently true of it, and
associated with some particular context. Pines and broadleafed trees are
both trees. But our chances of finding a tree in Scandinavia would be
improved were we to be instructed to look for a pine. In trying to find a
referent for the concept 'Scandinavian tree', that is an answer to the question 'Are there trees in Scandinavia? ', one might be grateful for the additional information that in colder climes pines are likely to be predominant.
This fact is not part of what it means to be a tree. J. J. Katz, in an excellent
discussion of reference, has suggested a distinction between 'type-
reference' and 'token-reference' that combines neatly with Roberts's DC/IP
distinction. It is not part of the meaning (intension) of the term 'okapi' that
specimens gather at this particular water-hole at sundown, but if one wants
to pick out an okapi from the ground of mammalian life it is well to know
this contingent fact about the local mammals. In certain cases these incre-
ments of descriptive specificity may go so far as to be identificatory of an
individual. So in working out the details of the material practices associated
with Roberts's DC mode of referential discourse one must be prepared to
add whatever scraps of useful information about token beings will be useful
in finding an individual specimen. The Katz distinction is needed to explain
how experimentation, as a material practice directed to particulars, *can* lead
to discoveries of exemplary instances, tokens. It can be no part of the meaning of the concept of neutrino that such beings produce bubbles in bubble
chambers. To assume that would be to prejudge the outcome of the debate
as to whether it is truth-conditions or conditions for warranted assertibility
(or neither) that are the basic and constitutive components of meaning.
Experimental equipment is a human artefact, and so it will be only

accidentally true of certain token neutrinos that they have just this effect. Even the amorphous allotrope of gallium may be a human artefact. The 'token reference/type reference' distinction is needed for 'keeping the books' with respect to what is to count as the intensional core of sortal concepts involved in both DC and IP modes of referential discourse.

In both Roberts's formulae the first component ('D' or 'I') is likely to involve token reference, since an *act* of reference can occur only in a context of material particulars. The second component ('C' or 'P') is likely to involve type reference since there is no a priori limit to the extension of a class. Expressions like 'the one and only', 'the first and only the first five members', etc. , are part of the first component, if they occur at all. The theoretical context of the use of a sortal term determines via the hierarchy of theories thought appropriate in that context how predicates are to be distributed between essence and proprium, while the exigencies of the practical context determine which accidental properties are to be taken as significant for picking out veritable tokens of the type of interest. One might be tempted to use the 'nominal essence/real essence' distinction in this kind of discussion. The distinction between the intensional conditions for DC and IP reference matches that distinction but the concept of nominal essence is too strong to explain the behaviour of natural-kind terms in practical contexts. The properties with the help of which we pick out exemplars in practical contexts may not, in the full scientific context, be counted essential, that is be tied in to the theoretical account of 'nature's joints'.

The defeasibility of essences

The argument so far could be interpreted as a demonstration that the strict distinction between nominal and real essences, which tended to nescience in the hands of Locke, can be replaced by an account of the behaviour of natural-kind terms, each of which must be seen as embedded in two contexts, each having its own characteristic practices. It seems as if 'necessity' and 'contingency', within the contexts of science, can be treated as expressions of attitudes, rather than as epistemic standings. They represent attitudes towards the defeasibility of the beliefs and conventions that the community has adopted at some moment of relative stability in the evolution of a terminology and its semantics.

Instead of nominal essences the community has sets of rules for applying natural-kind terms in practical contexts. The rules are ordered by reference to the willingness of the community to allow context-dependent exceptions. Can the community allow that, though usually yellow, gold is sometimes red? To explain why the 'Gold is a yellow metal' rule is low in the hierarchy at a particular moment, while the 'Gold has a specific gravity of 19. 6' rule is more elevated, the relevant theoretical context would need to be invoked. In keeping with the thrust of the argument in the preceding sections I claim that extensions of natural-kind terms are not given, but are created in accordance with the principles of 'intensive design'. According to those principles the extension of a kind is the set of beings which turn out to be sufficiently similar, in relevant respects, to an exemplary instance, from the study of which the intension of the set was confirmed. For Realm 1 kinds the choice of an exemplar could precede the fixing of the intension, but for Realm 3 kinds priority must be given to theory-derived intensions. We may never be able to produce the exemplary instance, *in propria persona*. The phrases 'sufficiently similar' and 'in relevant respects' reflect the historical contingency of the material practices and theoretical context available for the scientific study of some field of phenomena. Once Berzelius had improved the standards of quantitative chemistry and the Cannizaro hypo-thesis had tidied up the notions of atom and molecule, the concepts of 'sufficiently similar' and 'in relevant respects' were considerably changed from their significance in the days of Dalton's rough and ready experimental methods and his hard, spherical atoms. The effect was greatly to sharpen the distinctions that marked off natural chemical kinds. But, as I have argued at length in part one, the concepts of truth and falsity must be abandoned to the strict system and restored to the uses of the scientific community only as part of the resources of the scientific moral order. Kinds are identified not by the discovery of truths, but by the success or failure of practices. Changing practices and evolving theoretical contexts mean that no claims to have nailed down the essences of this or that natural-kind are indefeasible.

But what about the token reference of Katz? Are not the statements which purport to describe *this* okapi true or false? For all practical purposes that is so. And I have defended a kind of commonsense, everyday notion of truth (and falsity) with which in ordinary contexts of practical action and decision human beings assess claims and beliefs. But relative to the demands of the strict system there is not one of those claims and assessments that would not have to be revised in quite easily imagined circumstances. It is the fact that these circumstances are rarely realized in practical life that permits to humankind the illusion that in everyday assessments 'true' and 'false' are used in ways that are identical with the demands of the strict system.

Having got our okapi we find that in no way (except metaphysical category) is it exactly like the exemplary description that guided our search. But there is another kind of case. Once we have succeeded in finding a specimen, it can turn out that revisions within the relevant theoretical context force reconsiderations of beliefs about its nature. Another dimen-sion of defeasibility opens out, now with respect to the practical analogue of that which in the strict system is the real essence. The contrast between the fate of the singular referring expressions 'Pluto' and 'Vulcan' is instructive.

In the discourse in which Pluto was proposed as a putative planet the term 'Pluto' was used as a referring expression, directing attention to a certain portion of the sky at a definite moment. A pale patch of light, which could have been how a large lump of rock, or perhaps a ball of frozen gas, would look from that distance, was seen at the right time and place. So far so good. But really to secure reference other more robust material practices are required in Roberts's DC mode. Sending a space probe to land on the object or, failing that, to take some close-up pictures would still further disambiguate the matter. But in whatever way those further explorations turned out the astronomical community had found *something*. However, some astronomers now want to say that Pluto is not really a planet, but a captured comet. It is reclassified into a different natural-kind. The community's conception of its 'true nature' has changed, though all that we now believe about its properties as an observable thing may remain unrevised. We thought Pluto was a planet but it is really a comet. How much of the original theory-derived prescription which guided such a search as that which was made for Pluto, can be revised without undermining security of reference?

The technique of search that dominates this or that material practice of referent hunting is determined by two features of the content of the DC attribution in question, the ontological (metaphysical) category, be it substance, process, relation, and so on, and the natural-kind, be it planet, ion exchange, electrical discharge, etc. What is to count as a finding of a putative referent may, in certain cases, be tightened down with individuating descriptions. In the case of Pluto and Vulcan, both putative planets, such matters as mass and trajectory provided individuating descriptions. There are limits to the reassignment of beings to different natural-kinds as research continues. These limits are reached when the ontological category comes into question. Vulcan was thought to orbit the sun inside the track of the planet Mercury, and to influence its behaviour. A being was observed at roughly the right time and place. But later observational failures have since led the astronomical community to discount the existence of Vulcan as a planet. What was observed? It seems likely that it was a sunspot. However, no one has ever suggested that the community should adopt the name 'Vulcan' for that sunspot. While it seems reasonable to say that Pluto is the name of something that was once thought to be a planet but is now thought to be a comet, it is not reasonable to say that Vulcan should be the name of something that was once thought to be a planet but is now thought to be a sunspot. The shift of ontological category is too great. Sunspots are not the sort of beings which generally get names. But hurricanes do these days.

Relative to human affairs they display a persistence and integrity that justifies the practice though they are of the same natural-kind as sunspots (cf. Leplin, 1979).

The idea of 'natural-kind' is conveniently loose. It can be tightened up should the context of discussion seem to need it. In some contexts it would clearly be wrong to place hurricanes and sunspots and the red spot of Jupiter in the same natural-kind. It was known for some time that there were micro-organisms in putrefying wounds. But they were first thought to be human body cells which had become detached from the main structure and 'gone wild', so to speak. At one level of analysis bacteria and body cells are of the same natural-kind, say when the problems of growing cultures of human cells for research purposes are in focus. In other contexts, and the developing science of medicine was one of them, it would be more fruitful to mark off single-cell organisms from the specialized cells of an advanced animal or plant, as a distinction in kind. But one should not draw too relativist a conclusion from these observations. In most contexts the distinctions of natural-kinds do mark real differences, that is differences in superficial appearance and behaviour that can be explained by reference to current theory.

These examples can be connected to Katz's distinction between token reference and type reference. An entity can be 'held in focus' by satisfaction only of token prescription. When type prescription fails, conservation of reference can be maintained, at least for the purpose of further research, through token reference. It might not have been a planet but it was that thing at that place and time. This covers the case of Pluto in its transition from planet to comet. But if token prescription fails there is nothing about whose nature there can be any further research or any dispute.

I must emphasize again that in talking of natural-kinds I am using a notion a good deal weaker than that traditionally understood by this term. The implication of fixedness that seems to go along with the idea is misleading. Close examination has shown that the descriptive vocabulary of a scientific community is controlled by a shifting, historically conditioned network of contexts, conceptual clusters, material practices and social influences. At any moment it is possible to pick out a set of natural-kinds, but the instability of the network means that another division of the world may recommend itself. Does a later moment in the history of descriptive schemes provide the community with a better way of classifying natural beings? At this point I have not yet accumulated a sufficiently powerful philosophical armoury to dispel the spectre of relativism or exorcize the spirit of the coherence theory of truth.

In summary, then, I have tried to show that referring is a material practice, success or failure in which is registered by the use of certain characteristic linguistic forms. Once these linguistic forms are established members of a community can refer to non-existent beings or to beings of whose existence they have no surety by imitating the logical grammar of deictic expressions. But achieving reference, and thus fixing, for the moment, the denotation of a term, is a material practice. It is something we do. It involves capturing something, landing on something, photographing something, revealing something previously hidden, and so on. To achieve reference we need to identify beings only at the generic level, that is at the level of the metaphysical categories that define the ontology of a realm. Astronomers were looking for the third Jovian moon. They found a *thing*. But is it a rock, a ball of ice, or, if the imagination is sufficiently inflamed by science fiction, perhaps a huge alien spacecraft? The identifying description under which we search for the individual or for the exemplary token of the type may turn out not to be the most acceptable description once it has been found. 'Achieving reference' is not managing to satisfy some predicates. It is using a revisable prescription to establish a physical relationship with a thing.

5

Furnishing the World:
Referents and Natural-Kinds

A semantic theory for natural-kind terms

In the last chapter a general account of the meaning of sortal terms and of the grammar of denotational aspects of scientific discourse was offered. Scientific knowledge is ultimately organized around an evolving system of natural-kind terms. It became clear in the last chapter that natural-kind terms straddle two contexts of application, practical and theoretical. Their use, I shall argue, is controlled by two, partially independent, sets of 'deep grammatical rules' or 'semantic conventions'. One set derives from practical contexts, the other from theoretical.

A practical context is one in which human activity involves the manipulation and transformation of material things and substances. Actions in a practical context are directed to ends, and the intentional objects of such actions are primarily states and conditions of things.

A theoretical context is one in which the main human activity is the production of a discourse. In scientific theorizing many of the substantive terms are taken to denote beings which can exist independently of human kind.

Acts such as identification, selection and classification of observable things, processes, and so on, are performed in practical contexts in accordance with rules (not always fully and explicitly formulated) which regulate the use of each natural-kind term within the totality of the descriptive repertoire of that community. It is now widely agreed that when these rules are expressed verbally they appear to embody some measure of necessity. But unlike true definitions they are only quasi-analytic, and subject to revision or replacement. As Wittgenstein insisted, we cannot be prepared in advance for all possible concrete applications of our terminologies. An established natural-kind term might be the best to hand, but the existing rules for its use may not be exactly appropriate to new circumstances. This situation has often arisen in zoology and botany when specimens have turned up that straddle the borderline between existing species. In general there are two strategies open to a taxonomist. One could conserve the existing terminology, maintaining the rules which govern, its use and invent a new species term. Or one could make suitable changes in the existing rules of use to allow the new specimen to be accommodated within a modified terminology. Such modifications usually involve the resolution of existing but tacit ambiguities in terminology. By whichever route a new specimen is accommodated a decision has to be made on a balance of advantage. The natural sciences have had to deal with albino tigers, allotropic forms of chemical elements, quasi-stellar objects, isomers and isotopes, particles with momentum but no rest mass, and so on. Decisions as to how to allocate these beings to kinds will involve tightening, loosening and modifying systems of rules governing terminologies. Sometimes such discoveries force the community to notice, for the first time, the tacit criterial role of some property hitherto not particularly emphasized. (For a detailed discussion of historical cases cf. Wonsor, 1976.)

But, when embedded in theoretical contexts, the very same vocabularies of kind terms are controlled by other considerations, based on discoveries about the inner constitutions of the beings in question. As a preliminary rough characterization we could say that these considerations express empirical and revisable hypotheses about the real essences of natural-kinds. Though as hypotheses they are revisable, they may turn out to denote features of the kinds in question which the community is inclined to regard as necessary. Taken criterially as rules considerations of this kind do not denote observable properties of the things, materials and processes of interest, but molecular structures, genetic codes, internal circulations, and the like. A statement like 'Benzene is based on a hexagonal molecular structure of six carbon atoms' functions both as a rule for the use of the term 'benzene' and as part of the explanation of why phenols, for example, are a distinctive chemical species.

Kinds and natures

The use of sortal terms by a scientific community to pick out natural-kinds is stabilized by considerations of practical convenience and by the hierarchy of theories appropriate to the subject matter. For example chemical-kind terms are controlled by two sets of rules, one derived from practical techniques of experimental chemistry, the other from chemical theory, invoking atomic architecture, electron configurations, and the like.

Kripke (1980) and Putnam (1983) were right to insist that science is about real essences, but it is also about material practices, including classifying.

What, then, does 'gold' denote? It cannot just be to that metal which has such and such a real essence, whatever that may turn out to be (a Roberts IP referential mode). It must also pick out that metal which can be manipulated by material practices, such as mining, refining, jewellery making, and so on. The naming model of meaning is inadequate for analysing such a complex matter. 'Rigid designation' of real essences as the key to a theory of the meaning of natural-kind terms downplays the role of material practices in determining their use. There are two sets of rules for each term, neither of which is created by anything so simple as the baptismal dubbing of a suitable paradigm instance. Both are extracted from practices. Each may and often does undergo subtle changes. It is continuity rather than conservation that guarantees the diachronic intelligibility of natural-kind terms and makes their referential uses possible (cf. Papineau 1977).

The analytic-synthetic distinction, it has often been pointed out, is a procrustean bed when used as a device for classifying statements which express the sense of natural-kind terms. The distinction is part of the meta-linguistic apparatus appropriate to idealized vocabularies and is thus part of the strict system. When it is applied in a real context its lack of fit leaves room for such feline fantasies as Putnam's 'cats' and Kripke's 'tigers', 'look-alikes' with non-terran innards, or limping around on three legs. In this context, the problem for the philosopher of science is to design a pair of concepts that are more or less opposed in the same manner as the poles of the analytic/synthetic distinction, but do not suffer from the rigidity of concepts that are at home in the strict system. Putnam's suggestion that, because 'Tigers are stupid' is not an analytic statement, it is not anything like an analytic statement, when we use it to help us pick out members of this species, goes too far. Only by drawing on the Wittgensteinian notion of a language game and the deep grammatical rules with whose integrity the very existence of a linguistic convention and its associated practices are bound up, can we understand working distinctions that approximate those of the strict system.

Recent discussions of essences can be thought of in terms of a polar opposition between 'descriptivists' who hold that the extension of a kind term is determined by the prescriptions which a being must satisfy to fall under it, and 'essentialists' who hold that the extensions of kind terms are determined by the natures (sometimes unknown) of the beings which fall under them. At the risk of boring the informed reader to distraction I take up the oft-discussed example 'Water is H_2O' to illustrate what I believe to be an error that unites both sides in this dispute. Descriptivists and essentialists both take as an exclusive disjunction what ought to be treated as a pair of complementary contexts. Descriptivists emphasize cases where the demands of the practical context dominate those of the theoretical context, while essentialists emphasize cases where the weight of influence is reversed. But in any real case there is a dialectical interplay between the contexts. They are complementary. (See Harré and Madden, 1977.)

If an expedition were to find a substance which could serve as water in most practical contexts but competently performed analyses interpreted within an accepted theoretical context showed it to be of a different chemical composition (of a different nature) from that of the liquid with which we are familiar, would the *standard* linkage between practical and theoretical contexts created by our scientists, and expressed in the statement 'Water is H_2O' be in jeopardy? Putnam (1983, p. 73) approves of Kripke's view that we should not take the the stuff to be water. The theoretical context must dominate the practical. Those who hold that kind terms rigidly designate real essences must take this line. But it seems clear that the reaction of the community of chemists would depend on the exact content of the discovery. Let us first try to imagine some curious compound of unfamiliar elements found during an extragalactic expedition. Perhaps we would follow Putnam along Kripke's route. But such a reaction would surely be excessive if it turned out to be mostly composed of deuterium oxide (heavy water). Mellor's (1977) suggestion that in these circumstances we might say that water had a variable composition would do very well for deuterium and tritium oxides. The practical context would outweigh the theoretical context if the variations were minor. It is hard to comment on the hard case since we have no idea what other matters would be germane to our decisions in a world so different from our own. But it will not do to generalize Mellor's treatment to all cases either. The eighteenth century generic concept 'air' turned out not to mark a natural-kind. Dephlogistated air, fixed air, and so on have been shown to have distinctive chemical natures. Despite many similarities in their behaviour (as gases, arguably a physical kind) they are not treated as varieties of one chemical natural-kind but as chemical kinds proper.

Whence come the intuitions that I have deployed in the above discussion? Though Putnam and Kripke overstate the case, they are right to emphasize that in real natural science it is ultimately the theoretical context that exerts the greater influence on the way we use kind terms. Practical distinctions need, in the end, to be certified by theoretical arguments which guarantee or undermine such distinctions by reference to chemical constitutions or physical natures, such as atomic architecture. Only in this way can those behavioural differences which are induced extrinsically by differences in context be differentiated from those which are the effect of different intrinsic properties. Putnam and Kripke are mistaken in taking the theoretical context to be absolute. Mellor's argument errs in the other direction.

I am grateful to the anonymous author of an excellent article on this topic.

He or she arrives at substantially the same conclusion. According to that author the issue is not what the extension of a term really is. Rather the development of accepted usage within the life of a scientific community 'extends custom'. The apparently irreconcilable semantic theories of descriptivists and essentialists, are really two possible 'strategies for the development' of a terminology. As Madden and I showed in our discussion of the history of the term 'copper', one or the other will tend to be favoured depending on the current state of the scientific speciality in question. That includes material practices such as experimental techniques as well as the theoretical context of shared beliefs. The meaning of natural-kind terms is fixed, moment by moment, by their complementary locations in the dual contexts of theory and practice, each of which influences the other.

I turn now to deal with certain objections that could be raised to the idea of making 'same nature' the dominant (though not, as I have argued, the exclusive) kind criterion.

1   In the natural sciences the semantic rules governing some group of kind terms can continue to be used to pick out proper members of a set of beings, by descriptive criteria, when it may be known that there is no single common nature. Mellor in his 1977 article has offered the case of the isotopes of chlorine, chlorine 35 and chlorine 37. They are both chlorine though there are differences in the structures of their constituent atoms. We call them both 'chlorine' because the distinctions between chemical elements are rooted in the practical context. Both chlorines behave in accordance with the chemical criteria for the second lightest halogen. To call them both chlorine, mere variants of the same natural kind, does, however have a footing in the theoretical context. Theory explains chemical behaviour by reference to electronic configurations, rather than nuclear structure. I claim they are both taken to be chlorine not because of the identity of their chemical behaviour, but because that identity is rooted in an identity of relevant atomic structure, that is electron configuration. The rare earths manifest nearly identical chemical behaviour but they are classified as distinct elements because their constituent atoms are believed to be different in electronic configurations, but only in those shells that do not control manifest chemical behaviour. This example makes clear how the two contexts interact. Electron configuration is relevant only to the extent that it is explanatory of behavioural differences in the practical context, while similarities and differences of behaviour count as significant relative to kind determinations only if they can be grounded in a 'real essence' distinction created within a theoretical context. But we cannot make any claim we like about essences to save a definition based on a material practice because claims about essences must be certified by reference to theory.

2   Along with the idea of kind terms as rigid designators of real essences has gone the baptismal model of meaning creation. Putnam (1983) refers to various 'paradigm' instances, which determine all future usage. There is a historical continuity of linguistic practices spreading from the ceremonial dubbing of that instance with the kind term in question. But this is inadequate as a theory of the meaning of kind terms in the natural sciences. Putnam himself notices one obvious refinement. Room must be made in the theory for the fact that better samples are often introduced displacing the originals. This has certainly been true of the chemical elements and for many other domains. It can be followed in recent discussions of the nature of quasars.

But the most telling point is simply this: in many cases in the natural sciences work in the theoretical context provides the community with an identifying description of a typical member or sample of a kind before that kind has been identified in a practical context. The anticipation of experience is a central feature of scientific method. The Odling–Mendeleev 'gappy' periodic table was used to prescribe the identifying features of chemical elements yet to be picked out in the laboratory. Astronomers did not find superintensive gravitational fields and then dub them 'black holes'. Theory suggested that they should exist. None have yet been identified, but we can grasp the meaning of the natural-kind term 'black hole'. But Putnam's account firmly puts the existence of an exemplar prior to the creation of meaning for the relevant kind term. He says (1983, p. 73) 'A term refers to something if it stands in the right relations (causal continuity in the case of proper names; sameness of 'nature' in the case of kind terms) to these existentially given things. In the case of proper names, the existentially given thing is the person or thing originally 'baptized' with the name; in the case of natural-kind words, the existentially given things are the actual paradigms.' If Putnam means this account to be taken seriously it would confine the denotation of all natural-kind terms to the beings of Realm 1.

It will be worth working out two examples in some detail to hammer home the point of this section: that in general the theoretical context has priority in determining the intension of kind terms, but that these terms are located in two contexts, and that the way they are used at any moment is the result of an interplay between them. For my first example I take the discovery of the positron and I shall simply quote the excellent summary of that history by J. Leplin (1979).

The case is more straightforward for 'positron' and 'photon' being terms whose initial reference was fixed by their role in a certain theoretical context, rather than on the basis of some experience attributed to the causal agency of the referent. Initial reference to positrons was achieved by Dirac's quantum theory of the electron which required that there be 'negative energy' solutions to the wave equation. The realization that such solutions must refer to positrons resulted from Weyl's demonstration that they have electron mass, and predates Anderson's experiments which provided an independent basis for fixing reference to positrons, and which actually occasioned the first use of the term 'positron'. The realization that the particle Anderson detected is the particle Dirac's theory requires was evidently due to Blackett's observation that the small life span of the particle needed to acount for its appearance only in cloud chamber experiments is a consequence of Dirac's theory. The idea that the particle could be created and destroyed in interactions and need not have a role in the constitution of stable matter removed a major impediment to its acceptability.

This is a beautiful example of the interaction of the practical and theoretical contexts in fixing the meaning and stabilizing the reference of a natural-kind term. One might also consult Leplin's detailed discussion of the development of the meaning and denotation of the term 'electron' as used to refer to the 'atom of electricity'.

For my second example I shall take Pasteur's discovery of the attenuation of 'viruses'. It is often said that it is only the prepared mind that can make accidental discoveries. There already exists a conceptual structure incorporating an implicit kind prescription. The 'discovery' is a slotting of an entity into a total structure formed of the theoretical system and the practices that define the limits of current experience. It is not that someone finds 'something' and then wonders just what it is and what it would be apt to call it. Pasteur had prepared some cultures of the chicken cholera microorganism. He left them in his laboratory when he went away for the summer. He delayed his return that year and the cultures sat untouched for some months. When he did restart his researches he found that the chickens which he inoculated with those cultures did not develop the disease. In subsequent trials he found that even when infected with fresh chicken cholera culture those chickens were immune. Pasteur had already worked out a complex conceptual system, based on an analogy between fermentation and disease. Something, analogous to the loss of potency in yeasts, had been going on during the summer in his neglected culture flasks. He was already in possession of the concept 'attenuation of the potency of a microorganism'. The concept now had a putative referent in some unknown process within those very flasks. Its expression goes nicely into the Roberts IP form: 'Whatever went on in these flasks is the cause of the attenuation of chicken cholera "virus".' The example shows the inadequacy of the Putnam-Kripke account of how meaning and denotation are secured for a scientific concept. 'Attenuation of "viruses"' did not get its meaning as the name of the process whose nature was first unknown. Its meaning was created in a displacement of concepts from oology to microbiology. It is a very good example of Boyd's 'obtaining epistemic access'. Pasteur now had epistemic access to the process of the attenuation of viruses. He knew when and where it occurred and its natural-kind. It was certainly a microbiological process. From this position, and only from this position or an equivalent one, could more be found out.

Can anything more now be said about the structure of substantive scientific terms that would explain how referential acts are possible? And how is it possible for anyone to know that some attempted referential acts have been unsuccessful? I have already suggested in chapter 4 that the intension of kind terms should be thought of as a conjunction of three components. There is a metaphysical or ontological component (thing, process, disposition or whatever); a natural-kind component (animal, chemical element, etc.) and a specifying component, whose exact status will depend on context and content. The two latter components shade into one another, and a boundary can be drawn only case by case. The metaphysical component locates the working kind concept within a categorial framework, to borrow Korner's useful term. It appears in assumptions about the kind of material practice that would be appropriate to demonstrate the existence of an instance or a sample of the kind in question. The kind component and any tighter specifications that are called for are manifested in the properties by which an observable 'something' is recognized as a member or sample of the kind.

Natures and necessities

We are now in a position to tackle the question of the logical status of the relation between kinds and natures, as this relation is expressed in various ways in scientific discourse. An absolute analytic/synthetic distinction is evidently inappropriate to the analysis of these relations. A good deal of the difficulty which even well-disposed philosophers have found with the idea of a necessary relation between kinds and their natures has come from the realization, sometimes implicit, that there is an unavoidable duality in the contexts in which natural-kind terms are used, and in which their meanings are created. In different examples these contexts have different weight, a sure recipe for philosophical confusion and empty debate. In what follows I make occasional use of Bostock's unpublished paper of *c*.1978. Kripke's (1980) argument to the necessity of statements linking nominal to real essences must be undermined to permit my dialectic account of the relation between observable and hypothetical natures to flourish. To continue with the old example: 'Water is H_2O' is necessary according to Kripke because it is a singular identity statement and both its terms are rigid designators. That is to say they refer to the same thing in any possible world in which they do refer at all, that is to the real essence of water. They behave on the model of proper names.

Putnam's (1975) argument is similar and I shall discuss the issue through Bostock's useful summary.

The argument	*My gloss*
1 'This [particular] is dihydrogen oxide.'	An empirical discovery about the nature of the sample under study which could have been picked out by pointing; provided we had some notion of which category to attend to.
2 'This particular is to be counted as a sample of its kind.'	That is this particular is a Putnamian paradigm.
3 'Whatever is of the same kind as this sample is dihydrogen oxide.'	Kinds are defined in theoretical contexts, relative to contexts.
4 'Whatever is water is of the same kind as this [sample].'	This is a sample of a kind defined in a practical context.
5 'Whatever is water is dihydrogen oxide.'	

The proposition I have numbered 2 is presumably meant to make both 3 and 4 necessary truths, since 'this' refers to a paradigm sample of a kind in both contexts, practical and theoretical (Zemach, 1976). But 5 can be inferred from 3 and 4 only if a further premise is added, that kinds in the practical context must be coordinate with or reflect the kinds of the theoretical context. This surely is the force of Putnam's 'paradigm'. Such a proposition might be justified by pointing out that in the natural sciences the behaviour of the sample in the practical context is explained by the nature of the sample worked out within the theoretical context. That is the sample must be paradigmatic in both contexts. How then can it be a contingent matter, subject to further research, whether the cluster of properties picked out as criterial in the practical context has or does not have a backing in the discoveries controlled by the theoretical context? Furthermore the behaviour of the sample in the practical context is the joint effect of situational conditions and intrinsic dispositions. Thus water by virtue of its molecular constitution solidifies in cold and vaporizes in heat. But for Putnam's argument to succeed there must be some way of discounting some aspects of the behaviour of things and samples in the practical context. It cannot be part of the nature of water to be solid, liquid and gaseous, though whether in a particular context an actual sample will be in this or that phase will be explicable in terms of the nature of water. If contextual features enter into the explanation of behaviour in practical contexts then the strict correlation between nominal and real essences, upon which the argument depends, is lost.

In chapter 4 I expressed some cautions about the use of essentialist language, on the general grounds of the revisability of the conceptual structures of both practical and theoretical contexts. However the terminology does have its place. It does make sense to say that being composed of molecules of dihydrogen oxide is the essence of water. But why? How can the essential and non-essential aspects of the total ensemble of the properties of a natural being be differentiated in a principled way? Mellor (1977) for one has raised doubts about this possibility, but an answer is readily found by taking account of the hierarchical organization of scientific knowledge. (See also Fales (1979) for an argument to a position very similar to mine.) In a later chapter I shall be calling on Aronson's idea of explanation as a mapping from phenomena to aspects of a common ontology, to tidy up the idea of hierarchies of explanations. For the moment it is sufficient to point out that the assumption that a particular sample of a material substance is a swarm of dihydrogen oxide molecules is essential to explaining why that sample has just those boiling and freezing points it exhibits in a suitable practical context, why it has a certain latent heat of fusion, and so on. But none of these facts about that substance serves to expain why it is a collection of dihydrogen oxide molecules. The direction of an explanatory hierarchy is not arbitrary (*pace* Mellor) but determined by such powerful principles as the part-whole relation and the direction of the influences of causes. That its molecules are mostly built out of two hydrogen atoms and one atom of oxygen, that this is the essence of what it is to *be* water, follows from the way that relatively theoretical properties of water figure asymmetrically in explanations.

But there is something yet deeper to be brought out. At the back of the philosophical theories of both Putnam and Kripke is a radical extensionalism, which manifests itself in their attempt to create a theory of meaning for kind terms on the model of the way a proper name gets its meaning. Possible worlds and rigid designators strike me as flamboyant extentions of the crude extensionalist theories of language against which Wittgenstein directed the arguments of Part One of the *Philosophical investigations*.

The view I have been defending takes real essences as the constitutions of material beings, expressed in revisable hypotheses derived from the best current theories. At the same time the best current theory is used in support and extension of current material practices of assigning particulars to kinds. In the revisable conventions of taxonomies are to be found what remains of nominal essences in our sciences. But the route from real to nominal essences and back is a crooked one, since typical manifestations are influenced not only by the natures of things but by the circumstances of their manifestation. The natural sciences must offer the means for accounting for the distinctive clusters of different criterial properties needed by virtue of the fact that manifestations are relative to the circumstances in which material beings find themselves.

This analysis points to the need to avoid the kind of jokey fictional cases cited by Putnam. They mystify just because neither practical nor theoretical contexts for the employment of the vocabulary have been fully imagined (Mellor, 1977). The philosophical question upon which the theory of reference and of meaning depends is whether statements, the acceptability or unacceptability of which is criterial for deciding whether acts of putative reference have succeeded in a practical context, must be backed up by theory-based descriptions of the unobserved and perhaps even unobservable natures of those putative referents. The argument of this chapter suggests an affirmative answer.

These considerations have consequences not just for the theory of reference. They help one to deal with the puzzles raised by Goodman's (1954) ingenious revamping of the problem of induction with his synthetic predicate 'grue'. It must be studied as a possible addition to a scientific vocabulary. It is to be used of those beings which are currently seen to be green but will become blue at some future time. For those with our sensory make-up grue cannot be a phenomenal property. There seem to be two cases.

In one case the change from green to blue, when it occurs, is circumstantial, the real essences of the material beings involved remaining unchanged. For instance a sheet of white paper which looks green under green light will look blue under blue light. In that case there is no inductive puzzle involved since no one who knew the facts of the case would be tempted to say the paper itself was grue, and no reasonable person would be tempted to induce a law like statement one way or the other from noticing that a piece of white paper which once looked green now looks blue. In the other case suppose grue is an essential property, something in the nature of a certain kind of thing. In traditional terminology it must be a secondary property, a power to induce a certain phenomenal experience. Powers of this sort are grounded in some feature of the constitution of the being in question. Now Goodman's puzzle does arise, since the current green appearance of a thing is as good a reason to suppose it is really green, that is has a nature such that it permanently possesses the disposition to appear green, as to suppose that it is really grue, that is has a constitutional property such that it sometimes has the power to look green, at some other time the power to look blue.

Creatures who were capable of perceiving a thing staying grue would not see it as either green or blue, but as whatever primary quality it was that grounded the disposition to look one way at one time and another way at another time to human beings. For human beings the difference between green and grue could not be settled by inductive evidence based on appearances but would, so this fictional tale illustrates, require reference to predications in a theoretical context. Goodman's puzzle is a problem for him just because he accepts a logicist account of theory and an empiricist account of the content of scientific discourse. But once one has to hand the distinction between powers, natures and appearances – the common stock in trade of scientific thinking – the grue joke becomes a *reductio ad absurdum* of logicist empiricism. This analysis illustrates the enormous importance that the concept of a natural-kind plays in real science. Emeralds, as a natural-kind, cannot change spontaneously from green to blue at some moment. This is because as a natural-kind they are defined in the dual contexts of theory and practice as those beings with such a molecular constitution that in normal circumstances they will look green. Martians, as it happens, can perceive the property that we, as theoreticians, have introduced to explain the apparent spontaneous change of colour of certain very rare gem stones, namely 'grue'. Their philosophers have pointed out that, on the basis of evidence culled from appearances alone, it is just as rational to infer that in future these stones will appear bleen as grue. For people a gemstone which changed from grue to bleen would have looked green all along. Just as grue would be an unobservable primary quality for people, so green would be an unobservable primary quality for Martians.

Examples like the green/grue puzzle do not constitute problems for a realist philosophy of science because the theoretical context of kind predications is elaborated until as many as possible of the observed empirical irregularities and discontinuities in some field of interest are accounted for in terms of theoretically defined stable natures. We humans do not believe emeralds will always be green because they always have been, but because what it is to be an emerald is to have a certain molecular constitution. Things with this constitution usually look green to well-placed people. As Eddington remarked one should accept only those facts which are well confirmed by theory. We can make claims about natural necessities, that is we can sensibly use modal qualifiers like 'must' and 'should', to the degree that we are convinced that our theoretical sketches of the natures of things are correct. I shall discuss the grounding of these kinds of judgements in detail in part 4. None of these concepts is strict. Their behaviour and relations in the strict system provide an idealized template for the construction of a philosopher's version of the actual system of concepts employed by scientific communities.

The discussion so far has turned on what now can be seen as a particular case. Locke's influential treatment of kinds is the ultimate source of the distinctions I have worked up into a form appropriate for their application to contemporary sciences. But the Lockean model is an expression of a generally microstructural explanatory scheme. Real essences existed, but could not be known to human science. They were the unobservable textures of the minute *parts* of particulars. The examples I have discussed have all been drawn from this genre of cases. But if the question to be addressed is 'How is it possible that there are many beings which display contextually interesting similarities? ' then a more general answer is needed. This question is at the heart of the theory of classification because it is from clusters of observable similarities that those criterial properties we use in something like the way nominal essences would be used, are drawn. There are many beings which, it seems, have the properties they do because of the relations in which they stand to material contexts of other beings. This is all very obvious in the case of social beings and their social contexts. The categorizing of two people as 'ward' and 'guardian' makes use not only of a type distinction based on reciprocal and internal relations between any pair of beings properly so described. It also depends on the origins of their several dispositions and obligations in the social order within which they live. The criterial properties by means of which people are classified as 'wards' or 'guardians' are not free-floating or arbitrary, but neither are they grounded in the similarities between the microstructures of other wards and guardians as particulars. It would very odd to speak of the real essence of guardianship as some set of socio-legal conventions. Nevertheless those conventions play the same role with respect to the nominal essence of guardianship as the electronic structural similarities of constituent atoms do for the nominal essences of chemical species. The Machean theory of inertia is a macrostructural account of a property routinely taken as criterial for the identity of observable physical beings.

These examples illustrate that what matters is that there should always be a duality to the cognitive setting of kind-distinctions. As opposed to mere superficial classifications, the criterial distinctions or nominal essences of a working kind taxonomy are *grounded* in super- or subordinate properties. There has been a tendency, not wholly resisted by Putnam and Kripke, to analyse talk of essences only in the microstructural context, of which the philosophical logic of chemical species is typical. And indeed this tendency seems to be bound up with the way 'essence' is used in such discussions. But any serious theory of kinds must be developed in a larger context in which both microstructural and macrostructural explanations are invoked to defend the raising of the contingency of a merely practical kind classification to the natural necessity of a taxonomy.

How far do the sciences use natural-kind concepts?

Having developed a working concept of natural-kind, sufficiently subtle to survive standard philosophical criticisms, we can still ask whether, outside chemistry, scientists do or perhaps should make use of it. Natural-kind classifications are based on the conjunction of a set of criterial properties fixed by human fiat in a context of practice with an empirically revisable theoretical grounding in a context of associated theory. Is this structure found in all those sciences where classifications abound? We know that it is found in chemistry since it was from that science that the dual-context account was abstracted.

Are biological species natural-kinds? Or to put the question more generally has biology any use for natural-kind concepts? The use of the criterial component to pick out individuals as members of species does entail that those individuals will be similar in the relevant respects. Hull (1974) argues that species considered in the context of evolutionary theory 'need not be and frequently are not comprised of similar individuals'. For instance members of polytypic and polymorphic species may differ from one another more than they each differ from members of other species. Hull argues that 'even when the members of a species are fairly similar to one another they are *not* included in the same species *because* they possess any prerequisite degree of similarity' (p. 333). Species within the framework of evolutionary theory can only be populations, whose 'unity' is a matter of common descent. According to Hull populations are not to be understood in terms of class inclusion, but rather of the part-whole relation. Cohen (1974), however, seems to want to claim (following Ghiselin) that both the similarity concept (class) and the descent concept (population) are required in biology. The former is needed for taxonomy (the practical context) and the latter for explanations (the theoretical context). The species of traditional Darwinian theory are dual context natural-kinds, populations whose observed similarities are explained phylogenetically. Cohen at least allows the two components of a genuine natural-kind taxonomy to coexist, even if, as Hull seems to think, there is no systematic way of uniting them. But it seems that even in the most liberal reading biology does not really use natural-kind concepts. Gene pool accounts are tempting but the flow from genetic code to phenotypic adult form is a stream with many tributaries, including epigenetic influences and complex feedbacks from the moment-by-moment state of the developing organism.

Hull (1984) reintroduces the idea of a natural-kind. He says (p. 146)

The crucial factor is the relative primacy of similarity and descent. If similarity takes priority over descent, then the entity is a class and at least a candidate for inclusion in a scientific law. For example, all particular samples of gold may have developed originally from hydrogen, but that genesis is irrelevant on current physical theory to something being gold. Gold is a genuine class, a natural-kind. If descent takes priority to similarity, then the entity is not a class and hence reference to it must be excluded from any genuine laws of nature.

In biology descent is given priority over similarity. In recommending the idea of a lineage he remarks:

That we conceptualize lineages as individuals and not classes can be seen by the decisions we make when similarity and descent do not universally covary. Usually entities related by descent are similar to one another. A is similar to B because A gave rise to B. However they need not be similar, and even when they are not, they remain part of the same lineage. Human family trees are paradigm examples of lineages.

A metaphysics of biology based on lineages needs neither classes nor populations as basic units. At best a population is a cotemporal slice of a set of lineages.

The ways in which decisions as to whether or not some being is a sample or exemplar of a natural-kind emerge in a historical process can be illustrated, and the treatment of kinds as stabilized by the location of kind concepts in the dual contexts of practice and theory can be further recommended, by a brief look at the history of the 'four elements', earth, water, air and fire. In ancient science they were billed as basic natural-kinds, whose dispositions were their natures. Now only water survives as a natural-kind, significantly chosen by Putnam and Kripke for the leading role in their instructive fables. What happened to the others? Fire has turned out to be not a substance but a process. A liberal reading of the ancient concept might just permit it a ghostly persistence as the ultimate substance energy. As a process it has a nature, and so might be a process natural-kind. As an ultimate substance it has no nature other than its defining powers. Air as a mixture is a blend of independently existing gases, each a (lower-order) natural-kind, because the bizarre examples which might tend to force us because the properties by which they can be physically separated, such as atomic weight or respirability, depending on whether we have a gas centrifuge or just a mouse to work with, can be grounded in the theoretical context by reference to their several real essences, namely their distinctive atomic constitutions. Water has already occupied our attention, surviving as a natural kind, because the bizarre examples which might tend to force us back to an arbitrary and merely man selected nominal essence are strictly unintelligible. Earth is the most interesting of all. It is not a natural-kind, even of a higher order, because chemistry has revealed too great differences in the constitution of earths. There are mixtures and compounds, but there are also elements and compounds, there are alkalis and salts, and so on almost endlessly. Unlike nitrogen and oxygen, the main constituents of air, which are lower-order kinds of the high-order *kind* gas, the constituents of earth do not have sufficient in common *in the theoretical context* for it to be scientifically profitable to treat 'earth' as a higher order kind.

6

Referential Grids

The concept of 'grid'

'Terms denote; people refer.' I owe this crisp formulation of the underlying point of view of this part of my study to Mary Tiles. Referring is a human activity and reference is an achievement. In the last two chapters I have tried to show how both cognitive and material practices are involved in referential acts and in judging their success or failure. Importantly the cognitive achievement of giving meaning to a natural-kind term (or a term denoting an individual) may be prior to the *physical work* of establishing or trying but failing to establish a causal relation between the embodied observer and the being in question, be it token of type or individual. From a criterial point of view spatio-temporal location and causal efficacy come to the fore. In this chapter I shall try to tie spatio-temporal location to thinghood conceptually, and thence to eventhood, by arguing for the view that the spatio-temporal manifold is a property of the material system, and not an independent being.

Two sets of arguments will be advanced. The first set is aimed at showing that the most primitive concepts of 'spatial and temporal interval', 'thing' and 'event' are mutually dependent. In separating them we are in effect enlarging a conceptual circle, not establishing a synthetic correlation. Without the spatial and temporal manifolds we could have distinct (indivi-duatable and reidentifiable) things or distinct events. But without things and events there would be no spatial and temporal manifolds.

The second set of arguments goes further by linking considerations of indexicality in scientific discourse with the conceptual consequences of the relativity theories, further to substantiate the relationist point of view. The effect of these arguments will be to set off the spatial from the temporal mani-fold ontologically, the concept of velocity serving in Minkowski style to map the one on to the other.

The argument of chapters 4 and 5 was dominated by Roberts's concep-tion of referring as a theory-led material practice by which a figure is singled out from a ground. This view was set squarely between the extremes of descriptivism and essentialism drawing on the strengths of both. The discussion was directed to discovering those features of the 'figures' that were required for the material practice of referring to be possible. Nothing was said about the necessary features of the 'ground'. I begin with the assumption that the ground for acts of reference by the community of physical scientists must be some differentiated extension, some field of beings of the same Kantian category, but more extensive than the figure. Strong exclusion relations must obtain between individual beings composing the field and the target of an act of reference if it is to be capable of being used as a ground. For instance an array of things could form a spatial ground for a material figure if all the beings involved were impenetrable to one another. Temporal grounds are more complex. Not only is the exclusion of past, present and future events from one another more difficult to explain, but two events can occupy the same location in the temporal manifold. Two things cannot be at the same location in the spatial manifold, nor can two properties which are determinates of the same determinable. The relevant exclusion relations, as I shall show, can be tied to the use of the Principle of non-contradiction to structure a scientific discourse. Only those things and properties which exemplify the associated exclusion relations could form the physical basis for a ground for acts of reference for a science whose discourses are framed within that constraint. Such a physical basis I will call a 'grid'.

However the development of physics could show that the system of relations we call space-time may be best seen, not as a permanent structure underlying all manifestations of the physically real, but rather as a universal manifestation of certain *dispositions for order* which are grounded in something unimaginably different. I will touch on this speculation again in part 5.

A Leibnizean genesis for a spatio-temporal manifold

This exercise is designed to show how the most primitive spatial and temporal relations arise through the exigencies of discourse in which some simple exclusion relations obtain. Suppose we are given the ideas of individual and property, and the correlative linguistic acts of naming and predicating. (In the end it will emerge that we cannot really be given the ideas of individual and the act of naming without at the same time being given the idea of some primitive spatial manifold. The object of this exercise is to open out this basic interdefinition.)In the first case to be considered let us imagine sentient beings whose worldly experience requires them to assert propositions of the form 'Fa & $not\text{-}Fa$'. Let us suppose further that their conventions of scientific rhetoric include the prohibition of self-contra-dictory statements. In respect of what worldly experience would the above sentence form express an acceptable statement?

The violation of convention apparent in the above statement could be remedied in two ways:

1　The individual described in that statement, called a is *extended*. While it displays the property F at one 'end' it displays some other property, which is not F at the other. Without a temporal manifold the question of whether or not the acts of predication were simultaneous does not yet arise. This little fable introduces the concept of spatial interval, and with it, the intelligibility of multiple acts of reference, individuated by virtue of the spatial difference of the 'ends' of the being in question. Of course the spatial difference just is the fact that the 'ends' are mutually exclusive indi-viduals.

2　The individual described in that statement, called a is *enduring*. While it displays (the tense of this verb is now proto-temporal) the property F at one moment it displays some other property which is not F at another. Without a spatial manifold the question of whether or not the acts of predication were colocated does not yet arise. This little fable introduces the concept of temporal duration, and with it, the intelligibility of multiple acts of reference, individuated by virtue of the temporal difference of the two 'moments' of the process in question. And of course the temporal difference just is the fact that the moments are exclusive events, for instance the having of different determinates under the same determinable.

Combining the two sets of relations so defined allows each to sharpen the conceptual structure of the other. The concept of 'spatial interval' depends on simultaneous acts of predication and that of 'temporal duration' depends on collocated acts of predication. The fables make clear how these concepts are appropriate to a universe in which some things and events physically exclude one another. The important 'part-whole' relation is just barely adumbrated in this simple universe.

The analysis assumes that one individual can be distinguished from any other by whether it does or does not possess the property F. This property cannot be a spatio-temporal relation. It must be an intensive magnitude. The discernibility of the 'parts' of the extended being and of the moments of the enduring process are assumed in both fables, and is used as a ground for the introduction of the concepts 'spatial interval' and 'temporal endurance'. The concepts of individual thing and of individual event are then finally linked tightly to spatio-temporal location. The possibility of the one is a necessary condition for the possibility of the other. Thing individuation must be related primarily to space since space has been introduced as a system of relations based on thing exclusion. Pure numerical difference *is* difference in location. But things can be reidentified and so their conditions of individuation must involve time. It is not a contingent fact that things endure. Event individuation is related primarily to time. Events just are changes in properties and/or relations of things. But events are located so their conditions of individuation must involve the spatial manifold.

Up to this point in the analysis there has been a thorough-going symmetry between space and time as the totality of relations of each kind. (For a detailed examination of alleged asymmetries between the spatial and temporal manifolds, see Schlesinger, 1980.) What more is needed to distinguish them unambiguously? To go any further I believe we must take account of features of the way our world presents itself to us. The spatial manifold is three-dimensional and the temporal manifold one-dimensional. Further, in Minkowski's representation the temporal parameter is introduced in a way that is algebraically asymmetrical to the way the spatial parameters are introduced. Finally there is a marked asymmetry in the way metrics are imposed on each manifold. A slow transport of standard rods is similar to the repetition of a standard process in a clock. However a signal travelling with uniform velocity is an alternative possibility for the measurement of space. But there is no analogue for this in the measurement of time (Angel 1977, p. 72). Metrical practices for both manifolds are, of course, shot through with conventions the exploration of which has been a central interest of philosophers. For my purposes the importance of the various conventions upon which the effective use of physical measuring devices depends is that adherence to them ensures that spatio-temporal relations are non-causal. Changes in properties other than spatio-temporal location, which are correlated with spatial and/or temporal change, are to be put down to spatio-temporally non-uniform influences, for instance fields. It follows that any thing or event meeting the implicit criteria of identity and individuation built into the structures of space-time must stand in spatio-temporal relations to any other thing or event meeting these criteria including the scientist whose referring acts may, with luck, achieve a physical relation with a referent. Therefore *the spatio-temporal grid must be the basic framework for acts of reference, whether successful or unsuccessful.*

In sum, then, we need a spatio-temporal grid in order to make reference possible. It is one of the conditions of unambiguous communication for both lay and scientific communities. As I have argued in the two preceding chapters, referring is a practice by which individuals of various categories are *picked out* from among others of the same generic kind. These others form a manifold, a field of alternative referents. The topological properties of such a field are constructible in terms of exclusion relations. The treatment in this section has been Leibnizean but similar exclusion principles are invoked by Kant (1781) in his discussion of space and time. In the *Critique of pure reason*, 'Transcendental aesthetic', II, sect. 5, he remarks that 'only in time can two contradictorily opposed predicates meet in one and the same object, namely, *one after the other.*'

The manifolds so far considered are discrete grids of actual existents. But the exigencies of human life and scientific practice require acts of reference beyond the current reach of those observable locations and moments that are marked by real things and events. Space and time are extensions of the grid of locations and moments, both 'outwards' to infinity and 'inwards' to the infinitesimal. As human constructions our ideas of these extended grids are clearly the result of cognitive rather than empirical activities. What, then, is the ontological status of the manifolds which the concepts of space and time might be taken to denote? And how do the special and general theories of relativity affect this simple picture?

The reality question

No realist treatment of the physical sciences could tolerate an idealist interpretation of the system of spatio-temporal relations. Even the modest form of scientific realism defended in this work needs a robust sense of spatio-temporal location as the basis of existential proof by reference. Any of the community's beliefs about such partially known beings might be revised. Only spatio-temporal location remains to bear the burden of a demonstration of existence. The first ontological contrast marks off traditional idealism from all other accounts of the nature of space and time. If all the objects of experience are mentalistic, including things and events, as they might be according to some extreme phenomenalists, then space and time as systems of relations between such entities must also be mentalistic. Existential proof by establishing reference to a putative being among other beings does nothing to extend the realm of the real. (One way of dealing with such an extreme view is to argue that it does not really differ from the commonsense view, since the familiar distinctions between the real and the non-existent, the illusory, and so on, must be able to be reproduced within this ontology). But abandoning the extreme phenomenalist account of nature and experience does not lead straight to a realist interpretation of the grids of space and time. Kantian theory must first be eliminated.

The familiar Kantian theory of space and time treats them as differentiated orders of exclusions which are imposed upon an undifferentiated flux by human mental activity. The name of this ontological status is transcendental ideality.

It is convenient to express Kant's theory in statements taken from the 'Transcendental aesthetic', I, sect. 3 (Kant, 1788).

1 'How then can there exist in the mind an outer intuition which precedes the objects themselves, and in which the concept of these objects can be determined *a priori*? Manifestly not otherwise than in so far as the intuition has its seat in the subject only, as the formal character of the subject, in virtue of which, in being affected by objects, it obtains *immediate representation*, that is, *intuition*, of them; and only in so far, therefore, as it is merely the form of outer *sense* in general.' Space (and time) as the form of intuitions can exist prior to these intuitions only in the human subject, not in the world.

2 'It is therefore, solely from the human standpoint that we can speak of space, of extended things.' but 'Space is *ideal* in respect of things when they are considered in themselves through reason, that is, without regard to the constitution of our sensibility.' So the ontological status of space and time, for Kant, is ideality. 'We can indeed say that space comprehends all things that appear to us as external, but not all things in themselves, by whatever subject they are intuited or whether they are intuited or not.

Kant notes that if we took space and time to be manifolds abstracted from ordered fields of mutually exclusive beings by human mental activity we would be obliged to deny the *apodeictic certainty* of mathematical doctrines relative to real things. But this is just exactly what we now do. The modern view in a nutshell is that certain mathematical structures apply to the real world because they have been abstracted from it. And the question of whether structures which have been freely created by human imagination are useful in ordering natural or social beings is an empirical matter. We are not driven Kant's way because we do not share his assumption of the apodeictic necessity of just *one* form of geometry. We are free to consider geometry and the topology of time and the structure of the physical world as independent orders and to discuss the relation between them.

The generalized Leibnizian derivation with which I began this chapter leads to two different sets of acausal relations between material bodies and their changing properties. In this way two discrete manifolds of locations and events could be constructed. By supplementing these manifolds with further sets of locations and moments counterfactually defined as possible locations and moments, manifolds that are dense and of unlimited extent can be conceived. By adopting a mathematical description of the totality of point locations in each manifold in which they appear as continua of the order of the real numbers, we seem to be describing a remarkable and ubiquitous being which could exist independently of the material system from whence it was derived. Furthermore, with the idea of uniform velocity the manifolds can be mapped on to one another (Lucas, 1973). Conceived as a notation, these manifolds, when anchored to suitable material beings, provide the scientific community with an economical, unambiguous and ubiquitous nomenclature for locating parts of the material system through the material practices associated with skilful use of Roberts's DC-type referential statements. Conceived as real beings they promote the kind of dangerous fantasies once deplored by Leibniz. Unfortunately they are not wholly the preserve of writers of science fiction. The reification of space, time and space-time by philosophers must be dealt with (Hinckfuss, 1975).

How does space exist?

The reality of space, time or the spatio-temporal manifold which is described in a four-dimensional geometry such as that of Minkowski can be understood in two ways. It could be argued that space-time exists as an independent being of the same ontological status as the causally interacting system of material things. But from the point of view of geometro-dynamics that independence is only apparent. The material system is but a manifestation of certain geometrical properties of the spatio-temporal manifold. I believe that such a theory of space-time can be shown to be flawed. Alternatively space-time could be thought to be real because it was a property of the material system. On this view 'matter' is ontologically prior to space-time and embodied observers to their indexical acts. I shall try to show that the spatio-temporal manifold is an abstract and idealized set of relations, developed out of certain non-causal but real relations of coexistence and succession among the entities of the material system.

A strong case for the view that that the manifold has properties which are independent of the material system has been developed by Nerlich (1976). It is based on the idea that some of the geometrical properties of the spatial manifold can be treated as 'shape'. Only of concrete particulars can a shape be predicated. But how could one arrive at any idea of the shape of space? There is no standpoint from which space itself could be examined and its shape discerned. Nerlich sets out to make sense of the idea by introducing a distinction between intrinsic and extrinsic geometry. This distinction can be illustrated in the two ways the form of a sphere can be expressed. Regular figures (e.g. isosceles triangles) laid out on its surface will have distinctive properties different from figures of the same geometrical form laid out on other surfaces. For instance the internal angles will add up to a total greater than 180 degrees. But the unique shape of a sphere can also be expressed in terms of the rotation of a plane figure (a circle) in three-dimensional space. The latter description specifies a shape in terms of the extrinsic geometry of the body. We can now make sense of the idea of the shape of space itself. It could be expressed in terms of its intrinsic geometry.

The progressive development of ideas about the shape of a single manifold, space-time, can be followed through successive developments of the 'line-element law'. In classical physics the length of an element of geodesic in free space (ds) is calculated from the relation

$$ds^2 = dx^2 + dy^2 + dz^2$$

In the Minkowski representation of space-time the expression for the line element becomes

$$ds^2 = dt^2 - (1/c)(dx^2 + dy^2 + dz^2)$$

reflecting the basic idea of special relativity.

However, in general relativity the density of the system of material bodies affects the calculation of the line element. According to the Robertson–Walker metric

$$ds^2 = dt^2 - (1/c)(R\ dt)(dx^2 + dy^2 + dz^2)$$

Calculation of distances in accordance with this theory requires attention to the distribution and quantity of matter. Measures of space, time and matter-energy are functionally related. The latter conclusion is susceptible of a number of alternative readings, not all of which require that space-time and the material system be treated as independent realities in mutual inter-action. In favour of the independent existence view it could be argued that the interrelation of measures of space-time and of matter-energy is a natural consequence of a physical interaction between the space-time manifold as a real being and the material system, each an independent substance. In support of this proposal one could cite the fact that there are solutions for the field equations defining universe models even in the absence of any matter, solutions which imply a residual structure for space-time. The fact that mathematical descriptions of model universes admit of solutions which ascribe properties to the space-time manifold in the absence of matter need not entail any metaphysical consequences. Equations frequently admit of solutions for which there are no reasonable physical interpretations, and physicists are accustomed to deleting them in the light of their intuitions as to what is plausible physically. From a philosopher's point of view such intuitions express the basic metaphysical assumptions of that community of physicists. If vacuum solutions are declared meaningless on metaphysical grounds it might be perhaps because in the absence of a material system no concrete spatio-temporal relations could exist, and hence there would be no way of relating an abstract referential grid to material individuals. These considerations are not to be confused with the discussion of phenomena like the Lamb shift, for which the 'vacuum' provides a non-zero energy ground state. That vacuum is not an empty space–time. The concept of 'emptiness' has become more complex in contemporary physics than it was in the Newtonian scheme.

A more radical explanation of the appearance of relationships like the Robertson–Walker expression for the line element would be to deny that it reflects the interdependence of two substances. Space-time and matter-energy distribution could be two experientially distinct manifestations of the same underlying reality. Adopting this explanation would allow us the luxury of Occam's razor, at the same time as we permit ourselves two sets of relations among material beings, the one non-causal and the other causal. These 'intrinsic geometries' are descriptions not of space–time, but of the way material bodies influence each other's motion.

Nerlich's reply to this objection turns on a thought experiment. We imagine a region of space in which the intrinsic geometry is non-Euclidean. Geodesic paths of freely moving particles will be 'curved'. Let us suppose the space is a two-dimensional manifold with a structure as represented in figure 6. 1. In an adjoining region of space the intrinsic geometry is Euclidean. A large rubber sheet is drifting through space in such a way that each of its component molecules is describing a geodesic path. The sheet has been provided with strain gauges, again as in figure 6.1. In the flat region of space these gauges register zero. According to Nerlich as the sheet drifts into the non-Euclidean region the gauges will begin to show positive readings as the sheet takes up a new overall configuration. There is a physically real effect, but it does not stem from a causal influence. It seems reasonable to adopt the principle that whatever is responsible for a real effect is real. It follows, then, that the 'shape' of the non-Euclidean region is a real property. It would seem to be a simple step to the conclusion that the being of which it is a property, namely space, is a concrete individual. There is a fairly obvious objection to the effectiveness of this thought experiment in establishing Nerlich's point. In real physics one can always ask why a certain region of space differs from the Euclidean in its intrinsic geometry. Cosmologists use evidence of space–time distortions to postulate massy bodies which are responsible for disturbed geodesics. Furthermore the general relativistic equation which sets the metric tensor and the mass-energy tensor equal to one another can be read from right to left as a causal law. Distortions in trajectories of freely moving bodies are caused by massy bodies. The Nerlich thought experiment is incomplete. Perhaps a neutron

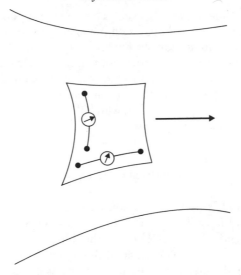

Figure 6.1 A rubber sheet on a geodesic trip in non-Euclidean space

star and its binary partner are responsible for the 'shape' of that inter-mediate region. The positive readings of the strain gauges are just the effects of the gravitational fields of the neutron star and its partner. Nerlich's argument does not go through unless it is supplemented by a thoroughgoing critique of the concept of field. Space is not a concrete particular, nor is it any kind of substance. The word 'space' names a set of non-causal relations between material bodies based on the principle of exclusion, supplemented by an abstraction and extension of the set of relations to include possible exclusions. Space is real, but its reality is exactly that of the material system of which it is a property.

The alternative defensive stance against an idealist treatment of space–time is to argue that exclusion and ordering relations among things and events are as real as their relata. Leibniz expressed the relationist point of view in the well-known remark (Leibniz, 1717) 'Space denotes, in terms of possibility, an order of things which exist at the same time.' As well as experientially grounded statements like 'The red body is between the blue and the orange bodies' the referential grids for the physical sciences must include locations and moments described in sentences like 'The brown body could be put between the blue and the orange bodies.' When an abstract manifold is 'drawn off' from the material system possible locations and moments as space–time points must proliferate very rapidly. What are the grounds for allowing modally qualified sentences to be used to make true statements in these contexts? The substantialist defence amounts to the claim that it is possible to show that such a statement is a good description of a real being, ontologically on a par with the material system. The defender of relationism needs an account of the meaning of 'possible location' and 'possible moment' as well as an explanation of how the truth of the modally qualified statements which refer to them can be defended. A correspondence theory which depends on the idea of a manifold of 'real possibilities' would be ruled out for any ontology in which the concept of 'possibility' was given a cognitive (ideal) interpretation.

How does time exist?

There are two kinds of temporal manifold that would threaten the strict connection I have been trying to establish between referential acts, the material system and existence. There is the 'block universe' in which all actual events in some sense coexist at all times. Then there is the idea of a temporal plenum, distinct from but 'housing' the events of cosmic history.

The block universe view requires that there are both successive and contemporaneous totalities of events. I believe that the idea of the temporal block universe involves confusions between disjunctive and conjunctive totalities that come about through insufficient attention to the consequences of the necessary indexicality of all acts of temporal reference. In the spatial manifold, at least in principle, every cognitive act of denotation can be realized in a physical act of reference. But this does not hold for the temporal manifold. (For a very careful discussion of some of the alleged contrasts between spatial and temporal expressions see Schlesinger, 1980.)

Ostensive acts of reference to moments, unmediated by any system of representation of events, can occur only in the present. But pointing as a physical act of ostension to materially marked locations can indicate place even on a cosmic scale. Relativity qualifies this aspect of our relationship to the spatial manifold in a logically inessential way. For practical purposes we must keep in mind the reservation that the material beings by which locations are marked may have perished at the time human ostensive acts involving them occur. But acts of reference to past and future moments must be cognitively mediated, via names of moments that do not now exist. 'Now' seems to occupy an ontologically privileged position in acts of temporal reference. There is no other moment at which material beings can exist but 'now', so, *a fortiori*, changes and rearrangements of them can happen only in the present. The manifold of events of the sempiternally real 'block' has been called the B-series. Those who believe that it is ontologically fundamental must suppose that it is progressively revealed to people through a sequence of subjective events. Past, present and future could be thought of as contingently distinguished regions of the 'block' accidentally marked off by the current focus of the beam of human consciousness.[1] An ideal physics would describe the structure of the block and would have no use for a category of 'becoming'. Temporal reference would be just like spatial reference, to events as the empirical markers of the moments which are the basic elements of the block. On the block universe view past and future are symmetrical and unique (Grunbaum, 1964). Opposed to these ideas are the advocates of an ontology of time tied to 'becoming'. Past and future are asymmetrical, and the future is not unique. For instance it has been argued that contemporary physics seems to show that there is an element of irreducible and real spontaneity in the coming into existence of the totality of properties of physical events. It follows that human thought about the future, and so the concept of the future itself, must involve an ineliminable concept of 'possibility'. The manifold of events in which 'now' marks an ontological separation between those which have happened and what is to come has been called the A-series. In a treatise on space and time discussion of the various ways that the uniqueness of the past and the open character of the future could be interpreted would involve detailed analyses of notions like the 'determination' and the 'determinateness' of events. For my purposes only one contrast is important. In the 'becoming' view there could be no complete description of the history of the universe as the logical sum of dated descriptions of past, present and future at least until the last moment of recorded time. The block universe view seems to require some sense to be given to the non-temporal existence of all events, as stable referents of dated expressions whenever they are uttered. (See Weingard, 1972.)

The philosophical project of eliminating tenses from scientific discourse would, if successful, have some bearing on whether the temporal manifold should be interpreted as a block (Gale, 1968). It has been suggested that tenses mark the temporal properties, pastness, presentness and futurity which are successively taken on by sempiternal events. I will be lunching; I am lunching; I was lunching. But Smart (1963) and others have argued, I think convincingly, that nothing is lost if all tenses are eliminated in favour of expressions which relate events to moments which are earlier or later than the present. The present is marked by the indexical qualification of acts of statement-making, 'now'. Past, present and future are not properties.

The idea of the block universe involves two collectives of events, one successive, the other contemporaneous. I shall offer arguments against a block universe interpretation of both kinds of event collective by exploiting the difference between disjunctive and conjunctive totalities. The collective of successive events that make up cosmic history can be only a disjunctive ontological totality. Each act of reference through which an ontological claim is settled for a human observer can occur only in the present. All human acts of reference are temporally indexical. They mark 'now'. At the moment of utterance of a plausible descriptive statement about the existence of events of the moment, only a disjunction of former and future temporal indexical statements can be formed, since each and every such statement is false. Neither the bud nor the seed pod exist now, though the flower does. If we tried to form a conjunctive ontological statement it would be false. But the universe does exist. So a disjunctive totalizing of indexical existence statements is possible. However an epistemic conjunction is possible, since at any one moment we may have reason to believe that the state of the universe was thus and so, and will be thus and so. But reference for this conjunction must be mediated by names not by acts. Block universe advocates have illegitimately inferred a conjunction from a disjunction, or alternatively thought that the epistemic conjunction had ontological force.

The difference between block universe and indexicalist views of the successive manifold of time can be summed up as follows:

	'now'	past and future
Block universe	ideal	real
	(beam of awareness)	
Indexicalist	real	ideal
	(physical existence)	(memory and anticipation)

Support for the indexicalist treatment comes from drawing out the consequences of the tight connection between existence and 'now'. Does the past exist now? Clearly not. Does the future exist now? Again obviously not. And this is true of every now. Things and events exist only in the present. On the indexicalist view, past and future are human constructions out of present traces and anticipations. The relations between past and future events are relations between ideal entities. This reminder provides an explanation of the ineliminability of 'now'. Since existence and the present mutually define one another, any form of realism must preserve the special informational quality of indexical expressions. They settle the all important question of what exists.

But what about the contemporaneous collective of moments? The position is perfectly complementary to that I have proposed for the successive collective. Because all indexical acts of reference must relate to real events there can be a contemporaneous ontological collective. But special relativity requires that not all space-like hypersurfaces orthogonal to all world lines in Minkowski space can be used to define simultaneity slices. (See figure 6.2.) tw could be simultaneous with any time between t1 and t2.

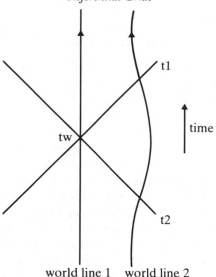

Figure 6.2   The forward and backward light cones from an event at tw

If 'now' is created indexically by each observer then there can be no universal now. But if existence is tied to the present it would seem to follow that there can be no universal existence claim. But all that follows from special relativity is that there is no universal 'now' which is the indexical referent of an epistemological conjunction of all the present-tense, indexical knowledge of all observers. The logical conjunction of all acceptable present tense statements describes what exists, but even if a human being could form it it could not be known to be true, since all that is available to an observer is a disjunctive collective of indexical statements.

The block universe view is based on a mistake about the logical form of the synthetic totality of moments. Each human observer can establish him or herself indexically at their own 'now'. There is an objective 'now' for each observer created by the utterance of indexical sentences. Furthermore each observer knows the truth of his or her own indexical statements. But no one observer can know the truth of every other observers' indexical 'now' statements now. By special relativity no one observer can form a conjunctive totality of 'now' statements. But since each observer might reasonably conjecture that every other observer is making indexical statements each observer can utter a disjunctive totality of 'now' statements, each indexed with its appropriate observer and moment. Thus anyone can say

$$O1 \text{ v. } O2 \text{ v. } O3 \text{ v.} \ldots$$

But this does not entail

$$O1 \mathrel{\&} O2 \mathrel{\&} O3 \mathrel{\&} \ldots$$

It is the collective totality which would have to be possible for there to be a universal 'now' and a block universe. It is the conjunctive statement which represents the universal 'now', but it is the disjunctive statement which represents the extent of human knowledge. For all observers except God time must be taken as a distributive, not a collective totality. Temporal, like spatial properties, are relational properties of the material system, relative to the indexical acts of observers. So the block universe conception cannot serve as the basis for a theory of reference for the ontology of any possible human physics. Not all denoting expressions can be matched with acts of reference. A second issue concerns the proper interpretation of world lines in Minkowski space. Such lines are usually read as real sequences of real events. Past, present and future events cohere into a line and they all have the same status. But at any point on that line only the state of the universe indexically contemporaneous with and near to the observer is real. So the usual picture (see figure 6.3a) is misleading. When an observer utters a statement with the indexical I_2 tying its sense to the moment of its utterance the observer only remembers his or her statement which involved the indexical I_1. The balloon in figure 6.3b represents the fact that at the moment indexed by I_2, the moment indexed by I_1 no longer exists and is at most *represented* at the moment indexed by I_2. The world line that is made up of the set of indexed moments is not a track through a higher order universal geometry, but a set of iterated and embedded utterances. Minkowski space is not a map of the universe but a representation of a particularly detailed discourse about it. It is not that the historical events are not real. Each was tied to an indexical use of 'now' at least in principle. It is rather that the conjunctive totality of those events is not real. While each event on a world line exists, they do not exist as a totality.[2] (See Stein (1968) for a defence of the priority of the present.)

There are some difficulties with this view.

1   Augustine's paradox forces the user of indexical language towards a now which is an ontologically problematic dimensionless point. Every human discourse is a compromise. Were there some ground for believing that temporal instants were discrete hodons endurance and change would be less subtly related than they are in our present conceptual scheme. But our current scheme which makes use of ideas of density and continuity unknown to Augustine is at least a formal resolution of the difficulty.

2   I owe the following objection to James Crompton. In defending relationalism of space against the neo-absolutism of Nerlich I invoked the

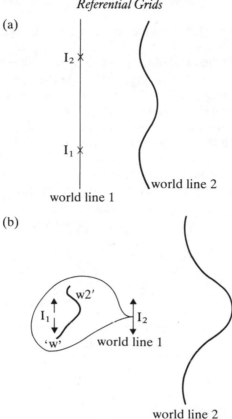

Figure 6.3 (a)   World lines as universal geometry
(b)   World lines as indexical discourses

principle that real effects have real causes. That strain gauges show a non-zero reading in the non-Euclidean region is to be explained by the presence of neutron stars, rather than referred to an anisotropic region of space. Applying that principle to the temporal case would block the idealist treatment of past and future in any theory that insisted on the reality of the present. If the present is real whatever causes produce it must be as real as the present is itself, and similarly what the real present produces as effects must share its reality. But the indexicalist does not deny the reality of past and future states of the universe. He does deny their coexistence with the only current reality, the indexed present. The relations between past and present, present and future, are not real relations, though there are some causal influences at work. Times are cognitive entities with which an abstract referential system, a nomenclature is created.

Are global space–time manifolds real?

Even the modest form of realism defended in this work makes a virtue of the principle that entities first conceived through the development of theory must usually be taken prima facie as candidates for reality. It is easy to show by example that for any given local geometry there are many global topologies. The simplest and easiest to visualize is the case of the embedding of a local Minkowsky metrical geometry in two different global space–times. The structures of both cylindrical and flat global space–time are compatible with the metric $ds^2 = c\,dt^2 - dx^2$, for a one dimensional space and a one dimensional time. The two cases are illustrated in figure 6.4.

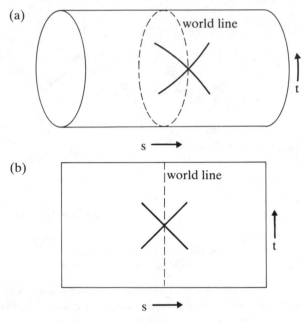

Figure 6.4 (a)   Cylindrical space—time
(b)   Flat space—time

In flat space–time, world lines cannot intersect themselves, since they are constrained by the geometry of light cones. But in cylindrical space–time closed time-like world lines are possible, indeed typical. If the global topologies described putative real entities then there ought to be empirical consequences which would enable *us*, at least in principle, to distinguish between them. A naïve reading of the situation would go something like this: if global space–time were cylindrical (or of an appropriately more complex form for a three dimensional space), human observers would experience repetitive historical cycles while if space–time were flat there would be an endless succession of distinct events. But these global space–times can be mapped on to one another. Unless we accept the Leibnizean law of the identity of indiscernibles, the cycle of cylindrical space time could be represented as a succession of numerically distinct but qualitatively identical sequences. The difference, then, between cylindrical and flat space–time is not an empirical matter but rests on the attitude of the scientists of that universe to Leibniz Law. It is a matter of commitment to a metaphysical theory rather than a question of finding a clinching empirical test.

The upshot of these arguments has been in effect to reduce the metaphysics of space–time to the logical grammar of indexicality, the properties of 'here', 'now', 'this' and so on. All other referential acts but those that tie existence to the immediate physical neighbourhood of token-reflexive utterances are tinged with theory, and in that measure speculative. The final step in defending relational space–time was the change to a conception of the world line not as a physically real being, but as a map of the successive speech acts of a community of ideal observers. Reality is the collective totality of what exists now, but only the distributive totality of what exists at each and every moment. While we can form a conjunction of indexical statements to describe the history of the universe, we can do no more than disjoin a totality of indexical statements of all the observers we may believe are our contemporaries. The block-universe of the temporal realists cannot be an ontological concept. Only indexical reference can securely prove existence.

To conclude we can now see that space–time is an abstract notation, facilitating the location of things and events relative to one another. It is a human construction on the basis of certain real relations of succession, coexistence and exclusion that obtain in the material world. Though conjoined into one manifold in relativity theory the spatial and temporal manifolds are ontologically distinct. While given time we can pick our way amongst the the material substances of the universe looking for the place of a being of interest, even given space we can do no such thing amongst events. Locating an event is finding a place in a story; locating a thing is finding a place in the world. There are other places from where we now are. There never has been, nor will there ever be any other time than the present. The construction of the full fledged space–time manifold, covering the material system with a dense network of actual and potential locations, is not just a mathematical generalization of the material practice of locating things with respect to other things, but also of the cognitive practice of telling histories ordered by reference to the changes recorded by observers.

Without techniques for locating the unobserved amongst the array of beings we can observe the case for a realist interpretation of theoretical sciences would be meagre indeed.

Other referential grids

By relating the defence of scientific realism so tightly to the possibility of successful acts of spatio-temporal reference I have made room too for a serious misunderstanding. The priority I have given to the spatio-temporal properties of the material system as the foundation of referential activities might suggest that scientific realism must needs be based on an ontology of material things and the events that occur in and among them. This would make any scientific-realist treatment of psychology automatically physicalist and reductive. But other referential grids are possible, which with other ontological priorities would support a scientific realist treatment of human sciences without reduction to the physical.

We have already noticed the close relationship between the irreducibility of the indexical terms of a discourse and the referential grid with respect to which existential queries are settled. The clue to other grids might be found in other important and typical indexicals. The main thrust of the 'new psychology' has been to give ontological priority to the network of symbolic, largely verbal exchanges between people that we could call the general conversation. For expository purposes we can concentrate on linguistically realized reticulations, the network of speech acts, of invitations, acceptances, pleas, insults, promises, warnings and so on. By and large it is not the place and time of a speech act that matters but who says it. People as social beings are often role holders, and in many cases a speech act has force only as uttered by the holder of a certain role. Declarations of love as much as declarations of war must come from the 'right' person. It is the one who insulted you who is usually required to apologize. But speech-acts are often delivered in forms like 'Look out! I can see a wasp on your shirt.' The completion of the meaning of such utterances requires a knowledge of who is the current speaker and who has been addressed. Along with 'here' and 'now' pronouns are the third kind of indexicals typical of our discourses.

For the purposes of studying conversations it is persons who are the prime referents, for it is 'at' persons that speech acts are significantly located. The array of persons becomes the prime referential grid for those branches of the human sciences for which the meaningful conversation is the basic object of study. This array is a multidimensional but discrete manifold. It has many interesting properties some of which are analogous to the properties of an anisotropic physical space and some not. Conversational time, created by the indexing of speech acts to moments in the conversation, is a manifold that is more complex than physical time. For instance speech acts that have been written down may lie dormant for centuries and become active only much later in the conversation. Scientific realism for those branches of the human sciences that deeply involve conversation has a parallel structure to that of the doctrine of realism for the physical sciences, but is based on a different referential grid and has a different ontology. (For a detailed analysis of social psychological, or conversational referential grids see Harré, 1983.)

Part Three

The Metaphysics of Experience

The causes we know everything about depend on causes we know very little
about depend on causes we know nothing about.

Tom Stoppard, *Travesties*

Introduction

To be a realist is to acknowledge an 'aboutness' in one's discourse, a referential tie to something other than one's own states. But for a scientific realist
that something must include a realm of active beings both independent of
oneself and only partially known. For the physical sciences this other is the
natural world. For the human sciences the other is more complex, since
people live not only within a physical but also within a symbolic universe,
the conversations of mankind. As I have argued, in the end one's adherence
to scientific realism is an act of moral commitment rather than a wholly
rationally grounded realization of some inescapable conclusion from incorrigible premises. That idea is part of the myth of the strict system. The
actual–ideal system is a network of human exchanges and practices based
on a morality of trust. But it must also be grounded in a genuine and interpersonal experience of such aspects of the natural world as our evolutionary
heritage has fitted us to take account of. The defence of scientific realism
must in the end be based on a realist theory of perception. We cannot escape
the obligation to delve deeply into the metaphysics of human experience.

Do we perceive the physical world, or only some representation of it?
This is the question on the answer to which hangs the possibility of
scientific realism. Traditional scepticism is usually taken to cast doubt on
the possibility of determining the truth or falsity of generalizations that refer
to cases beyond the possible reach of our limited perceptions in space and
time. It can be remedied by dropping the unrealistically strict demands
embodied in the concepts of truth and falsity. The problem of our right to
believe in the existence and nature of beings about which we know only
indirectly through theory can be resolved by attention to the way the realm

of scientifically validated experience grows, by the existential testing of the reality claims the scientific community makes on behalf of such beings. But, however successful these moves may be, both in the end depend on the willingness of the community to accept a residue of common experience as genuine disclosures of the natural world. In this part I shall try to show that, despite powerful arguments against foundationalist doctrines, rampant relativity does not reign. Realm 1, the realm of actual human experience, is, with suitable qualifications, a part of the natural world, and not a mere representation of it.

The history of the philosophy of science shows that there has been a gradual realization that the idea that facts are generated by the candid description of some pristine level of sensory experience is untenable. Nevertheless any treatment of the genesis of scientific facts must start with the psychology of perception. But the abstraction of knowledge from perceptual experience involves the use of conceptual resources which are put to work in the cognitive operations of categorizing, without which the description of our experience within the categories of human languages would be impossible. As Duhem (1914) put it 'a physics experiment is not simply the observation of a phenomenon. . . . It is . . . accompanied by the interpretation of these phenomena: this interpretation substitutes for the concrete given . . . some abstract and symbolic representation which corresponds to the given by virtue of the physical theories admitted by the observer.' But a further transformation of experience occurs. We must take into account the recent demonstrations of the way in which the certifying of facts as part of the corpus of scientific knowledge is accomplished through social negotiations.

7

A Psychological Defence of Common Sense

The trap of reliabilism

The representationalist tradition, which has played such an important part in the epistemological discussions with which the philosophy of science has been plagued for more or less the last 300 years, institutionalizes a radical separation of percept and (corresponding) world state. But, if *all* perceptions are representations how can there be any application for concepts like accuracy or verisimilitude of perception? Such concepts could only be applied if there were some way in which the object of perception could be compared with the percept. Since the objects of perception can never be contemplated except through representations no such comparison is possible. At most a kind of hypothetico-deductive testing of the consequences of forming this or that representation might stand in as a criterion for such assessments. A determined sceptic could make short work of such a proposal. Without some better solution to the traditional problem of the verisimilitude of perception the cause of scientific realism is lost and with it much of the moral authority of the scientific way of life. (See for example the dissolution of such authority in Rorty's (1980) attempt to dispose of all forms of foundationalism.) Many philosophers seem to have taken for granted that there could be no psychology of perception that could reinstate realism through a non-representationalist theory of common human experience. The doctrine that our senses give us accurate knowledge of the physical world through representations is 'reliabilism'.

Classical perception theory inserts two stages between world state and percept. In the first a causal relation is supposed to obtain between world state and sensation. In the second the sensation is reworked in some cognitive process to yield the percept. Reliabilism is the doctrine that scientific support can be found for confidence in the verisimilitude of the product of that causal relation, so that the sensation is, in some measure, a correct representation of the state of things that produced it. The reliabilist position takes for granted that the states and processes of the physical world act upon the sensory apparatus of human beings in such a way that *somewhere* in the chain of effects of those causal impulses is a 'representation' of those states and processes. Ultimately, it is supposed, scientific knowledge must rely on those representations. The basic epistemological problem is to find a defence for the reliability of these representations. The reliabilist move is to try to find that justification in the results of a scientific investigation of the causal conditions of perception.

The reliabilist theory of perception has two main versions. According to naïve reliabilism at least some of the properties of that which is perceived are accurately reflected, for example primitively represented via a similarity relation, in the person-state caused by that thing. And a perceiver is able to tell which of his or her ideas are of this class. No further cognitive activity is needed to perceive. That part of Locke's theory that deals with primary qualities and Descartes's doctrine of 'natural geometry' are naïve reliabilist theories (see Maull, 1978). The perceptual system, it is supposed, can be shown to be a reliable device for creating primitive representations of at least some of the states of the things perceived. For Descartes this comes about by geometric projection. This is the basis of Descartes's idea that the perceiver unconsciously uses 'natural geometry', a kind of reflection of scientific geometry, to work back, so to speak, from the projection to the thing.

The psychology of Thomas Reid

In naïve reliabilism physical science is the guarantor of the verisimilitude of the very experiences upon which physical science is based. With Reid's (and later Whewell's) hypothesis that there is a cognitive operation which transforms the caused sensation into the experienced percept, the naïve theory is transcended. Sensations are not reliable representations of that which causes them. But how can it be shown that the cognitive reworking of sensations produces percepts which are reliable representations? Both Reid (1787) and Whewell (1847) seem ready to accept an answer couched wholly in cognitive terms. In Reid's psychology the question of the verisimilitude of sensations is displaced in favour of the problem of the representational quality of percepts.

In certain important ways the psychology of Reid catches the essential shape of the theories of perception that developed much later, for instance the theories of J. Muller and Helmholtz. The descendants of those theories are the orthodox representationalist doctrines of the present day. Reid distinguishes between sensation and perception as follows: 'we must distinguish the appearance that objects make to the eye, from the things suggested by that appearance' (p. 91). In an earlier passage Reid had introduced the idea of 'suggestion', the mediating process between sensation and percept, with the example of the sound of hooves suggesting the passage of a carriage in a distant street. It is clear that Reid thinks that such a mediating process is cognitive. But it is not inferential. 'Perception, whether original or acquired, implies no exercise of reason ' (p. 210). 'Although there is no reasoning in perception, there are certain means and instruments, which, by the appointment of nature, must intervene between the object and our perception of it.' These include the impression on the brain and the immediately following sensation which is itself followed by 'the perception of the object' (p. 214). Reid describes this non-inferential cognitive process as follows:

We see only the visible appearance of objects by nature; but we learn by custom to interpret these appearances and to understand their meaning. And when this visual language is learned we attend only to the things signified; and cannot, without great difficulty, attend to the signs by which they are presented . . . we seem immediately to percieve the thing signified. (p. 204)

The project of the psychology of perception is first to become aware of sensations and then to try to understand the process of interpretation by which sensations become perceptions. The key to the awareness of sensations is attention: 'We cannot be unconscious of the sensations of the mind . . . it is essential to a sensation to be felt, and it can be nothing more than it is felt to be' (p. 214).

From the point of view of one who is intent on defending scientific realism this account of perception, and so of the main source of our knowledge of a putative realm of beings other than our subjective states, is deeply disturbing. Reid optimistically offers it in opposition to and as a redress for the scepticism of Hume and the idealism of Berkeley. But it is as fatally flawed by inductive assumptions and the threat of solipsism as is any doctrine of ideas and impressions. Solipsism is a threat because, though perception is a reading of a sensation, the sensation itself is a quality of an individual consciousness. There is no guarantee anywhere in Reid's scheme that the material referent of a perception is the cause of the relevant sensation, or if it is that it resembles it or the subsequent perception in any way. Furthermore the degree of sophistication that is involved in the reading of a green and branching sensation as a tree depends on inductive assumptions. For instance earlier experience of the tensile strength of wood is carried forward into any perception of a tree by a normal person. But what is the source of these inductive assumptions? To find them in previous perceptions begs the question, just as does Hume's idea of 'habits of expectation'. To assign them to nature opens up the thorny question of how an inherited physiological structure can be manifested in a culturally specific cognitive process. Let us look forward a few years to Whewell's imposition of progressivist dynamics on this essentially static picture.

The role of concepts in experience

I believe that Reid's theory is typical of all representationalist theories, even the most technically sophisticated. If percepts are cognitive constructions out of sensations, and sensations are produced by the causal influences of extrapersonal things, we can have no guarantee from the natural sciences that percepts accurately represent the things that caused the sensations. There must be some 'feedback' through which the use of inadequate cognitive resources shows up in practical difficulties, which then lead to changes in those resources. This thought is the basis of evolutionary epistemology, and though partially anticipated by Bacon must be credited to Whewell. In domesticating Kantian philosophy Whewell introduced a modification of great importance. The concepts which were prior to empirical experience were not a priori, but arose out of that experience at an earlier phase. The progressive cycle of ideas and facts touches on many of the dichotomies dear to philosophy, such as necessity and contingency, theory and fact, deduction and induction.

According to Whewell, Hume had 'asserted that we are incapable of seeing in any of the appearances which the world presents anything of necessary connexion; and hence he inferred that our knowledge cannot extend to any such connexion. . . . Our inference from Hume's observations is, not the truth of his conclusion, but the falsehood of his premises; – not that, therefore, we know nothing of natural connexion, but that, therefore, we have some source of knowledge other than experience . . . our ideas are not the copies of our impressions.' Whewell was among the first to see that facts arise as the product of a dialectical interplay between concepts and sensory experience. But, in common with nearly all epistemologists of science since Descartes and Locke, Whewell, like Reid, takes for granted that the elementary foundations of our experience of the natural world are sensations. Whewell's main contribution to the epistemology of science is a weakening of the distinction between theory and fact: 'in Theory the Ideas are considered as distinct from the Facts; in Facts, though Ideas may be involved, they are not, in our apprehension, separated from sensations' (Whewell, 1847, p. 40). To explain their involvement he invokes the image of Man as the interpreter of nature; 'whether taken as an example or a comparison [this image] may serve to show both the opposite character of the two elements of knowledge [fact and idea] and their necessary combination, in order that there may be knowledge' (p. 38). We see the needle turn towards the magnet – 'we assert that the magnet exercises an attractive force on the needle. But it is only by an interpretative act of our own minds that we ascribe this motion to attraction' (p. 41).

Interpretation according to Whewell, is a kind of inference. : Theory [is] a conscious, and Fact [is] an unconscious inference.' However, the relativist implications of this are not lost on Whewell. In none of the multiple antitheses such as Theory and Fact, Deduction and Induction, and so on 'can we separate the two members by any fixed and definite line'. Even indexicality of knowledge to the person who promulgates it is anticipated in a remark on p. 45: 'before we can estimate the truth [of the assertion that something is a Fact] we must ask to whom it is a Fact.' Each of us will be in possession of a different corpus of knowledge and will have acquired different habits of thought. But Whewell does not think that relativism leads to scepticism, since he believes that scientific method, while never producing knowledge that is without some colour of indexicality and relativity, is nevertheless the result of 'improvement of successive generalization'.

As theories of perception the doctrines of Reid and Whewell are not reliabilist in the obvious way of those of Locke and Descartes. Neither draws explicitly on a scientific defence of the thesis that the causal processes specific to the workings of the perceptual apparatus should cause states in the perceiver that are reliable representations of the states of the world that produce them. The verisimilitude of perceptions turns instead on an examination of the cognitive processes supposed to transform sensations into perceptions. In the end, for Whewell, it is the progressive inductions of natural science which support realism. Reliabilism of a sort is reinstated but not at the most primitive level of perception. It appears at the later stages of the dialectic of Fact and Theory. Some kind of coherentist criterion (for Whewell it is the consilience of inductions) must finally be invoked to support belief in both the Facts and the Theories of the later stages of the development of a natural science. But once one takes the cognitivist step of grounding perception in sensation, reworked though they may be, the threat of solipsism reappears. If sensations are the final point of anchorage for beliefs they cannot be compared with whatever physical conditions caused them. Relative to sensations, perceptions, which are sensations cognitively reworked, must have the status of theories. Scepticism easily takes root in this account, since there are always, in principle, indefinitely many theories for any data base.

The psychology of J. A. Fodor

Reid's theory has reappeared in recent years reclothed in the technicalities of 'cognitive science'. Since I am intent on clearing the way for the perception theory of J. J. Gibson, it is convenient to examine that reincarnation in a version that was specifically directed against the ecological theory of Gibson. Fodor's account of perception relies heavily on two technical notions unknown to Reid. First it is an exercise in the formal science of mind. Mental processes are treated as computations which take account only of the structural or syntactic properties of the states in which representations of external states of affairs are realized. The computational model necessarily cannot take into account any semantic properties of representations such as their meaning or truth. This strange dogma appears to rest on a logicist theory of language, according to which natural languages are 'really' instantiations of the formal predicate calculus, and as such linguistic operations are computational. The basic move in Fodor's (1980) account of perception is to be found on p. 64: 'strictly speaking there can't be a psychology of perception if the formality condition is to be complied with. Seeing is an achievement; you can't see what is not there. From the point of view of the representationalist theory of the mind, this means that seeing involves relations between mental representations *and their referents*; hence semantic relations' and these cannot be studied in cognitive psychology. Of course, if all mental contents are representations or cognitively (formally) reworked representations, there can be no place for a contemplation of the relation between a representation and its referent which is *a fortiori* never representable. This, says Fodor, is 'tantamount to a sort of methodological solipsism. If mental processes are formal . . . they have no access to the semantic properties of such representations.' Hence no mental (cognitive) process can be used to tell whether a representation is true or false.

But why should one accept the representationalist account in the first place? The second step in Fodor's argument involves the notion of 'opacity'. For those readers who may be unfamiliar with the idea of referential opacity I take the liberty of sketching the outlines of the idea. Common sense would suggest that all coreferential terms, say different names for the same person or thing, could be substituted in a sample sentence and all the statements made with any of the subsequent set of sentences would be true. However, logicians have noticed that there are some contexts (called 'oblique', 'opaque' or 'intensional') in which this does not seem to hold. For example the statement 'Jim believes the Isis runs swiftly in winter' may be true, while 'Jim believes the Thames runs swiftly in winter' may be false, even though 'Isis' and 'Thames' are two names for the same river. This same feature, which seems quite unproblematic for belief statements, also characterizes perceptual statements, according to Fodor 'Jim saw a bird on the bough' may be true even though it was 'objectively false' that there was a bird on the bough. From the point of view of psychology, so says Fodor, it is what Jim thought he saw that matters. It is the 'fully opaque' reading of Jim's experience that explains why he fired in that direction. As Fodor puts it (p. 67), 'in doing our psychology, we want to attribute mental states fully opaquely because it is the fully opaque reading which tells us what the agent has in mind, and it's what the agent has in mind that causes his behaviour.' This claim depends on our acceptance of the computational model, since, if Jim can perform only formal operations on the syntactical properties of his mental contents, he cannot make any semantic distinction between cases where he thought he saw a bird and those where he 'really' did. This is 'methodological solipsism'.

Fodor's 'derivation' of methodological solipsism is quite simple in essence. Representations are opaque, particularly when they appear in the form of psychological reports such as 'Jerry believes the ice will support him' or 'Jerry sees the Charles is frozen over.' Therefore the explanation of behaviour in terms of representations cannot involve semantic relations. But the argument is circular. It is only by already assuming that the effects of physical causes acting on the perceptual system are representations that they are demonstrated to be opaque. Methodological solipsism cannot be derived from the alleged phenomenon of 'full opacity', since the claim that mental contents are fully opaque depends on assuming that computational processes carried out on the formal properties of mental contents cannot disclose whether they truly refer. But to suppose that cognitive processes are exclusively devoted to formal computations is already to embrace methodological solipsism. A slightly more elaborate version of the circularity objection can be found in Carello et al. (1984).

There are both substantial and formal objections that are fatal to this argument. There is a confusion between what could be true on a particular perceptual occasion and what could be true in general. Who can deny that Jim may sometimes be unable to tell whether he has really seen a bird or only fancied it? But we need an explanation of how Jim fell into the practice of aiming at where he thinks he sees a bird. Unless he were right most of the time he would soon tire of his haphazard sport. That he remains trapped within a fully opaque perceptual predicament becomes more and more implausible, as he plucks, cooks and eats the birds he catches, and gradually learns to distinguish fleeting shadows from game. It is patent that we are being stared down by a boldly proclaimed *petitio principii*. According to Fodor (p. 71), 'it's our relation to these sorts of descriptions [namely of a state under whatever description the organism has in mind] that determines the psychological state-type we are in so far as the goal in taxonomizing psychological states is explaining how they affect behaviour.' But as I have pointed out above this can be true only in occasional particular cases. It cannot be true in general. If representations are inaccurate they will lead to ecologically inappropriate behaviour and so the organism will learn that they are defective. At this point a philosophically literate organism has two options open to it. Either it remains a Fodorian and never can solve the problem why pains appear spontaneously whenever it thinks it has shut its thumb in a door; or, if it is a really smart creature, it abandons methodological solipsism and looks more carefully after what it is doing. The concept of 'looking more carefully' can make no sense on the basis of the Fodorian perception theory. Of course this reminder that there are pragmatic tests for the correctness of perception is only required if one has already assumed the representationalist account. Fodor is not denying that there are such tests, but they are not, he seems to claim, part of the subject matter of the psychology of perception.

The argument Fodor offers not only is open to substantial objections such as those above, but seems also to be formally invalid. It runs as follows:

1   Representations might be thought to be opaque or transparent. For someone to have transparent representations he/she would need extra-representational knowledge of the referents.
2   But that kind of knowledge cannot be obtained from the formal properties of representations.
3   If personal knowledge is confined to the results of computational operations on the formal properties of representations there can be no extra-representational knowledge.
4   There can be no transparent representations.

So far as I can see 4 does not follow from the conjunction of 1, 2 and 3.

Fodor offers another independent argument in favour of the conclusion, 4. The reasons why this argument fails are of considerable importance for the proper interpretation of Gibson's realist theory of perception, so I shall set them out in some detail. Fodor's argument is intended to show that there could be no laws of perception. I shall call this the 'pencil' argument. According to Fodor any laws of perception would have to be so specific that they could explain how the utterance of the word 'pencil' would be prompted in the presence of a pencil. But this is precisely what no naturalistic psychology of perception could achieve. (We shall see that Gibson himself slips into thinking that there could be an ecological psychology of 'knives'.)The concept of 'pencil' is a cultural concept, part of the categorial apparatus by which classifying operations are performed on that which is delivered to the agent by his or her perceptual system, the sensory apparatus a human being has by nature. However, while one must concede that there could not be psychological laws which explained how someone came to see a pencil, it does not follow that there could not be psychological laws which explain how someone came to see long, thin things, causal sequences, and other generic perceptibles. Fodor slips from the correct observation that a computational psychology (which must be culturally neutral) cannot explain how there are culturally specific classifications, to the conclusion that no psychology of perceptibles is possible. Yet he concedes that 'there must be a naturalistic psychology since, presumably, we do sometimes think of Venus, and presumably we do so by virtue of a causal relation between it and us.' But a causal relation between ourselves and Venus would be only a necessary condition for our seeing *Venus*, and hence only part of the explanation of that event. A good many beliefs are needed as well.

The drift of the argument has taken us from a naïve to a sophisticated version of essentially the same old theory. Reid's account can be represented as follows:

O (object) causes S (sensation) which is interpreted (non-inferentially) as P (percept).

The process of causation is physical and the process of transformation is cognitive. Versions of representationalism vary by virtue of the variety of cognitive processes offered as the mechanism of interpretation. For Reid it is to be understood through the analogy of reading; for Gregory (1974) through the analogy of hypothesis testing. The idea that perception is *like* scientific hypothesis testing must rely on a presumption that we can know what hypothesis testing is independently of any theory of perception. But to understand how hypotheses can be tested in science we need a realist theory of perception.

Whatever form the representationalist theory takes, it must run counter to scientific realism. Belief in the existence of a causal relation between a world-state and some cluster of brain-states that is experienced as a sensation does not support the idea that sensation must be verisimilitudinous. Every theorist of perception has to cope with the fact that illusions also are caused by states of the world. Even if it turns out to be pragmatically useful to take account of one's sensations in everyday life it is conceivable that they may be useful despite gross distortions, provided they are systematic. Spear fishermen soon learn to aim below the presented location of the fish. Inference to the best explanation is not enough to restore confidence in the representational quality of pragmatically adequate perceptions if what is to be explained is an organization of sensations. The trouble lies deeply embedded in the foundations of the reliabilist point of view, in the ubiquitous assumption of the various versions of Reid's schema, that perception is built out of sensations. It is just this unexamined foundation of four centuries of perception theory that is challenged by Gibson's ecological optics. Both clauses of Reid's schema are brought into doubt, that percepts are cognitively transformed sensations, and that the basis of perception is an awareness of states of the brain that are the remote effects of physical causes.

Transcending reliabilism

Gibsonian theory

Once we have accepted the idea that states of the world cause sensations which somehow – by reading (Reid), by classifying (Fodor) or by hypothesis testing (Gregory) – are assembled and/or transformed into perceptions that represent those states, the cause of realism is lost. It is lost as much for van Fraasen's mean little world of current observations as it is for the grander landscapes of Bhaskar's transcendental tendencies. The traditional argument, used the world over in elementary philosophy courses to throw doubt on Locke's way of ideas, shows that there can be no epistemology of science, since there is no way in which ideas and the objects that cause them can be compared. The Gibsonian strategy is just to deny the empirical validity of the Lockean basis upon which the psychology and epistemology of the last 400 years has been based. There is a considerable literature occasioned by Gibsonian theory (cf. Michaels and Carello, 1981). In this chapter I set out the theory in sufficient detail only for the purposes of the argument. The basic Gibsonian ideas are as follows:

1   *Information pick-up and non-cognitive perceiving*. According to Gibson (1979, p. 242) physical objects and their properties are specified by information present in the 'ambient array'. The ambient array is a flux of energy shaped by the presence of both the perceiver and that which is perceived. Sensations do not specify physical things and their states. They specify only the current state of the sensory *organs*. Neo-Gibsonians prefer to reserve the term 'specification' for the way information in the ambient array specifies things. (See Michaels and Carello, 1984.) The concepts of 'specification' and 'information' need some further elaboration.

'Information' in the ambient array 'specifies' the object which structured the array. An organism in actively exploring that array for higher-order invariants, 'picks up' that information. It is as the 'pick-up' that perception occurs. Let us first see what Gibsonians mean by 'information' and 'specification'. The former is sharply distinguished from information in the sense of propositional content. Information of that sort might be embodied in premises from which one would infer the existence of an object. This popular model of perceiving is specifically denied by Gibson. Perceiving, Gibsonians argue, is not like doing forensic science. To quote Carello et al. (1981) 'This optical structure [of the electromagnetic field] is not similar to its sources, but it is specific to them, in the sense of being nomically dependent on them.' It is the 'conclusion', so to speak, which is embodied in the structure of the ambient array. There are no premises. This structure lawfully and uniquely maps the structural properties of the object. Such structures are the 'higher-order invariants' that the organism is seeking when it is using its perceptual system to explore the ambient array. According to Carello et al. 'It is because of the specificity of the information identified in [pick-up] that perception does not involve interpretative, elaborative, restorative, constructive etc. operations.' The organism does not perceive something by finding a pattern in its sensations either. The structures it recognizes are in the ambient array, not in the pattern of events at the retina, or any sensory representation of them. This is what is meant by 'direct pick-up'. It is at this point that a Kantian flavour enters the story. I take it that sensations are the raw material of perception, but that their organization as structured percepts comes from what has been non-sensorily 'picked up'. The 'schematisms' are derived not from a priori categories, but from information pick-up.

Great care needs to be taken in expressing this theory. At what level of particularity can things be specified? Even Gibson himself gets into a muddle. Reed (1983) expresses a sense of the worry as follows: 'Is a law-like relation between the structure of an object and the consequential structure of the optical array enough to support an intentional quasi-relation such as perception? ' The answer will depend on the level of description of the object perceived. Are we trying to explain how we can see things, three-dimensional persistent objects, against a ground? The senses, considered as perceptual systems, provide a world only relative to a generic categorization of beings. To explain how we can see some things as knives and other things as forks, a culturally specific categorization of things, we need to pay attention to the influence of concepts and beliefs. Gibsonian psychology, I believe, is properly a solution only to the problem of how generic perception is possible. Unfortunately Gibson himself said, as late as 1979, 'A rigid object with a sharp dihedral angle, an edge, affords cutting and scraping; it is a *knife*' (p. 133). But if this implies that there are 'Knife-to-"knife"' laws it is surely implausible. But this is just what Gibson seems to be committing himself to in his insistence on 'cognitive purity' (Gibson, 1979, pp. 75–9). And Fodor seems to have picked up just this aberration in his joke about perceiving pencils. The old theory requires that the totality of a perceptual categorization, things as knives, was the result of cognitive operations on physically caused sensations. If one accepts Gibsonian realism one must relocate the cognitive interpretative work at the point at which the active organism has *already perceived* something generic, a thing, an event, spatial, temporal or causal relations, and so on. 'Pick-up must be achieved by a device tailored to the property,' says Carello. But the only way a perceptual system could be tailored to anything would be by Darwinian selection. No *device* could be so tailored as to pick-up information that would specify

knives, forks or pencils, indeed any human invention, artefact or cultural
category. I suppose there could be quasi-devices, learned skills that do serve
to pick up beings that are more specific than those marked out at the level of
the Kantian categories, and yet less culture-bound than carburettors or
Venetian double choirs. But whether there do turn out to be such devices
does not touch the main thrust of the defence of ecological optics – that
there is no need to offer hostages to fortune by generalizing Gibsonian pick-
up beyond the level of a generic ontology.

2   *Perceptual system v. passive receptor channel*. Gibson says (1979) that 'the
external senses should be considered as active, exploratory, intimately
interconnected systems, rather than as passive mutually exclusive channels.'
'The world is specified in the structure of the light that reaches us. . . . Perceiving is an act, not a response, an act of attention, not a triggered impression, an achievement, not a reflex.' With these systems we explore the
ambient energy flux in search of the invariants it affords. It should follow
that evolutionary pressure must act on the senses as perceptual systems,
rather than as sensory receptors. If the biologically relevant items in the
physical environment are specified by higher-order invariants in the flux
then we would expect just those to be picked out as the salient things of its
environment by a highly evolved animal. One of Gibson's greatest experiments established the distinction between active exploration and passive
reception with great elegance. An immobilized hand on to which variously
shaped cookie cutters are pressed is unable to feel their distinctive shapes.
But if a person is allowed actively to explore the surface of the cutters with
the same palm of the hand the shapes of the cutters are easily distinguished.

3   *The modality of experience: affordances*. An affordance is that which an
environment offers this or that species of creature by way of possibilities of
action. According to Gibson we perceive things in terms of their affordances
for us, as affording, say, cutting or walking. As formulated by Costall (1983)
the concept of affordance is specified as follows: 'typically and primarily
[we] attend to the higher order invariant information which specifies what
an object affords for our actions, rather than lower order information which
specifies its isolated properties.' I see a bike as ridable rather than as five- or
ten-speed, red or blue. The same problem besets this idea as troubled us in
1. Gibsonians tend to describe the perception of things in terms of their
affordances as if interpretative, conceptualizing work had no place in it (see
Cutting 1982). Affordances are supposed to be real dispositions. Gibsonians
must find a way of distinguishing natural affordances from those made available to the perceiver through such cultural artefacts as language and
science. Concept learning and interpretative processes must enter into
everybody's account of the *full* story of perception. Again this polar distinc-

tion is meant to leave open a place for empirical studies of those cases in which a cultural category is so pervasively and deeply engrained that it mimics a natural perceptual capacity, allowing a direct pick-up of a percept from the culturally specified information embedded in the structure of an ambient array. A final step is needed to clarify the key notions of 'information' and 'pick-up'. Neither is intended in its ordinary meaning. This is not information in the sense of substantive content, nor is it information in the sense used in the theory of communication. Consider how, according to Gibsonian theory, we can see a cube as a solid object. Classical perception theory allows four of the corners to be represented on the retina, and somehow, by a high-speed (inductive?) inference, we conclude that there must be four more. It is this conclusion that is finally embedded in the seeing of the cube as a solid object. Gibsonian theory has the eight-corneredness of a cube expressed as a mathematical property of the structure of the ambient array, the flux of energy, which bathes the perceiver and his or her perceptual systems. It is this 'higher-order invariant' that is picked up as the array is actively explored by a perceptual system geared to pick up just such mathematical properties. 'Pick-up' is, then, a mathematical apprehension, not a grasping or taking out of anything. It is the same kind of act as that in which one sees the way of a proof. To apprehend this mathematical aspect of the structure of the ambient array is just to see the cube as a solid object.

By carefully qualifying the excesses of Gibsonian enthusiasm we can find much to accept in it. It explains how we can have experience of the physical world mediated by sensations yet unmodified by cognitive work. But what we perceive directly in the Gibsonian sense is coarse-grained. The world is presented as differentiated by no more subtle categorization than those from which Kant deduced the system of the schematisms. It is this feature of modest Gibsonianism that leads, through critical revision, to the illusion that Gibsonian theory is more Kantian than it is (see Ben-Zeev, 1981). In its basic standpoint Gibsonian theory shares with the Kantian account of perception the principle that the organization of experience as it is manifested in things, events, and so on, is not extracted from the sensory flux. But it is non-Kantian in that what corresponds to the schematisms, higher-order invariants, are not a priori, but are found in the exploration of the ambient array. Since that flow of energy is in principle inexhaustible so is the information potentially in the array. Accepting the broad outlines of Gibsonian psychology permits us to hand over responsibility for the defence of the reality of perceived things and events, and of certain general types of relations, to the psychology of perception. All representationalist versions of reliabilism are outflanked, and so solipsism, whether methodological or epistemological, no longer poses any kind of threat. Gibsonian theory is a reliabilist doctrine of a sort. Because it does not make sensations ontologically prior to things it does not fall into the trap awaiting all those forms of reliabilism that are built on representationalist foundations. Cognitive influences now appear where they should: at the point at which propositional knowledge is extracted from perception. Even though Gibsonian perception is direct it is never incorrigible. We do perceive things and events, but everything we believe about them, in extreme cases, even their ontological status, can be revised. Gibsonian theory does establish the essential contours of the Kantian categories as the metaphysics of perception without the Kantian commitment to the transcendental necessity of the categories a priori.

4 *Ecological reality and the ontology of physics*. It is now time to tie Gibsonian psychology into the considerations relevant to scientific realism. Realm 1, the realm of those existents that human beings can actually experience, is made of Gibsonian ecological reality. How is this related to the other epistemic realms I have roughly distinguished? Realm 2 consist of those beings which, though not actually experienced, are objects of possible experience. Realm 3 is the realm of beings which are beyond all possible human experience and yet which are the typical referents of physical theory. As I have emphasized, Realms 1 and 2 are ontologically continuous, and this relationship should be reflected in Gibsonian theory. Though they need microscopes to be able to so affect the flux of electromagnetic radiation that there is sufficient information to specify them, for an active perceiver, bacterial affordances are no different at the generic level from the affordances of cows. They both exist in the same ecological reality inhabited by other active and interesting animals, such as tigers, milkmaids, bacteriophages and microbiologists. The fact that cows afford milk is a cultural discovery. Ecological reality, the world as we perceive it, is an arena for both actual and possible action. This follows immediately from the fact that it is largely perceived in terms of affordances. Furthermore, different creatures will pick-up different Gibsonian information from it. There may be indefinitely many invariants of higher and higher order impressed upon the flux. There is only one world but it may secrete indefinitely many real worlds relative to the perceptual systems of different creatures.

Those beings that inhabit our Realm 3, the realm of 'things' beyond all possible human experience, may not be perceptual invariants for us. But we can see how they may still be real for us in Gibsonian terms. The point has been well made by Ben-Zeev (1984). Quoting Michaels and Carello's (1981, p. 99) distinction between 'information about' and 'information for', he says;

in the physical realm information is a pattern ... of energy. That pattern exists independently of any information system that may receive it. In the ecological realm, patterns of energy may qualify as information only if they have ecological significance. As anything else in the ecological environment, ecological information too exists only in relation to a certain animal.

We may be able to construct apparatus that explores some energy flux, seeking invariants that are information for it. In this way our equipment produces an ecological realm that did not exist before. But it explores a structured flux of energy of indefinite complexity, only part of the physical information in which becomes information for that apparatus. This is how the metaphysics and epistemology of Neils Bohr will become the basis for the analysis of Realm 3.

Philosophical commentary

Most philosophers, since Descartes, have tried to find a foundation for empirical knowledge. By a 'foundation' I mean an (open) set of incorrigible true judgements (beliefs with a characteristic propositional content) which are inferentially related to other judgements (beliefs with a characteristic scientific content). To be foundational the former set must be meaningful and decidable independently of all general theoretical beliefs, since everything general is subject to the reservations of inductive scepticism and so cannot be taken as incorrigible. To be foundational for scientific knowldge it has often been supposed that judgements must be concerned with the existence, qualities and relations of sensations.

It is now widely agreed that there can be no such foundations. Among the influential arguments that have led to the current consensus, Austin's (1962) version is distinguished by its brevity and depth.

Any description of a taste or sound or smell (or colour) or of a feeling, involves (is) saying that it is like one or some that we have experienced before: any descriptive word is classificatory, involves recognition and in that sense memory, and only when we use such words (or names or descriptions, which come down to the same) are we knowing anything, or even believing anything. But memory and recognition are often uncertain and unreliable.

Yet without some basis in veridical perception scientific realism, whether it be based on 'truth' or upon 'reference', must founder in a mess of relativism. Gibsonian psychology offers a way forward by showing how inference-from-a-sensory-basis can be eliminated from a scientific account of perception. By adding the idea of the organic evolution of a well-adapted perceptual system to ecological perception theory we arrive at a kind of reliabilist account of perception. But we rely on our perceptual systems without any knowledge of the psychological and biological theories that I have offered in justification of that confidence. There are even a few psychologists who have not fully accepted Gibsonian ecological theory.

It is worth noticing first that what we tend to trust and distrust corresponds pretty well to the contrast between the generic Gibsonian level of immediate perception and the specific Fodorian level of conceptually mediated interpretations we call observations and noticings. But in the end that reliance is grounded in experience of successful practice. From the point of view of the actor, knowledge is that which serves as a trustworthy basis for action. The nearer to the generic Gibsonian level we take ourselves to be, the more trustworthy we take perception to be. We may not be able to say for sure that it is a piece of oak, but we can be certain that it is at least a thing. (On a mountaineering trip a companion and I used what we later discovered to be a box of gelignite sticks to serve as the platform on which we burned our stove.) As practitioners we know what makes a trustworthy grounding for action – direct perceptual judgements at the generic level. But as philosophers we need an argument to support the thesis that practical knowledge reliably reflects certain features of the world. Gibsonian perceptual theory provides it. There are broader issues in philosophical logic that are affected by any demonstration that there can be non-inferential perceptual judgements. J. Kelly (1984) has argued that the existence of such judgements supports the doctrine that there are irreducible *de re* beliefs, beliefs whose referents are determined by context. But Kelly still does not go far enough. It would be best if we could establish the possibility of making successful or unsuccessful acts of reference prior to the satisfaction of any specific description. These would be pure acts in the practical context, those which the psychologists call 'deixis'. They are satisfactory or not depending on practical consequences. If Gibson is right our perceptual systems enable us to perform just such deictic acts. Gibsonianism provides us, as philosophers, with a context variable, but in each context a quite definite way of distinguishing between reference and sense. Reference is a practical achievement in a context of material practices, such as picking out, picking up, and so on. Sense is a cognitive matter in a theoretical context and is germane to the formulation of communicable belief. If reference is always indexical, that is contextually determined, then it must be based on actual human discriminatory skills. This connects the discussion finally back to Roberts's distinction between the two sentential formats for expressing referential practices. The DC format, by which referring as an act in the public domain of interpersonal discourse is expressed, depends on just those kinds of discriminatory practices and material skills, of picking figures from grounds, that are required for there to be *de re* beliefs.

The case I have been making for a qualified perceptual realism is an argument within the general framework of 'naturalized epistemology'; the view that attempts to understand what it is for a human being to know or believe something ought to belong in natural science, and particularly psychology (if we are willing to grant it the status of a natural science). The way I have adapted the argument between Fodor and the Gibsonians to sustain qualified perceptual realism can also be taken as a 'middle way' resolution of the 'naturalized epistemology' debate. Quine's original (1969) formulation of his neo-psychologism has the merit of both clarity and uncompromising generality. But the connection to biological and particularly natural selection theory is most sharply formulated by Annis (1982). The explanation of the persistence (though not the origin) of an epistemic (knowledge-garnering or assessing) practice is to be looked for in its survival value to the culture which employs it. It does not matter much how strictly biological such an account might be, since it is the reference to factual, historical matters which relocates the critical discussion of human knowledge. It is no longer part of the programme of philosophy but belongs in biology and/or cultural history.

The vagueness of the notion of 'epistemic practice' is, in part, I believe, responsible for the persistence of the debate. I am indebted to a discussion by Stone and Stone (1985) for the impetus to tie the problem of clarifying the idea of an epistemic practice to the Gibson-Fodor debate. Mark and Maria Stone mount a general attack on both the literal and the metaphorical use of evolutionary biology to explain the knowledge garnering value of epistemic practices. They argue that survival value is not enough to show why *that* and not some other equally efficacious practice persists. Explanations must draw on the existing belief-systems, fantasies and fallacies characteristic of the culture. Many practices of some epistemic quality continue to be used despite their non-adaptive results. But their examples of epistemic practices, such as the Eskimo technique of laying out bones to find caribou, or that of a gambler following a run at roulette, presuppose the existence of generic categorial schemes. Without such schemes the specific practices they cite would be unintelligible to us and useless to those who perform them. Any scheme for finding caribou is in debt to the existence in the repertoire of concepts of space, time and thing. In considering the possibility of viable evolutionary explanations we must distinguish between the practice of using a generic conceptual scheme at the level of Kant's categories in perceptual activity (say in picking out long things) and the practice of using customary and particular ways of 'finding out' such as experimentation (running the thumb *across* a knife blade to test its sharpness).

The Stones' arguments, with some refinements, count against a selectionist-adaptationist justification of the latter, but leave room for an evolutionary biological account of the former. Generic concepts and the ability to use them could be thought of as cognitive reflections of adaptive features of human perceptual systems. For instance the Stones' argument that the Eskimo persistence with the bone ceremony can be explained only by reference to the religious-metaphysical theories of that culture presupposes that, like all of us, an Eskimo can pick out a thing, which has some spatio-temporal integrity, from a complex environmental ground.

Again the most general argument against any selectionist-adaptationist form of naturalized epistemology under which some of the Stones' exemplary cases could be subsumed would turn on Clavius' paradox, that the instrumental efficacy of theories is independent of their truth or falsity. But this argument requires a common ontology, by means of which the phenomena to which a range of alternative but equally efficacious theories can be applied could be singled out perceptually. Nothing in the Stones' arguments rules out the possibility of a naturalistic evolutionary explanation for the largely and perhaps universally and culturally independent appearance in perceptual practices of the Kantian categories. The polar distinction between generic perceptual practices and culturally relative 'ways of finding out' does not, of itself, prove that the claims of the latter are properly the province of philosophical discussion. A philosophical argument, for instance Clavius' paradox, that there are indefinitely many theories in deductive relation with any given data base, is needed, case by case, to show that considerations relevant to the assessment of the practical adaptiveness of a practice, such as experimentation, are not adequate to decide how far the practice conforms to some theoretically formulated ideal, for instance the possibility of experimentally grounding a claim to universal knowledge.

A speech-act theory of Realm 1 discourse

The argument of chapter 1 gave priority to the moral order of the scientific community over all other considerations germane to the understanding of scientific thought and practice. This priority was realized in the substitution of the interpersonal relation of trust for the person–world relation of truth. Falsity was displaced by distrust. A scientist's claim to knowledge is to be assessed within a moral framework of obligations and commitments one person with another, rather than in an impersonal context of one statement judged against a neutral state of affairs. On the traditional account Realm 1 discourse is made up of observation statements, which, at least in principle, are capable of being exhaustively assessed for truth or falsity. The revised account, presented in this work, requires a reinterpretation of the role of observation statements within the whole scientific discourse. We must ask for their illocutionary and perlocutionary force as performative utterances, rather than for their truth or falsity as simple descriptive statements. I owe this way of putting the matter to S. P. Norris (1981).

According to Norris, to utter an observation statement is to perform the illocutionary act of 'reporting something to be or to have been the case as witnessed by the speaker or, in some situations, by someone other than the speaker' (p. 134). Roughly translated into ordinary English a scientific observation statement is to be thought of as prefaced by 'Trust me . . . ', or 'You can take my word for it . . . ', and then follows the ground for the demand put upon the listener's trust: 'I saw it with my own eyes.' The speaker then (in Searle's (1979) words and my emphasis) 'is *committed* to something's being the case'.

The conditions for a successful illocutionary act of this sort are summarized by Norris as follows (pp. 140–1):

I   *The Essential Condition*: The point of the report is to represent some specific events that have happened or are happening, or to represent the states in which some specific things are or were, as witnessed either directly using the human senses or indirectly using some sensory apparatus instead of or in conjunction with the human sensory apparatus.

II   *The Sincerity Condition*: In reporting that such-and-such is the case, the speaker believes that such-and-such is the case.

III   *The Propositional Content Condition*: To meet the preparatory condition the following set of conditions must be satisfied:

A   The speaker occupies a position of superiority compared to the hearer because the speaker's report is substantially immune to criticism from the hearer. [Notice the reappearance of the very social structure upon which the morality of trust was based in chapter 1.]

B   There is a community of language users the members of which would readily affirm the speaker's report, if they received the same sensory stimulation as the speaker [*pace* Gibson], and the speaker and hearer belong to that community.

C   The report serves as a foundation or part of the foundation for knowledge in the field in which it is an observation statement.

D   The illocutionary point is presented more forcefully than if the same illocutionary point had been made by reporting an inference because, in general, there are fewer places in which an observation report can go wrong.

In line with this analysis we can take a fresh look at the act of reporting experimental results. In addition to incorporating the above 'performative' analysis which locates these acts within the moral network of interpersonal trust between the members of the community (involving shared commitments to sincerity and care) one must take account of the fact that members of the community generally report only those results which they obtained when they believed the experimental apparatus was *working properly*. Sometimes it takes months to achieve this happy state of affairs. When the apparatus is working properly it produces the kind of results one has anticipated and has built this very apparatus to obtain. (The assessment of the moral quality of suppressed results is very difficult, and there seems to be no formula for making a judgement. Cf. Millikan's 'fraud' as described by Holton (1981).

The reporting of experimental results can hardly be just the bland stating of facts neatly corresponding to robust, unambiguous states of affairs. I suggest the most plausible account of this linguistic practice is that it is rhetorical. The report of a successful experiment is a persuasive anecdote, which, within the belief-system and social conventions of the scientific community, lends credence to the complex of theories, concepts and other assumptions within which the doing of the experiment and the telling of its best results is framed. It is no wonder that no one has succeeded in devising a satisfactory 'logic' of inductive support, if the act of reporting results is rhetorical and its force illocutionary.

What, then, is the perlocutionary force of the act of reporting experimental results and observations? It can only be an enhancement or diminution of the degree of belief of the members of the community in that part of the context upon which the current discourse focuses attention. Perlocutionary force is indexical, in the sociological sense. The level of belief is dependent on the illocutionary force, not on any purported 'logical' relation between the report as a true or false or even probable statement and a hypothesis or theory abstracted from the context as a focus of interest. The moral concept of dependability displaces the epistemic concept of incorrigibility in defending the relatively foundational role played by observation reports (see Norris, 1982).

Foundations or groundings?

The failure of those philosophical projects which were aimed at identifying and justifying claims for foundations of knowledge seems to be irremediable. The idea that there are recognizably incorrigible statements has to be dropped. But need one dash off, with such as Rorty, to the opposite extreme? Are there then nothing but equally commendable human 'conversations', from one to another of which one might wander, giving one's loyalty as fancy takes one? There is a shifting but always distinguishable shoal of accepted beliefs on which our claims to knowledge, that is to be trusted by our fellow scientists (and eventually by the lay community) are *grounded*. Grounding is not in propositions or statements, but in material practices. We trust beliefs that have been produced by reliable people using reliable methods. Reliability and trust are tied into one another through the idea of beliefs as a basis for action. The policy realism to be defended in part four is just such a programme of action based on beliefs. It is action and the material upshot of action which justifies beliefs, not the fulfilment of argument schemata. But if our groundings in action and common experience are to be reliable as a guides to better beliefs about the natural world we cannot do without something like the Gibsonian psychology of perception. It bootstraps its way into our regard, since it is in the end recommended by its concordance with the theory of organic evolution. Perception must rest on the existence of evolv*ed* perceptual systems and evolv*ing* conceptual systems.

As I have argued, Gibsonian reliabilism can go no further than a guarantee of the realism of perceptual discriminations at the level of the distinctions marked by the Kantian categories: things from events; spatial from temporal relations; causal from accidental sequences, and so on. Of course the forms of judgement should be *correlated* with the categories, but only if language has reliabilistically evolved to manage Gibsonian metaphysical genera. Other beings, equipped with different perceptual systems adapted to the pick-up of different classes of information from the ambient array, the energy flux, would no doubt have developed different systems of categories, since other aspects of the world from those that interest us would be important to them. But this consideration does not make our sample of the higher-order invariants any less reliable.

8

The Construction of Facts

Knowledge-garnering in general

Given the success of Gibson's project we can assume that we do touch, see and physically operate with and upon things, constituents of a world that exists independently of ourselves. But much of our knowledge-garnering depends on interpretative procedures in which belief-systems are intimately involved. While every human being is so endowed that he or she can pick out things as stable beings against a background, only the members of certain cultures can tell a hawk from a handsaw. To identify the point at which the propositional expression of the knowledge we garner from experience should be called 'scientific knowledge' I turn to an admirable discussion of this matter by F. Dretske (1969). In robust Gibsonian style Dretske describes a generic kind of apprehension as follows (p. 76): 'what we see . . . is a function solely of what there is to see and what, given our visual apparatus and the conditions under which we employ it, we are capable of visually differentiating.'

One can freely acknowledge the relativity inherent in *other* ways of seeing, a relativity which depends on the conceptual background . . . of the individual percipient, *without undermining the objectivity and publicity of what we see*. For the objectivity and publicity of the world resides in the fact that we can all, *regardless* of our conceptual background . . . see. m [the generic visual achievement] the same objects and events. (p. 77)

But to see how a thing is behaving, to see what properties it has or whether it is changing, is seeing of a different sort. Gibson's analysis does not provide a certification of any form of 'seeing that . . .' To accept Gibsonian realism is not to slide back into a new form of foundationalism. The truth account of realism does not run in Realm 1 any more than anywhere else in the epistemic realms of scientific referents. Gibsonianism does certify realism in general, in the referential sense, since it gives us very good grounds for the belief that, in describing the things and events we perceive, we are talking *about* the things and events of a world independent of our perceptual systems. In the more familiar terminology of Boyd we could say that Gibsonianism provides us with the grounds for believing that we can obtain epistemic access to the physical world as it exists independently of ourselves, but that it gives us no reason to believe that that access can be exploited in such a way as to provide the scientific community with a sediment of absolutely unrevisable nuggets of truth.

Knowledge-garnering as 'seeing as . . .'

According to Hanson (1958) a good model for treating the difference that differences in belief, and, in particular, that differences in belief in different theories, makes to how different people see the world is the gestalt switch. We have no reason to believe that there was any difference between what Lister saw when he saw the micro-organisms in infected wounds and what Pasteur saw when he saw them. But Lister thought they were wild human cells and Pasteur thought they were hostile invaders. The difference is in no way comparable to that between seeing a mass of lines as a rabbit and seeing the same mass as a duck. Think 'rabbit', see rabbit; think 'duck', see duck. The perceptual gestalt model is a poor analogy. In a gestalt switch the perceiver passes from seeing a duck to seeing a rabbit. It is only in those conditions that the small shift in focus of attention from what is salient to duckhood to what is salient for rabbithood brings about the change in gestalt. The transition that matters for the understanding of how knowledge is garnered from what people perceive is not like that between one visual gestalt and another. As Aronson (1984) puts it (p. 98), 'Hanson's mistake . . . was to confuse seeing with knowledge based strictly on visual means.' When Lister changes his mind there is no reason to think that any difference occurs in what he sees with the help of his microscope. Hanson's model is inadequate to show that 'going from see, to seeing that on the basis of applying a theory indicates a perceptual achievement'. 'Seeing that . . .' is not a species of 'seeing as . . .' So the difference between mere seeing and seeing as does not mark the difference between perception and knowledge-garnering. Whatever 'seeing that . . .' on the basis of seeing might be, it is not a perceptual achievement, so it is not likely to be illuminated by the psychology of 'seeing as . . .', *even though the latter requires attention to the role of the perceiver's beliefs*.

Knowledge-garnering as 'seeing that . . .'

In her important discussion of Hanson's views Ruth Putnam (1972) pointed out that scientific knowledge-garnering differs from everyday perceiving in the way that 'noticing that . . .' or 'observing that . . .' differs from just seeing this or that thing. By these key phrases she means to refer to some kind of concept-guided attending. For example on the day that Tinbergen made his great discovery we could imagine him saying 'I saw a stickleback, and I noticed that it had turned red just as the red mail van passed outside the window.' This saying presupposes that he saw the stickleback turn red and that he saw the mail van. What he noticed was dependent on seeing but as he tells the story he had seen those things before. One day it struck him . . .

A more complex example from the history of science is Mendel's 'fraud'. Ever since Fisher demonstrated that the chances of Mendel's getting results as good as those he reported, from a patch of peas the size of the monastery garden, is about 1:30,000, scholars have pondered on what actually happened. Since his notebooks were destroyed by his successor as abbot, any reconstruction of his methods must be speculative. A most interesting solution has been proposed by Root-Bernstein (1983). He argues that in Mendel's time there were 'two fundamental ways of viewing nature'. The 'biological view' saw individuals as varying continuously in all their common characteristics. Darwin shared this view and formulated his idea of the accumulation of small intergenerational differences within that frame-work. The 'statistical view' was based on counting the frequency of occur-rence of attributes within a population. To be countable, attributes must be discrete. An individual must be either green or yellow, if a head count of green peas and of yellow peas is to be possible. Greenish-yellow things are an embarrassment. In order to apply statistical methods to biology it was necessary to solve 'the problem of assigning continuously variable charac-teristics to discrete categories' (p. 279).

There was, then, 'an irreconcilable tension between the discrete, categorized perception of inheritance, and the "fuzzy" biological one' or, to put the matter another way, 'the "reality" of nature confounds the "ideality" of systems of classification' (p. 280), at least systems of classification that could yield materials capable of statistical treatment. Mendel's problem was what to do with the 7 per cent of peas which did not unambiguously fit his predetermined discrete categories. He had to *assign* them to the discrete categories which were already well filled with specimens. According to Root-Bernstein, 'what in fact Mendel published was not a "real" description of his peas, but his perception of how those peas could be categorized into "ideal" discrete groups' (p. 282). Root-Bernstein presents very good evidence derived from his replication of the Mendelian experiments and from his study of Mendelian literary fragments to show that the abbot was well aware of the need to 'make a decision' the outcome of which was not strictly determined by nature. Fisher's criticism is, in the end, beside the point. It would only be germane were there indeed such discrete categories in nature. But they are theoretical constructions *by the help of which* nature is segregated. 'Mendel's peas did not represent an "objective truth" that Mendel could unambiguously interpret . . . [they] represented a "fuzzy set" of data which required subjective analysis to fit into discrete categories' (p. 289). Root-Bernstein's choice of the expression 'subjective' is unfortunate. Rather Mendel's analysis depended on the use of relatively a priori categories which emerged not from his experience of nature, but from the exigencies of the method he had chosen for studying the phenomena.

What if Tinbergen had gone on to say, 'I saw that the stickleback was aroused'? This is the same kind of step that is marked by such comments as 'I see that the electroscope is charged' when one contemplates divergent gold leaves. I return to Dretske's analysis of the deep grammar of expressions like 'seeing that . . .' for further guidance. Such expressions are used to express the result of some knowledge-garnering effort in which perception is inextricably involved. (There is also a use for this kind of expression to mark a purely cognitive act of apprehension.) The point of such a remark as 'S sees that b is P' is to indicate how S came to know that b was P, namely by looking. But that cannot be a simple Gibsonian seeing. The kind of categories involved in the predication of attributes of interest to science are far more specific than the bare-bones Kantian distinctions that the human perceptual systems are evolved to pick up. Dretske proposes four conditions for the correct use of this kind of 'seeing that . . .' expression.

1　b is P.
2　S sees b.
3　The conditions under which S sees b are such that it would not look the way it does look, say L, unless it were P.
4　S, believing 3, takes b to be P.

If any of these conditions fail we can rightly say that S did not see (could not have seen) that b was P. These conditions pick out the structure of the process of the acquisition of knowledge by perceptual (and, for this example, visual) means. It is in condition 3 that the corpus of prior belief, available to S, enters into the process of knowledge-garnering. Amongst S's beliefs there must be some representation of a law-like relation between P and L. There is an enormous variety of possibilities. P might be a presumed cause of L-type experiences; L might be the perceptual manifestation of P, and so on. Whatever is involved in any given case the relation between P and L can never be stronger than the natural necessity of a law of nature which licenses only plausibility assessments. Revisable beliefs enter into the process of knowledge-garnering at just the point at which scientific knowledge emerges from pre-scientific experience.

It is worth noticing that Aronson, for instance, cites cases of the ascription of dispositional attributes as instances of Dretskean 'seeing that . . .' Seeing a steaming kettle the Dretskean observer remarks, 'I see that the kettle is boiling'. But ebullition is the grounding of the disposition to emit steam. I believe this is the typical case. When Tinbergen says, 'I see that the stickleback is aroused', the ascribed predicate refers to the presumed grounding of a cluster of dispositions including the tendency to turn red. And the same analysis applies to the case of the electroscope, and a myriad other examples.

We have been following a progression that leads from Gibsonian seeing to the perceptual/cognitive genesis of scientific knowledge. The results of Gibsonian seeing are, I claim, immune to conceptual change. They are defeasible only by the demonstration of defective functioning of the perceptual systems. For instance the claim that one could see canals on Mars is finally disposed of by showing how under certain circumstances the perceptual system is fooled into the creation of a false gestalt. An observer must see lines before he or she can see that there are canals. But that observer need not see these lines as canals before being able to make a factual claim. Canals, at that distance, may indeed look like lines. Dretske's analysis shows that the input from the belief-system occurs at just the point at which propositional knowledge is drawn off from experience. But the defeasibilty of that knowledge comes from the tacit involvement of law-like beliefs which carry the perceiver from manifestations to the groundings of dispositions. The basic referent (b in our Dretskean formulation) is a Gibsonian invariant. And that is the basis of the modest realist construal of the science of Realm 1.

Decontextualization: negotiating entry to the corpus

The account of the creation of facts is still not complete. Claims of the kind I have been describing are liable to become the subject of negotiation by members of the scientific community. The final acceptance of a 'fact' by the community is mediated by a social process. This point has become a commonplace of contemporary philosophy of science, but it is instructive to turn back to an account of it from which, whether acknowledged or not, the current view derives. As T. S. Kuhn admits, much of what he has to say about the social genesis of scientific fact is derived from the work of Ludwig Fleck (1935). Fleck's aim was twofold. He set about revealing the social processes by which facts were acknowledged by the community, and at the same time he tried to explain why the illusion that there were no such processes had been so persistent. His account makes use of two main explanatory concepts, 'thought-style' and 'thought-collective'. Each thought-collective has a distinctive thought-style. It is a 'readiness for directed perceptions' that constrains the way the members of that thought-collective perceive reality. This adds a social dimension to the story, since a thought-collective is first of all a social unit of some profession, medical, chemical and the like.

Why do facts appear to be independent of the thought-collectives in which they are generated? An utterance or inscription is transformed in the act of publication. The thought-collective rewrites the history of its discoveries and indeed its own history to present itself and its programmes of activities as rationally ordered research efforts intentionally directed to what, in any external account, would be seen to be only retrospectively recognizable as 'results'. Fleck distinguishes between 'journal science', the first tentative publication of results that are presented as revisable, and 'vademecum science', which in becoming exoteric and popular has lost its provisional character. This transformation is very similar to that which sociologists describe as the loss of indexicality, that is the loss of marks of origin which label a putative fact with the name of the laboratory in which it was formulated and the time and identity of its 'discoverer'. Less happily perhaps Fleck distinguishes between the passive part of science, the deliverances of the senses, and the active part played by a thought-collective which imposes its thought-style on everything that it presents as knowledge. A very similar account of the genesis of facticity can be found in Latour and Woolgar (1979). Successive acts of publication delete indexical markers, such as date and place of discovery. A fully decontextualized report may even omit the name of the person who claims the discovery. Decontextualized publication presents the 'fact' as wholly independent of the human world. Loss of confidence in the trustworthiness of the claim expressed in the decontextualized style may lead to the successive reintroduction of marks of indexicality until the putative fact appears as the eccentric opinion of just one man.

Knowledge-garnering as selection: the use of analytical analogues

Concept-guided perception provides the community with too rich a diet of facts. The world of common experience, including what are seen or heard as the reactions of instruments, is complex and superficially ambiguous to the point of being almost inchoate to human contemplation. Research projects begin only when a further measure has been imposed on the beings of Realm 1. The most potent device for inducing the appearance of pattern in the world of common experience is the 'analytical analogue'. I shall illustrate its power with a couple of examples.

Case 1   Forcing a 'closure'.   I owe the idea of a closure to Roy Bhaskar (1975). To pick out a particular pattern of events or properties or arrangement of things or whatever it might be from the complexity of the common-sense world is to eliminate, in thought (and in well-designed experiments also in practice), all but a very few of the many influences that are actually at work in the production of that world. This is to force a closure on natural tendencies. Analytical analogues are often used for this purpose.

Unguided by scientific theory our commonsense perceptions of the conditions surrounding disease are notoriously both complex and cloudy. We organize our perception of illness with a mix of traditional folk practices and surviving fragments of antique theories. Both physical and psycho-social conditions clamour for our attention. The ubiquity of human malevolence is at least as obvious as any biological conditions might be. Even at a late stage in medicine, long after the bewitchment theory had fallen from favour amongst medical practitioners, the aetiology of the suppuration of wounds was unclear. To continue with an example I have discussed already, it was well known that such wounds were alive with 'wild cells'. By this time confidence in the microscope had risen to the point at which microbes were as much creatures of common sense as cows. If disease was a metabolic disorder, wild cells were probably the effects of suppuration, detached human cells. Pasteur did not reach what we now take to be the correct understanding of the origin and role of the wild cells by straightforward experimental tests within the framework of Mill's canons. Pasteur's innovation was conceptual, and depended on the deployment of an analytical analogue. His microbiological experience had mostly been as an oologist, studying the role of yeasts in fermentation. This became his analytical analogue. If suppuration is analogous to fermentation, what is analogous to yeast? Clearly the wild cells. They are an infection. At one blow they are shifted from concomitant status to that of causal agent. In inducing a closure the analytical analogue had opened up a research project, which culminated in the discovery of the so-called 'attenuation of viruses'. At that time 'virus' was the generic term for all infective agents. Analytical analogues work in something like the same way as stains in cytology. Different stains enhance the visibility of different structures within the cell. In the absence of a theory as to what the cell structure ought to be, one must acknowledge the ever-present possibility that some induced appearances of structure are artefacts. The same reservation applies to the reliability of the results of using an analytical analogue.

Case 2   Guided selection.   Social worlds of which we are not ourselves members are often opaque. How can we make a guided selection of events that will be a first inroad into an alien order? Sociologists still make use of an ancient technique, the comparison of an alien social order with a drama. This is sometimes called the 'dramaturgical model', and is not to be confused with 'dramatism', the sociolinguistic theory of Kenneth Burke. In a typical research project football riots were compared by the sociologist Peter Marsh to staged performances. The riot, as an opaque social event, is searched for analogues of actors, staging, costume, director, critics, audience, perhaps even proscenium arch. This analogue has proved particular fruitful in the social-psychological study of football hooliganism, since it can be further deployed in suggesting a search for analogues of plot, script and of the relation of actors to these controls. Further analytical analogues can be applied to study each of the components selected under the guidance of the macro-model. For instance episodes of violent encounter can be fruit-fully compared with jousting (ritual combat in the pursuit of honour) and with the tests traditionally used in *rites de passage* (see Marsh, Rosser and Harré, 1977).

There are deeper reasons than the pragmatic for selecting one analytical analogue rather than another. The choice of analogue is partly determined by the metaphysics of the underlying theory. But further investigation of this constraint must await the detailed analysis of Realm 2 theorizing in part four. One can make similar methodological observations on the analogue at work in Darwin's selection of significant patterns from among the huge diversity of natural phenomena with which he was presented when he stepped ashore from the Beagle. I think it is no exaggeration to say that Darwin saw the whole of the natural world through the eyes of a Shropshire countryman, that is in terms of lines of descent. The creatures of nature then appeared grouped as a cattle or horse breeder would group bloodstock.

No doubt in practice the steps I have presented sequentially go on together. Patterns emerge before the educated eye with little sense of progression. But from the viewpoint of the philosophy of science the steps to a fully 'trust-worthy' fact are a discrete series. From the categorizing stage the world appears to be sorted into kinds – collocated, coexisting clusters of charac-teristics. From the analogizing stage there emerge observable patterns of change, development, dissolution and decay. Can these kinds and these sequences be the matter of science? Or, to put the issue more transparently within the terms of the moral order of the scientific community, can we put our trust in the persistence and reliability of the kinds and sequences so revealed? Those exemplars of moral probity, the members of the scientific community itself, show by their practice that trust should still be witheld. If this is all that has gone into the selection of facts it is not enough.

It seems that facts are created by applying fine-grained conceptual systems, *ceteris paribus*, to the coarse-grained deliverances of our perceptual systems. The metaphysics of experience, guaranteed by the plausibility of Gibsonian psychology, gives us a basic ontology of relatively stable beings endowed with causal powers, and of events as changes within the system of things that forms our physical environment. The application of concepts yields taxonomies and knowledge of temporal regularities. The facts so created cannot be used as evidence for taxonomies or causal generalities, in the traditional sense, since they cannot stand independently of the theories and conceptual systems involved in their genesis. Citing the facts is the telling of an anecdote. We recommend conceptual systems to one another with exemplary tales, illustrating the power of this or that analytical analogue and conceptual system *to engender order* in our experience.

One final difficulty must be faced. In criticizing van Fraasen's ontology I drew on an objection entered by Musgrave. In order to sustain his position van Fraasen needed to accept a status for scientific theories that his views denied. In drawing support for scientific realism from Gibson's psychology do I not have to presuppose a realist interpretation of experience in order to use the experiences of Gibson, his associates and those who assisted him in his experiments as anecdotes to exhibit the power of Gibson's theory? But I need the theory to interpret those experiences in such a way that they will support it. I must presuppose a status for Gibson's theory that I am intent on proving, in so far as I can show that theory to be plausible. However, it has been my intent all along to deny the epistemological theory on which the alleged independence of theory and supporting fact is supposed to rest. As Whewell (and before him Humphrey Davy) saw with such clarity, fact and theory can never be radically separated. The history of science shows a dialectical development, a widening circle of intelligible experience. At any moment, for rhetorical purposes, a scientist can make an arbitrary cut, declaring him- or herself satisfied or dissatisfied with one or other of the segments created by the act of division. This provides an occasion for the use of the rhetoric of evidence, test, confirmation and disconfirmation. But, as I have argued, these metaconcepts are not part of the epistemology of science. They are *themselves* part of persuasive rhetoric.

9

Kinds and Causes: Constraints on a Science of Experience

The characteristics of proto-science

Could there be a science of the beings of Realm 1, their properties, their relations and the changes among them? To put this in the now familiar terms of the activities of the scientific community – could there be a discourse concerning the beings revealed in common experience, based solely on that experience, which referred to nothing but those beings, and yet met the moral standards that the community has set for trustworthy discourse? Gibsonian psychology gives us confidence in the possibility of extra-mental reference to the beings of a rather coarse-grained ontology – to things, events, surfaces, and so on, and their basic affordances. The ordering of these beings, as distinct referents, seems to invoke nothing more sophisticated by way of referential grids than Euclidean space and Newtonian time. Were referential acts to beings other than the Gibsonian beings of Realm 1 to be proscribed (say on epistemological, metaphysical or even moral grounds), could we sustain an enterprise like that which our science has actually become? I think the answer is no. It is an answer which emerges from the standard criticisms of positivism.

Classical positivism, though the most thoroughly worked out, has not been the last attempt to proscribe serious reference to the unobservable from scientific discourse. We have already looked at van Fraasen's form of 'empiricism'. I shall confine myself to taking up those criticisms of classical positivism (and its associate, the belief in logical essences) that help in coming to see why a Realm 1 discourse is so constrained as to be incapable of expressing as trustworthy a repertoire of beliefs than we have in traditional science. (By talking of 'serious reference' I mean to exclude pseudo-referential acts to convenient fictions.) A dramatic consequence of the positivistic proscription of serious reference to the unobserved is the enthronement of psychology as the most important source of concepts for analysing those aspects of scientific discourse that are not captured in

revelations of logical form, relative to the resources of the first-order predicate calculus. From the positivistic proscription it follows that there could
be no non-psychological concepts of explanation, cause, law, natural
necessity, kind, etc. , to take up the slack. I hope to show that if a science of
the beings of Realm 1 were a possibility it would involve the redress of
inherent instabilities in the Realm 1 discourse by covert reference to the
states and relations of beings in the realms beyond actual experience. This
would be to abandon the enterprise of a pure Realm 1 science.

Attempts at the construction of a scientific discourse apropos the beings
of Realm 1 can be broadly divided into two kinds of studies. There is work
on the correlations of properties and states of beings individuated by
reference to the common grid of classical space and time. By taking
temporal matters into account this work can be divided into studies of coexisting and collocated properties (taxonomy) and studies of regularities of
concomitance and sequence (behavioural sciences such as kinematics). The
practices of the scientific community seem to be based on the tacit assumption that this kind of work is radically incomplete. Biological doctrines like
'transformed cladistics' and chemical ideologies like the anti-atomism of
mid-nineteenth-century chemical operationism tend to be rarities. These
are 'advertised' as pure Realm 1 endeavours, leading to discourses in which
no referential acts to beings other than those available to common perception, are admitted. With one instructive exception they tend to be short-
lived. Ethnomethdology and behavioural psychology were quickly
challenged by rivals such as ethogenics and cognitive psychology respectively. The former invoked unobserved entities, such as tacit rule-systems
and the latter hypothetical processes such as unconscious information-
processing in explanations of the regularities described in the more primitive corresponding proto-science. Pure Realm 1 discourse seems to be
incomplete. The kind of supplementation instanced in social psychology
leads inexorably to a Realm 2 discourse and beyond. But since in the
general argument for scientific realism reference to the beings of Realm 1
provides the essential grounding of the claim that scientific discourse is
about a world independent of human material and cognitive practices, the
properties of the proto-sciences of Realm 1 must be explored. I emphasize
once again that by a grounding I do not mean an incorrigible foundation.

The proto-sciences of Realm 1 discourse arise by the pulling together of
fragmentary experiences into a network of correlated properties and
states, classifying when the properties are considered synchronically and
collocated, predicting and retrodicting when they are considered dia-
chronically. The discourse of Realm 1 proto-science will serve both to
express the results of such work, and to facilitate the practices of classification and prediction. The former appears as a semantic network of kind

concepts, the latter as a network of expanded versions of basic ontological concepts.

For a proto-scientific discourse to be trustworthy these networks of correlations must be understood to pick out kinds and causes. But, it will emerge, neither kinds nor causes can be distinguished from arbitrary or accidental coincidences unless reference is made, tacitly for the most part, to matters beyond actual experience.

Classes and kinds: the cladistics controversy

Though neglected in many contemporary works on general scientific method the community has devoted a great deal of effort to the classification of Realm 1 beings – plants, animals, rocks, gemstones, geographical features, and so on. Classification requires two steps. One must first acquaint oneself with as many of the properties of samples of the beings in question as one's conceptual and practical resources enable one to pick out. Since what can be picked out as a basis for comparison between Realm 1 beings is relative to the conceptual system currently in use, it is quite possible for later scrutiny deploying another conceptual scheme to reveal previously unnoticed distinguishing properties, the sex of flowering plants for instance. The second step in classifying is comparative, to use likenesses and differences to set up tentative groupings that will eventually crystallize into taxa. There are any number of problems concealed in this simplified exposition.

Is the practice of classifying beings into discrete groupings a matter of convenience and human convention or does it reflect disjoint natural kinds? The elucidation of Mendel's 'fraud' shows how complex is this issue. Borderline cases are intolerable and yet they seem to be forced on us by nature. The scientific community has indulged in all kinds of shifts to bypass this difficulty, the latest of which is the technique of fuzzy sets. But fuzzy-set theory is an evasion of the deep question that is prompted by the clash between the apparent continuity of instances of naturally occurring properties and the discreteness of taxonomic practice. Are borderline cases a disturbance of some true natural order?

The right answer seems to be that the imposition of those boundaries which serve to maintain discrete groupings in any human classificatory practice cannot be justified without reference to unobservable properties and structures of the beings in question. Manifest properties are the realization of dispositions which are grounded in the natures of things. The philosophical groundwork for this crucial assumption has been laid in part two. Sometimes the theoretical account of natures is enough to show that the taxonomy must be discrete. For instance the discrete classification of the chemical elements is grounded in the electronic theory of chemical atoms, so that each element differs from the next in a series by just one electron. The rare earths have almost identical chemical properties but they are treated as discrete elements on the basis of the electronic constitution of their constituent atoms. They differ by the number of electrons in an 'inner' shell. Only the outer shell of electrons is effective in determining distinctive chemical behaviour. The philosophical arguments of part two, directed to elucidating the concept of natural-kind, showed that if taxa are to be reliable they must mark off natural-kinds. But natural-kinds can be demarcated in a stable way only if each natural-kind concept can be located in both a practical and a theoretical context. The latter, as instanced in the case of the chemical elements, requires reference to beings of Realms 2 or 3 certainly unobservable in practice and probably, in the case of electrons, in principle. This seems to depend on the possibility of classifying unobserved and unobservable beings into natural kinds too. Hierarchies of kinds and natures cannot be avoided if chemical elements, biological species, minerals, and so on, are to be treated as natural kinds. Must such hierarchies terminate in a natural diversity of basic kinds? This question can be answered only when we have studied the natures of the beings scientists suppose are in Realm 3.

The 'cladistics' controversy illustrates most of the philosophical issues that have arisen in considering the proto-science of Realm 1 discourse. The main features of this biological technique are described, though not wholly coherently, by Patterson (1980). He enunciates the basic axiom of biological discourse as follows: 'Features shared by organisms (homologies) manifest hierarchical patterns in nature.' Such patterns can be expressed in branching diagrams or 'cladograms'. 'The nodes in cladograms symbolize the homologies shared by the organisms grouped by the node.' A cladogram is shown in figure 9.1 where n_1 represents the homologies shared by B and C,

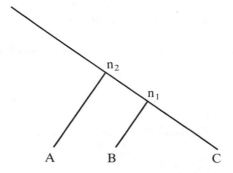

Figure 9.1   A cladogram

and n_2 represents the homologies shared by A, B and C. B and C are more closely related than are A, B and C. Each 'twig' is distinguished by features that are unique to it, and necessarily not shared by any taxa to the right of the closest node. These diagrams are created by considering properties. Can they bear any further interpretation? One should have in mind the situation in chemistry. The halogens, fluorine, chlorine, bromine and iodine, have sufficient observable properties and dispositions in common to be taken as a group. We also believe that the grouping can be interpreted in terms of some common feature of the electronic structure of the constituent atoms of samples of the halogens. So this sector in the periodic table is susceptible of *two* readings: one phenomenological and the other ontological. Can we justify a similar duality of readings for cladograms? Different answers to this question define rival schools of taxonomists. The issue arises over how far biologists should develop a relationship between a taxonomy and a phylogeny, between a system of classification and a representation of the evolutionary history of the organisms classified. In classical neo-Darwinian biology taxonomies are used as evidence for phylogenetic hypotheses, which are in their turn implicated in taxonomic decisions such as determining whether certain similarities between groups of organisms should be discounted because they seem to be the result of convergent evolution. The use of taxonomic evidence as support for phylogenetic hypotheses depends on various auxiliary assumptions, the most important of which is the assumed rarity of convergent evolution. In general things which 'look alike' do not stem from different ancestors. To a positivist all this looks distinctly fishy. As T. S. Kemp (1986) has rather charitably put it, 'Recognition of the frailty of the explicitly evolutionary models available for converting empirically derived taxonomic patterns into phylogenetic hypotheses has led to a number of attempts to exclude as much assumption about evolutionary processes as possible.' Not only is there a whiff of circularity about the use of evolutionary evidence, but the associated hypothesis of the rarity of convergent evolution seems both to be speculative and to beg the question. To abandon the use of morphological similarities in theorizing about descent seems an excessive response to these caveats. Such a reaction makes sense only when coupled with a positivistic hostility to theory. (Pheneticism, a purely statistical correlational taxonomy based on unweighted characteristics, is a taxonomic practice that comes closest to a biological variant of the phenomenological strand of extreme Machean positivism.) It is from this metaphysical standpoint that the idea of a 'transformed' cladistics has been promoted. It would be a pure taxonomy purged of all neo-Darwinian or other theoretical elements. These are castigated by transformed cladists as mere speculation, since the processes referred to would be unobservable, introduced for theoretical reasons. Differences

between postivists and scientific realists come to a head over the interpretation of the nodes in the cladograms. According to phylogenetic
systematists, n_1 refers to an ancestral species from which B and C evolved,
while n_2 refers to an ancestral species from which both A and n_1 evolved.
For Hennig (1966) and almost all systematists the nodes refer to or
represent ancestral species, while for Patterson, (1980, p. 239) 'the assumption has been found to be unnecessary, even misleading and may be
dropped.' The judgement 'found to be unnecessary' turns out to be relative
to two old friends from vulgar positivism – 'parsimony' and 'predictive
power'. Transformed cladistics turns out to be ordinary taxonomy without a
realist or referential interpretation of the nodes. As such it is just a vulgar
positivist reduction. This is made abundantly clear in the debates that have
followed its claim to be the 'real' theory of biological classification.

The opponents of transformed cladistics have little difficulty in showing
that unless the nodes are given a realist interpretation as referring to
historical entities, ancestral forms, then the choice of a particular cladogram, out of an indefinite range of alternatives for any given set of
characteristics, is arbitrary. Transformed cladistics is beset with the
classical and insoluble problem of all positivistic movements in science,
the underdetermination by data of the residual formal scheme. Choice
among alternative cladograms can depend only on mere formal considerations. And these formal considerations turn out to be the formalistic and
scientifically shallow positivistic criteria, parsimony and predictive power.
It is worth noticing how closely this controversy parallels the sixteenth-
century disputes about the ontological status of rival planetary theories.
Then too parsimony and predictive power were on offer as criteria for
choosing among rival theories. The astronomical dispute was resolved in
favour of a realist reading of the geometrical models, finally opting for the
best of the heliocentric schemes.

Patterson's paper is instructively incoherent when he enters into a discussion of how to apply the formal criteria. One must 'know', he concedes, that
not all characteristics are of equal standing when it comes to creating a
cladogram. There are two classes of 'false characteristics', superficial
similarities, for which non-transformed cladists have a Darwinian explanation. These are the results (in Darwinian terms) of convergent evolution and
irrelevant homologies. The latter are able to be assigned to every species in
the cladogram by invoking disappearing embryonic forms to eliminate
anomalous species. These are evidently *biological* criteria, which invoke
theoretical considerations from outside the statistical correlations of species
attributes. Without these external considerations the resolution of the
problem of an over-abundance of cladograms relative to any given data base
cannot be achieved by the device of deleting false homologies in anything

but an arbitrary way. The claim by transformed cladists – that they are revealing a 'natural order' – is rightly rejected by Charig (1981) in a masterly paper. If evolutionary theory is dropped from the considerations germane to constructing taxonomies, and that is the consequence of abandoning a realist treatment of the cladogram nodes, then the alleged 'natural order' is wholly arbitrary. It is no longer connected with hypotheses of origin, that is with phylogenetics. It collapses into 'a random assortment of characters – some due to common ancestry, some being similar adaptations to similar causes, and others being purely fortuitous' (p. 19).

Unlike transformed cladistics, evolutionary systematics closely resembles the taxonomic practices of the physical sciences. It is an 'attempt to ascertain the phylogeny, an objective reality, and to represent it by means of a branching diagram' (Charig, 1981, p. 19). Martin (1981, p. 127) sharpens the distinction between a classification and a phylogenetic reconstruction. The degree of fit between a cladogram representing an empirically based classification and the branching diagram representing the phylogenetic hypothesis could appear, at first sight, as a test of the hypothesis. This is another of Patterson's exemplary philosophical errors (1980, p. 239). It is clear that the elimination of false homologies which is required to produce a determinate classification, that is just one cladogram, is dependent on the phylogenetic hypothesis of organic evolution. The history (and the philosophy) of science show that theory and fact must evolve *together*, each correcting the other. (Cf. Martin, 1981.)

In terms of the distinctions with which I have been working, the philosophically (and theoretically) confused effort to advocate 'transformed cladistics' is no more than an attempt to purge biological classification of references to beings from Realm 2 or Realm 3, that is real entities we cannot or could not observe, but in whose existence and efficacy we have good reason to believe. It amounts to a self-defeating attempt to formulate a technique for marking off stable kinds, wholly within the practical order. It would be as absurd to attempt to purge the periodic table of all reference to the electronic configurations of atomic structures. And, because of the existence of the rare earths, a transformed cladist taxonomy of the chemical elements would also be indeterminate.

Taxonomies as meaning-relations: the search for self-sustaining necessity

From the point of view of a pure empiricism, such as that of Hume or the Tractarian Wittgenstein, there can be no semantic structures underlying discourses which refer to beings 'given' in experience, that is by the use of the perceptual systems. Atomic propositions are concatenations of names, and there can be no contradiction in asserting any one of these names, say one which names a cause, and the negation of another, say that which names its customary concomitant, or effect. In this framework the analytic/ synthetic distinction is strictly dichotomous, and every statement in a scientific discourse must fall into one category or the other. The unpacking of implicit component concepts in a complex descriptive concept yields sequences of analytic propositions which express the conceptual structure of the taxonomic system as nothing but man-made groupings. All descriptions of coexistence or succession are synthetic. The scientific community uses taxonomic systems as devices for focusing attention on some subset of the properties of a being of interest to facilitate its management by comparison with other beings. We could speak of degrees of attention, depending on how detailed were the comparisons. At one degree of attention tigers are obviously distinct from alligators, at another they are as obviously members of the same kind.

According to Leibniz the difference between truths of reason (something like our post-Kantian analytic statements) and truths of fact (something like our synthetic statements) is but the difference between statements involving nominal concepts constructed out of finitely many and hence humanly knowable unit concepts, and those involving nominal concepts with infinitely many components. No human being could ever come to know the internal composition of such concepts, and so statements involving them must be tested against experience. Waismann's (1968) way of undermining the alleged dichotomy between analytic and synthetic statements was to remind us that conceptual clusters are human constructions which can be abandonded if their use proves to be an embarrassment. For instance a concept may be so internally structured that our use of it in a classificatory project leads to the collecting up of an excessively diverse group of beings for the project in hand. Again Waismann makes the point that analytic statements are not dressed up logical tautologies, and can be reached by substitution in such linguistic forms only by using substitution rules which are in effect reports of usage. Analytic statements which might be offered as expressions of the content structure of a way of thought do not provide a self-sustaining necessity for classification systems.

From each vantage point, taxonomy in general, the cladistics controversy and the viability of the alleged rooted inviolability of analytic statements, the stability of a taxonomic system and its capacity to deal with borderline cases must depend on something other than the observational data upon which its structure was originally based.

Though the position of Leibniz seems extravagant it does suggest some kind of polarity in the kinds of meaning-relations which mark off the semantic network of Realm 1 discourse. There are cases in which our awareness of a correlation between types of properties or events strikes us as no more than a coincidence. But gradually some psychological process as commonplace as the formation of habits of expectation, as Hume once put it, can begin to force the inexorable incorporation of facts into meanings. 'Cigarettes' become 'coffin nails', then 'cancer sticks'. These conceptual changes in the meaning of the term 'cigarette' take up into the very concept those facts which appear in the Government Health Warnings that now decorate cigarette packets in the more socially responsible nations. The synonyms for 'cigarette' are quasi-scientific nicknames.

In the middle ground are predicates whose meaning is affected by pervasive natural phenomena. The association between heat and combustion is taken up into the meaning of 'fire', just as cold is taken up into the meaning of 'ice'. But statements such as 'Fire is hot' are not analytic in the strong, Kantian sense. 'Hot ice' and 'cold fire' are dramatic poetic tropes, not self-contradictions. Further removed still from the wherewithal to report the merely accidental are the vocabularies of botanical and zoological classifications. Once established, they are very nearly immune from disturbance, even when there are discoveries of massive clusters of novel organic or mineral forms. This cannot be due to some superior inner logical force in the component statements of taxonomic discourses. But it has to do with the way the concepts of a classification system are derived from classificatory practices and the appearances of actual samples. In a sense we discover the *right* meaning for 'loris' by closely studying lorises.

At the opposite pole are the interconnected definitional relations that obtain between the concepts of certain branches of physics. For instance the statement '$v = s/t$' expresses part of the structure of the concept of velocity in terms of two more fundamental concepts. Further refinements of the concept are made along similar lines, for instance in the statement '$v = ds/dt$', and so on. Statements like '$F = ma$' cannot be interpreted without attention to the metaphysics implicit in the system within which they appear. In a Machean interpretation of classical mechanics '$F = ma$' is just like '$v = st$'. In the Newtonian interpretation 'F' refers to an independent dynamic parameter which is measured by the product of mass-acceleration. So arguments about the modal status of putative laws of nature cannot be conducted in isolation from consideration of the metaphysical schemes in which one might express the presumptive ontologies of rival views.

Every facet of the contexts of use of the proto-scientific concepts of Realm 1 discourse contributes to the rules for their use. The use of the word 'rule' in this discussion is justified by the thought that the uses of words in the typical discourse of a community are normatively constrained. But that should not be taken to imply that there is some kind of psychological reality in which rules exist as the causes of linguistic regularities. The 'rule' metaphor stands in for whatever it is in psychological or social reality that does maintain normative control. The content of a Realm 1 discourse within the scientific community is not a mere aggregate of authenticated beliefs, 'facts', but a structured network of concepts, some of the relations between which surface as laws of nature (see Dretske, 1977; Aronson, 1984), while others manifest themselves in the principles of a taxonomy.

But why is Realm 1 discourse merely proto-science? In discussing the beginnings of true scientific discourse in which reference is made to beings in Realm 2, we shall see that the conceptual structures of isolated Realm 1 discourses are vulnerable to shifts in the respect offered to some key theory. This is for the important reason that it is within the framework of a theory that there occurs the next level of beings, whose putative existence both grounds our trust in the persistence of patterns of collocation and succession of properties in the world of ordinary observation, and guides the efforts of those realists in the scientific community who are intent on finding ways of making the existence or non-existence of such beings manifest. Sometimes the change in status of a theory is freakish (such as the anti-Darwinism of 'transformed cladism') but sometimes it reflects genuine revisions of the ontology. No thing, event or relation, substance or attribute, to be found within the universe of reference of Realm 1 discourse, is likely to be so simple that it can be exhaustively described in terms of its ostensible properties. Realm 1 things may have dispositions that are quite unknown to those who, at some historic moment, make daily use of them. They may be manifested when the historical conditions have changed; for instance the electromagnetic properties of physical things have become commonplace. Even events which appear simple as Realm 1 beings, such as flashes of lightning, may turn out to be complex hierarchies of collocated events, differentially identified by reference to the concepts of relevant Realm 2 and Realm 3 discourses. Sheet lightning and forked lightning are not both 'lightning' from the point of view of the theory of electrical discharges.

It follows immediately from the foregoing that there is no one modal status to which each and every statement of a Realm 1 discourse can be assigned. At some moment there will be parts of the discourse that are treated as purely contingent assertions, vulnerable to the next experiment or observation. Even exceptionless correlations may be treated with caution. But most Realm 1 statements are taken to be naturally necessary, that is to exclude certain alternative possibilities. And some are taken to be truly analytic statements, whose purpose in the discourse is to reveal the semantic structure of this or that concept. These modal assignments appear not as overt modal qualifiers of the main verb, but are often manifested in the practices of the community, such as a reluctance to abandon a conceptual relation even in the face of apparent exceptions. In holding on to that relation the community tacitly rejects the exception as a genuine alternative to the relation in question. But why is scientific practice the way it is? It will become clear in the final section of this chapter that there is no way in which these intuitions and the practices which realize them can be rationally grounded in beliefs which concern Realm 1 beings alone, however well attested.

Correlations are not causes

The usual target for critics of the positivist doctrine of causation is Hume's regular concomitance analysis. Hume did not think that the concept of causation was exhaustively analysed in terms of mere sequential order. He thought the concept did include the idea of necessitation. It was his account of that idea that was startlingly radical. He tries to convince us that the idea derives from a psychological phenomenon and not from a real-world relation of production between cause and effect. His argument depends on his atomistic analysis of human experience, which is supposed to show that we do not, indeed could not, have impressions of the engendering or necessitating *relations* that productively unite causes with their effects.

Even if one is confined to proto-scientific discourse, the referents of which are all revealed by the use of human perceptual systems, one has no great difficulty in upsetting Hume's reasoning. The metaphysics of experience which emerges from Gibsonian psychology of perception requires that the properties of the things perceived be largely given as affordances – which, in philosophy, are a special class of dispositions. These are the dispositions which have to do with the facilitation of human activities. To treat the kind of a thing as in some measure revealed in its dispositions requires that, *ceteris paribus*, what is known of the past behaviour of that thing, and what can be expected of it in the future, must realize at least those dispositions, and perhaps others not yet manifested. Failure to perform up to specification is good grounds for entertaining the suspicion that the thing had been wrongly assigned to a kind, or that the picking out of that cluster of occurrent properties and dispositions as the marks of a kind had been unwise. Notice the terminology – 'wrongly assigned', 'unwise'. The discourse of Realm 1 supports a great range of material practices, and it is in terms appropriate to that role that it must be judged. But confidence in the manifested behaviour of things as revealing real dispositions realized from time to time in real causal production requires the community to take account of the beings of Realm 2 and 3 in the properties of and relations among which those dispositions are grounded.

In real science the distinction between causes and coincidences is drawn by turning to the putative referents of the implicit ontology of causal mechanisms of the appropriate theory-adumbrated realm. Here is a nice piece of primarily Realm 1 discourse from the *Guardian* (1983). Notice particularly how instabilities in the Realm 1 story are remedied by including reference to unobservable processes sketched by the appropriate theory.

Coffee is all but cleared this morning of the suspicion that it might cause cancer. After tracking the dietary habits of more than 14, 000 men for 17 years scientists have found no association between the drink and the disease.

Three years ago a US survey prompted researchers to suggest that coffee might cause cancer of the pancreas. The findings have been hotly disputed ever since.

A report today in the Lancet from Professor John Yudkin, diet specialist from Queen Elizabeth College, London, and colleagues at Oxford, the City University, and the Office of Population Censuses and Surveys, appears to settle the issue.

The men in their survey were all Londoners, aged 45-60 when the work started in 1967. By 1982, 47 had died of cancer of the pancreas. They had been drinking an average of 0.8 cups of coffee a day. The other 14, 038 men had been drinking an average of one cup of coffee a day.

Why did the US researchers find a relationship between coffee and pancreatic cancer? One answer, says the British team, may be that the condition itself causes sufferers to drink more of everything including coffee, *because it disturbs the body's glucose tolerance*.

They examined the records of four men who had died from pancreatic cancer within a year of entering the study. It turned out that they were drinking slightly more coffee. But they were also consuming more tea, milk, and fruit squash, and their total intake of these drinks was 20 per cent above average.

This factor, and others which would affect the amount of coffee consumed, were not taken into account by the US researchers, say Professor Yudkin and his colleagues. [Italics mine.]

Most of the work is reported in a typical Realm 1 discourse and concludes, unexcitingly but perhaps comfortingly, that there is no correlation between coffee drinking and cancer of the pancreas. The explanation of the apparently contradictory results obtained by the American researchers does invoke a causal relation, namely that marked by the correlation between the occurrence of the disease and increased drinking. But notice that this crucially important comment which defuses the contrary force of the US research is not left as a correlation. Yudkin and colleagues need to drive home this point in such a way that any suggestion of coincidence, statistical artefact, etc. , is ruled out. But how to raise the status of a correlation between cancer and increased drinking to a causal relation *from* cancer *to* increased drinking? Characteristically the Yudkin team drop out of Realm 1 discourse into that of Realm 2. They cite a causal mechanism, at the core of which is a substance that, relative to the observability of people drinking cups of coffee and pancreatic tumours, is an unobservable. Glucose molecules are probably beings of Realm 2, since a technique for their identification does exist. A study of the exact form that that identification takes would be needed to decide whether perhaps they should be cast into Realm 3. But whatever the outcome of such a study the point is clear. To distinguish a causal relation from a correlation one must leave the discourse and the ontology of Realm 1.

In the case of a more fundamental science, namely mechanics, the same pattern is realized. Aronson (1984, pp. 57-60) has shown how certain key features of causation, for instance the 'agentive' direction from cause to effect, can be consistently sustained and so causal relations picked out from among others which are manifested in correlations, only by reference to a quantity which is transferred in the interaction. This quantity turns out to be a typical Realm 3 being. Depending on context it might be energy or it might be momentum. A cause is materially related to its effect, while an effect is merely statistically related to its cause.

Part Four

Science for the Realm of Possible Experience

Flash fights the dirt you can see and germs you can't.

Introduction

There are, as we have seen, two ways of defining realism in relation to the epistemological claims of science. The bivalence principle interprets scientific realism as the thesis that every scientific statement (and particularly every non-definitional statement in a scientific theory) is true or false by virtue of the way the world is. Since we found good reason to think that no scientist or scientific research programme could ever tell whether any theoretical statement was strictly true or false, a defence of realism based on the bivalence principle came to seem hopeless. The alternative approach was to build a more modest idea of scientific realism on the results of successful and unsuccessful acts of reference in which a real physical relation is established between an embodied person (acting for the linguistic community) and an exemplary thing, event etc. Referential realism was developed on the basis of the thesis that many of the referring expressions that occur in theoretical discourses have referents in the world that exist independently of human cognitive and practical activity, and that we have good reason to believe that thesis. The philosophical argument to defend this form of scientific realism depends on the demonstration that at least some such putative beings had been shown actually to exist and some not to exist.

To establish a referential relation between a denoting expression and something in the world, two criteria must be satisfied.

1 The demonstrative criterion: it must be possible to locate a being in the appropriate referential grid which satisfies criterion 2.

2   The recognitive criterion: the being so located must exhibit properties which satisfy some prescription as to natural kind. In certain cases the recognitive criterion may prescribe marks of individual identity.

Once such a being has been found *any* of the component demands within the prescription that was criterial at the search–find/fail-to-find phase of the investigation may be revised. Revision of those demands that prescribe generic metaphysical status have, of course, the most radical effect on the putative ontological standing of the being in question.

As both sceptics and defendants of scientific realism are only too well aware, there is a problem about that doctrine, in whatever form it comes. The referents of many of the referring expressions found in well-regarded scientific discourse, such as 'chemical atom', 'intermediate vector boson', 'material dialectic', 'grammatical rule', 'super-ego', and so on are so located relative to common human experience that neither of the above criteria can be satisfied unproblematically. Progress can be made, I have suggested, if the putative referents of substantive terms in scientific discourses are divided into three realms, relative to the possibilities of human experience. Realm 1 is the world of common experience, and a very complex web of theoretically influenced perceptions it turns out to be. Realm 2 comprises those beings which, technical and other practical difficulties having been surmounted, might be available to human perception. The denizens of Realm 3 are beyond all possible experience. If beings located in Realm 2 are to become objects of experience, they must be roughly of the same natural kinds as the beings of Realm 1. When the idea of micro-organisms was first put forward in the early part of the seventeenth century the referents of the then current theoretical terms for such beings (perhaps van Helmont's *archae*) were in Realm 2. The microscope was known to transcend common experience, so it would not have been unreasonable to conjecture that with the improvement of the microscope such beings might be revealed. If it were to be possible to observe micro-organisms (if the project of searching for them was to have any chance of success) then they must be of roughly the same natural-kinds as larger organisms, and both must fall within the generic metaphysical category of individual substances.

The boundary between Realm 1 and Realm 2 is contingent on the state of the technology of instrumentation and, as illustrated with the case of the improving microscope, can change. Realm 3 is heterogeneous. There are several ways in which a being can be 'beyond all possible experience'. Some Realm 3 beings are of such a kind that advances in science would lead to their being thought to be, after all, capable of being observed given appropriate technical developments. Viruses were micro-organisms too small to be resolved with optical microscopes, and hence, *circa* 1900, in

Realm 3. But the discovery of the wave-particle dualism as expressed in de Broglie's rules opened up the technical possibility of microscopes of hitherto unimaginable resolving power. The change in physics shifted the boundary between Realm 2 and Realm 3 for micro-organisms. The serious consideration of the wherewithal to carry out empirical tests of existence claims for such beings now becomes possible. But this transformation of epistemic status is not confined to the physical sciences. Freud had the idea that the contents of dreams were symbolic representations of repressed material, unavailable to a person in waking life. This is a change of psychological theory which, given some lexicon of dream symbols, would shift the boundary between Realm 3 and Realm 2 for psychological beings, such as thoughts, feelings, attitudes, etc.

To defend a realist interpretation of that part of scientific discourse which has referents in Realm 2, I shall first develop the idea of a kind of cognitive object characteristic of those theories which concern beings located in that realm. I shall call it a 'theory-family'. I hope to show that this idea helps to make clear how new kinds of beings are anticipated in thought, and how projects for trying to find exemplars of such beings can be rationally designed. I call this 'policy realism'. Before I turn to setting out the structure and ways of evolving characteristic of theory-families I must first develop the idea of policy realism in a good deal more detail. Only then can it be made clear how the construction of a theory-family and the assessment of its current state facilitates projects of the kind that policy realism will justify. The kind of realism appropriate to assertions about the beings of Realm 3 will be tackled in part five.

10

Policy Realism

The idea of policy realism

We could say that tidying up our theory-driven beliefs about the furniture of the world is one of the prime aims of science. But that is an aim of science considered as a material practice. In our enthusiasm for that insight we must not neglect the traditional scientific aim of making our experiences intelligible. What is it to render an event, an action, a process, even the appearance of a thing, intelligible? I believe intelligibility is achieved by the answering of two questions:

1   To what kind does the being in question belong?
2   By what process (or mechanism) was it brought into being?

I hope to show that theory-families, those cognitive objects which I undertake to show lie behind sequences of successive theories, are just what is needed to answer the questions which encapsulate the idea of intelligibility.

Under what conditions does it make sense to initiate an exploratory/technical project to try to push back the frontiers of experience in search of an exemplar of a natural kind whose characteristics have been adumbrated and whose existence has been anticipated by cognitive (theoretical) means? There are several relevant conditions:

1   The community must have some idea of the metaphysical category to which the being belongs. Which category – substance, relation, quality, process, and so on – it is will determine the way the search is conducted. For example if the being is thought to be a substance a search of space-time may turn up an exemplar.

2   The way the 'expedition' is finally put together, the equipment set up and the personnel recruited will be determined by the natural-kind to which an exemplary being would be supposed to belong.

3   To be sure that one has found an exemplar or to be satisfied that no such being exists, a description sufficiently detailed to be both identifying as to kind and (in the appropriate circumstances) individuating as to particularity must be available.

4   The expedition must have equipment adequate to achieve the appropriate enhancement of human sensory and motor capabilities necessary to make contact with such a being, if it exists. From the viewpoint of the philosophy of science, the wherewithal for looking for the Loch Ness monster must meet the same kind of general requirements as that needed to look for the anthrax bacillus: nets, filters, microscopes, sonar, and the like, equipment through which a physical relationship can be established between the thing sought and the person seeking it, if the thing exists.

Conditions 1–3 are met by the development of theory, while condition 4 is a requirement for technology, not itself innocent of theory.

To establish policy realism for theories whose major referents would be in Realm 2, that is would be objects of possible experience, it must be shown that a way of theorizing has developed in the sciences which meets conditions 1–3 above. These must be met in such a way that the mounting of exploratory 'expeditions' under the control of that kind of theory is a rational way of proceeding. By 'rational way of proceeding' I mean that by using a theory-family, of the kind to be described in what follows, to control search projects, one is in a better position to answer the existential questions prompted by theorizing than one would be if one had merely guessed, or adopted some other non-scientific strategy. It will also emerge that if one uses the methods of theorizing that scientists actually use as a model, rather than, say, the D-N conception of theory, one will also be at an advantage in the game of science, as scientists see it. A realist interpretation of theoretical terms, I shall argue, will make better sense of the practice of policy realism than any other reading.

The idea of epistemic access

In the course of several asides I have hinted at the repudiation of the idea of a science which accumulates once-for-all, unrevisable and definite discoveries. The old truth realism proved vulnerable to simple sceptical arguments just because it shared with foundationalisms of various kinds the idea that a science is composed of cognitive entities which, whether we can know it or not, are true. The favourite candidates for such entities for truth realists like Newton-Smith are laws of nature. Referential realism is not grounded on cognitive entities but on those material beings thrown up by the search procedures of the community. To break with truth realism I have had to emphasize the revisability of beliefs about such material beings. Could all such beliefs be revised? Referential realism would look pretty fragile if the very ontological category, belief in which grounded the search for the being in question, had to be revised in such a way that we would have to say the being did not exist. If this makes sense it would be analogous to the fatal discomfiture of a putative law of nature: not that it had some counter-examples, but that there was nothing to which it could be applied.

In a way this issue has been dealt with already in the discussion about the status of Pluto and Vulcan in chapter 2. As a general rule, when a search is successful, it reveals a being whose existence, relative to some generic ontological category, is not further revisable. This strong conclusion follows from the close relation between ontological category and method and realm of search. One searches for a putative thing in a rather different way from that in which one searches for a relation or an event. (Even this parallelism can be broken in extreme cases. As an ephemeral sunspot Vulcan can never be treated as a kind of planet.)But the more particularizing the *description* of the being in question the more vulnerable it is to revision. Bacteria do exist as hostile micro-organisms, but they do not fall under many of the same descriptions as did the alien *archae* of van Helmont.

Though still, it seems, hankering after referring as a cognitive rather than a material or practical activity, Boyd (1979) has introduced the term 'epistemic access' to describe what is achieved by communal agreement on the subject matter of discourse and research, the social act of fixing a referent. Once the entity is, so to speak, pinned down, knowledge-garnering can begin, including revisions of the criterial predications with which the search was directed and its conclusion assessed.

From the point of view of philosophical logic any search must begin with acts of Roberts's IP reference – 'Whatever is the cause of anthrax is a micro-organism' and must conclude with an act of DC reference: 'This rod-like being is a micro-organism and is the cause of anthrax'. The ontological category of the final term of an IP formula, derived from the metaphysical element in the kind of theorizing to be further described in chapter 11, determines the general mode of search, say a progress through likely locations of some region of space–time. Theorizing in Realm 2 must be capable of yielding IP referential statements. In so far as these formulations are possible, theorizing can be the basis for the kinds of projects typical of policy realism. One must remember that the point of the search is to establish a physical relation between an embodied person and a physical being resembling the model one set out to match. The physical relationship may be mediated by an apparatus. It is just as important to convince oneself that no such relationship could be established because no instances of the kind of being in question exist. Under what conditions is a pre-indicative reference of the Roberts IP type suitable for guiding a search, which may, of course, have a negative outcome? In what follows I shall be setting out a number of conditions the degree of fulfilment of which I believe is a useful basis for the assessment of theories as plausible or implausible. The twin concepts 'plausible' and 'implausible' are, I hope, sufficiently close to the cluster of concepts by which real scientists assess the products of scientific theorizing – that they can be treated as idealizations of the concepts in actual use. I will show that when the plausibility conditions are well satisfied it is reasonable to take the corresponding IP formulations of existence claims as good guides for searches of the material world. The policy of setting off to try to find exemplars of the beings whose properties are anticipated in theory is policy realism. Notice that policy realism is vindicated by both successful and unsuccessful outcomes to IP-controlled searches. The whole of this makes up an argument for policy realism as the variety of referential realism defensible for the sciences of beings that are located in Realm 2.

Formal structures for Realm 2 theorizing

Logicism offers an account that is meant to include the formal structure of any kind of theorizing, and so of Realm 2 theorizing. This is the familiar Cartesian deductive picture, recently revived as the D-N model of explanation. But for any given data base an indefinitely large set of alternative 'theories' can be created, from each of which the data base is deductively recoverable. There is no independent criterion for law-likeness available within logicist philosophy of science. It follows that successful D-N theorizing can have no ontological significance. Any research-guiding ontological assumptions, say that beta rays are streams of negatively charged particles, are, *from the point of view of a deductive account of the structure of theorizing*, merely optional extras. This unsatisfactory state of affairs appears in several aspects of the logicist account of the inner nature of theorizing. It appears for instance in the troubling consequence that explaining and predicting can differ in no other way than in the moment at which the logical operation of D-N deduction is performed.

I propose to accept, with only minor revisions, a truly radical proposal set out in Aronson's *A realist philosophy of science* (1984). The basic idea is that theories are mappings. But they are not mappings which project statements onto statements, say descriptions of initial conditions on to pre- or retrodictions of so far unobserved states of affairs. They map manifest phenomena (those which form Realm 1) on to unobserved states of affairs (those which are located in Realms 2 and 3). A theory links *real-world beings* just as a topographical map links my real-world journey with a material terrain, both real-world beings. (This idea was toyed with by Toulmin (1959).) The mapping which is a theory represents two kinds of real-world relations, material identity and cause–effect. In Realm 1 there are all kinds of phenomena, most of which are apparently independent of one another. Theory mappings, if successful as theories, map apparently independent phenomena on to the states of afffairs of a common ontology. Depending on the kind of beings that ontology countenances search projects, on the look out for exemplary instances, can be mounted. The molar properties of gases are mapped onto properties of swarms of molecules by kinetic theory. The kinematic properties of material bodies in fields, say accelerations, are mapped onto properties of the field, potentials. The kinetic theory of gases is a Realm 2 science because the common ontology to which its substantive terms refer involves beings of the same generic natural-kind as some category of observable beings, namely free chunks of tangible matter. Dynamics is a Realm 3 science, since the beings in its ontology of fields and their potentials have no analogue in the observable beings of Realm 1.

Aronson says (p. 171) that

theories explain by showing how phenomena which seem, at first, to be physically unrelated are actually aspects of a common or underlying ontology; that is *theories explain by virtue of their reference to objects*. Theories that are committed to different types of entities – different ontologies, such as atoms, waves, fields etc. – then explain phenomena differently and, hence, assign different probabilities to combinations of events [and coexistence of properties].

The art of theorizing is to 'reduce the number of independent phenomena'. But everything depends on how that trick is pulled off. The attempts by crypto-logicists like Kneale (1949) and Friedman (1974) will not do. They try to define 'independence' in logical terms, as lack of a common derivation from a higher level of logical order. Such a move was already shown to be unworkable in 1602 by the paradox of Clavius, the logical property of theories we now call the underdetermination of theory by data.

The first step in Aronson's treatment is an account of that 'independence' which is reduced by the creation of the mapping. On p. 174 he says that 'two phenomena are independent in that it is (physically) possible for one to occur without the other and vice versa.' At this point Aronson's doctrine is in debt to the reader for an account of physical possibility. The debt is paid, perhaps somewhat sketchily, in terms of the non-violation of known laws of nature. A state of affairs is physically possible if it does not violate any known law or combination of laws of nature. But what is it to reduce this independence? In general the apparently independent phenomena occur in Realm 1, within an ontology specified by the Kantian categories. This gives us some idea of what sort of independence to expect.

1   'Individual events [co-occurring] under a single set of conditions.' Thus one sort of reduction of independent phenomena involves showing how a cough and a fever are non-independent by a theory which treats them both as symptoms of the same disease, that is maps them on to states of affairs obtaining among a common set of beings, say viruses and human cells.

2   Another kind of independence obtains when there seem, at first sight, to be no real connections which could be described in a law-like way between any of the properties of one phenomenon and those of another. In this kind of reduction the scientific theory shows how it is possible for there to be one kind of being (ice) under some conditions, and another kind of being (water) under others, by mapping the phenomena on to different states of the same being, namely ensembles of water molecules.

How do theories bring about these kinds of reduction? According to Aronson (p.   175), 'theories reduce the number of independent phenomena and thereby explain them *by providing them with a common ontology.*' What is it to provide a common ontology? It is to show that 'these seemingly separate and diverse phenomena are all manifestations of the same system of objects.' Aronson himself places great weight on the identity relation as the (almost) exclusive interpretation of the mappings. Theories, then, from a logical point of view, are identity statements. Thus for him the way one shows that diverse phenomena are manifestations of the same system of objects is by discovering identity relations. The logical status of theories is therefore whatever is the logical status of identity statements. On Aronson's view it looks as if these must be analytic a posteriori. Identity relations are expressed in a variety of characteristic substantive-hungry predicates such as 'aspect of . . .', 'manifestation of . . .', etc, each having its own field of use.

But this will not do as an exhaustive account of the mappings. In some cases lengthy causal chains intervene between the states of affairs obtaining among the beings of the common ontology and the manifest phenomena. The gene theory of inheritance requires an identity relation between the blueness of eyes and a molecular structure in the iris, in so far as the former is treated as a secondary quality on Lockean lines, and the latter is the occurrent grounding of the appropriate power. But these molecular structures are linked by causal relations via messenger RNA, protein synthesis, and so on, to the structured ensembles of atoms that appear in DNA molecules, and are 'the' gene. The blueness of eyes is mapped on to some combination of genes, certainly, but not just by an identity relation. Similarly the line of silver atoms on the photograph of the track of a subatomic particle is mediated not only by various identity relations (the visible track *is* a vast assembly of such atoms) but also by the complex of causal processes we call collectively 'ionization'. The supplementation of Aronson's theory by the addition of causal to identity relations is entirely within the spirit of his account of the role and purpose of theory, and serves to strengthen and extend it. Two deep principles must lie at the back of the Aronson treatment. To accept it one must subscribe to Frege's notion of identity rather than to any version of Leibniz law. In an Aronsonian mapping, identicals are discernible. An aspect of the common ontology would be manifested in one way in Realm 1 and in quite another way in Realm 3, were there to be beings capable of perceiving in the mode of that realm. The Aronson treatment also requires one to subscribe to some principle of causation, which requires at least that causes and effects are distinct existences.

But there is still one key concept not yet explicated, that of 'ontology'. For Aronson an ontology is not a metatheory about what may be taken to exist, but a set of objects which have 'some properties in common'. In Aronson's book the notion of an ontology is sketched in only lightly. Clearly it bears some relation to Korner's (1974) categorial frameworks and Bunge's (1973) basic models. However, since for Aronson an ontology is a set of objects and not a cognitive entity which describes, prescribes or in any other way refers to or describes objects, it is not of the same order as Korner's or Bunge's 'ontologies'. For my part I propose to take 'ontology' in a more traditional way as a component of the cognitive apparatus of scientific thought. Whichever way the concept is taken, the Aronsonian account of theories is incomplete. Ontologies are simply treated as *there*. In the next chapter I turn to a further step in the analysis of theorizing, by which the formal treatment I have just described must be matched. This will be an analysis of theorizing in search of those features of content which mark out scientific explanations.

11
Theory-Families and the Concept of Plausibility

Cognitive objects and content structures

A number of authors, including T. S. Kuhn (1962) with his 'paradigm' and I. Lakatos (1970) with his 'hard core of a research programme', have pointed out that the unit of scientific thinking is not the theory, as it might be 'the Clausius–Maxwell theory of gases' or 'the theory of cognitive dissonance'. These are static, synchronic descriptions of moments in the development of cognitive entities of higher order. For various reasons I prefer to call these higher order cognitive entities 'theory-families'. They are the bearers of the content of the successive theories that are 'taken off' them as they evolve. Their structure is the content structure of a set of theories, unified by the incorporation of a common metaphysics, or a common categorial framework (in the terminology of Korner, 1974) or a common ontology (to adopt Aronson's vocabulary).

At the heart of a theory-family is an entity I shall call 'an ideal cognitive object'. I believe that what we recognize as theories and as taxonomic systems are manifestations of states of such ideal cognitive objects. An object of this sort can belong to an individual human being, or it may be distributed among several people, or it could be the possession of a wider community. When anthropologists of science claim that the social structure of scientific communities reflects the necessary conditions for the production of scientific texts, these texts are best seen as drawn off from a more fundamental kind of cognitive being, the ideal cognitive object. Such beings are extended in time, but they have no special mode of existence. They can be represented in several different ways, iconically, linguistically or by means of abstract mathematical structures. In writing about such beings I shall be using language to describe iconic expressions of such objects as a matter of expository convenience. In discussing the role of visualizability in the formation of physical concepts, Miller (1984) has highlighted the subtle influence of iconic expressions on the thought of physicists. His quasi-psychological observations closely match a philosophical point to be emphasized in this chapter, namely the natural-kind constraints on conceptions of unobserved entities upon which the possibility of policy realism depends. A distinguishing feature of the structure of such objects is that their constitutive relations are semantic and intensional, creating an organization of content. They are not ordered, in any fundamental way, by principles drawn from logic.

The structure of theory-families

Behind explicit scientific discourses lie ideal cognitive objects formed by the union of two major components. There is an 'analytical analogue or model' through which the world of human perceptual experience is made to manifest patterns of various kinds of order. And there is the 'source analogue or model' from which theoreticians draw their concepts for building plausible explanations for the existence and evolution of such patterns.

As I have argued in detail in chapter 8 one must assume that common experience is first differentiated and categorized with respect to some cluster of loosely organized common sense schemes, scarcely well integrated or simple enough to be described as theories. There are no brute facts. But further selections from common experience and more refined categorizations of phenomena require the use of supplementary schemes. Many of these take the form of analogues 'brought up to' items of common experience. They sharpen our grasp of the patterns that are implicit in the experience or that can be made to emerge from it, by the similarities and differences they force us to take account of. When an analogue is used for such a purpose I call it 'analytical'. Analytical analogues can be used in a great variety of ways. Sometimes entertaining an analogue simply helps an observer to see a pattern that is already there, so to speak, in what ordinarily can be seen. The young Darwin looks at the bewildering diversity of plants and animals, both living and extinct, with the eye of an English countryman, that is with the analogy of farming, gardening and breeding in mind. He sees lines of descent, blood ties, etc. , where another observer (Captain Fitzroy, for instance) might see the manifestation of God's munificence. But sometimes the analogue transforms experience by suggesting an experimental programme. Largely I believe by reason of its theological implications Boyle had a keen interest in the nature of the vacuum and in finding an explanation for the apparent absence of vacua in nature. If the air were springy it would expand to fill any vacua that tended to form in natural processes. A natural phenomenon forbade vacua, if that were so. To study the 'spring of the air' Boyle made use of an explicit analogy between metal springs and the way they could be studied, and air springs and how they might be investigated. His famous apparatus is a gaseous analogue of a coil spring suffering progressive compression under increasing weights.

I have described these analytical analogues iconically, but they could just as well have been described as conceptual systems. I claim that it is cognitive entities of this sort that are an essential part of the ideal cognitive objects that underlie theorizing, and so must form part of evolving theory-families. Their role is to provide the classificatory categories by means of which experienced reality is given texture, both as a patterned flow of phenomena and as differentiable into kinds. There will be as many clusters of phenomena available in common experience and its experimental extensions as there are analytical analogues to engender them. Nature, as experienced, may not 'take' a particular analytical analogue. There may be no emerging facts. The theory of 'signatures' was just such an analytic analogue – that there were iconic illustrative properties by which plants, flowers, fruits, and so on, with medicinal virtues, were marked. In Boyle's researches into the spring of the air, the patterned phenomena (volume/pressure proportions) are not natural phenomena, but are properties of an artefact, the apparatus constructed on the basis of the analytic analogue. In other cases analytical analogues serve to reveal texture and pattern without the use of an intervening apparatus. Darwin's 'agricultural' point of view is a case in point, but the use of such analogues is ubiquitous in good science. Goffman (1969) asked his readers to look on the loose groupings of people that act together in everyday life as 'teams', intent on maintaining the impressions they make in the eyes of others. This famous analytical analogue brings out aspects of the behaviour of all sorts of people, including nurses and receptionists in health clinics, that would have been difficult if not impossible to discern without the potent Goffmanian image. There are no 'given' patterns in nature and human behaviour. The results of observation and experiment are the product of sometimes quite complex chains of analogical reasoning.

The second major component of a theory-family is its source analogue. It is from the source analogue or analogues that the material for building concepts or representations of unobservable processes, mechanisms and constitutions is drawn. Deep within the cognitive foundations of the kinetic theory lies the analogue relation that molecules *are like* Newtonian particles. The way the concept of 'molecule' is developed in successive theories of the behaviour of gases (within the framework of the one developing theory-family) is controlled by the possibilities inherent in the concept of the Newtonian particle. One of the most elegant and one might even say spectacular uses of an explicit source model is in Darwin's own exposition of the theory of natural selection. The steps that lead up to the introduction of the concept of natural selection are managed through an analogy with domesticity. The first part of Darwin's book is occupied with detailed descriptions of the breeding of plants and animals in domesticity, together with discussions of the variation that is found in successive generations of domestic animals and plants. The upshot could be expressed in a kind of formula:

> Domestic variation acted on by domestic selection leads to domestic novelty (e.g. new breeds).

As the second chapter unfolds Darwin takes his readers through a great many examples of natural variation and natural novelty, the appearance of new species. We are carried along by the narrative to the point where we are driven to contemplate another 'formula':

> Natural variation acted upon by (. . . ? . . .) leads to natural novelty (e. g. new species).

The rhetorical force is irresistible and we find ourselves making Darwin's great conceptual step ourselves. The unknown and unobservable mechanism of speciation must be natural selection.

The reasoning is analogical, and, as the theory-family develops the limits of the analogy need to be examined through explicit statements of the positive and negative components in the analogy relation. Darwin systematically deletes some of the common implications of the term 'selection' from his scientific concept. His deletions include volition and any personifications of the natural forces involved.

The basic structure of the theory-family derives from the exigencies of explanation. In a great many cases the use of analytical analogues reveals patterns among phenomena, for whose explanation the community may be at a loss. The deficit is made good by imagining causal processes which could produce them. But, in the first instance, these processes will usually be unobservable, if real, in that people could not experience them in the same way as they experience the patterns the existence of such processes would explain. Reference to unobservable causal mechanisms and the beings upon whose existence they depend must involve the use of terms which denote beings which are, at that time, beyond experience. In short the community cannot tell what is producing the phenomena of interest by looking, touching, or listening. Just to guess is to leave open too wide a range of possibility. It is to remedy the lack of 'microscopical eyes (and ears)' that the *controlled* imagining of what those processes and beings might be begins. The role of source analogues is essential to this cognitive activity. It is from these that the community of scientists draws the images and the conceptual systems, with the help of which the cognitive work of pushing the imagination beyond experience is achieved in a disciplined way.

Looked at this way the methodology of theorizing can be described in four steps.

1   Methodological step: an analytical analogue is used to elicit a pattern or patterns from nature.
2   Theoretical principle: observed patterns are caused by unknown productive processes, and the clusters of properties that mark putative kinds are manifestations of unknown constitutions.
3   Theoretical principle: an analogue of the observed process can be thought (imagined, for instance) to be caused by some analogue of the real but unknown productive process.
4   Methodological step: the analogue of the real productive process or 'inner' constitution is conceived (imagined) in conformity to the source analogue.

I illustrate how this activity creates a semantically organized theory-family for the explanation of an observed process, a patterned sequence of event-types. Within this structure there are three analogy relations:

  (i)   An analytical analogy between the analytical analogue and the observed pattern.
 (ii)   A behavioural analogy between the behaviour of the analogue of the real productive process and the behaviour of the real productive process itself (which we already know, since it is revealed in the observed pattern).
(iii)   A material analogy between the nature of the imagined productive process and the nature of the source analogue.

The behavioural and material analogies control the way the community conceives a hypothetical generative mechanism or process which would, were it to be real, produce the patterns revealed by the use of the analytical analogue. It is important to see that hypothetical generative processes so conceived are, strictly speaking, analogues of whatever the real productive processes might be. We know from experiment and observation, within the conceptual possibilities constrained by the analytical analogue, how the real productive mechanism behaves. We imagine, through the joint constraints of the behavioural and material analogies, what that mechanism or process might be like. These relationships can be summed up in the following schema, representing the structure of a theory-family. In the schema the double arrow represents a real-world relation; all the other relations are conceptual. In some treatments the conceptual entity I have called an imagined generative mechanism or process is called an 'explanatory model'.

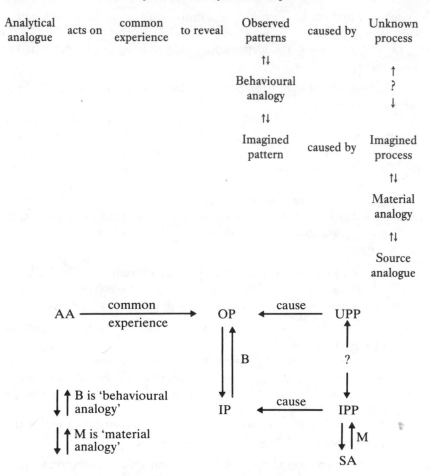

Figure 11.1   Schematic representation of a theory-family

Schematically the structure of a theory-family can be laid out as in figure 11.1.

The realist reading of this account of theorizing is created just by adding a fifth step to the methodology.

5   Epistemological claim: the hypothetical productive process or mechanism, conceived with the aid of the constraints embedded in the relevant theory-family, represents, to some degree, the nature of the real productive process or mechanism, when the theory-family is in a condition such that the theory which describes that moment in its evolution is plausible. The justification for picking out certain observable clusters of

properties as something like the nominal essences of natural-kinds by reference to the relevant constitutive (and unobservable) micro- or macrostructures as real essences follows exactly the same pattern.

The next step in the analysis will be to give an account of plausibility and implausibility of theory-families, by reference to their momentary condition. I must emphasize that I am defending policy realism, not truth realism. It is no part of my account to suppose that the plausibility of a theory justifies the claim that the hypothetical productive mechanism or process it describes is just like the real one, or that implausibility would ground the dismissal of such a claim. Rather I argue that in the condition that a theory is plausible it represents a moment in the history of a theory-family, when the policy of undertaking a search through the appropriate referential realm for exemplars of the entities imagined (conceived) in the act of theorizing makes good sense.

The above schema is to be read in the iconic mode, that is it refers to patterns, properties, things, processes, and so on, real and imagined. A corresponding 'discourse' schema could be constructed for a science, in which each element in the above schema is replaced by a description. Such a discourse schema could be used to analyse scientific publications. When the explicit formal discourse of the scientific community is matched against this schema it becomes clear that only a very small part of it is reproduced in normal scientific writing. Usually only the observed patterns and the hypothetical generators of those patterns are described. The rest of the discourse is taken for granted, with some notable exceptions. When great scientific writers such as Darwin or Hales are writing up their work, much more of the implicit discourse of the scientific community comes to be laid out explicitly. I believe that for expository purposes it is better to describe the components of theory-families and their interrelations in the iconic mode, since the complexity of a discourse which did justice to the implicit analogies and their interrelations in a discursive mode would be formidable.

A theory-family develops in response to two kinds of external pressures. There is the need to accommodate new experimental results, which refine our knowledge of the manifest patterns of behaviour of the real causal mechanisms operative in some field of phenomena. These are accommodated by adjustments of the behavioural analogy which spark off adjustments of the material analogy. But there are also changes in the theoretical background to the theory-family which come about by further developments of the source analogue. These lead to adjustments in the conception of the hypothetical generative mechanisms and processes at the heart of the theory-family, through the material analogy. And in their turn they suggest new domains of research through the behavioural analogy which links their imagined behaviour to manifest experimental or observational patterns. I reserve the detailed exposition of examples of these processes of adjustment to the section on plausibility and implausibility.

Any theory of theories that is to merit attention must account for the meanings of theoretical terms in the scientific discourse, in particular the way in which theoretical terms have an excess of meaning over that which accrues to them simply from the empirical consequences that follow from their incorporation into a theory. I propose that the cognitive processes (mainly judgements of likeness and difference) which are involved in working with structures such as that sketched above determine the meanings of the lexical items that appear in the corresponding discourse. Ideally the etymology of theoretical terms should parallel the way theoreticians come to conceive of the hypothetical mechanisms, processes and constitutions which the terms are used to describe. Since the hypothetical generators of observed patterns are conceived by analogy with known generators of known patterns, the source analogue of the relevant theory-family, the terms descriptive of those hypothetical generators should be thought to acquire their meaning by parallel processes. The tropes of simile and metaphor would seem to be the obvious candidates. Both are linguistic devices which create new meaning from within the resources of a lexical system, and make no use of ostension to extralinguistic exemplars. In the case of simile, extralinguistic input is required for the literal meaning of the term to be used, but its use as a simile does not depend upon a point-by-point comparison between the first and second subject. Rather it creates that comparison. It invites the reader to look at the second subject in such a way as to emphasize certain aspects of it. Metaphor too extends the contexts of use of terms already having literal meaning, which may indeed have been based on extralinguistic exemplars, but it is used for just those occasions when we do not possess the linguistic resources to express what it is about the second subject that has struck us. It is not a comparison, but a catachresis. (See chapter 3.)

So far I have left the source analogue unanalysed. The role of a source analogue in a theory-family is to provide and maintain a set of natural-kind rules within which hypothetical entities are to be designed. But for a realist construal of those entities in terms of a material practice of seeking concrete exemplary instances of such beings, a mode of reference must also be given. As we have seen in the general discussion of natural-kind concepts in chapter 5 modes of reference, for instance 'pointing to a spatio-temporal location', 'testing a material substance for its ability to display a certain disposition in appropriate circumstances' and so on, are bound up with the implicit metaphysical component in the structure of the intensions of such concepts. Source analogues as the progenitors of natural-kind rules should also be structured so as to incorporate the necessary metaphysics to prescribe this or that determinate mode of reference. It turns out that this is indeed just how source analogues are structured. Domestic selection as the source analogue for natural selection constrains the metaphysics of speciation within a 'material process' categorial framework. Its one-time rival, as a source analogue, creationism, constrains the metaphysics of speciation within an 'act' categorial framework. Each source analogue further constrains the hypothetical entities involved in the theory of speciation with regard to the kind of process or kind of act hypothesized. The metaphysical component of the source analogue determines what kind of demonstration is required to establish a physical relation between the entity in question and an embodied human scientist, the necessary link for a proof of the existence of the beings proposed in the theory. The natural-kind rules determine, in a general way, the features to be looked for in deciding whether a putative specimen should be recognized as an exemplar of the kind of being in question. The metaphysical component then plays a central role in the setting up of the search procedures that are consequential on a policy-realist reading of a moment of equilibrium (plausibility) in the evolution of a theory-family.

Finally I need to show that the content structure of Realm 2 discourse, theorizing aimed at working out what must be the characteristics of beings which could, with technical advance, become objects of human experience, is just the structure that would make theories considered as descriptions of the state of a theory-family at some moment of equilibrium, mapping functions of the Aronson type. That is to say, theories become devices by which phenomena are mapped on to aspects of some common ontology. I owe a neat formulation of this point to Craig Dilworth. The two analogy relations, which are the main structuring relations of the theory-family, create the mappings. The behavioural analogy relates the hypothetical generative mechanism to the nominal subject of the theory, say 'overt bodily characteristic', which would be the Aronsonian 'phenomenon' to which genetics as a theory-family is directed. The material analogy relates the hypothetical mechanism of inheritance to the source analogue. This is the concrete form that the aspects of an Aronsonian common ontology for genetics would take. In this way there is created a mapping to aspects of the nature of genes, as complexes of chemically defined units, which are the real subject of the theory. Aronsonian mapping is the abstract or formal structure of theories considered as expressing or representing moments of temporary equilibrium in the unfolding of a theory-family. They play the role that deductive-nomological structures played in the logicist-empiricist view of theories.

Plausibility and implausibility

Judgements of the relative plausibility of theories are based, I believe, on a sense of the structure of the implicit content of the theory. This content is the current state of the cognitive object underlying theories of that kind, the theory-family. There seem to be five main aspects of a theory-family that influence asessments of plausibility and implausibility. I set them out as successive necessary conditions for making such a judgement.

1   The strongest condition necessary for a theory to be judged plausible is that it should represent a moment in the history of a theory-family at which there is a balance in the behavioural and material analogies. Precisely what is meant by a 'balance of analogies'? The idea is this:

(i)   Behavioural analogy: the better the imagined behaviour of the hypothetical generative or productive mechanism simulates the behaviour of the unknown real mechanism which actually produces the observed patterns, the more plausible is the theory which represents that moment in the development of the theory-family. The worse the simulation, the more implausible the theory.

(ii)   Material analogy: the more fully the imagined properties of the hypothetical generative or productive mechanism match the essential properties of the source model, that is those properties that define the natural-kinds it represents, the more plausible is the theory. This condition on the material analogy ensures that the reality-determining natural-kind rules which express the ontological commitments of this theory-family are conserved.

Balance has to do with the way the behavioural and material analogies are restored when a theory-family is disturbed either by new empirical discoveries or by theoretical innovations, or both. This can be illustrated with the later history of the gas laws.

When Amagat discovered systematic divergencies in the behaviour of gases at high pressures from those predicted on the basis of Boyle's law, the simple point molecule conception of the mechanism responsible for the behaviour described by the law had to be revised. Amagat realized that gas molecules would be more plausible existents if they were thought of as having volume as well as position and momentum, since they were modelled on Newtonian particles which are essentially extended. At high pressures the volume of the molecules themselves ('a') would reduce the effective space in which they could move to 'V − a'. By so modifying his conception of a gas molecule, adjusting the positive and neutral components of the material analogy, Amagat changed the theory-family in such a way that its new state could be represented in a theory which took the form of a revised gas law 'p(V − a) = k'. This law was deductively consistent with his results. In short he restored the behavioural analogy between the way the real but unknown structure of the gas manifested itself in the new conditions he had created, and the imagined behaviour of the hypothetical nature of gas as expressed in the theory. A theoretical 'gas', imagined now to consist of spatially extended molecules, would behave more like real gases had been shown actually to behave in experiments. The analogies had been rebalanced, restoring plausibility to the modified theory as it represents a moment in the life of the theory-family.

The history of the discovery of the positron (described in detail in Hanson, 1967) is a good example of the re-establishment of equilibrium after a theory-led disturbance in the relevant theory-family. Dirac's theoretical work led him to postulate the possibility of positively charged particles of the same order of magnitude as electrons. The actual story of the eventual matching of Anderson's experimental results with Dirac's theoretical concept is rather complex, but from the perspective of this analysis it represents the restoration of the balance of behavioural and material analogies in that theory-family. This example is borderline in that both electrons and positrons are perhaps best considered to be Realm 3 entities, not of the same metaphysical status as ordinary kinds. It is worth a reminder that what I have in mind in this discussion is not the demonstration of the existence of a hitherto unknown kind of being, but the restoration of the key analogies, so that the behaviour of a hypothetical generative mechanism, which theory describes, is analogous to the behaviour of the real corresponding mechanism of nature, which experiment has revealed.

Since the body of data upon which intuitive judgements of plausibility and implausibility are based includes both observed patterns of phenomena and the content of the source analogue which specifies the natural-kinds of the proposed hypothetical entities, and since plausibility is adjusted to the strength of the analogies based upon both the observed patterns and the source analogue, the assessment of plausibility and implausibility is fully determined by the data. In this scheme the difficulty which Quine called the underdetermination of theory by data does not occur. It is easy to see now why, if data are confined to experimental or observational results, there seems to be underdetermination.

The first component in the concept of 'plausibility of *a* theory' can be set out as follows:

A theory is plausible in so far as it represents a condition of a theory-family in which the material and behavioural analogies are 'in balance'.

A theory-family is in an imbalanced state, and the theory representing that moment is implausible, if either a behavioural advance has not been remedied by a change in material analogy (Amagat) or a change in material analogy has not been remedied by an advance in the behavioural analogy.

2   A theory-family in balance is the more plausible as its component analogies are strong. Various intuitive formulae can be developed for the representation of the comparative strength of analogies. The strength of an analogy depends on the relations between its positive component (likenesses between source and subject), its negative component (differences between source and subject) and its neutral component (those properties of the source whose likeness or difference from properties of the subject has yet to be explored). Generally an analogy is the stronger as the positive analogy outweighs the negative analogy, and both outweigh the neutral analogy. There are various matters of philosophical interest in defining 'measures' of weight and I postpone a detailed discussion of the assessment of the strength of analogies for a separate section. For the moment it will be enough to suggest that the more the comparison between source and subject, the two terms of the analogy, has been explored, and the more of the aspects studied that have turned out to be likenesses, the stronger is the analogy.

Part of the difficulty that geologists found with the early versions of Wagener's hypothesis of continental drift and plate tectonics (Hallam, 1973) seems to have been the fact that the analogy between continental masses and floating bodies had not been thoroughly explored. The neutral analogy was too large.

3   A theory-family which at a certain moment in its development is in balance, with strong analogies, is the more plausible in so far as the material analogy preserves the natural-kind rules for beings from whom the source analogue of the material analogy is derived. When Pasteur used analogical reasoning to develop his theory of disease he made an explicit comparison between suppuration and fermentation. Using the natural-kind conservation principle he inferred that if suppuration is like fermentation then there must be micro-organisms involved (bacteria) that are like yeasts. The causal agents of the infection of wounds are of the same natural-kind as the causal agents of the fermentation of liquors. And so the theory of disease as caused by micro-organisms is the more plausible. But when the attempt to balance the behavioural and material analogies calls for changes in the natural-kind rules characteristic of the source analogue in defining the entities of the theory the theory-family can slide into a state of implausibility. The putative reality of the imagined entities is undermined. It is this kind of difficulty that made it seem unreasonable to undertake a search for biological entelechies.

4   Since there are two independent sources of concepts for any theory-family, namely the analytical analogue (or model) and the source analogue (or model) the question of their interrelation can be raised. This provides us with a fourth feature that seems to go into judgements of relative plausibility, namely the degree of co-ordination between analytical analogue and source analogue. A theory-family in balance, with strong analogies, preserving natural-kind rules, is the more plausible in so far as its analytical and source analogues are co-ordinate, that is drawn from the same general conception of the empirical realm to which they apply.

For instance in ethogenic psychology the analytic scheme for picking out relevant social patterns is based on an analogy between social action and staged performances, the dramaturgical model. A co-ordinate source analogue would be 'person as actor following a script'. An ethogenic account of a social event is the more plausible in so far as the the explanatory theory, developed for the problematic behaviour in question, uses concepts based on those of actor and script, such as 'knowledge of role'. A measure of implausibility would infect an explanation for which the material analogy for the generative process was a socio-biological source, with concepts like 'gene selection', while the analytical analogue continued to enforce an analysis of behaviour in terms of concepts appropriate to the description of a staged performance.

This component of (im)plausibility can be given a Kantian turn. It is equivalent to the principle that the schematisms by which experience is ordered should be in one-to-one correspondence with the categories in terms of which one's whole cognitive apparatus is organized. But in the building of a plausible scientific theory it is by no means sure that such a correspondence can be achieved. It is a desideratum which has to be actively pursued.

The four components of the concept of '(im)plausibilty' could be mapped on to a four-dimensional space somewhat as in figure 11.2. The breadth of the trace represents the degree of co-ordination between analytical and source analogues. But there is a further consideration.

5   Popper and others have pointed out that our confidence in a theory grows with its successful passage of tests of various kinds. This idea was originally proposed for a deductivist conception of theories and their testing, but the same principle can be applied to the more elaborate structure described here. Meeting the above four desiderata can be thought of as passing tests. If a theory-family has the resources to develop so that it still meets the four desiderata late in its history so much the more plausible must that late moment of equilibrium appear as a particular theory. The fact that the kinetic theory of gases has survived successive modifications, but all

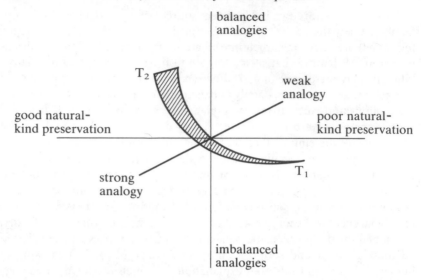

Figure 11.2   A graphical representation of the concept of plausibility

within the basic overall scheme defined by its analytical and source models, is, I believe, a ground for holding that the most recent version merits our assent as a plausible theory. I offer these five conditions for plausibility as contributions to spelling the useful but the rather vague terms, 'disadvantage' and 'advantage', which I have taken up from Miller's arguments cited in chapter 2. But one must bear in mind that each successive 'theory' is a representation of a moment of equilibrium in a continuous history of adjustments within a theory-family. The Darwinian evolutionary theory-family and the theory-family developed around the concept of 'electron' can easily be shown to have evolved along the same lines as the kinetic theory-family.

If all five desiderata have been met, something more can be said about the nature of the cognitive object I have called a theory-family. The fact that the interrelations between the parts are constitutive of those parts, that is the analogy relations serve to determine the meanings of the concepts in the theory-family at this or that moment in its history, shows that a theory-family is a *structure*. The changing balance between the behavioural and material analogies preserves this structure against the disruptive effect of certain disturbances. There are internal mechanisms of adjustment which maintain the integrity of the whole. The existence of these mechanisms suggests that a theory-family is not only a structure but could be usefully thought of as a *system*. This suggests the possibility of further study of theory-families directed to a more detailed analysis of their system properties. It may also be the case that the social structure of scientific teams that work with theory-families mirrors the structure of those theory-famiies, and that the conversations within the team apropos their researches have system properties.

With the strict system of theory assessments displaced to the ethics of science, and the deductivist scheme of analysis reduced to a reflection of a mere heuristic and pragmatic aid to using parts of theory-families more effectively, plausibility, implausibility and complex structures of analogical relationships must fill the gap. But there are several ways in which (im)plausibility judgements differ from truth and falsity. For instance the grounds for plausibility judgements cannot be mapped on to either of the grounds implicit in the traditional theories of truth. (Im)plausibility is not measured by degree of correspondence with the facts, nor is it an expression of the degree of coherence of the theory in question with other theories. Relative (im)plausibility assessments partake in some measure of each. There is a kind of correspondence in the use of observed patterns as a test for the behavioural analogy between the unknown real generators of those patterns and the hypothetical productive process imagined in accordance with the content of the theory-family. There is a kind of coherence in the requirement that our conceptions of the hypothetical mechanisms assumed in theories should be constrained by a material analogy to a source analogue which represents the kind of world we think we are exploring.

An important aspect of the concepts of truth and falsity is their use in defining the logical particles or truth-functions. If theory T_1 is true and theory T_2 is false then their logical conjunction T_1 *and* T_2 is false, and so on. If T_1 is true then not-T_1 is false. And there are many other familiar combinations. If 'true' and 'false' are transferred to the moral universe of the social order of scientists, what sort of meaning are we to give to the logical particles in theory-family discourse? I owe to Jonathan Bennett the idea of testing the way 'plausibility' and 'implausibility' work, and of more carefully establishing the meaning of 'and', 'or' and 'not' in so far as they are used to form complexes of theories.

Certain useful qualifications of the use of these concepts immediately become obvious, when Bennett's suggestion is pursued. Time must be taken into account. Two successive states of equilibrium of the same theory-family may be equally plausible, since their plausibility will be relative to the state of empirical knowledge and theoretical sophistication at any time. But to form a conjunction of the two theories, except in the purely historical sense that perhaps the scientific community once held the former *and* now holds the latter, makes no sense. Boyle's law and the Clausius model and

Amagat's law and his model cannot be conjoined, since when the interface is 'zipped up' contradictions appear. A molecule cannot both have and lack volume. This points up the fact that, in this way of looking at science, and the same goes for Lakatos' view as well, successive theories are determinates under the same determinable. The fact that Boyle's and Amagat's laws cannot be conjoined is the same kind of fact that blue and red cannot be jointly predicated of the same thing at the same time.

However, determinates can always be disjoined, and indeed one way of interpreting the determinable under which they fall is as the disjunction of its determinates. A disjunction of plausible theories within the same theory-family is that theory-family. And if the disjunction contains at least one plausible theory and it is the latest in the the development of that family, then the family is plausible, by condition 5 above. Again a temporal condition must be imposed on the 'molecular' structure.

If we try to form conjunctions or disjunctions of theories drawn from different theory-families, in any other sense than as mere catalogues of what the French Academy, say, believed in 1775, we run into further complexities. A conjunction of plausible theories could be assessed for epistemic value, and the infection of an implausible conjunct represented only if there were some melding of source analogues (in Aronsonian terms, some degree of mapping on to a common ontology). Consilience (non-contradictory conjunction of empirical hypotheses on a combined data base) would increase plausibility of the conjunction over any of its conjuncts taken separately only if ontological melding had occurred. There would be an increase in implausibility if there were an ontological clash. Further pursuit of these minutiae does not strike me as likely to prove fruitful, since the discussion so far has brought up two extra-logical matters which seem to exert a determining influence over how our intuitions should go. These are the temporal order of theories, as they reveal the way a theory-family has unfolded; a theory-family might unfold in various ways. The second matter is the degree to which a common ontology (common source analogue) can be created out of the theory-families relevant to each conjoined or disjoined theory. And this last seems to me to be a matter of content not form.

Finally, is the negation of a plausible theory implausible? It will depend a good deal on how much of the engendering theory-family is expressed in the theory, and thus to what parts of the theory-family structure negation is to be applied. If it is no more than that which appears in the printed scientific paper, not much can be said. The negation of a plausible theory is nothing. However, if the source model is contradicted (molecules are not point masses) then it might seem that something like the truth-functional relation between affirmed and negated theories does hold. At least the negation, in this last sense, of an implausible theory, may be plausible – *but only if the content is right*. It certainly now looks very unlikely that the meaning of the logical particles, as used in a metatheoretical discourse is particularly illuminated by the study of the relationships between plausibility and implausibility.

The strength of analogies: a metrical metaphor

Assessments of (im)plausibility, I have suggested, depend on a theoretician's intuition of the balance between the strength of the behavioural and material analogies of a theory-family. I offered a mere sketch of the idea of 'strength of an analogy' above. It can usefully be filled out a little. The strength of the behavioural analogy is greater if the positive analogy – that is, the similarities between the imagined behaviour of the hypothetical generative mechanism and the actual behaviour of the real generators of natural patterns – predominates over the negative analogy (the dissimilarities). But the more aspects of the possible behaviour of the hypothetical generative mechanisms which have been tested, whether they turn out to be similarities to or differences from the behaviour of the real generators, relative to all the ways these behaviours could be compared (the neutral analogy), the stronger the overall behavioural analogy. These relations can be expressed in an algebraic metaphor. Let pA, nA and tA 'measure' the positive, negative and neutral analogies.

Consider two behavioural analogies A_1 and A_2, say a gas behaves as a swarm of point particles behave, and a gas behaves as a random ensemble of 'plump' molecules behaves. We might compare them for strength by reference to the preponderance of likenesses and differences. There are more differences and fewer similarities in the former analogy than in the latter, so we believe. Thus

$$pA_1 - nA_1 < pA_2 - nA_2$$

expresses our intuition that the latter analogy is stronger than the former.

But we might also be impressed by the extent to which the neutral analogy of some model had been explored, compared with another. For instance some of the opposition to Wagener's hypothesis was the degree to which features of the 'floating continent' idea (A_2) were unexplored. Thus

$$pA_1 + nA_1 - tA_1 > pA_2 + nA_2 - tA_2$$

These formulae are not intended to be the basis of a serious calculus for 'strength of analogy' measures. For one thing they do not take into account the quality of the similarities, differences and undetermined properties of the relata. Similarities in behaviour may be few, but involving important properties, while dissimilarities may be many involving only unimportant properties. How is the relative importance of properties to be decided?

Any suggestion of a numerical measure of the relation between source analogue and subject presupposes criteria for individuating and identifying properties. For instance, it might be important for comparative purposes to treat degree of heat and hue (determinate colour) as distinct properties in assessing the balances of likenesses and differences. But whether they should be treated as distinct will depend upon the level of analysis. In some contexts, such as metallurgy, hue is used as a measure of degree of heat. Relative to some underlying conception of molecular behaviour, hue and degree of heat might not be considered distinct. This is another sort of case illuminated by Aronson's concept of 'mapping on to a common ontology'.

But this suggests a way of ordering properties by relative importance. The greater the number of distinct superficial properties that can be grounded in a deeper property (mapped onto an item in a common ontology) the more important the deeper property. Thus, electron configuration of the sub-atomic structure of the atoms of an elementary substance is an important property, while atomic mass is of lesser importance. But one should not be tempted into trying to devise a quantitative index of importance on the basis of what seems to be a purely ordinal notion. And how do we pick out 'distinct superficial properties' from one another? How many of these are there in the colour spectrum for instance? I have touched on the problem of imposing a discrete parsing on a property continuum in discussing Mendel's researches. Again there is no general solution to the problem of how this can be done. In Mendel's case the basis was the atomistic concept of genetic factor, and this overrode the continuity characteristic of the varieties of any property found in nature.

Assessment of the strength of the material analogy is more complex. There are certain minimal conditions an entity must meet to be said to have a certain mode of being. Different ontologies will set different metaphysical limits to the possibility of existence. For instance a Cartesian materialism requires that a material being be spatially extended. Dynamical materialism, in the manner of Boscovich, required only that the centre of a field of force emanating from a material being be located at a point in space–time.

In assessing the strength of the material analogy one must take into account the requirement that the negative analogy between source analogue and the basic entities presumed in the physical groundings of a productive process does not transgress the minimal conditions for the existence of things of the natural-kinds of the source analogue. The fewer of the properties that define the minimal conditions for existence that appear among the similarities and the more that are in the neutral analogy and so undetermined, the more likely it will be that in further developments of the theory the metaphysical limits of the source analogue will be transgressed in the specification of the analogy in the associated hypothetical productive process. The worse the transgression, the weaker the material analogy and the less plausible the theory. For instance, the original kinetic theory of gases was weak, *vis-à-vis* the material analogy. Molecules, though analogues of the material particles that formed the source analogue, were imagined as mere points, and it was undetermined whether they should be thought of as having volume. The addition of volume to their properties in the later theories strengthened the material analogy relative to the Newtonian source analogue.

The relation between properties whose status has been determined and those so far undetermined has a similar effect on our intuitions concerning the strength of a material analogy as it does on intuitions about behavioural analogies. While much of the neutral analogy remains undetermined, it is full of potential surprises. The larger the neutral analogy relative to the positive and negative analogies, the weaker the analogy overall, and the less plausible the theory.

A place for the 'semantic' theory

The relationship I have called the 'behavioural analogy' can be represented as a similarity relation between the forms of laws. One law sentence describes the behaviour of the natural causal mechanism, the other that of the hypothetical or imaginary causal mechanism which is the heart of a Realm 2 theory. Thus in physics we often have cases of similarity between empirical laws like those describing the structure of the electromagnetic spectra of incandescent elements and laws describing a 'model universe', for instance those Bohr deduced from a description of his planetary model of atomic structure. There are very many such cases, for instance the pheno-menological general gas law $PV = RT$ and the formula derived within the Maxwell–Clausius kinetic theory $pv = \frac{1}{3}nmc^2$. (Or Stefan's law and Planck's description of an ensemble of mechanical oscillators).

It is to this small corner of the sentential expression of the cognitive structure of Realm 2 theoretical science that the Sneed-Stegmuller account of the nature of theories in physics applies, so far as I can see. This becomes clear when we look a little more closely at the relationship between a pair of laws which represent a behavioural analogy. The similarity relationship between laws can be described in set-theoretical terms as a mapping from one set on to another. The first set is the ordered list of observational results representing the behaviour of the natural causal mechanism under study, relative to the imposition of a conceptual system on its field of behaviour powerful enough to engender data. The second set is the set of pairs, triples, etc., represented by a function which is the mathematical core of the hypothetical law of the imagined behaviour of the hypothetical generative mechanism which is the cognitive core of the theory. Any set of experimental results is, of course, a member of the 'Sneed' set of intended applications of the theory. So the 'semantic' account of theories is just another (and, I am inclined to say, more obscure) way of describing the situation that obtains when the behavioural analogy at a moment in the history of an evolving theory-family is good (cf. Sneed, 1971, pp. 250, 252–3).

From my point of view theory-families are maintained by preservation of main features of the intensional structure of the source analogue. I have identified these main features as rules specifying the natural kinds of that universe. They are the specific form that the ontology of *that* theory-family takes. For Sneed (1971) and Stegmuller (1979) something roughly like a theory-family is created by structural morphisms (mappings) between specialized laws (the set of which is the totality of (possible) intended (and intendable) applications), say $F = m\omega^2 r$, and the mathematical structures of the 'core', including in this case $F = ma$.

Both Sneed and Stegmuller (and I) deny that theory-families have a top-down structure – for instance axioms and boundary conditions leading deductively to specific law forms. We share the view that the structure is, so to speak, 'side-by-side'. But my account allows for a great many importantly different side-by-side relationships that could emerge as morphisms of mathematical structure. So far as I can see Sneed certainly, and Stegmuller probably, are committed to the view that their mappings are mediated by sets of numbers. By adopting the set-theoretical terminology Sneed and Stegmuller are unable to make the crucial distinction between extensional and intensional structural isomorphisms. Multiple analytical analogues coordinate with the source analogue, correspond to Sneed's 'I', the set of intended applications. But in my account these analytical analogues are not generally mediated by quantitative techniques, even in physics. When they are it is a very special case. Finally it is worth pointing out that the philosophically subordinate character of Sneed and Stegmuller's 'core desideratum' is acceptable only as a surrogate for a content rich-account of what is at the heart of a theory.

Networks or hierarchies?

It should now be clear why the 'network' image as an expression of the way conceptual systems or scientific discourses are organized will not do. Conceptual systems as embodied in the cognitive objects that underlie particular moments of explicit theoretical discourse are indeed structures of interconnected parts, but their organization is hierarchical. In the Aronsonian formal version of this account of theories they are mappings from real beings to real beings. This mapping imposes a hierarchical order on the concepts that would be needed to express the mapping discursively. Two hierarchical relations emerged in my discussion of Aronson's formal account: part to whole, and cause to effect. There may well be others. These relations are asymmetrical and transitive. As such their presence within the cognitive object from which theories are drawn off ensures a hierarchical inner organization to the conceptual core of the theory-family.

Hesse's (1974) account of the network image (echoing Quine, 1953, pp. 42–3) runs as follows (p. 28): 'any predicate may be more or less directly ascribed to the world in some circumstance or other, and that none is able to function in the language by means of such direct description alone.' This is precisely the consequence that would follow for the theory of scientific predicates from the dialectic account of the growth of theories (and kind concepts) brought about by the interplay of relatively practical and relatively theoretical contexts in governing the use of a term. But construing this in the *network* image suggests that there is no hierarchy in our beliefs. A much better image is that of a dialectical development, an image we owe to Whewell. The network picture tends to suggest that there is no difference in principle between the way a concept like 'Halley's comet' functions and the way a concept like 'intermediate vector boson' is used, while both differ from the way a concept like 'Africa' is used. With suitable equipment a human being could stand in the same physical relationship (or very nearly) to Halley's comet as they can to Africa. There could be no circumstances in which an embodied human being could become aware of an intermediate vector boson by landing on it, that is by establishing an unmediated physical relationship to it. Since the core of Halley's comet has turned out a roughly cylindrical lump, about 12 km. by 5 km. , about the size of the island of Sark, making a landfall is only a technical problem, and will no doubt be achieved next time it comes round.

There is a second dimension of hierarchy. The concepts by which hypotheses about possible generative mechanisms are formulated are controlled by the natural-kind rules implicit in the source analogue of the theory-family. A discursive expression of that source analogue, say in an explicit statement of the metaphysical presuppositions of a certain theory-family, Boyle's *Origins of forms and qualities*, for instance, must make use of concepts which subsume but are not subsumed by the concepts of any particular theory of this or that phenomenon. Boyle's generic mechanical concepts, 'bulk', 'figure', 'texture' and 'motion', take on specific characters in the theory of colour and others in the theory of chemical composition.

12

The Reasonableness of Policy Realism

An inductive argument for adopting policy realism

In my account of science the crucial moments in the continuous assessment of a theory-family are instantiation events, demonstrations of existence by the material/cognitive practice of locating a being in a prescribed referential grid, so establishing a physical relation between that being and an embodied scientist, and then finding that it satisfies a theory-based prescription as to individual or kind. Arriving in Australia, seeing Neptune, finding anthrax bacilli in the gut of earthworms – these are instantiation events.

What is the epistemic force of a successful or unsuccessful instantiation event? On my view it is not the confirmation or refutation of a hypothesis, for example of a universal law-like proposition. Rather, a series of favourable instantiation events leads to growing confidence in the use of the natural-kind rules embedded in the source analogue. Unfavourable instantiation events, finding nothing or perhaps something quite different where one was looking for an exemplar, tend to make a theoretician and indeed eventually the whole community lose confidence in those natural-kind rules as fruitful determinants of theoretical concepts. One would use natural-kind rules in deciding on the confirmatory power of the experimental or observational instantions of hypotheses, and one would certainly use them in grounding one's confidence in the counterfactuals associated with law-like statements. It is important to see how different is this idea from that of the traditional conception of evidential support. Evidential support has to do with explicit discourse, and in particular with discussions about isolated hypotheses. The theoretical liasons of such hypotheses are mere background information. According to the theory-family point of view, the assessment of the belief-worthiness of theoretical statements is based on the opinion of the community as to the plausibility of a theory-family at that moment in its development. A 'law' is usually assessed as an integral part of a theory-family, rarely in isolation.

The next step in the defence of policy realism is to link (im)plausibity of the theory-family to the (un)likelihood of the discovery in Realm 2 of beings meeting, more or less well, the prescriptions derived from the theory that represents that moment in the history of a theory-family. The satisfaction of the five plausibility conditions set out in the last chapter ensures the maintenance of the natural-kind assumptions that ground the identity of the theory-family during its development, whether it maintains its place in the body of scientific beliefs or falls away. They make possible the drawing up of existential prescriptions. The ontological component in the intension of a natural-kind term, the thinghood of bacilli for example, implies certain methods of referring. For germs this would be some form of of deixis, physical pointing. For each mode of reference there is a referential grid (in this example, space–time) which defines the matrix of real locations which are germane to the setting up of a search programme for entities of the kind mentioned in the theory and accepted or taken for granted by the community. The material analogy ensures that the way theoretical entities are conceived is by analogy with beings of natural-kinds which the community already knows exist – and for which, *a fortiori*, there is a method of referring and a referential grid. The 'balance' condition ensures that the entities conceived within the discourse of that theory-family are causally efficacious in the way required of them, namely that they should be capable of generating the patterns that show up in experiments and are seen in observations. Since we already know that domestic selection of domestic variants produces domestic novelties, new strains and breeds, the use of this schema as the analogue for natural selection only extends the domain of a causal/generative process which is already well known (though much about it remained to be understood in Darwin's time). A prescription 'drawn off' from a theory-family with that degree of integration is more likely to find an instantiation in the realm of possible experience than a mere invention at random or just a guess. Realism *as a policy* is still vindicated if the prescription, however plausible the theory-family, is not able to be instantiated. Theory can anticipate experience, and prescriptions can become descriptions. To have demonstrated that capillaries exist is to have settled the question of the referential force of the term 'capillary'. A being of the kind the term denotes can be causally related to the embodied observer. And, since they have been found, the search that Harvey's hypothesis ultimately prompted vindicates policy realism. As a theoretical term in Harvey's theory of the circulation of the blood the term ' capillary' or rather Harvey's (1649) synonym, 'invisible anastomoses', *must have already denoted something* and continued to do so through the long years before Malpighi's microscopical demonstration. During that time people were actually referring to little tubes whenever they used the term 'invisible anastomoses'.

Thus is Putnam's cry 'Oh for an argument to block the meta-induction that theoretical terms never refer [denote]!' answered. Some did, and no doubt there are plenty that still do.

There is an epistemology implicit in scientific practice. But unlike the epistemology of the 'bivalence' philosophers it makes use of the attainable judgements 'plausible' and 'implausible', and these are close to the scientific community's many and various surrogates for the unattainable 'true' and 'false'. Intuitions of plausibility and implausibility, which reflect the state of theory-families, most of whose content is not subject to explicit assessment, serve the rational man or woman as reasons for believing or disbelieving theories, provided they are members of that community which shares the tacit content of that fragment of the scientific culture.

The argument that links plausibility to representational quality runs as follows:

1   The commonsense truth or falsity of singular, descriptive statements can be decided for referents in Realm 1. Well-informed veterinary surgeons can say with a good deal of confidence whether or not a cow has contracted anthrax. There are characteristic symptoms.

2   Theoretical concepts, the content of which has been created by analogy with the content of concepts well established for Realm 1 discourses, if they have referents, will refer to Realm 2 beings. Anthrax bacilli, conceived as micro-organisms, are offered as the hypothetical agents responsible for anthrax symptoms. According to the criterion of balanced analogies the bacterial theory of anthrax is plausible. Expressed in words the theory would take the form of a Roberts IP statement: 'Whatever is the cause of anthrax symptoms is a bacillus.'

3   Some kinds of beings, originally in Realm 2, that is possible observables, become observable by virtue of technical advances, say in microscopy. Such advances gave Toussaint the capability to find anthrax bacilli by finding a definite space–time location (several in fact) in which there were beings which more or less fulfilled the prescriptions of the theory. As I showed in some detail in part two this transition of epistemic status is matched by a change in the form of referential sentence to Roberts's type DC: 'This micro-organism is the bacillus responsible for anthrax.' The deictic relation is a physical link mediated by microscopes.

Since it is unlikely that the community will generally be able to say in advance whether or not the boundary between Realms 1 and 2 is likely to 'move', we must allow that possibility for any plausible theory. Therefore the only reasonable strategy is to give a tentative realist reading to any referring expression in such a theory. We could call the principle that the plausibility of a theory makes it reasonable to undertake the material practice of searching for exemplars of its putative referents, 'Lenin's Rule'.

At this point a reminder of the particular form taken by the realism defended here might be in order. It is not just that plausibility is an inductive ground for a belief in the referential success of the appropriate expressions in the discourse, and implausibility grounds for believing referential success unlikely. The important phase of the argument is that the plausibility of a theory (as a moment in the evolution of a theory-family) makes it reasonable (and its implausibility makes it unreasonable) to pursue the *policy* of setting up a search for the putative referent. It seems clear that in some cases searching on the basis of a plausible theory makes it more likely that a being of the right sort will turn up. But that is not the basis of the argument. It is rather that the maintenance of ontological control by the conservation of the natural-kinds that are embedded in the source model, through the balancing of analogies, makes the policy of searching through the appropriate referential grid a reasonable policy. This is so even when, as in the case of palaeoanthropology, the chances of finding hominid remains to complete a convincing series of prehuman forms are low. The plausiblity of an evolutionary theory of human origins does not entail that there is a high probability of finding the immediate precursor of *homo sapiens* (now thought to be a latecomer). On the contrary – but it makes the search for such remains very reasonable.

In summary: when one offers a scheme such as the theory-family as an *ideal* and not just as an accurate description of a historically relative practice, one must provide an argument that the scheme will, indeed must, do the job. If the 'job' is the controlled formation of a conceptual system to provide 'epistemic access' to the hitherto unobserved, then the arguments set out above have shown that the theory-family does just that. The balance between behavioural and material analogies controls concept formation, while the co-ordination between analytical and and source analogues ensures that the natural-kinds involved are realistic. Contrary to Feyerabend I believe that, since a great many pieces of actual research were controlled by cognitive structures which were a good approximation to the structure of the theory-family as described in chapter 11, the attempt to describe a finite methodology makes sense.

Conditions for the scientific use of cognitive objects

The cognitive objects I have been describing are used to control the formulation of reference claims of the 'Whatever is the cause of . . . is a . . .' form.

In their turn these lead to the setting up of material searches controlled by features of those very same cognitive objects. These activities and uses do not happen in a vacuum. There are at least three kinds of conditions that have to be met for the proper use of a cognitive object.

1   Since applications require the tacit acceptance of auxiliary theories, other cognitive objects are always involved. Obviously, unless they are plausible, material searches which involve them will be unsatisfactory. For instance the 'kinetic theory-family' is applied with the help of instrumentation. The correct way to read the scales of such instruments as manometers and thermometers assumes the correctness of geometrical optics, another theory-family, with its roots in Kepler's *Paralepomena*. There may be research projects which tacitly invoke theory-families that have not been formulated explicitly by the community.

2   The people who use a certain theory-family must know how to apply it. Each cognitive object is accompanied by a set of tacit rules through which the community that uses that object applies it in particular cases. These cover such matters as the precision with which we expect predictions to be fulfilled.

3   Finally it is no use making use of a cognitive object whose ontology encompasses beings, states and processes that the scientific community has neither the manual skills nor the technical expertise to identify, even if the referents are, for that community, in Realm 2. This condition may seem so obvious as to be scarcely worth stating explicitly. However, Latour and Woolgar have shown that it may be of central importance in research. They point out that existence claims are indexical, that is must be interpreted relative to the available skills and equipment of some laboratory. A *special* process of decontextualization is required to establish existence *tout court*. Decontextualization is not a logical process but a social-moral one, since it depends in the end on the degree of trust that exists between the claimant and his/her audience.

Limits to system transformation

A feature of this account of scientific work is that it does not admit of comparisons between successive returns to plausibility for a developing and evolving theory-family. Longterm comparisons between 'states of the art' in the service of arguments for realism need to be based on something other than the plausibility of theories, in my sense. Further, if plausibility is offered as a surrogate for truth and stands in a relation to implausibility analogous to that in which truth stands to falsehood (for instance that a theory-family cannot be both plausible and implausible at the same time), no defence of realism in terms of an analogue of bivalence could succeed. There is no way in which a superior 'realism' of a later stage of a theory-family could be defined in terms of a superior plausiblity. Plausibilities are not comparable, since at successive high points in the history of a theory-family they may touch the same maximum.

As we have seen in the discussion of the justification for Lenin's Rule, realism is to explicated in terms of the policy of trying to establish referential relations between expressions in a theoretical discourse and exemplars of natural-kinds by comparing the imagined beings of which that discourse is a description with those very exemplars. Realism is not to be defended through discussions of the possibility or otherwise of demonstrations from evidence of the truth and falsity of general statements. The 'logic' of realism is that of existential statements, not of universal laws. This shift in viewpoint leads to somewhat different conceptions of the kind of evidence that should be taken into account in assessing the current state of a theory-family and, vicariously, the epistemic quality of the laws that appear in a description of that moment of stasis.

If a theory-family continues to be assessed as implausible - that is, the analytical and source analogies persistently fail to provide material adequate to remedy disparities in behavioural analogies, and/or experiments cannot be adjusted, refined or corrected to alter the empirical basis of the theory-family to remedy theory-driven changes in the explanatory hypotheses (the conception of the hypothetical generators of observable patterns) – then that theory-family is usually dropped and replaced by some other. The latter may have coexisted with the former for some time. We have had dramatic descriptions of this process from Kuhn and Lakatos. However the lack of fine detail in their formulations of the idea of that which I have called the theory-family ('paradigm' and 'research programme') has made it difficult for either to give an adequate explanation of the course of such replacements.

In terms of the idea of the theory-family, we can see that moments of restoration of equilibrium in the structure of the evolving theory-family come about through the community's drawing further on the resources of the 'outer' models, the analytical and source analogues. Both include content which can be expressed as sets of natural-kind rules. A new theory-family is created by changing these rules. This has the effect of redefining the ontological basis of the theories which represent successive moments of stasis in the evolution of the family. (Remember if you will that a theory-family is *not* a family of theories. It engenders such a family.) For instance in the change from atomistic to field theories of electromagnetism one can observe a change in at least two of the rules that define the natural-kinds of physical beings. The rule that a being must have a particular and discrete space–time location was abandoned, and so was the rule that at least one of the defining properties of a kind of being must be occurrent. Fields were introduced as extended ensembles of dispositions or powers.

Transition among and cross-comparisons between theory-families

Both Laudan ('research traditions') and Toulmin ('explanatory ideals') have identified, though somewhat mistily, the cognitive objects I have called 'theory-families'. Both conceive of merit or demerit for their cognitive objects in terms of runs of successes or failures in problem-solving. Both seem to think that such successes and failures can be described without recourse to the concepts of truth and falsity. Both have been decisively criticized. (Cf. McMullin, 1979; and Siegel, 1983.) What is right in their views can generally be subsumed under the account of the dynamics of theory-families set out in this chapter. Both Laudan and Toulmin distinguish between 'conceptual problems' and 'empirical problems'. The former arise within a theory-family, sometimes involving issues of coherence with larger cultural assumptions (e.g. contradictions between causal accounts of human actions and the agency component of concepts of personhood). The latter arise in programmes of experimental research and observation guided by relatively stable theory. The Maclaurin–Boscovich demonstration of the internal contradiction in the Newtonian system that arises when its physics and metaphysics are brought together created a conceptual problem within the Newtonian tradition to which a variety of solutions were offered. The criticism of Newton's reference to God's intervention to correct the motion of the planets, with which Leibniz opens his correspondence with Clarke, is an example of the diagnosis of a conceptual problem arising by the embedding of a theory within the general cultural assumptions (natural religion) of the time. On the other hand Amagat's discovery that gases under very high pressure did not obey Boyle's law posed an 'empirical problem'. We have seen how 'solutions' to both kinds of problem are created in the moves by which 'balance' is restored within a theory-family. The use of the source analogue to control the conceptual innovations needed to restore the equilibrium disturbed by a novel empirical finding comprehends Laudan's vague references to 'ontology'.

Siegel, in particular, has shown how the 'problem-solving' approach, espoused by both Toulmin and Laudan, quite fails to deal with cases which straddle two or more 'research traditions' or sets of 'explanatory ideals', those which Toulmin calls 'cloudy cases'. Toulmin's analogy with case-law is weak, because of the intrinsic ambiguity of the historical examples each side can cite in the dispute (cf. Siegel, 1983, p. 99). Laudan's attempt to compare rival 'research traditions' by measuring the internal problem-solving success of each seems to be a clear case of *ignoration elenchi* (cf. Siegel, 1983, p. 105 ff.).

But, since I too want to dissociate myself from a view of science which makes any practical use of truth, does not the plausibility view also fall victim to vicious relativism, with each theory-family incomparable with every other? I turn now to look at the means by which scientific communities make cross-familial comparisons.

The five conditions by means of which I have explicated the concepts of plausibility and implausibility allow for a moment-by-moment assessment of the stages of development of a theory-family. Clearly the concepts of plausibility and implausibility, as thus defined, cannot be used to make comparisons between discourses representing stable moments drawn from different theory-families, as rival theories for explaining patterns of phenomena from the same empirical field. The matter is quite complex. Two theory-families may share a common analytical analogue, but draw on distinctive and perhaps incompatible source analogues. In such a case it is proper to speak of the 'same phenomena' calling for explanation. But there are many cases, and these have been much emphasized by Koyré and Feyerabend, in which differences in analytical analogue make it improper to speak even of the same phenomena. Just these problems arise with the more loosely defined 'paradigms' of T. S. Kuhn and the 'research programmes' of Lakatos. Can the more finely structured notion of the theory-family help towards the development of an account of a possible assessment system for the making of cross-familial comparisons?

We have noticed that theory-families provide not only explanations but classification systems as well. Through the interplay between analytical analogues and source analogues powerful conceptual clusters, something like nominal/real essence pairs, are constructible upon which taxonomies can be built. Strictly speaking a pair of contrasting explanations can be rivals only if they are putative explanations of the same patterns of phenomena. Since the co-ordination requirement between analytical analogues and source analogues of a theory-family is weak, the theory-family scheme can admit of cases in which analytical analogues are the same but source analogues differ. Darwinian and Lamarckian evolutionary theories both used a genealogical analytical analogue, seeing lines of descent and 'blood' relationships between plants and animals. But they differed in their source analogues. This example illustrates cross-familial comparisons of type 1. The alleged phenomenon of 'meaning variance' is of no moment for type 1 cases, since the common analytic scheme guarantees a common core of rules for the use of descriptive and classificatory terms, as defining putative nominal essences. I propose three levels of comparison for discussion.

1   *Logical structure*. We prefer a logically coherent to a logically incoherent logical structure. So Boscovichian physics is to be preferred to Newtonian. This preference is to be explained sociologically, and not epistemologically or metaphysically. As I have argued throughout, the presence of logical structure in scientific discourses is to be explained by reference to the rhetorical necessities of the literary conventions of scientific controversy, and heuristic and pragmatic utility. But since a scientist will not get a hearing these days unless he or she subscribes to this convention, adherence to the canons of deductive logic is a powerful criterion for assessing the discourses that are momentary spin-offs from rival theory-families.[1]

2   *Metaphysical compatibility*. We prefer a theory-family, the source analogue of which is compatible with the general metaphysical climate of the age. We prefer explanations of criminal acts that draw on a social-dispositions source analogue to those which use concepts like 'natural wickedness', Satanic temptations and so on.

3   *Existential success*. We prefer a theory-family which has promoted successful 'search and find/fail to find' programmes over one which has not. So, for example, Harvey's account of the circulation of the blood, giving rise as it did to the many existential discoveries of Malpighi and Hales, is to be preferred over the Galenic theory-family.

In each case the patterns of phenomena to be explained, mechanical interactions, criminal acts, haemic quantities and qualities (arterial and venous), are identified for the rival theory-families by a common analytical scheme.

I propose that the three levels of comparison stand in increasing order of strength. To take the most extreme case, we prefer a theory culled from one theory-family over a rival culled from another, differentiated in these type 1 cases by differences in source analogue alone, if the existential search programmes controlled by it are more successful. And this is so even if the metaphysics of the proposed theory is incompatible with the *Zeitgeist*, and even if there appear to be flaws in the overall logical structure of the total theory complex based on the preferred theory-family. I believe we have reached this stage in the epistemology upon which we based our scientific culture after much bitter experience in which we have allowed logical coherence and the power of contemporary world-views to sway our judgement. Now it is the *Zeitgeist* that must give way in the face of existentially successful research programmes and the theory-families which animate them.

There is a fourth criterion, much used in practice.

4   A theory-family which engenders explanatory and classification schemes that encompass a greater variety of phenomena is to be preferred to one with a narrower reach. It is one of the virtues of Aronson's view of theory, discussed in chapter 10, that the principle of explanation by reduction to a common ontology has the effect of implicitly supporting this criterion. It is also connected with Nagel's non-demonstrative criterion for reality (cf. his old but still valuable work *The structure of science*, 1961), a criterion one might call 'triangulation'. In this sense criterion 4 seems to be a special case of criterion 3. Theoretical unification by the use of some purely formal mathematical device, without independent existential implications, belongs in the technical repertoire of Realm 1 and Realm 3 science, and has no place in the science of Realm 2. (See Zahar, 1980.)

In considering the possibility of a type 2 comparison between theory-families which have nothing in common, neither analytical nor source analogues, the basis of comparison can be judged relative only to common-sensical descriptions of phenomena, which they purport to explain. Here we enter the treacherous waters of what has been called 'paradigm change', to be menaced by the submerged rocks of relativism and the unmarked shoals of discontinuous meaning variance. However, the problem in a way takes care of itself. I do not believe that there has ever been a case of a substitution of one theory-family for another in the course of which conceptual continuity has been wholly ruptured. Reconsideration of the alleged cases, the Copernican 'revolution' for instance, seems to me to have shown that there were always continuities of analytical and source analogues and the taxonomic and explanatory discourses they controlled.

Revisability

So far in this part I have been concentrating on creating an idealized and unified version of a cluster of assessment concepts I believe to be actually in use in the scientific community. But arguments and disputes as to the standing of a theory as worthy of belief involve, I believe, another cluster of concepts, not explicitly entertained by the community but demonstrably at work in their discussions. I shall call this (philosophers') cluster of concepts 'revisability'.

I claim that the actual working assessments of the scientific community are arived at from the balance struck between informal and implicit versions of assessments of the relative plausibility and implausibility of theories, representing moments of stasis in the development of theory-families. The generic concept of revisability is something like this: the (informal) likelihood, given the total corpus of science at that moment, including experimental and observational technology and associated conceptual systems, of the relevant theory-family being disturbed. All that is needed to identify the four modes of revisability has already been introduced as the discussion has advanced. The four modes and their interconnections are as follows:

1   *Empirical revisability*. 'How likely is it that further experimentation or observation will upset the behavioural analogy, by disclosing new empirical relations, the conceptual, theoretical and metaphysical aspects of the theory-family remaining stable? ' Darwin's oft-expressed anxiety to accumulate more and more 'observations' reflects, I think, an anxiety to reduce the empirical revisability of his theory. Instead of interpreting inductive procedures positively, as has been the custom in the formal science of 'confirmation theory', or negatively in the fallibilist style, I propose to treat inductive procedures as precautionary. They are indulged in to guard against the possibility of revision. This reading would give a happy turn to Cohen's (1970) 'variants of a variable' idea. Popper's view could be turned quite upside-down, though without transforming him into an inductivist, and his insights concerning corroboration preserved, if instead of accepting his advice in the form 'Always seek the falsifier' he were read as telling the scientific community to dread it.

2   *Conceptual revisability*. Thanks to Whewell's admirable analysis of how scientists create the facts they garner, and the recent revival of his ideas by Koyré, Feyerabend and others, we can be sure that the instability of the descriptive conceptual system is as much a matter for anxiety as is the inscrutability of the natural world. The revisability of that part of the theory-family I have called the behavioural analogy is a function of both these sources of anxiety. I have sufficiently emphasized the relativity to one another of facts, concepts and problems in part three. Since the conceptual element in observing and experimenting, in most theory-families, is co-ordinate with the metaphysical basis, the sense of vulnerability to revision must be a (non-metrical) function of the degree of co-ordination of the theory-family. One would expect 'revisability anxiety' to be greatest when analytical and source analogue are independent of one another. Through this consideration one can see that low revisability and high plausibility are linked to one another, but weakly, since co-ordinativeness is one of the

weaker internal properties of any theory-family. Though co-ordinativeness is a weak necessary condition for high plausibility, it is a strong necessary condition for low revisability. A new conceptual system for creating facts is unlikely to 'pop up' and merit the attention of the community when the relevant theory-family is highly co-ordinated.

3   *Theoretical revisability*. The likelihood that theory will be revised (independently of disturbances to the behavioural analogy arising from new empirical findings) has to do with the confidence that the community places in the material analogy. Against the background of a stable source analogue this must concern the extent to which existential hypotheses generated by taking the referential terms of plausible descriptions of hypothetical mechanisms seriously have been substantiated. For example Harvey's theory of the circulation of the blood becomes progressively less revisable as first Malpighi discovers the capillaries and then Hales charts, in detail, the hydrodynamics of the system. But it is also at just this point that an analyst in search of the sources of communal conviction must take account of the influence of metaphysical assumptions, theological commitments and subtle social influences. All bear upon the willingness of the community to take an interest in attempts by members (or outsiders) to revise the source analogue of a well-established theory-family. As I have argued in chapter 1 the fact that such influences exist is not a ground for a debilitating scepticism, since they can be at least partially identified. Recent work in the philosophy of psychology illustrates how it is possible to disentangle social from other influences on the thoughts and judgements of a scientific community.

4   *Metaphysical revisability*. Revision anxiety and its correlate, confidence in a theory-family, must finally depend on the sense the community has of the stability of the metaphysics embodied in the source analogues of favoured theory-families. At any moment in the history of a culture there will tend to be clusters of favoured theory-families with markedly similar source analogues. The history of science shows few moments of a truly broad consensus. The mythical Newtonian synthesis, as a mechanistic metaphysics of atoms in the void, was never without a dynamicist rival even in the works of the great Sir Isaac himself (as witness the metaphysics of the *De natura acidorum*).

In the light of all this, what are we to make of the fact that 'classical' theories play such a large part in both scientific education and scientific practice? The fact is that in many cases old theories, actually discredited, nevertheless continue to live on. Sometimes this is because the up-to-date theory is not a replacement for the old theory but a refinement of it, a development within the same theory-family. Kinetic theory of gases, neo-Darwinism and relativistic mechanics are all examples of refinements of the classical theories, and presuppose them. Sometimes as in the case of kinetic theory and relativity the classical theory survives in those contexts for which it was originally formulated. Within a certain range of values of the variables of the laws expressing that moment in the history of the theory-family the classical theory is, for all practical purposes, adequate. One can design distillation equipment on the basis of the classical stagnant film theory without needing to draw on the more correct but horrendously complicated theory of Kishinevski and Pamfilov. Moon shots do not travel at relative velocities great enough to require the special theory of relativity to place them accurately at their destination.

A note on terminology

The terminology that I have adopted for the description of evolving theory-families is a version of a vocabulary already in current use. Many authors share the basic idea that a theory (or, as I prefer to call it, a theory-family) is an evolving conceptual structure, the continuity of which is maintained both by conservation of reference and by a tacit commitment to a relatively stable metaphysics. The similarities between their views and the analysis I have proposed can be brought out by a comparative table of equivalent terms used by some of these authors.

1   *N. R. Campbell (1957)*   *My terminology*

Dictionary	Material analogy
Hypothesis	Source analogue

Campbell's intuitions were a great advance on deductivist accounts of theorizing. (Indeed Campbell must be credited with the first and perhaps the most devastating criticism of deductivist accounts of theorizing.) However, largely ignored during the reign of logicism, his ideas were not carried far enough to reveal fully the inner structure of theory-families.

2   *S. Korner (1970)*   *My terminology*

Categorial framework	Source analogue
Inexact logic	Material and behavioural analogies

The main drawback of Korner's scheme is the way in which the use of the concept of 'inexact logic' obscures the essentially analogical nature of internal conceptual links within a theory structure.

3   *I. Lakatos (1970); followed by some*   *My terminology*
     other philosophers of the LSE school

Hard core	Source analogue plus aspects of hypothetical causal mechanisms
Heuristic (negative)	Material analogy
Heuristic (positive)	Behavioural analogy
Theoretically progressive research programme	Equilibration by adjustment of the material analogy
Heuristically progressive research programme	Equilibration by adjustment of the behavioural analogy

The main drawback of the LSE terminology is the way its use obscures the structural properties of theory-families, in particular the analogical relations that tie fragments of content together. This means that the essentially 'system' character of the process of theorizing is obscured, though the idea of 'progressive and degenerating research programmes' seems to need positive and negative feedback loops.

4   *J. R. Aronson (1984)*   *My terminology*

Common ontology	Source analogue, particularly its metaphysical component, the natural-kind rules
Mapping	Material analogy
Induced mapping	Behavioural analogy

The Aronson scheme, while a great advance on any other alternative leaves two matters obscure. No clue is given as to where to look for the origins of a common ontology. And the concept of 'mapping' sometimes must be read as an identity relation, sometimes as a part-whole relation and sometimes as cause-effect relation. This is not brought out by Aronson's scheme, but can be added without strain.

There are many cases in a degenerate scientific field, such as classical experimental psychology, where the methodology becomes detached from the metaphysical foundation which grounded its right to be considered a knowledge-garnering process. In my vocabulary this would be described as a case of the breakdown of the material analogy. For instance most classical psychological experiments make sense only against a background of behaviourist metaphysics. The persistence of a methodology which governs a practice of looking for naïvely identified effects of naïvely identified causes when the metaphysics has been repudiated leads to the production of 'data' which are strictly pointless. In the LSE terminology classical experimental psychology would be called a 'degenerating research programme'.

The kind of theorizing I have been analysing in part four has involved referential acts to unobserved beings prior to the establishment of deictic relations between any of those beings and members of the scientific community, at least in ways that would enable the members to realize that they were indeed in a physical (experience-engendering) relationship to them. The structure of analogies, unearthed at the base of such theorizing, provides a matrix of semantic relations through which meaning can be created prior to the establishment of reference. It is thus possible for a Realm 2 theory to be used to guide an exploration of the world, and a project for the building of suitable instruments, to try to find exemplars of those beings whose descriptions have been adumbrated prescriptively in theory. Policy realism is not a claim of inductive support for the idea that plausible theories *do* refer to real things, states, processes, substances and relations. If a theory is plausible it is rational to look for one of its referents, token, type or individual. Even one example of a successful search guided in this way is enough to defeat global antirealism. I have already remarked that the appearance of a strong case against any variety of scientific realism that requires acceptance of the possibility of theoretical entities entering the domain of accepted beings is sometimes given by a choice of examples that flatters the argument. These are examples drawn from the frontiers of physics. In part five I press on to test out the idea of a further tentative extension of this modest policy form of referential realism to some of the ways of theorizing about beings which, were they real, would be forever beyond human experience. A third philosophy of science, analogous to those I have constructed for Realm 1 and Realm 2, will have to be taken 'on board'.

There is a cluster of philosophical questions that arises naturally in the context of a discussion of theorizing. It includes all those questions that have to do with the nature, purpose and distinguishing marks of scientific and other kinds of explanation. The topic is a large one and it needs an extended and independent treatment, including many other fields of human endeavour than the natural sciences. For my purposes in this study, directed at the defence of scientific realism, it is enough to identify the variety of ways of theorizing described in parts three, four and five, as encompassing some of the variety of scientific explanations. Structural, teleonomic and causal explanations can all be found places as species of the genus of theorizing described in this part. However, I do not intend to pursue this cluster of important questions any further here.

Part Five

Science for the Realm beyond Experience

We apologize for the fact that in the title of a recent talk in the last newsletter, the words 'theoretical physics' came out as 'impossible ideas'.

Reported by J. Partington from a Cambridge University newsletter,
Punch, 26 February 1986

Introduction

The insight upon which this discussion is based is that realism – roughly, the doctrine that science describes, somewhat imperfectly and certainly incompletely, the world as it exists independently of the cognitive and material practices of mankind – cannot be defended by any global argument. There is no argument that could justify a realist reading of all the kinds of theories we find in the writings and conversations of scientists, nor one which could cover all the domains to which those various kinds of theories purport to denote. The domain of referents for the descriptive terms of a discourse which describes only objects of actual experience I have called Realm 1. The referents of terms which are among items of possible experience I have called Realm 2, while those items which, if they were real, would be beyond all possible experience I have called Realm 3. Two features of this scheme should be remarked upon. The discourses of most sciences invoke referents in all three realms. And the boundaries between realms are ill defined. In practice, where such boundaries are drawn is historically and technically conditioned. However, central cases for each realm are easily found.

Realism takes a different form in each realm. In consequence realist readings for the discourses appropriate to each realm stand in need of distinctive defences. The explanation of how reference is possible in each realm will be different, and the methodological and metaphysical principles that define the knowledge-garnering project for each realm will also differ. The pursuit of the philosophy of science becomes the effort to develop an adequate theory of science for each realm, a theory which explains how knowledge concerning the beings of each realm is possible, and defines the extent to which the methodologies of science can achieve it. Nevertheless the defences of realism form a hierarchy. The policy realism appropriate to the science of Realm 2 depends on the successful defence of the perceptual realist account of Realm 1. And the transcendental realism of Realm 3 science, modest though it is, is defensible only if the policy realism of Realm 2 has been persuasively demonstrated.

A realist account of Realm 1 science was developed through an exposition of Gibsonian psychology. This led to a realist metaphysics of experience at the level at which the Kantian categories were incorporated in our way of experiencing the world. Realism for the science of Realm 2 was defended by an inductive argument in favour of policy realism. The policy of searching for hitherto unobserved beings whose existence has been suggested by the theoretical discourses of Realm 2 science was shown to be justified on the basis of the success of that policy in the past. The rationality of the practice was defended by demonstrating that it depended on the way that iconic theorizing conserved the generic natural kinds of the world of Realm 1, whose observability was already given. Iconic theorizing is based on the balance of behavioural and material analogies, the latter controlling the formation of conceptions of the unobserved by building them on characteristics of known natural kinds. Each source analogue engenders a theory-family, and theories are moments of stasis in the development of theory-families. The success of these cognitive practices in guiding the material practices of researchers like Pasteur and Koch is an inductive ground for realist readings of contemporary and future Realm 2 theories such as plate tectonics.

This style of argument cannot be extended to include Realm 3 theories in general. Their referents, that is the beings their terms denote are beyond all possible experience. They cannot be the objects of a material search, and those who enunciate existential hypotheses about them must look to some other way of establishing their belief-worthiness. Historical shifts of the boundary between Realms 2 and 3 do occur, such as the technical innovation that made viruses possible objects of visual study with electron microscopes, but the distinction between the realms remains robust. However, Realm 3 is heterogeneous. A being which belongs to Realm 3 may or may not be of a familiar metaphysical category and of one of the common natural-kinds. At least some of the beings that theory allows us to conceive of as denizens of Realm 3 are not of familiar natural-kinds. We shall shortly encounter such puzzling beings as the intermediate vector bosons of quantum field theory. In rejecting van Fraasen's neo-Berkeleyan philosophy of science I committed myself to the rejection of the principle that only those beings which belong to familiar natural-kinds can be said to exist. Our current conceptions of the ontology of Realm 3, as it has developed under the pressure of the mathematical epistemology to be described in this part, is surprisingly conservative, depending as it does on the continued use of concepts of substance, and a current revival of a shadowy corpuscularian metaphysics. Yet it is also very radical, since the properties of the substances and corpuscles it invokes are very different from any of the material properties we usually accept as observable in principle.

A realist reading for Realm 2 theories depends on the central role of theoretical prescriptions of the natural-kinds of the beings which the theory seems to denote. It is the fact of the conservation of natural-kinds that makes policy realism rational. Because of it we can promote sensible search programmes on the lookout for exemplars of the kinds in question. Is there any aspect of Realm 3 theorizing that can play the same role as the conservation of natural kinds? The techniques of iconic modelling that play so large a part in the theories of the middle sort cannot in general serve for Realm 3 science, since we have no reason to suppose that beings that we can never observe must be like those we can. But there is a form of analogical reasoning that, while not iconic, has a similar structure to the way scientists develop theory-families of the kind typical of Realm 2 science. In this part I try to defend realist readings of certain Realm 3 theories, those which display a very striking mathematical property. The feature on which I pin my hopes of stemming the rising tide of irrationalist antirealism is the cluster of interlinked mathematical and metaphysical aspects of Realm 3 theorizing we call covariance, symmetry and conservation. For example covariance under the Lorentz group of transformations is very nearly a necessary condition for a hypothesis to be taken seriously as a putative law of nature.

Our investigations will lead to a surprising conclusion. The Kantian category of substance exerts a very powerful influence on the way symmetries are classified as 'good' and 'bad'. In this way our conceptions of Realm 3 beings are constrained to the same genera of metaphysical categories as are the beings of Realms 1 and 2. The vogue for covariance works to support the influence of a conservative metaphysics on how symmetries are chosen. Though not exactly what Kant had in mind as the noumenal, central cases of Realm 3 are beyond all possible human experience. The conservation of metaphysical categories through the favouring of certain mathematical forms seems to contradict one of Kant's most sweeping doctrines, the prohibition of the transcendent use of the categories through which experience is ordered as the phenomenal world. The escape route that I shall map out depends on a detailed study of the kinds of properties which physics requires us to ascribe to the substances and corpuscles of Realm 3. They are different but not wholly distinct from those which characterize the beings of Realms 1 and 2. Theorizing for Realm 2 was under the constraint of Lenin's Rule. I owe to M. Feher notice of Theon's Rule, which can serve as a summary of the constraints on Realm 3 theorizing. According to Theon we should adopt that hypothesis which is consistent not only with the facts, but with the metaphysical first principles accepted by the community. However, it will be necessary to give this story a further twist. The new properties we ascribe to the imagined beings of Realm 3, beings a realist would like to admit into the common ontology accepted by the community, are dispositions. But their grounding, unlike that of the dispositional properties ascribed to the beings revealed in Realm 1 and confidently imagined for Realm 2, is problematic. Furthermore, as manifestations of the causal powers of beings of Realm 3 they depend in uncheckable, and even unknown ways on the apparatus we have chosen for revealing them. The resolution of these difficulties will be found finally in a tightened-up version of the philosophy of physics of Neils Bohr.

To illustrate the kind of thinking typical of Realm 3 science I invite you to imagine a ball attached to an elastic string, whose further end is fixed to a hook firmly embedded in a wall. Suppose I draw the ball towards me, away from the point of attachment of the string. This will stretch the rubber cord. I hold the ball for a moment and then release it. It starts to move back towards the wall and the string shortens. A scientific account of these events requires two levels of description. At one level the events can be described in terms of dispositions, in particular in terms of the disposition of the ball to accelerate and of the string to contract. In that descriptive frame, 'force' is merely the dispositional counterpart of mass-acceleration. But physicists offer another account, invoking beings from Realm 3, such as 'work' and 'energy'. In pulling on the ball and stretching the cord I do *work* against the elastic *force* in the rope. That work is stored as potential *energy* in the rope. When the ball is released, the subsequent motion is to be described in terms of the transfer or transformation of potential into kinetic energy. A Lagrangean description of the system could be written in which this trans-action becomes the main focus of attention.

What is the relation between these levels of description? Philosophers have long been aware that a systematic use of dispositional predicates requires that each disposition be grounded in an occurrent state of the substance to which they are ascribed. The pantemporal attribution of dispositions, whether or not they are manifested, makes sense only if there is some attribute of the relevant substance that does persist in time. This is the grounding state. The presence of free hydrogen ions grounds the attribution of acidity to the vinegar while it is still in the bottle. The potential energy of the medium grounds the attribution of dispositions to accelerate test bodies even when none is present. In Aronson's terms the groundings of dispositions are the common ontology from which explanations are forged. We will be looking for the common ontology of fundamental physics. Occurrent phenomenal descriptions belong in the scientific discourse appropriate to Realm 1. But phenomenal descriptions relevant to Realm 3 must be dispositional, that is they are used to ascribe tendencies, powers and liabilities to unobservable beings. The dispositions are tendencies, etc. , to manifestations in Realm 1 or 2. Thus the ball and string set-up is such that, if the ball is (were to be) released, it will (would) accelerate at such and such a rate towards the wall. In grounding this disposition in the energy stored in the stretched string we introduce another kind of Realm 3 predicate, whose 'deep grammar' is part of the metaphysics of Realm 3. In the simple fable of the tennis machine, descriptions like '$F = ma$' are ways of introducing dispositional concepts via their typical manifestations, while terms like 'work' and 'energy' refer to items in a common ontology. I hope to show that the general structure of Realm 3 science is captured in this simple exemplar. But the ontology is not reached by the same kind of route as it is in Realm 2 science. I shall be demonstrating the enormous ontology-creating power of the triad 'covariance–symmetry–conservation', which plays such a large role in the foundations of contemporary physics. In adopting this triad the scientific community is acting in a thoroughly rational fashion.

In this part I turn to reasons for realism which are based on an analysis of the significance of the constraining role of certain mathematical features of physical theories, covariance under co-ordinate transformations, for relativity, and gauge invariance and renormalization for quantum field theory. I have called these the elements of a mathematical epistemology. Like all epistemologies they too will turn out to be at work as principles for garnering and winnowing knowledge because of the metaphysical principles they favour. Though I use such terminology I do not intend it to pre-empt solutions to the interesting problem of the actual importance of mathematics to physics.

There are two interconnected questions involved. Does the use of formalistic modes of expression and algorithmic ways of drawing inferences within such a mode entail that all aspects of the mathematical system of which that formalism is a part must be indicative of features of the ontology of that science? This is the question raised by Hartrey Field (1980). To take a very simple case: does the use of the formalism of differential equations throughout mechanics require that the space–time manifold be actually of the order of the real numbers? In many cases the formalism, if treated as bringing with it characteristic mathematical structures, seems to carry 'excess baggage'. This issue will be taken further in the section concerned with auxiliary mathematics and its ontological irrelevance.

I owe to E. Scheibe (1981) a further refinement of this issue, germane to the discussions of this part. He shows that 'the mathematical part of every physical theory . . . presumably can be reformulated as a species of structures.' Further, the concept of a species of structures is essentially defined by a condition of invariance. Scheibe calls this kind of invariance 'canonical invariance' and shows that for many important cases it is 'essentially equivalent to the common invariances of physical laws'. He goes on to show that, while the principle that physical laws should be invariant under arbitrary differentiable co-ordinate transformations is relatively trivial, the achievement of covariance is of physical significance. It is not always possible to reduce the group of co-ordinate transformations under which some set of physical laws is covariant. I hope to display the ontological importance of the covariance constraint in what follows.

I do not need to take these issues very far for the argument of this part. Both covariance and gauge invariance will be seen to be dependent, for their criterial power, on other, metaphysical principles. The referential force of the theories that adherence to these mathematical desiderata favours will be shown to be realized only through the derivation of conservation principles and their interpretation, within conservative metaphysical (categorial) frameworks.

13

Covariance and Conservation

The limits of the iconic

The argument of part four showed that the theory-families which develop through the imperative to explain phenomena by reference to the properties and relations of contingently unobservable beings are cognitive *systems*. They are structures which incorporate the conditions for the restoration of their internal equilibrium. When the system has been disturbed by a novel experimental result, equilibrium is restored by a process of concept adjustment controlled by the source analogue. The source includes a categorial cluster which serves as a metaphysical basis and a set of natural-kind rules. The theoretical concepts of middle-level theories purport to refer to beings which could be observed. It follows that the metaphysical basis necessarily repeats the cluster of Kantian categories which I have argued reflects the generic structure of human experience.

But deep theorizing, whether in the physical, psychological or sociological sciences, makes reference to beings which, if they were real, would be denizens of Realm 3. Two questions suggest themselves.

1   Without the constraint of 'in-principle observability' which limits the metaphysical basis of Realm 2 theorizing, and which provides the basis for the argument in support of policy realism, is there merely metaphysical anarchy among Realm 3 theories?

If a metaphysical basis can be identified then we can go on to ask the second question.

2   Do deep theory-families have similar system properties to those of the middle level, the theory-families whose referents are in Realm 2?

I hope to show not only that deep theory-families are tightly constrained by a metaphysical basis, but that they do have a system structure. The metaphysical basis is carried by the almost ubiquitous survival of conservation principles in the physics of Realm 3. I believe that the popularity of symmetries as constraints on the mathematical structure of theories is to be explained by their standing behind many important conservation principles. The role of the preference for conservation is generic, at the level at which the Kantian categories appeared in Gibsonian perception theory. What is conserved differs greatly between theories. That something is conserved in all interactions is a generic principle that embodies the traditional concept of substance. By juxtaposing analyses of relativity and quantum field theory I try to support the intuition that the generic category of substance is fundamental to both. Mathematical epistemology has come to play a more and more important part in the ways in which physicists assess putative laws and theories, because the use of co- and invariance to select laws ensures that definite conserved quantities can be found for each type of interaction.

Referential realism was based on the idea of the ontological possibilities of acts of reference to beings or typical members or samples of classes of beings, which, for technical reasons, were beyond ordinary observation. The imperative to shift to a mathematical epistemology came, I believe, from a widespread recognition of the limits of iconic theorizing. It was by no means always so obvious that iconic theorizing could not be a universal technique. The ontology of Realm 2 theorizing as it developed in the sixteenth and seventeenth centuries closely resembled the world of ordinary experience. A spatio-temporal array of discrete things formed the basic icon. Newton himself laid down a principle of iconic theorizing when he declared that the mechanical properties of bodies should be 'esteemed the properties of all bodies whatsoever'. But the success of the corpuscularian philosophy was short-lived. Why should it be right to assume that unobserved beings at either end of the scale of natural magnitudes must be in all essential respects like those we can observe? However, iconicity in deep theorizing may not be just a heuristic device. (Cf. Miller, 1984.)

This intuition concerning the 'limits of the iconic' seems to reflect radical methodological differences between the techniques of theorizing in Realm 2 and Realm 3 science. The former must so construct theoretical concepts as to maintain a strong similarity to the beings of Realm 1, while the latter, it might be thought, could make use of abstract mathematical structures constrained only by logic. But as I have argued, logic is, at least without further justification, a rhetorical, not an epistemological or metaphysical constraint on scientific theorizing. The community may come to esteem some system other than classical logic. But covariance imposes a tighter rein on theorizing. I hope to show that the basis of theorizing in both realms is substantially similar. Each can be represented by an ordered pair. For Realm 2 theorizing it is ⟨source analogue: iconic theoretical concept⟩, while for Realm 3 theorizing it is ⟨covariance/symmetry: conserved quantity⟩. Just as the iconic theoretical concepts of Realm 2 theorizing provide the basis of the material practice of searching for their exemplars, so the conserved quantities of Realm 3 science hint at the existence of substances as the beings denoted by theory.

Formal properties: covariance and symmetry

For physicists the concept of symmetry is the result of the union of two more primitive notions. There is the idea of the geometrical replication of form as in mirror reflection. And there is the more abstract idea of invariance under transformation of co-ordinates, which may take many forms. As Redhead (1975) put it, 'A symmetry is a set of invariants together with a set of transformations, usually a group of transformations, which express the changes for which the invariants are unchanged.' By treating spatial displacement, temporal displacement, rotation, mirror reflection and some kinds of property exchange such as the substitution of positive for negative charge as transformations of co-ordinates a wide variety of symmetries can be identified. For example the relation between a left hand and a right hand can be represented by the 'parity' transformation, $x' \to -x$, $y' \to y$, $z' \to z$. (See figure 13.1). It is important to distinguish between two kinds of 'unchanges'. A symmetry is a group of transformations which leaves *something* unchanged. But that something can be the form of a law or laws (covariance) or the quantity of some property. Only the latter are generally called 'conservations'. The argument will be aimed at showing that the latter are more fundamental than the former. Here I am greatly indebted to a paper by Zahar (1980). Nevertheless the covariance of the form of a law can often be related to a kind of conservation principle. It is that, I believe, which provides us with the physical and perhaps the metaphysical meaning of covariance and which underlies the physicist's intuition of what is a good symmetry.

I propose to show, in a sequence of cases, that not all conservations are ontologically significant, but that those which are conserve a substance. This argument will show that the covariance condition functions as a *constraint*. It is a way of enforcing certain necessary conditions for a concept to denote something real. This is just the role that natural-kind rules embedded in the source analogue of a Realm 2 theory-family have in Realm 2 theorizing. But as a necessary condition the achievement of covariance does not prove that the law which is covariant describes a real process.

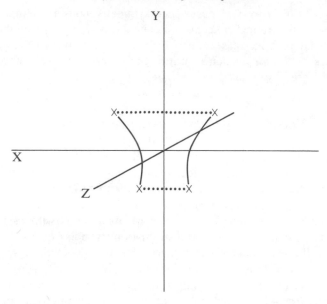

Figure 13.1   Parity transformation $y' = y, z' = z, x' = -x$

An elementary example: Cartesian extension

The basic idea of linking invariance to reality can be found at the very dawn of mathematical physics. J. Aronson has pointed out to me that it underlies Descartes's famous assertion that the essence of matter is extension. Framed in the Cartesian axes a rod will display only one provably invariant property as the Cartesian co-ordinates are transformed (the axes translated or rotated). That property is linear extension. From whatever pair of Cartesian axes we chose to assign co-ordinates to define the location and dimensions of the rod,

$$l = \sqrt{(x_2 - x_1)^2 + (y_2 - y_1)^2}$$

In our terminology the Pythagorean length is invariant under translation of the axes, that is under the co-ordinate transformation $x' = x + a$, $y' = y + b$. Similarly that quantity is invariant under rotation of the axes, that is under the co-ordinate transformation $x^* = x \cos \theta$, $y^* = y \sin \theta$. If we follow Descartes in giving an ontological reading to this mathematical property of bodies in Euclidean space, that is in expressing the conclusion in some such form as 'The essence of matter is extension', the invariance of length under co-ordinate transformation appears to lead to a conservation principle. Extension, as the invariant associated with a conservation law, is real.

The ontological reading of the mathematical properties of length in Euclidean space could be grounded in the principle that whatever is independent of the particular situation of an observer is real, and translation and rotation of axes is a formal device for examining what happens when the point of view of an observer changes. The demonstration that length is not only independent of the situation of the observer but is conserved under co-ordinate transformation adds another necessary condition for an ontological reading of the mathematical demonstration.

Momentum conservation

Can anything more be said about the processes described by covariant laws? Mathematical epistemology permits a further step. Co-ordinate transformations are expressions of 'symmetries'. Roughly the physical system appears the same whichever co-ordinate system it is described in. But typically symmetries entail conservation principles. It is, I claim, the conserved quantities associated with the symmetries that are ontologically significant and justify realist-inspired hypotheses about the existence of unobservable processes in which those conserved quantities are implicated. In classical mechanics we can treat Newton's Third Law as a symmetry.

$$F = \frac{dp}{dt} \text{ where p is momentum}$$

But if the total force in an interaction under Newton's Third Law is zero

$$\frac{dp}{dt} \text{ is also 0}$$

It follows from this that p is a constant, that is momentum is conserved in classical interactions. More generally it can be shown that in the Lagrangean formulation

$$\frac{d}{dt}\left(\frac{\partial L}{\partial q_j}\right) = 0 \quad \text{so} \quad \frac{\partial L}{\partial q_j} \text{ is a constant}$$

The latter expression represents the generalized momentum.

Energy: the ghost of a category

What is the ontological significance of this mathematical phenomenon? Momentum, energy and angular momentum can be shown to be conserved quantities as an immediate consequence of the requirement that the laws of mechanics be covariant under space translation, time displacement and rotation of axes. In the categorial system underlying the metaphysics of experience that which is conserved is substance. I shall try to show that the ontology of Realm 3 is based on a straightforward extension of the domain of the concept of substance to the unobservable beings of Realm 3. The argument depends on linking covariance of law with a conserved quantity. The conserved quantity represents the stuff in which the process represented by the law really occurs. This is what sustains the analogy between the role of covariance in Realm 3 science and the role of natural-kind rules in Realm 2 theorizing.

The most important covariance we know of is that of the laws of electromagnetism and mechanics under the Lorentz transformation. Einstein's creation of special relativity could be looked at as a two-stage process. The first stage was the achievement of the harmonization of the laws under a single principle. The second was the bringing out of the ontological consequences of the harmonization. The example of special relativity will show very clearly why the mathematical harmonization of the laws is not a sufficient condition for their belief-worthiness. The harmonization step starts with the observation that Maxwell's equations are, or can be made, covariant under the Lorentz transformation. Their form is independent of the choice of inertial frame within which electromagnetic processes are studied. The laws of mechanics as formulated by Newton are not covariant under that transformation. But by modifying the concept of mass the laws of mechanics can be harmonized with Maxwell's Laws, in the sense that they are all covariant under the relevant co-ordinate transformation. But the revised concept of mass no longer represents a conserved quantity. In

$$m = m_0 \quad \sqrt{1 - v^2/c^2}$$

mass is a function of relative velocity.

If covariance had been 'the bottom line', so to speak, the matter would have ended there. But already by 1917 Kretchmann had shown that covariance was too easily achieved. Any laws could be rewritten to be covariant under the Lorentz transformation including the laws of Newtonian mechanics. As Zahar shows Einstein immediately acknowledged the force of this demonstration. A deeper conservation principle was needed to make relativity a genuine scientific theory. The harmonization of the laws was achieved by a modification of the concept of mass. So modified, the laws of mechanics become covariant under the Lorentz transformation. But only if this move leads to a common ontology does it make physical sense – at least so says the realist. Does the concept of the conserved quantity so arrived at obey the same deep grammatical rules as the generic notion of substance? We can test the viability of the idea of a mathematical epistemology, that the covariance constraint coupled with a derived conservation law leads to an ontology, by trying to answer this question for relativity. By drawing on an analysis proposed by Zahar I try to show that the sequence of steps that leads from classical mechanics to general relativity makes sense if we accept the principles of mathematical epistemology.

The 'relativities' as a theory-family

The Kretchmann proof shows that covariance with respect to any transformation of co-ordinates is not a sufficient condition for a law to be a description of the behaviour of a generative mechanism. But the application of the need for covariance to the special theory is relative to the Lorentz transformation. Is there something special about that particular transformation group? I have suggested in the foregoing that indeed there is. It sustains a new and powerful conservation principle. What was lost in the substitution of

$$m = m_0 \quad \sqrt{1 - v^2/c^2}$$

for the Newtonian concept of mass is regained when the energy-mass conservation emerges through the proof of $E = mc^2$.

This suggests that it might be worth trying to lay out the successive relativity theories as a theory-family in the sense described in part four. The common ontology (or metaphysical element in the source analogue) is expressed in the conservation principles that are sustained by each theory. This part of the argument depends heavily on the work of E. Zahar. His discussion of the continuity between the special and general theories of relativity is couched in the terminology of the LSE school (following Lakatos) but as I showed in part four, apart from minor differences in detail, their dynamics of theory construction is very similar to mine. I have already shown how that terminology can be mapped on to my vocabulary. In a passage of great interest Zahar lays down the main principle of 'mathematical epistemology' as follows: We start from some hypothesis H which we may want to modify. We express H in an equivalent form, $H^*(t)$, which brings out a certain mathematical entity t. [The entity] t is then given a realistic interpretation which subsumes it under a philosophical category, e.g. the category of substance; this category obeys some very general laws, e.g. conservation or symmetry laws. It is then found that $H^*(t)$ violates these laws. The breakthrough is achieved when $H^*(t)$ is modified into $H'(t)$ which conforms to the laws in question.' We can think of the modification of the laws of mechanics by the change in the mass concept so that the laws are covariant under the Lorentz transformation as an example. As Zahar says, 'Special relativity puts matter and energy on a par; so we can suppose that there exists a unique substance which our senses apprehend sometimes as radiant energy say and sometimes as hard impenetrable matter.'

Zahar shows that the step from special to general theory of relativity could have been motivated by two considerations. Einstein seems to have been dissatisfied with the privileged status of the set of all inertial frames. There should be no privileged frames. And the apogee of metaphysical plausibility for the special theory, namely the law of the equivalence of mass and energy, leads to some odd results when considered with respect to gravitation. Mass (the bearer of the category of substance) becomes the centre of the creation of the new theory. Newton's 'casual' equation of gravitational and inertial mass must be remedied. In a true substantialist theory such an equality must represent an identity. If all bodies of whatever mass fall with the same acceleration it must be because gravitational fields are local accelerations of the frame of reference. But most gravitational fields are spherically symmetrical. In Euclidean space the 'deep' solution to the mass problem would require an infinity of local frames of reference, each undergoing an infinitesimally different acceleration, in both quantity and direction. But once the Euclidean representation of space is abandoned the local frames of reference can be harmonized into a single Riemannian geometry.

The choice of title for this chapter represents, in part, an act of historical piety towards the actual method by which relativity was created. That the laws of electromagnetism and mechanics should be harmonized by so modifying the latter that both sets were covariant under the Lorentz transformation was the guiding principle, so I believe. As I remarked above it was not until 1917 that it was realized that the covariance condition was too weak. Any arbitrary set of laws can be so written as to be covariant under any arbitrary co-ordinate transformation. (As Scheibe shows, this result is not quite as debilitating to covariance as it might seem.) Einstein, it is said, supposed that the covariance requirement was equivalent to the principle of the equivalence of all inertial frames. But the latter is a much stronger constraint. For the purposes of the exposition of the development of the relativity theory-family I shall adopt the historical form of the 'covariance' criterion in terms of which to argue the case.

The story of the development of the relativity theory-family involves the re-creation of a central conserved quantity. The revision of the concept of mass leads directly to the popularly famous Einstein relation, $E = mc^2$. The elementary derivation of $E = mc^2$ clearly shows its dependence on the Lorentz transformation.

T is kinetic energy, in the usual convention.

$$\frac{dT}{dt} = \underline{f} \frac{d\underline{d}}{dt} = \underline{f} \cdot \underline{u}$$

$$\underline{f} = \frac{d}{dt} m\underline{u} \qquad\qquad m = \frac{m_0}{\sqrt{1 - v^2/c^2}}$$

So:

$$\frac{dT}{dt} = \frac{d}{dt} m\underline{u} \cdot \underline{u}$$

Changing from vectors to Cartesian components and integrating we get

$$T = \frac{m_0 c^2}{\sqrt{1 - v^2/c^2}} + c$$

But kinetic energy $= 0$ when particle velocity $= 0$, so:

$$0 = m_0 c^2/1 + c$$

$$c = -m_0 c^2$$

Therefore:

$$T = \frac{m_0 c^2}{\sqrt{1 - v^2/c^2}} - m_0 c^2$$

So:

$$T = mc^2 - m_0 c^2$$

Defining E (total energy) as $T + m_0 c^2$ we get

$$E = mc^2$$

This relation can be interpreted as introducing a new conserved quantity, 'energy'. Or, to put the matter another way, the existence of this relation within the theory shows that the laws which are covariant under the Lorentz transformation can be interpreted as being about a 'substance' of unknown constitution but known dispositions: energy. A realist interpretation then calls for the postulation of a being, 'energy', to be the heart of a common ontology for physical theories. Whatever it is, the energy *concept* behaves like a substance concept. Some of the principles controlling the way a 'substance' concept can be used are as follows:

1 Substance is conserved: that is the quantity of a spatio-temporally determinate sample of a substance does not vary with its location in space

and time. Newtonian matter is a substance with respect to the quantity measured by its inertia. Or to put the matter another way it is because inertia is invariant under all spatio-temporal transformations in Newtonian physics that it is a measure of the quantity of substance. One of the first deep things that children learn in physics is the distinction between mass and weight. Weight is the measure not of the substance, but of a locally varying force. The conditions for the application of the rule 'Substance is conserved' turn out to be quite complex. They must include the choice of an associated property which, because it is insensitive to spatially and temporally diverse causal influences from other substances, can serve as a measure. I call such a property 'indicative'.

2   Considered under its indicative property (ies) the quantity of a substance is subject to arithmetical rules of addition and subtraction. It is conserved.

3   With respect to its indicative property or properties the quantity of a substance is always positive. Negative measures of quantity of an indicative property must be artefacts of the choice of measuring scale. If the property is genuinely indicative of a substance then the negative measure can be eliminated by a gauge transformation. If energy is a substance and temperature is one of its measures, there can be no negative temperatures. The expression 'Forty below' is an artefact of the choice of zero. On such a chilly day the 'real' temperature, that is the quantity which measures energy, must have been +233 degrees Kelvin. Physics now countenances negative energies. Metaphysical propriety is preserved by the creation of a dualist ontology, in which matter is the collection of manifestations of one substance, positive energy, while anti-matter is the other.

4   In the course of a physical process a quantity of substance can be transferred from one part of a physical system to another. Losses are 'leakages'. In this respect that which the concept of 'energy' refers to behaves no differently from wine. When wine is drawn from the barrel, poured from the jug to a glass and from thence to the innards of a toper, decreases in quantity during the process are put down to spillage.

These are some of the more obvious and naïve conditions that any being which falls under the metaphysical category of substance must fulfil.

In classical mechanics, which it is convenient to discuss in the Lagrangean formulation, the substantial character of energy is obvious. The concept obeys rules that are, at the very least, compatible with the metaphysics of substance. The total energy of the field together with that of the material system is a constant described in the Hamiltonian $H = T + V$. The

Lagrangean formulation itself describes changes in the distribution of that energy between field and material system under the constraint of Hamilton's principle. If $L = T - V$, the integral of L over time is a minimum. In relativistic and quantum mechanics, energy budgeting also follows the Lagrangean formulation. As I remarked above the negative energies that turn up in Dirac's discovery of the positron can be made to fit the substantialist metaphysics by the positing of two substances, one of which is manifested as matter, the other as anti-matter.

Arguments to explain the attraction of covariance and conservation as criteria

The argument of the last two sections has been offered in support of the thesis that the achievement of covariance is ontologically significant because laws which are covariant under a certain transformation can be shown to entail conservation principles. That which is conserved falls within the general category of substance, a 'stuff' for the common ontology needed for *some* yet to be spelled-out variety of realist reading of mechanics and electromagnetism. However the argument shows only that the achievement of 'covariance' and 'conservation' are necessary conditions for a realist reading of a physical theory. The paradox of Clavius reminds us that no argument from the properties of a theory alone could show that they are jointly sufficient. For sciences with Realm 3 referents the theory-motivated real-world search for an exemplar of the kind of beings assumed to form the common ontology will prove abortive. In the relativity case the 'substance', mass-energy, is systematically experientially elusive. Policy realism, of the robust sort outlined in part four, must fail as an account of the practice of sciences whose substantive terms denote beings of Realm 3. However, a suitably weakened version of policy realism will emerge in the next case to be studied, quantum field theory. (See Zahar (1980), pp. 41-2, for a clear statement of the status of the covariance principle, as a principle whose field of application is discourse, not that which a discourse may denote.)

Before taking that step, however, I want to examine several other arguments in support of the methodological pre-eminence of covariance. The first argument to be considered is implicit in Einstein's Pythagoreanism. He opens his 1905 paper with a general Pythagorean argument in favour of the reality-confirming power of symmetry considerations. Perhaps with the Lorentz force law in mind he criticizes the traditional account of electromagnetic induction on Pythagorean grounds. When the magnet moves and the conductor is stationary the Lorentz law requires the existence of an electric field throughout space. The force on electrons in the stationary conductor is due to the referent of that term in the law. But when the magnet is stationary and the conductor moves there is no corresponding field. While the effects are symmetrical and depend only on the relative velocity of the magnet and conductor, the proposed underlying physical processes are not symmetrical. Einstein seems to have held to the principle that superficial or empirical symmetries must reflect deeper-lying or theoretical symmetries. He seems to have used this principle as at least a negative criterion for physical plausibility. Any theory which did not manifest it should be rejected. The principle that what is true of phenomena must be true of the processes which generate those phenomena is surely specious. For example physics is full of cases of phenomenal regularities which are believed to be the effects of large numbers of randomly distributed micro-processes. The general problem of 'co-ordination', of how the emergence of regularity or stability out of disorderly tendencies among the micro-processes is to be explained, is unresolved. 'Co-ordination' is a principle of statistical mechanics, not a consequence of it.

There is another class of arguments which attempt to explain the attraction of covariance and conservation without referring to their ontological aspects. These arguments relate the community's predilection for laws and theories which exemplify the Pythagorean properties to the necessary conditions for the possibility of certain human practices. Meyerson (1930) develops such an argument. He distinguishes clearly between covariance and conservation and suggests an explanation for the apparent ubiquitous indispensability of the former in utilitarian terms. For him, lawfulness and causality are distinct metatheoretical properties. The former, the principle that laws should be ubiquitous, holds in all circumstances. Covariance under the Lorentz transformation is clearly a special case of the 'lawfulness' requirement. Meyerson's account of lawfulness (p. 41) shows that it amounts to the requirement that the deductive conclusions of lawful explanations should be determinate. This is the pragmatic basis for our predilection for laws. It is a condition both for animal existence and for the successful prosecution of practical tasks in the contemporary human world. 'Foresight', he says, 'is indispensable for action' but that foresight must yield a determinate picture of the future. The causality requirement leads to another kind of sameness, the conservation of some quantity through time. As Meyerson puts it, 'the original properties plus the change in conditions must equal the transformed properties' (p. 41). Zahar has pointed out that Meyerson did not defend causality (conservation) in the same detailed way that he supported the 'lawfulness' or covariance condition. No doubt an argument of similar form could be constructed to relate the causality condition to practical utility. In a brief sketch Zahar proposes such an explanation of the ubiquitous appearance of the conservation principle. He argues that the assumption of substantial continuity is a more efficient way of orienting myself in the world than the mere accumulation of laws representing phenomenal regularities.

This argument is vulnerable to anthropological counter-examples. If there is only one culture which does not make use of either of these principles but manages to survive, then the argument fails. It is a question of the depth at which the 'same law' is supposed to hold. The Azande are ever ready to deal with unpredictability and diversity in the world of Man and nature, by resort to a theory of magic which explains untoward happenings as due to the malice and whim of sorcerers. There is an underlying law that all events are produced by something, that is there are no accidents. Meyerson's argument is about the preservation of phenomenal lawfulness whatever the circumstances. But the Azande and many other cultures do not seem to subscribe to that principle. Nor does it seem to me that Zahar's anthropological argument for the universality of the conservation principle (the category of substance) does much better. Greek metaphysics swayed between non-conservationists like Heraclitus and conservationists like Parmenides. And Parmenides had to locate his 'one' beyond the disorders of experience.

Meyerson's argument could be taken as a primitive form of transcendental argument. In general such arguments are aimed at showing that some category must be assumed or some principle taken to be of universal application, because that category or that principle represents one of the conditions for the possibility of human experience, or more generally for the possibility of some ubiquitous human practice. The Kantian form of transcendental argument can get no grip on theoretical physics, since the beings denoted by its discourses are supposed to be beyond the realm of all possible experience. But physics would be forced to stand paralysed at the portals of the unobservable were its discourse to collapse into unintelligibility the instant it should be directed towards describing the nature, behaviour and causal powers of the denizens of Realm 3. Perhaps we can ground the attraction for the category of substance, and its mathematical partner the principle of covariance (and the general relation between symmetry and conservation), in the conditions for the possibility of unambiguous communication.

This last phrase will no doubt have a very familiar ring to anyone interested in the philosophy of physics. It is the famous condition with which Bohr introduced the 'correspondence principle'. All physical theories must have a realization in a description of a physical set-up, usually an apparatus hooked up to the material world, which can be fully described in terms of the concepts of classical physics. At times Bohr seems to have linked this condition with an assumed priority of ordinary language over all technical conceptual systems. Ordinary language embodies a conceptual scheme which includes the concept of substance (conservation) and, it could be argued, a principle of determinate causality.

But ordinary language embodies a very complex conceptual repertoire including not only substance concepts, but also dispositional and phenomenal concepts. A language would seem to need to be equipped not only with substance concepts but also with a repertoire of concepts for a wide range of kinds of properties in order to ensure the possibility of unambiguous communication. In chapter 14 I shall be examining the property-making tactics of particle physicists, particularly in the context of quantum field theory. It will then be possible to see whether Bohr's trust in the power of the conceptual structure of ordinary language as a necessary condition for the possibility of unambiguous communication is vindicated. It will become clear that certain 'deep grammatical' constraints on the behaviour of property concepts do recur and do reflect the conceptual structure of classical physics.

But can the argument be taken further to ground the common substantialist ontology of classical and relativity physics in something more robust than the grammatical necessities for the linguistic practice of unambiguously communicating our experiences one to another?

The first step in the argument is to take up the oft-quoted aphorism of Feynman that invariance (covariance) is the mark of reality. Or, to adopt another of Feynman's expressions, that which is invariant (covariant) under some significant co-ordinate transformation is 'robust'. But we have already seen that covariance has been shown to be too readily available for its one-time criterial role in selecting belief-worthy laws. Nevertheless the demonstrations of conservations from symmetries does remain as a possible criterion, as does the original Einsteinian idea of reconstructing the forms of laws so that they are independent of choice of inertial frame. This is a narrower constraint than that expressed in the simple idea of a law being expressed in a form that is independent of co-ordinate system.

If the quantity of a substance is the same no matter from which reference frame (observer standpoint) it is measured, then it has some claim to be real, that is to exist independently of human experience, concepts and intentions. There is a further qualification of this argument – that that which may manifest itself to us as substance or as a conserved quantity is, to be sure, the result of poking and prodding at 'something', which may, in itself, be quite unimaginably different from anything of which we could form a concept. This possibility will be explored in a discussion of Bohr's philosophy of science. I believe that the general principle that links early Einsteinian covariance to reality is just a consequence of the generalization of the above argument to include processes as well as properties. So, if the form of a law is covariant under a co-ordinate transformation *that represents frames of reference moving with uniform velocity with respect to one another*, we can take the law to be describing a real process. The preservation of form from one reference system to another would suggest that whatever the process that is being described it is independent of the observer's point of view.

It is worth remarking how similar this argument is to the standard arguments advanced by Galileo and Locke among others for making the distinction between primary and secondary qualities and for grounding the latter as powers in the former as the real qualities of bodies. The variability of the experienced quality (idea) with the conditions of observation and state of the observer marked off ideas of secondary qualities from ideas of primary qualities. And it was the main ground for denying that the secondary quality was anything but a power in the body to excite such an idea in us. Such powers were grounded in clusters of primary qualities which produced stable ideas in human experience generally resembling them. The fate of that theory at the hands of Berkeley need not discourage us, since no experienced stabilities but only experiential measures of conservation are involved, and there is no suggestion in modern physics that our ideas of primary qualities should resemble those qualities as they are in the real world. Nevertheless a kind of Berkeleyan critique might be mounted if the measures of conserved quantities could be referred to the nature of measuring equipment. If variations in the state of that equipment are reflected in variations in the measures of quantity of putative substances, our confidence in a conservation law, and in the existence of that which is conserved, would be undermined.

To sum up: what is the explanation for the appearance of a generic conservation principle as a methodological commonality in nearly all reasoning in contemporary physics? There seem to be two main lines of argument, Feynman style and Bohr style. In the former, *un*changingness through various kinds of external changes is taken as a mark of reality. Whatever is invariant under co-ordinate transformation is real. But is the robustness thus signalled a sufficient condition for a claim to have pinned down reality? The argument has leaned rather to the more modest claim that it is at best a necessary condition. Recently, at a debate about the methodology of history at Moscow State University, I heard a somewhat similar point made. Since the past is both fixed and real we can pick out what is a genuine historic reality by the way that it bears the same appearance in different kinds of historical narratives.

But, according to Bohr, we have no access to a final reality beyond the manifestations which are elicited by our material practices, including experimenting. But the conditions of unambiguous communication require that the conceptual repertoire be confined to the categories of the classical conceptual scheme. This scheme is, he thought, either a variant of or closely similar to the scheme embodied in ordinary descriptive language. Taking the Kantian categories as an expression of the generic characteristics of that scheme it becomes clear why conservation has taken such a large role in physics. I believe that contemporary particle physics has developed in such a way that practically all that survives of its classical predecessor is a generic conservation principle. In the form of the bookkeeping rules by which the quantum numbers descriptive of states of evolving systems are regularized and the menagerie of particle concepts and prescriptions is controlled, it exerts a powerful influence on the way unobservable beings and their novel properties are conceived. It is the route to a common ontology.

Auxiliary mathematics

Which mathematical symmetries carry ontological commitments in the mathematical apparatus? Roche (1986) uses the idea of 'auxiliary mathematics' to issue a warning against too great a readiness to step from symmetries to real properties of a physical system. The harmonic oscillator provides a simple context in which to discuss the issue. In simple harmonic motion the oscillations can be reproduced by constructing an auxiliary circle with centre at the centre of the simple harmonic motion and radius equal to half the amplitude. When the uniform motion of a point in the circle is projected on to the diameter, a simple harmonic motion is reproduced. The geometrical symmetry of the circle reappears in the isochrony of the period of the motion.

By what criterion do we judge the circular motion to be 'auxiliary mathematics'? One could imagine a Victorian mechanism of steel and brass, with wheels, rods and sliding couplings which realized the 'auxiliary mathematics' in a quite concrete way. But a simple harmonic motion of identical periodicity and amplitude could be produced by a weight hanging from a suitable spring, the symmetry of the motion ascribed to forces (symmetrically) arranged along the line of motion. Roche's intuition, that the mathematical description of the circular motion is auxiliary, is then tested by an empirical criterion. Does the mathematical formalism describe an abstract or schematic version of some real generating mechanism? If not it is auxiliary, 'mere geometry', as Kepler might have put it. But there could also be a conceptual criterion. Does the mathematics describe a schematic world which, for internal, conceptual reasons, could not be realized as our world? Then too the mathematics is auxiliary.

Hilbert space is a basis of a mathematical representation in physics that needs to be assigned its place in the epistemic firmament with some care. It too, I believe, is auxiliary mathematics. But is it like the auxiliary circle in the elementary analysis of simple harmonic motion, or is it like the Hamiltonian, which represents the relationship between momentum and displacement? If it is the latter that provides the proper comparison, then consequences drawn from the Hilbert space representation may not be like the conservation laws which can be derived from symmetries and from the covariance requirement. The argument by which Hilbert space is assigned to auxiliary status depends on the nature of the mathematical concept of phase-space.

To continue the example of the simple harmonic oscillator: a suitable phase space is created by taking the relevant physical properties as co-ordinates of the space. We could choose displacement 'x' and momentum 'p_x'. The Hamiltonian for a classical harmonic oscillator is

$$H(x,p_x) = \frac{p_x^2}{2m} + \frac{\kappa x^2}{2}$$

In phase space the harmonic oscillator generates a sine curve as p_x varies with displacement. The sine curve is not a schematic representation of any possible generator. A phase space in general is a piece of physics torn away from its moorings in an implicit ontology. We look simply at the structure of its mathematical description. The trouble is that phase space mathematics does not describe a unique, realizable physical process. A phase space representation must be auxiliary mathematics in an even stronger sense than that in which the auxiliary circle is auxiliary. In the latter case it is an ascertainable empirical fact that no mechanism realizing the circle exists surrounding and driving the spring. In the former any one who set out to look for the sine curve would reveal a radical misunderstanding of the role of the mathematics that generated it.

In Euclidean phase space any vector representing a physical process in real Euclidean space can be resolved into a linear combination of an 'orthonormal basis', that is of three unit vectors lying along the axes, i, j and k. It is an empirical question whether, in real space, there are powerful particulars generating physical forces corresponding to those vectors. In some cases at least Euclidean phase space could be interpreted as a Eucli-dean physical space and its orthonormal basis as a physical system, say lift, thrust and wind. When Euclidean phase space is auxiliary it is auxiliary in Roche's sense. Let us now consider the orthonormal basis for the Hilbert space representation. Generalizing from the Euclidean case we reach the condition that a set of vectors $\langle A_1 \ldots A_n \rangle$ is an orthonormal basis if $\langle A_m | A_n \rangle$ = 1 for m = n and ≤ 0 for m $\neq$ n. Any vector in Hilbert space can be repre-sented as a linear combination of the vectors of the orthonormal basis. But the vector algebra of Hilbert space is constrained by the properties of the phase space, not by the metaphysics of a physical interpretation. For instance in Hilbert space the inner product of two vectors, V_1 and V_2 is the complex conjugate of the inner product of V_1 with V_2, because in Hilbert space scalars are complex numbers. As it happens this result is physically convenient, but notoriously the attempt to interpret this operation within a coherent metaphysics has proved intractable. Hilbert space is auxiliary mathematics in just the way that the sine curve representing the functional relationship between momentum and linear displacement is auxiliary in the mathematical description of the simple harmonic oscillator. Similarly the use of the mathematics of the two-colour problem by Kocken and Specher in their proof of the impossibility of inserting a hidden variable into the existing structure of quantum mechanics has no ontological significance. It is auxiliary mathematics. Quantum mechanics differs radically from relativity in the significance of its mathematical structures. The structure of the Hilbert space representation is neutral in debates about the ontology of that province of Realm 3. It neither helps nor hinders realist arguments concerning quantum mechanics.

14

Deeper into Realm 3: Quantum Field Theory

The origin of the concept of 'intermediate vector particle'

The philosophical interest of quantum field theory, with respect to the interests of referential realism, centres round the interpretation of its major generic concept, the intermediate vector particle. Where did the concept come from? The creation of quantum field theory can be thought of as the implementation of the following steps: Classical field theory assigns a number to each space-time location. This number represents the field strength at the point. Quantum field theory assigns a quantum mechanical operator to each space-time location. Thus the theory engenders a probability distribution of possible states of affairs at each space-time point, that is possible values of the observables corresponding to the quantum mechanical operators. Interactions, say between two electrons, are described by a suitable wave equation. The exact form of the equation is determined by the requirement that it be locally gauge invariant. Amplitudes can be expanded into sets of terms, representing possible states and their probabilities. Each such term can be parsed so as to expose a particle style expression, analogous to the standard expression for the particle aspect of some already well established quantum mechanical entity, in particular the photon.

This act of parsing is nicely illustrated in Aitchison and Hey (1983, p. 29). They consider the lowest order amplitude term for electron–muon scattering. The term is parsed so as reveal three components, those representing the electron and the muon, and a third 'mystery' component. It takes the form $-ig^{\mu\nu}/q^2$. How do we know what to *call* this term? Aitchison and Hey build its meaning by reference to photons.[1] Very significantly it is called the 'photon propagator'. In the Feynman diagram representing the lowest order transition amplitude it is this term which is visualized as the 'intermediate vector particle', the exchanged photon. Taken literally the term represents not a photon, but another being of the photon *genus*. It is not massless, since the 4-momentum, q, is such that $q^2 \neq 0$. Each such interpretation is represented in a Feynman diagram, such as those presented in figures 14. 1 ff. Each diagram represents a possible state of the system expressed in particle terms. Does a Feynman diagram have any ontological significance?

Feynam himself warns us against reading his diagrams realistically. Yet when one looks at the way certain experimental research programmes have been developed the corpuscularian model does seem to be functioning ontologically. The corpuscularian reading of quantum field theory provides a genus of beings, of which the 'virtual' particle is a species. The model quantum field theory uses for the intermediate vector particle of the electromagnetic interaction is the ordinary photon, thus ensuring the IVP is of the same genus as the photon, at least in *concept*. We now have a situation in which there is a virtual and real species under the same genus. Extending this model of quantum field theory reasoning for weak and strong interactions would suggest that for every species of IVP there might (should?) be a real particle of the same genus. This line of argument seems to me to lie behind the design of experimental research programmes directed to 'looking for' such beings as the W and Z particles. The corpuscularian reading of the diagram enables the formulation of a project: the 'search for the "particle"'. The search for the 'particle' consists in trying to find a *track* or *tracks* in a suitable recording medium. In this way the whole of quantum field theory might at first sight appear to lie within the framework of policy realism. The corpuscularian reading of a Feynman diagram does not, by itself, licence any existence claims, but it has turned out to provide a reasonable guide for the policy of looking for a kind of particle of the genus adumbrated in the corpuscularian parsing of the amplitudes, and visually presented in the Feynman diagram.

But one can go a step further. It seems that the distinctive properties of the two species, IVP and free particle, under the common genus, can be explained by reference to their distinctive contexts. Perhaps, after all, it is not so absurd to think of there being a real exchange, and to think of a new status of being, and of 'virtual' as a new ontological mode. In the case of the electromagnetic interaction the concept of the IVP was modelled on that of the known free particle. In the case of the weak and strong interactions the concept of the free particle was modelled on that of the IVP. The next step must be look closely at what it is that counts, in experimental physics, as finding the free particle.

Finding it is *always* in a display of effects, not of intrinsic properties. The tie-up between tracks as displays and a particle reading of a Feynman diagram, however tricky the latter may be, is mediated by an important technical consideration. The functions describing quantum field theory interactions are superpositions not mixtures. This means that each possibility can occur, 'one at a time', rather than as in a mixture as simultaneous contributions to a combination of the total possibilities. Without this feature it would make no sense at all to take each term of the amplitude expansion, give it a particle interpretation and go on to an ontological (mis)reading of the diagram representing that possibility. The slide in the metaphysics of quantum field theory towards corpuscularianism also entails a complementary change in the implicit treatment of the probabilistic 'wave' aspect of any quantum mechanical treatment. Within the general framework of quantum mechanics, and quantum field theory is after all just second order quantum mechanics, a wave interpretation of the terms of an expansion of an amplitude is quite legitimate. But the exigencies of the experimental programme and the kinds of material practices that are possible within it have so highlighted the particle aspect of matter that, so far as I can see, the wave aspect has effectively been transmuted into behavioural propensities of particles, represented as the probabilities that this or that level of complexity of virtual particle exchange will occur. It is an implicit corpuscularian metaphysics encouraged by the existence of experimental techniques for recording *tracks* that seems to push towards a particulate ontology.

This is how *Science News* (Janurary 18, 1986) reports the 'fifth force' suggestion:

Fischbach and his coworkers relate this suggested force to a quality of matter called hypercharge or baryon number. The baryon number is related to the number of neutrons and protons, and therefore to the chemical composition of a material – thus explaining the differences in force for different materials. The researchers propose a formal similarity between this hypercharge force and electromagnetism. Just as electromagnetic forces are carried from object to object by intermediary particles called photons, so this hypercharge force would be carried by 'hyperphotons'. A number of experiments could test for the existence of the hypercharge force, including a direct search for the hyperphotons themselves. (D. E. Thomsen)

Of course this is scientific journalism, not a quote from a textbook. A textbook quote would be expressed in algebra. Hidden within that algebra would be the move by which amplitude terms are parsed in such a way that simulacra of photon forms appear, and from then on function within the framework of a corpuscularian metaphysics, particularly when the move from genus to species is made. It is that move that lies behind the very possibility of a research programme. When the wave aspect of matter does happen to be emphasized apropos an empirical domain, and hence relative to some possible experimental programme it is experimentally interpreted in terms of ensembles. This idea is already built in to the Feynman images, since each member of the ensemble is represented by a separate diagram, each with its own repertoire of IVPs. So looking for the W particle, the details of which I shall attend to more closely below, depends on taking a member, usually that of lowest order, of the total set of Feynman diagrams, as the marker of the genus to which the other species, the free particle, belongs.

I am not suggesting anything as absurd as that the masters of quantum field theory are so naïve as to be simple minded corpuscularians. Rather that the totality of cognitive and material practices of which quantum field theory is a part, involves a submerged preference for corpuscularian thought, which is evident both in the terminology and in the experimental programmes. Since there could scarcely be any other way of doing experiments in high energy physics except by recording tracks in various media, the exigencies of experimentation exert a gentle pressure towards that preference. In this I am making a similar point to that made by A. I. Miller to which I have already referred. Backstage in relativity is a notion of visualisability. Neither Miller nor I are making psychological observations. It is rather that within the conceptual structures operative in high energy physics and particularly in quantum field theory, corpuscularian concepts exert a certain hegemony over the complementary picture.

In the next chapter I shall be making a comprehensive plea for affordances, a species of dispositions introduced in part 3. Irritating though it is to referred forward in a book, I would like to complete this brief sketch with a remark about the role affordances might play in explicating what could be meant by a claim to the reality of a virtual particle. Free particles are products, I shall argue, of the effect of apparatus of a certain design on the basic stuff. We are not entitled to say that the stuff consists of particles, only that it can afford particles when shaped up by our equipment. To say that the virtual species of a genus of particle whose free species has been found, that is has engendered tracks or the equivalent, is real is to say something like this: were we able to probe the region in which, say, an electron interacts with another, it would afford particulate phenomena in a piece of equipment, if we could have it, of the same kind as that which forces the basic stuff to display an affordance of that genus in free particle experiments. This is a counterfactual statement. It would be justified by reference to the free particle case. In that case equipment of the right sort has forced the basic stuff to appear as the free species of the genus under discussion.

Corpuscularian metaphysics and the structure of quantum field theory

The use of covariance to select putative laws, that characterized the research programme of relativity, is matched in quantum field theory by the criterial use of local gauge invariance under well-chosen symmetry groups. This constraint effectively selects those laws which retain the same form no matter how the scales are set for assigning values to their constituent variables. The interactions between particles in the subatomic realm, including decay processes, appear experientially, that is are manifested in Realm 1, as permanent records of ionization tracks in various sensitive media, such as photographic emulsions. Sometimes the absence of a track is a significant event. The analysis of these events and the attempt to explain them within the framework of quantum field theory is the business of high-energy physics. This proves to be a second context in which certain features of the mathematical description of the episodes in question turn out to be ontologically significant. The recent rapid development of quantum field theory provides another useful instance of Realm 3 methodology. There is a constraint on the mathematical form of the expression of laws of nature, that they be gauge invariant and renormalizable. The coupling of this constraint with a strict set of conservation principles (to be called 'book-keeping rules') and the further constraint of the corpuscularian metaphysics creates the physical significance of the theory. Again we find, given empirical adequacy two necessary conditions for a realist reading emerging. Together they are not sufficient. But the constraining of the plurality of theories still further, by the metaphysics of corpuscularianism (which permits the application of the other two principles), does not enhance its putative realist reading though it makes a sufficient condition for selecting theories. The categorial framework of 'corpuscularianism' is somewhat weaker than the substantial-ist metaphysics that grounds relativity theory. The relationship between gauge invariance and renormalizability of the mathematical forms of the putative laws of nature applicable to this realm will need to be spelled out. I begin with a summary of the salient features of quantum field theory, as it strikes a philosopher.

1   *The meaning of the gauge invariance constraint*. In *Symmetries and reflections* Wigner (1967) places great weight on the physical irrelevance of the absolute value of potential energy. Thus he introduces the idea of a global symmetry, general gauge invariance. Laws which involve differences in or differentials of potential energy are unchanged in form under the trans-formation

$$V(x') = V(x) + C$$

where $V(x)$ is the potential energy term, and C is a constant, representing a change in bench-mark, common to all observers. But could a local change in bench-mark be tolerated, one which would represent a different change in measuring conventions for each observer? Suppose C were to be a function of position C(x). The observer O_i would recalibrate his or her measures of potential energy by adding $C(x_i)$, but the observer O_j would recalibrate his or her measures by $C(x_j)$. Could there be laws which were invariant in form under the transformation

$$V(x') = V(x) + C(x)?$$

It seems that certain laws can be reformulated to be locally gauge-invariant, including Lagrangeans and wave equations.

For example in the wave equations of quantum mechanics the absolute value of the phase of the wave front is not relevant to the form taken by these equations as laws of nature. It is only phase difference that counts in quantum mechanics. This is a global phase invariance. But the Schrodinger equation can be modified so that it is locally gauge-invariant. A change of phase representation by each observer can be accommodated by making the phase a function of x and t. The overall form of the Schrodinger equation is preserved if, when we change ψ to $e^{ie\psi(x,t)}\hbar\psi$, we change A to $A + \nabla\chi(x, t)$. One could say that the requirement of local phase invariance has provided a reason for introducing the vector potential.

Quantum field theory is that branch of high-energy physics that is concerned with the creation of hypotheses about the exchange processes that stand for forces in the subatomic realm. As I understand it the current research programme in this sector of scientific research is to make the Lagrangeans describing the electromagnetic, the weak and the strong interactions, locally gauge-invariant. This has been achieved for quantum electrodynamics by adding the photon as a 'gauge particle' to compensate for local changes in the electric field. Though it would not be historically accurate to say that there was a coherent programme of extending this treatment analogously to all interactions, this is roughly what seems to have happened. The theory of the weak interaction was achieved by introducing the W^+, the W^- and the Z_0 particles to 'carry' the interaction (the conditions for this step will be tackled below), and to be the gauge particles which make the Lagrangean description of the weak interaction locally gauge-invariant, under some well-chosen symmetry group. The further generalization of the programme to the strong interaction depended on a number of further considerations, which amount to the need for the theory to entail the existence of very weak 'forces' at short distances. I understand that only non-abelian gauge theories behave like this. It will emerge as the argument unfolds that this empirical-cum-mathematical feature chimes in well with the metaphysical constraints that lead to the gauge theory programme in general.

2 *The basic physics of interactions.* The essential step is the replacement of any explanatory apparatus that refers to forces acting between corpuscles

with a scheme in which all interactional phenomena are mediated by the exchange of particles. Collisions between particles and decays of particles, as well as the forces that bind together the components of the atomic nuclei, are comprehended under the same scheme. This class of phenomena are represented in Feynman diagrams as in Figure 14.1. Such a diagram represents the simplest mode of exchange commensurate with the demands of the conservation laws relevant in each case. The contributions of more complex modes of exchange to the interaction are dealt with by a technical device, 'renormalization'. I shall discuss the relation between renormalization and gauge invariance below. The expressions which refer to intermediate vector particles are theoretical terms, whose place in theory is justified by their role in maintaining the 'book-keeping' conservation principles germane to the kind of interaction being described.

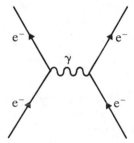

Figure 14.1   Electromagnetic interaction by photon exchange

3   *The properties of virtual particles.* The properties of the intermediate vector particles can be deduced directly from the conservation principles of the 'good' symmetries which are supposed to hold overall in each class of interactions. But in general it turns out that the rule

$$E^2 - p^2 = m^2$$

which links energy, momentum and mass for real observable particles is not obeyed by virtual particles. For example $E^2 - p^2$ is not zero for the virtual photon of electrodynamics.

So far I have discussed the use of conservation principles as book-keeping rules in quite general terms. However, the methodologically prescriptive force of the adoption of a general principle of conservation does not come out fully until one looks in some detail at the physics of a particular class of interactions. The electromagnetic field appears in the form of an exchange of virtual particles in any coupling mediated by that field.

The naïve picture treats the coupling as the conjunction of the emission of a photon at one vertex and its absorption at the other, as in Figure 14.2. Suppose the energy of the initial state is E_A and of the final state E_B. Then

$$E_A = E_B$$

But if E_N is the energy of the intermediate state of the system it can be shown that neither E_A nor E_B is equal to E_N. Book-keeping rules germane to the deduction of the properties of photons as IVPs of the electromagnetic field break down.

$$E_1 + E_2 - [E_1' + E_2 + \hbar\omega] \neq 0$$

that is

$$E_A - E_N \neq 0$$

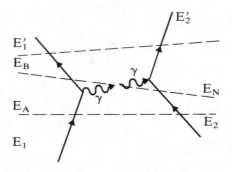

Figure 14.2   The naïve emission/absorption picture

To get a more sophisticated picture we must incorporate the Feynman 'covariance'. The above picture includes the process direction $A \rightarrow B$. But from the point of view of equivalent reference frames we must also consider the equally likely picture displayed in Figure 14.3. The total description will be a superposition of the two equally likely descriptions. From the analysis of the joint picture we get an expression for the amplitude which is Lorentz covariant. And in the combined picture both energy and momentum are conserved. According to the substantialist metaphysics to which we seem committed we are once again at least in touch with reality.

The properties of the IVP can now be calculated by using the restored conservation laws. 'Its' energy is $(E_1 - E_1') = (E_2 + E_2')$, and 'its' momentum is $(p_1 - p_1') = (p_2 - p_2')$. And for the virtual photon as IVP

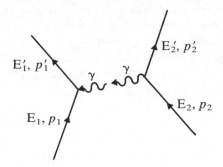

Figure 14.3 The alternative process

$$q = (E_1 - E_1')^2 - (p_1 - p_1')^2 = (p_1 - p_1')^2$$

which is an invariant.

For the ordinary photon $p^2 = E^2 - c^2p^2 = 0$, but for the virtual photon $(p_1 - p_1')^2 \neq 0$, that is the virtual photon has mass. From a philosophical point of view the 'anomalous' property of the virtual photon seems to arise directly out of the Feynman restoration of the full bouquet of conservation principles typical of the substantialist metaphysics.

The choice of symmetry group and the achievement of gauge invariance relative to that group and the ascription of properties to IVPs through the use of strict conservation book-keeping rules on the basis of a conservative 'grammar' both seem to be mutually motivated pairs of operations. The empirical basis of this elaborate, internally supported structure is simple, namely the preservation of the observed initial and final states of an interaction or decay. Despite the complexity of the structure of quantum field theory the IVPs are apparently typical hypothetical entities of an advanced corpuscularian physical theory. The diagrams are, then, despite Feynman's disclaimers, treated as quasi-pictorial representations of the mechanisms of processes. We have already seen how the diagrams are *both* corpuscularian metaphors and guides to research designed to find the free species of beings whose genus is defined by their 'hidden' constituents, that is those which do not have or cannot be assigned tracks in the real world on the basis of photography, computer reconstructions, and so on, but which can be associated in some way with particles which do leave tracks.

But should we call the electromagnetic IVPs 'photons' ? After all, they have one startlingly anomalous property, 'mass'. The justification for the assimilation that the use of the common term implies lies, I think, in the natural history of quantum electrodynamics. Once the decision to separate the Hamiltonian for matter from that for radiation is taken, the theory of exchanges must develop from the conjunction of two 'pictures', one representing the emission of a free photon and the other its absorption. Thus the basic physics invokes standard photons as elementary quanta of excitation of the electromagnetic field considered as an infinite array of elementary oscillators. In this way the genus of the electromagnetic IVPs is fixed. It is only in the further development of the theory that we come to see that the IVPs of quantum electrodynamics are a different species from the photons of tradition. (Some would say that all photons are virtual. Those which are 'free' link distant vertices and are of near-zero mass.) Thus far the existence of virtual photons remains open. The framework of thought is still exactly that of the policy realism of part four. A free 'X' need not have exactly the same properties as a captive 'X' provided they belong to the same kind.

Suppose theory tells us of a necessary condition that must obtain for a certain, quite definite phenomenon to be possible. When the phenomenon turns up, physicists make a confident claim for the existence of the necessary condition, in just the same sense as the phenomenon exists. A cause, after all, must be at least as real as its effect. This reasoning is apparent in the following quotation:

The researchers do not actually 'see' gluons in their apparatus [for instance they do not manage to photograph their trails]. At the highest energy at which [the apparatus] runs they find that a small fraction of electron-positron collisions produce three sprays or 'jets' of particles ... [of] three pronged appearance ... which all lie in the same plane. . . . the physicists believe that the jets originate in a gluon, quark and anti-quark that materialize from the electron-positron annihilation. (Quoted by Pickering, 1984)

But the imperative to accept such particles is stronger than the force of a necessary physical condition. The 'intermediate vector boson' comes not only from the 'book-keeping' rules of the relevant conservation principles, but also from the conditions for the gauge invariance of the relevant Lagrangean. IVPs are also gauge particles, GPs.

A particular case of the use of this kind of reasoning is the Gargamelle experiment. On the basis of the properties assigned to the Z particle of the weak interaction a phenomenon called the 'neutral-current event' would be expected (see figure 14.4). But neutrinos are involved in this episode. Since they are uncharged, they leave no ionization tracks, so a real-world neutral-current event would look something like the track in Figure 14.5. It is not hard to visualize the photograph of real tracks which would count as a picture of a neutral-current event.

At first sight this looks like a simple case of hypothetico-deductive reasoning. It seems to make gauge invariance under whatever group of transformations is popular (in this case SU (3)) as ontologically pregnant as

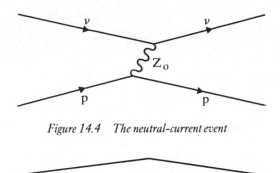

Figure 14.4   The neutral-current event

Figure 14.5   Schematic track of a neutral-current event

was covariance under the Lorentz group. But the matter is not so simple. In the relativity case the choice of the Lorentz group as the relevant 'base-line' is based upon considerations that are independent of the particular form that covariance takes in the harmonized laws. The 'contraction' rule can be deduced directly from the Michelson–Morley experiment. But, so far as I understand the reasoning that leads to the choice of symmetry groups in quantum field theory, it involves choosing a symmetry group just so that the favoured Lagrangean will turn out to be gauge-invariant. This makes the gauge invariance condition more potent than the group of transformations. However, there is another way of reasoning which leads to the community accepting the IVP in question.

The photograph which *we* read as a picture of a neutral-current event appears in the discussion *as interpreted*. I have already pointed out the importance of the balance between plausibility and revisability of theories. When the neutral-current event does turn up, that balance shifts slightly towards the left. But in a recent study of the history of the development of this approach to subatomic physics Pickering (1984, pp. 188–95; 300–2) points out an interesting feature of the control of the experimentation. The 'observability' of neutral-current events is relative to the measures taken to eliminate from the tables of results another class of events, neutral background events. The latter are interactions between neutrons, which like neutrinos leave no tracks, and the circumambient environment, apparatus, etc. Pickering shows that the conventions of interpreting were so set in the 1960s as to strike out all events initiated by trackless particles as neutral-background events. Only when the convention was reset in the 1970s did neutral-current events, initiated by neutrinos, become observable. He argues, no doubt with justice, that the resetting of the convention had to do with growing confidence in the theory that said that neutral-current events should exist. Of course confidence in the theory will not make neutral-current events come into existence. Neutral-current events might not have been detected within the reset convention. Resetting is a necessary but not a sufficient condition for their discovery. This point hardly seems worth emphasizing, but one must remember that there is a reading of the programme to sociologize all explanations of scientific decision-making which seems to suggest that conventions make existents, rather than making possible the setting up of experimental programmes for their detection.

But the history of the study of the weak interaction shows that it is actually much closer to the kind of example that I used to ground the case for policy realism for the beings of Realm 2. Experiments at CERN have produced sprays of particles, the immediate antecedent of which, though not itself leaving a trail, seems to have the physical properties assigned to the W particles by quantum field theory. If by 'free' particle is meant a being which leaves an ionization track that can be photographed or otherwise recorded, and which is the only particle required to explain the length, curvature and density of the track, then the CERN experiments have not quite identified a free W particle. But at least it is the next best thing. Quantum field theory then looks very like a theory-family in the sense outlined in part four. The difference lies in the mode of manifestation of the hypothesized beings when they are 'free'. Realm 2 beings appear to ordinary observation within the world of perception. Any problem about their existence is reducible to a philosophical problem about the status of Realm 1 beings. But even the most robust 'free' particles in high-energy physics are distanced from the naïve observer by the causal processes that intervene between the moving particle and the ionization track it leaves. These processes are epistemically ineliminable. It follows that when we, the scientific community, are using observational predicates in our description of these beings, they must appear in *dispositional attributions*. These are the characteristic attributions of Realm 3 discourse.[2]

A summary of the methodology

From the point of view of quantum field *theory* there are two interlocking steps.

1   The mechanism of the fields (forces) is described in terms of exchanges of virtual particles. They are introduced as intermediate vector particles, IVPs, and their properties are determined by the 'bookkeeping' requirements of the conservation principles that control the attribution of

quantum numbers for such properties as 'charge', 'spin', 'colour', etc. The properties that are conserved differ between the three interactions, strong, weak and electromagnetic. This aspect of the theorizing goes on within the framework of a corpuscularian metaphysical model.

2   Virtual particles also appear as gauge particles, GPs. Their properties are determined by the requirement that they compensate local field changes so that the Lagrangean for the whole interaction is locally gauge-invariant under some appropriate symmetry group. The choice of symmetry group is not independently motivated as is the choice of the Lorentz group for relativity. The symmetry groups which 'discipline' the invariances are derived from the rules for the conservation of quantum number properties, rules found necessary to keep the books in the descriptions of the results of experiment. Properties and symmetry groups 'grow up together' so to speak.

If, by each route, we get concepts such that

$$IVP = GP$$

the community seems to be satisfied with the theory. It is plausible in just the sense of that term I developed for the assessment of theorizing for Realm 2.

The story of the W and Z particles also illustrates this procedure. By the use of the methodology sketched above the weak interaction is pictured as a process mediated by particle exchange, and the properties of that class of corpuscles worked out in the standard way. The Gargamelle experiment shares the weakness of all attempts to prove the plausibility of a theory conceived hypothetico-deductively, by the test of a prediction of phenomena of the same natural kind as the lowest-level 'facts' encompassed by the theory.

But if the parallel with Realm 2 methodology is taken more seriously the policy realist treatment of quantum field theory suggests a different kind of experiment, an existential search for examples of the beings referred to in the theory.

The quasi-pictorial reading of the Feynman diagrams, or if you like the taking of W *particle* talk fairly literally, motivates the 'search for the free W particle'. This amounts to the conceiving of and realizing experimentally a physical situation in which the vertices of the W process are well separated and the 'particle itself' can become manifest.[3] In fact the W particle does not manifest itself, *in propria persona*, but rather the phenomena are such that any alternative explanation of the 'cross-section' of the process is ruled out. Nevertheless the argument hinges on the general point about the difference between the status of 'virtual' and 'real' particles – that it is a matter of the genus encompassing two species, one of which can be tracked. But we are still in Realm 3. The W particle is not manifested by virtue of generating its own unique track. It has to be inferred from the tracks of a shower of particles to which it is antecedent. But that last and crucial condition can be satisfied at all only through the use of the appropriate book-keeping rules – even when free, Ws are, in some sense, virtual!

The case against subsuming the virtual status as a species of physical reality turns on the unclarity of the particle concept in the context of exchanges. The analysis above, in which IVPs seem to have most particulate a representation, is the lowest order of exchange. The 'true picture', so to speak, is a superposition of the higher-order modes of exchange as well – for instance, figure 14.6. In the 'true picture' the number of virtual photons is not sharp, since the system fluctuates over an infinity of superposed states. On the reasonable principle that ontologically photons are entity-like and have some of the 'grammar' of individuals, the unsharpness of the number of virtual cousins counts against their reality. But the upset of the metaphysical clarity of the virtual particle picture goes deeper.

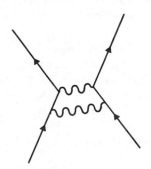

Figure 14.6   Higher-order exchange

The metaphysics and methodology of quantum field theory in terms of particles meshes only with the simplest kinds of exchange. The more complex modes of exchange are conceivable within the discipline of the conservation rules which are represented by higher-order terms in the mathematical description of the interaction or decay. Integrating over these possibilities should give a gross description of the actual interaction. But the result of these operations are infinite values for momenta and other relevant physical properties, such as charge. It was shown by Feynman, Tomonaga and others that in general one could absorb all the infinities into a redefinition of the mass and charge of the beings adumbrated in the theory. When these quantities are replaced by the measured values of the same parameters, finite values are imposed. This technique is called 'renormalization'. The same way of cancelling infinities was extended from quantum electrodynamics to the combined theory of electromagnetic and weak interaction by 't Hooft, by adding scalar fields to the Lagrangean descriptions of the interactions.

Essentially what we are viewing here is a series of adjustments to the mathematics to make the ontology of the theory 'right'. But there are also adjustments to the ontology to save the mathematics. This comes out clearly in the history of the Higgs mechanism. In the gauge-invariant version of quantum electrodynamics the intermediate vector particles are not massless photons but the theory is renormalizable. However, this is not the case for the weak interaction. The conventional theory of massive charged vector particles is not renormalizable. Such a theory would be renormalizable if a gauge symmetry could be imposed. But the mass of the quanta are such that all gauge symmetries are violated. Suppose there were a 'hidden' gauge symmetry. This is the motivation behind the introduction of the Higgs mechanism.

Just as covariance depends on a commitment to conservation, so do the mathematical adjustments and ontological hypotheses that make up the story of the use of renormalization. But what are the properties whose conservation exerts such a powerful effect on the development of theory? We shall see that in general these properties are created so that there shall be conservation.

The unification programme conforms exactly to Aronson's analysis of theoretical science as directed to the construction of a common ontology for the phenomena in a domain. Suppose quarks are the basis of both electro-weak theory and the theory of the strong interaction. They become a common ontology for all three theories. All the corpuscles invoked in the preceding theories are now thought of as complex and composed of quarks. Two independent sets of quantum numbers (new properties) were proposed for quarks. Electro-weak gauge theory corresponded to local invariance of quark flavours, while strong gauge theory corresponded to local invariance of quark colours. The IVPs (which in a well-ordered theory are also the gauge particles) are coloured gluons. Looked at in this context colour, is a property that behaves 'grammatically' like charge. Later a further quantum number (property) 'charm' was added. In sum flavour, colour and charm, through conservation principles, maintain the bookkeeping, so to speak, of the initial and final stages of the subatomic event. Their bearers, quarks and gluons, provide the fields, whose adjustment to some suitable symmetry group results in a locally gauge-invariant Lagrangean description of the interaction. As I remarked above the choice of symmetry group does not seem to be animated by independent physical considerations, as was the choice of the Lorentz group in special relativity. Instead it seems to have been arrived at as the most elegant group of co-ordinate transformations under which a Lagrangean with the necessary gluon content is locally gauge-invariant.

Once again it is evident that the most fundamental metaphysical dogma, that which controls the way in which ever new ranges of hypothetical Realm 3 properties are invented, is the preservation of conservation principles. But that is only half the story. These uses of conservation do not lead physicists back to rooted properties. There is no hint of the a priori generalization of the primary qualities of bulk, figure, texture and motion to all existing beings, observable or unobservable, that set Newtonian science firmly in Realm 2. It was only our lack of microscopical eyes that prevented our experiencing those 'arrangements of [Newtonian] particles in the super-ficies of bodies' that were thought so to effect light as to cause our different colour sensations. Can anything further be said about the new properties? I shall argue in the next chapter that all these properties are affordances, a kind of dispositional property with which we became acquainted in the exposition of the Gibsonian version of the metaphysics of experience.

Quantum field physics as a theory-family with a typical system structure

Looking back at the exposition of quantum field theory one must be struck by the remarkable extent to which the evolution of this branch of physics conforms to the developmental scheme outlined in part four. The corpuscularian metaphysics seems to be a source analogue in just the way Newtonian metaphysics was a source analogue for classical physics. Disturbances to the internal balance of the theory-family structure lead to restorations of equilibrium by adjustments from within the structure. In this way it behaves like a system. These adjustments have characteristically taken the form of the invention of IVPs and gauge particles *under the discipline of the conservation principles* and the requirement that the Lagrangean descriptions of the inter-actions be locally gauge-invariant. Furthermore the introduction of new properties is controlled by the traditional menu. There are really only three kinds of properties. There are scalars like charge and mass–energy. There are vectors like momentum. And there are polar vectors like spin, isospin and parity.

But the conservation principles are yet more powerful. It is relative to them that new properties are introduced to permit standard bookkeeping exercises through which the physics of the events in question is developed. A theory-family in Realm 3 science could be described as an ordered pair consisting of a mathematical structure and a metaphysical scheme, which is itself composed of a categorial prescript (such as the corpuscularian scheme) and a set of appropriate conservation rules. The latter controls the readjustments we make in the former. For example, in the face of the non-conservation of parity in the weak interaction, physicists continue inventing properties, with the 'grammatical' constraints of existing physical theory, until they reach a set of quantum numbers which are conserved. And of course they may invent the particles to go along with them. This last step, as became clear, I hope, in the exposition of the way Feynman restored conservation to the lowest-order exchange picture of quantum electro-dynamics, is constrained by a key feature of the mathematical structure, namely covariance. But why covariance?

The close link between covariance, symmetry and conservation, even in the context of the obscure affordances of quantum chromodynamics, suggests one obvious and commensensical explanation of why physicists use symmetry considerations. It is summed up in Redhead's introduction of the generic term 'stabilities' to describe the gamut of these principles. The commonsense principle, implicit too in Feynman's notion of the 'robust', runs something like this: Whatever persists unchanged through change is real. Call this the 'robustness principle'. It is an exceedingly powerful principle, since it would permit very direct inferences from Realm 1 phenomena, certain kinds of observable changes, through some bookkeeping calculations, to phenomena of Realm 2 or 3.

The robustness principle should be distinguished from the Kantian doctrine that whenever there is a change there must be a non-change against which it is picked out. Kant's doctrine of conservation licenses his transcendental deduction of the category of substance in B225. Physics does not seem to need a principle quite as strong as this, to support modest realist attitudes. The robustness principle has the advantage of linking hypotheses concerning conserved quantities, substances, to empirically testable conditions, namely whether or not the accepted current bookkeeping rules can be applied. There is a measure of circularity in the genesis of these rules, that is the cluster of covariances, symmetries and conservations are mutually adjusted to one another. But that adjustment is not indefinitely flexible, as the history of particle physics amply demonstrates. The robustness principle is both metaphysical, controlling the formation of scientific concepts, and empirical, contingent in any specific application on the actual affordances. However, the robustness principle will be qualified in the last chapter, in which favourable consideration will be given to Bohr's warning that there can be no unequivocal *specific* application of any metaphysical principle to the ur-stuff of the physical universe. All principles are applied to that which Bohr called 'phenomena', those queer things which are half artefacts and half *objets trouvés*, and which we call experimental set-ups. Only the affordances for these phenomena are ascribable to the basic stuff of the universe. How remarkable it is that conservation principles can be applied to them!

The two stabilities upon which the edifice of Realm 3 science depends are both susceptible of commonsense explications. They both pick out what remains the same through changing points of view, that which is independent of the 'condition' of the observer. Stabilities differ from seventeenth-century primary qualities only in the non-subjective quality of what modern physics takes to be the 'condition of the observer'. In the seventeenth century the primary qualities were distinguished against the background of the subjective/objective distinction. 'Point of view' had as much to do with the qualities of independent consciousnesses as with differing location in space and time. (Galilean invariance and the principles of indifference associated with it were treated at the time as conditions governing the appropriateness of citing a cause in an explanation of change.)

Both of our stabilities have to do with independence of choice of a basis for measurement and physical description. Relativistic covariance is a stability which is defined just so as to be independent of the inertial frame which an observer uses as his or her bench-mark for the measurement of kinematic variables and the investigation of their relationships. Gauge invariance is a stability which is defined just so as to be independent of the particular calibrations which an observer choses as his or her personal zero or bench-mark for the measurement of dynamic variables and the investigation of their relationships. I think that the reasoning which underlies the place these stabilities currently hold is essentially simple.

Whatever description (or measure) of a physical process whose form (value) depends on the arbitrarily chosen conditions of observation cannot be real. The robustness principle follows immediately as a necessary condition for the referent of a description (a process described by a law of nature; a quality whose value is given in a measurement) to be real. And this is just the sense of 'real' which crystallized out of the search for a coherent account of scientific realism undertaken in chapter 2.

Finally we can see in a very simple and commonsensical way why renormalization has to be achieved for any quantum field theory to be taken seriously as a description of an unobserved reality.[4] The idea of the conservation of infinite quantities in a finite process, say beta decay, is incoherent. It is incoherent in just the way that the infinite forces required by Newtonian corpuscular theory during infinitesimal contact times were incoherent, against the background of Newtonian metaphysics. Unless renormalization can be achieved, a quantum field theory of a class of interactions would be at odds with the metaphysical basis of the overall enterprise. As a theory-family the system would not be in equilibrium. Renormalization restores the balance between the source concepts and the theory they inspire, and the experimental results which are taken up into the revised theory by the very act of renormalization.

Can the persistence of the same metaphysical basis from the proto-Newtonian physics of the seventeenth century to relativity and quantum field theory be explained in some fundamental way? We *could* say 'Nature has so far proved to be well disposed to open up its secrets to those who adopt the techniques which depend upon the robustness principle.' Or is it that by tacitly adopting the robustness principle our explorations of diverse phenomena have drifted towards techniques which promote the display of just those affordances whose manifestations are susceptible of that particular kind of bookkeeping? Perhaps that kind of bookkeeping is a reflection of the conditions for constructing an intelligible discourse about the phenomena our manipulations bring into being?.

The robustness principle seems to be closely linked to an a priori commitment to a realist epistemology. The route to reality passes through symmetry and conservation. So the system structure of the quantum field theory-family is reality-preserving. But it became clear that at best the Feynman approach led only to necessary conditions for a theory to be susceptible of a realist construal. Particle physics, under the control of the general conservationist attitude, has been elaborated by the addition of a repertoire of particle properties that, despite their exotic appearance, are classical in the sense of obeying similar principles of 'deep grammar' to familiar dispositional attributes. Their general coherence with classical concepts is guaranteed by the overall control exercised by the corpuscularian metaphysics and the generic conservation principle. So we, as philosophers, on pain of circularity, cannot use the replication of classical 'grammar' in support of a general adherence to corpuscularian metaphysics and conserved quantities. It was an interest in the conditions of unambiguous communication that led Bohr to his 'correspondence principle'. Could we find an argument that would justify adherence to the generic conservation principle as a condition for a theory-family to engender *intelligible* theories?

If it could be shown that the conditions for our organic survival favoured creatures built to look for and make use of conserved quantities (stable entities) then that would be a reason why physicists, being just such creatures, find conservation principles so deeply attractive. Meyerson's argument for the importance of 'lawfulness' is based on the necessity that to master nature we must achieve reliable forecasts of the immediate future. I have criticized this argument above. The successful evolution of organisms that detect and make use of stabilities in their environment would seem to entail that there are such stabilities at least among objects of daily use. But the deeper principle that the realm of the unobservable should also contain stabilities does not follow from the evolution argument. At best it would follow that physicists tend to imagine that realm in those terms. It will be intelligible to them only if it is thought of as containing the physical stabilities which appear as symmetries and conserved quantities. Even if it could be shown that only theories based upon conservation principles could be intelligible to human beings, it would not follow that such theories picked out the true architectonic principles of nature. At best this would leave the basis of physical science exactly where Kant located it, in the synthetic a priori principles by which we construct a phenomenal world that would thereby be intelligible to us. It would come as no surprise to discover that we imaginatively extended that world in accordance with the same principles.

It has turned out that the force of both the 'mathematical' methodologies, covariance and gauge invariance with renormalization, is metaphysically conservative. At the end of the day the philosopher of science interested in the impicit ontological foundations of natural science is presented with the age-old problem: how does substance underlie phenomena? This is just the problem that Aronson's 'mappings' approach glosses over. In general there are two ways in which the problem can be tackled. In the one the part–whole principle is invoked, so that the tracts of substance presented in Realm 1 are treated as (structured) drifts of substantial individuals in Realms 2 or 3. But the analysis of quantum field theory has shown that this treatment is inadequate. A theory of properties is also needed. The right kind of ontological hierarchy to match the way in which hierarchies of theories develop in the physical sciences seems to be based on the principle that all properties are grounded dispositions. This idea will be confirmed by the analysis of the apparently 'new' properties invented to match the quantum numbers of the menagerie of particles called for by the corpuscularian trend in high-energy particle physics.

But the part–whole principle and the grounded disposition principle are in tension. If both principles are applied to natural science then an indefinite ontological regress is opened up, since there will be no properties which could serve as the attributes of the ultimate 'parts', because according to the grounded disposition principle it is always proper to ask how any property is grounded. I hope to find a resolution of this tension in the philosophy of science of Neils Bohr.

15

Dispositions
and their Groundings

Dispositions: their structure and conditions of attribution

The argument of the last chapter left a key concept unanalysed and undefended. The properties with which physicists endow the denizens of Realm 3 belong in the general category of affordances. These are dispositions which, though grounded in states of the world which are independent of human whim and convention, are manifested in phenomena which are brought into being through some human intervention. A phenomenon identical with that created in the Gargamelle experiment, for instance, may never occur in nature. Nevertheless on the basis of what happens during the activation of experimental set-ups the scientific community cheerfully ascribes properties to beings which are supposed to exist independently of the state of mind and level of technical expertise of the community. Such properties must be dispositions or at the least contain an irreducible dispositional component. Furthermore they are not just dispositions but causal powers, since they are supposed to be the properties that activate the equipment when it is switched on. But they are not simple dispositions, since the form of their manifestation is a function of the way the community has chosen to build its apparatus. (See my discussion of the role of the Stern-Gerlach apparatus in the physics of molecular beams and the fourth quantum number (Harré, 1983). Science is not only a cognitive enterprise but also a material practice!)

An entity may have a tendency, disposition or propensity to manifest itself in certain observable states or events in a particular environment, which, when deliberately created, we call the experimental conditions. For example a body in a gravitational field has a tendency to accelerate (exert a force) which would be manifested in a certain motion, *ceteris paribus*. An Atwood's machine is so constructed as to allow a human being to study systematically the manifestations of just that one disposition. To borrow a useful terminology from Bhaskar (1978), one might call the subsequent motion 'actual' and the tendency of which it is a typical manifestation 'real'. The laws of physics invoked to explain the behaviour of various parts of the Atwood's machine, and by analogy things in the world, describe the tendency and not the actual motions; $d^2x/dt^2 = mg$ is such a law. To interpret the laws of physics as summary descriptions of actual events is the 'fallacy of actualism', a special case of the product/process fallacy. The reason for insisting on a tendency interpretation of laws such as that cited above is simply that it is contingent that any actual motion occurs, and if it does that it is a clear-cut manifestation of the tendency described in the dynamic law. The fact that the world is full of beings with countervailing tendencies to the ones that are momentarily of interest to the scientific community will become a matter of serious concern as this argument unfolds. What happens is *always* a resultant of many coexisting tendencies, some of which are so related to the tendency or propensity of interest that they prevent any manifestation at all. The metaphysics of classical mechanics exactly exemplifies this sketch, with its concepts of force, potential, virtual motion, and so on. I shall argue that it extends to the deepest levels of contemporary physics, though not without some modulations.

Working physicists unreflectingly manage such concepts with ease. But from the philosopher's point of view they are highly problematic and their defence will require a careful dismemberment of the leading notions to enquire into the standing of their root ideas. Since Hume mounted his famous attack on the metaphysics of the science of his day, dispositions seldom rest undisturbed by philosophers for long. The latest, and therefore the one to which I shall mostly attend in this chapter, comes from N. Cartwright (1983). How is it possible reliably to individuate and identify elemental tendencies when even in the most carefully contrived experiment the actual course of events never reflects the nature of just one disposition? I shall also be addressing another problem, that of giving an acceptable account of the status of the possibilities which seem to be referred to whenever a physicist or anyone else ascribes a disposition to a real thing or substance. This is one domestic corner of the grand problem of the ontology of modalities and its relation to the truth conditions of modal statements. Tendencies are the dispositions of individuals. *This* cannon-ball has a tendency to fall, *this* electron has a tendency to accelerate towards a positively charged plate, and so on. In the simple case a tendency is individuated by reference to the material individual to which it is ascribed and to the kind of effect it is likely to produce. Within this framework the statement that two material individuals have the same tendency to turn green on exposure to light, say, should be read in the sense of qualitative identity of distinct individual dispositions.

The matter is made more complicated by the fact that the same material individual may properly be ascribed different degrees of the same tendency in different circumstances. For example the weight of a body differs depending on the gravitational field. 'Same tendency' in this framework must be read as 'tendency of the same kind'. Furthermore, manifest behaviour is not, in general, an unequivocal guide to the correct ascription of tendencies. In most cases there are several co-acting dispositions involved and manifest behaviour is the effect of their composition. Sometimes there is no manifest behaviour when two or more exactly countervailing tendencies are activated. How could we know that a univocal manifestation involves more than one tendency? The individuation of tendencies is actually a more complex matter than appears from the brief account above. A tendency is individuated by its grounding not just in the material individual to which it is ascribed, but in some particular state of that individual. For instance the tendency to fall is ascribed to the mass of a body, while its tendency to swerve in a magnetic field is ascribed to its charge. In the Millikan experiment the charged droplet displays a form of motion which is the manifestation of the resultant of three tendencies, each grounded in a different occurrent property of the drop – namely, weight grounded in mass, electrostatic force grounded in charge, and viscous resistance grounded in molecular states of the surface layer.

Tendencies are ascribed on the basis of our beliefs about the natures of things, and involve very special assumptions about manifest behaviour in usually highly contrived conditions in which each tendency-grounding aspect of the nature of a kind of thing can be manifested one at a time. In a certain sense there is no such thing as *the* disposition. There are various situations in which the common grounding can be manifested in some situation-specific behaviour. There may be several different conditional or action components of the total content structure of a disposition associated with a common grounding. In certain special circumstances such conditions can be achieved in the laboratory. Affordances are a special kind of tendency, one for which the typical manifestation must be related to something specifically human. In the perceptual case affordances reflect human intentions and interests, while in the case of Realm 3 science they reflect the choices of apparatus which the community decides to construct. But affordances are grounded in the objective properties of the beings to which they are ascribed. In these circumstances it is clear there can never be a wholly theory-free reading of the natures of things from the observable displays of tendencies.

Tendencies and propensities are exactly suited to a central role in non-Humean causal explanations. But in that role they are subject to further qualifications. These qualifications lead to a number of distinct schemata in which the variety of causal modes can be expressed. The structure of the causal explanation of an observable phenomenon is as follows:

A *Particular Being* has a *Tendency* which if *Released*, in a certain type of situation, is manifested in some observable *Action* but when *Blocked* has no observable effect.

Adding the releasing and blocking condition introduces the basic element of agency into the causal story. Further advance in the scientific under-standing of a causal process involves the discovery of the mediating mechanism and the precise state of the particular being in which the tendency is grounded. Sometimes a tendency is to be ascribed to a particular being because of some unique and idiosyncratic configuration of its components; sometimes a tendency is ascribed to a being just in so far as that being is a member of class of such beings and so can be expected to share a common nature with its fellows. Finally one must note that some beings have the tendencies they do because of their internal or intrinsic natures, while others acquire tendencies dependently through the influence of environmental influences upon them. I shall refer to this distinction as that between micro- and macro-grounding. In either case the tendencies ascribed to a particular being are to be accounted for by reference to a regress of explanations creating a hierarchy of tendencies.

Dispositions, together with all the other concepts of the same family, such as tendencies, propensities, powers and forces, are ontologically problematic. They are ascribed to actual occurrent beings, but, in most contexts, they seem to refer to possible rather than actual manifestations of the typical behaviour cited in the consequent of the leading conditional clause. Furthermore, as I have emphasized, these possible manifestations are both diverse and conditional on the obtaining of the appropriate conditions. Taken extensionally, concepts of the disposition family seem to include both actual and possible states of affairs. A great deal of confusion has been engendered, I believe, by attempts to create a uniform ontology for both the actual and the possible segment of such extensions. I have already argued for the need to accept a dual ontology, and dispositions provide yet another case in which it seems appropriate. But, as I argued in the first chapter, the idea of a such a dual ontology is a fable, called for only if a dogmatic extensionist account of meaning is taken for granted.

Developing a metaphysics of properties along these lines suggests another way of introducing the idea of a Realm 3 science. It seems that explanatory regresses are an inherent feature of dispositional explanations, which soon run beyond the limits of the observable. The technique of anticipating observation by using analogues to control the natural-kind hypotheses that enter into explanations soon runs into difficulties. This was strikingly exemplified in the way 'new' properties were required to maintain the hegemony of conservation principles in high-energy physics. To complete the general account of dispositionalist forms of scientific discourse a description of the form of such regresses will be required.

I begin with the idea of attribute stripping. To take a hackneyed example, colour is parsed out of the world of science and the real world stripped of colour as an attribute, by referring to the power of surfaces to reflect light differentially, and the power of light of different wavelengths to excite sensations differentially in a sensitive organism. The power of surfaces to reflect light is grounded in some feature of their molecular structure. Molecular structure has dispositional properties which are grounded in the natures of constituent atoms, and so on.

Power 1 is to be analysed in terms of dispositions 1 grounded in the nature 1 of beings of level 1. Such natures are usually associated with natural-kinds in ways that were brought out in part two.

Nature 1 is some (usually structured) ensemble of beings with powers 2.

Power 2 is to be analysed in terms of dispositions 2 grounded in the nature 2 of beings of level 2. Such natures are usually associated with natural-kinds.

Nature 2 is some (usually structured) ensemble of beings with powers 3.

And so on . . .

This rather coarse-grained analysis needs refining in several ways. There has been a general but by no means universal tendency for the number of distinct kinds of beings to be reduced as the regress develops through successive 'levels'. The obvious contingency of this tendency should warn us against any too ready acceptance of paucity of natural-kinds as a mark of progress towards a description of the real nature of the universe. The endeavour to arrive at a common ontology on which to ground dispositions with the most diverse observable manifestations does not at all depend on any principle of paucity.

Looking at the beginning of each statement in the above schema, one notices a sequence of powers, 1, 2, 3, etc. These are usually distinct powers, those lower in the sequence engendering the dispositions or tendencies involved in those higher in the list. That would be the proper way to describe the sequence of powers in the example above. Looking at the second part of each statement one notices a sequence of levels which seem to be ordered by the part–whole relationship. But for the whole to manifest different powers from those of its parts the whole must not be simply an aggregate of those parts. In general wholes which manifest different powers from their parts are a distinctive and stable structure of those parts. Mere aggregates do not exhibit emergent causal powers because they have no structure. So far in this discussion I have had micro-explanations in mind.

But with suitable adjustments of phrasing the schema will also capture the form of macro-explanations. While the part–whole relation is preserved, the cause–effect relation is reversed for macro-explanations. The powers of parts are explained by reference to the powers of the whole. When this whole is the physical universe I call this an ultra-grounding. This is the Machean form of explanation.

The general principle of superposition

Dispositional concepts began to play a central role in physical theory in the seventeenth century. Since that time there has scarcely been a physicist of note who has not subscribed to the principle that real tendencies are rarely, if ever, exactly manifested. In the real world there are many co-acting tendencies, and the actual course of nature is the manifestation of their combination. It has been an important task for physicists to find the rules of combination. The most general principle of combination of tendencies is the rule of superposition. According to this rule the total effect of a set of co-acting tendencies is the sum of the effects each would have were it to act alone. Subsidiary rules specify the algorithm by which the sum is arrived at case by case. For example the parallelogram of forces is an algorithm for discovering the effect of two or more forces acting on a common test body.

The parallelogram rule enables a physicist to relate components and their resultant. But the clarity of the algorithm may not reflect an equally clear ontological principle. I owe a useful pair of illustrative examples to John Roche. Applying the parallelogram rule to velocities, one can determine the resultant motion of an airship that would have had a certain forward velocity in still air, and would have had a certain lateral velocity merely drifting in a side wind. However, when the airship with motors running and actually blown upon moves in the direction of the diagonal of the parallelogram, the ontological situation is such that though the resultant velocity is real the resolved components are notional. There is no sense in which the airship is really moving sideways and really moving forward. The superposition rule must be read counterfactually. But when one applies the parallelogram rule to forces the ontological situation is different. The component forces are real, but the resultant is notional, a useful fiction to be used in calculating joint manifest effects. There is no general rule for distributing existence among components and resultants of superposition algorithms. In any real case the question is resolved by referring the components of the motion to independently identifiable physical causes. The resultant force has real components, one due to the engines and the other to the pressure gradient that powers the side wind.

Electromagnetic concepts as grounded dispositions

The vectors E and B refer to active tendencies or dispositions which are manifested in the motion of test particles in electric and magnetic fields. They could be taken to refer to forces which are manifested in accelerations of 'unit' test particles. I shall so take them. In the ontology I shall defend in this chapter 'force' is not an alternative term for mass-acceleration, but an ontologically independent being which as a causal influence produces mass-accelerations. E and B are associated in electromagnetic theory with potentials according to the following steady field relations:

$$E = -\text{grad } V;$$

$$B = \text{curl } A$$

V and A are the scalar and vector potentials respectively. Consider the relation between E and V. As I remarked above Ex_i refers to a causal influence exerted on a charged body at x_i. It is a tendency or disposition grounded in a state of the field at x_i. The scalar V is a substance concept and the quantity of 'it' present at x_i is measured by the work done to bring a particle to x_i against the field from a chosen bench-mark. Similarly the second of the above relations ties Bx_i to the field state referred to by A, the vector potential. To see that V and A are quantities it is enough to notice that Vx_i is the latent energy of the field at x_i, while Ax_i is the latent momentum. It is the momentum which would be delivered to a test particle at x_i if the field was reduced to zero.

Not only does electromagnetism involve a decomposition of the electromagnetic field into electric and magnetic components, but also each 'component' field is represented not by one but two vectors. The electric field is represented by E and D, while the magnetic field is represented by H and B. But this decomposition represents yet another aspect of the field ontology. Technically each pair represents two different averages of the field (see figure 15.1). B and H, E and D are just different ways of expending the energy of the field. They correspond to the case of dual dispositions associated with a common ground. They are 'really' distinct because each member of a pair is manifested differently. Maxwell said (1890, vol. 2, p. 27), 'when the magnetic field is explored by a moving wire, it is the magnetic induction, not the magnetic force which is directly measured.' H is measured by taking account of the cause of the field, that is of the current needed to create it.

Suppose we observe a large boulder slowly moving towards us along a muddy track. From our position in front of the rock we can give no

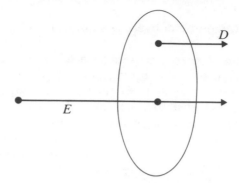

Figure 15.1   The meaning of electromagnetic vectors

unequivocal account of the sources of the motion and how it is to be decomposed into the pushes severally exerted by those presumed to be pushing it. By climbing the bank we can see that one huge and powerful man is pushing at an angle to the line of advance while one puny chap is shoving directly ahead with all his might. Two tendencies have been individuated by reference to their groundings in distinct powerful particulars. And these particulars are members of the relevant natural-kind, namely navvies. Provided we can find distinct groundings there is no danger of falling into equivocation. Gravitational forces are grounded in massy bodies in general (or distortions of the geodesics of the space–time continuum if you will, which just look like massy bodies). Electromagnetic forces are grounded in charges and poles, and these have quite distinctive material realizations.

The criterion by which real tendencies are distinguished from notional or fictional tendencies is represented in electromagnetism by the distinction between charges and fields. Both are real, but the former are the sources of the latter. A defender of a thoroughgoing action-at-a-distance version of electromagnetism must challenge that ontological claim, reserving his or her ontological accolade only for charges. In terms of the distinction between dispositions and their groundings, classical electromagmetism depends on an ontology that takes the field disposition (at x_i, y_i, z_i, and t) to be grounded in a local but spatio-temporally collocated state of the field, the potential (at x_i, y_i, z_i and t). In general that state is taken to be caused by the distant charge or charges. All this ontology is built in to Maxwell's equations. There is one important qualification to this account, which still further strengthens the case for an ontological reading of field terms. Field parameters can have a value in accordance with Maxwell's equations even when the charges are zero.

But can we go further and find an unequivocal way of decomposing the electromagnetic field itself into component vectors? These vectors are orthogonal and are always capable of being decoupled mensurationally. When a radio aerial detects an electromagnetic field it is sensitive only to the electric vector. Hertz was the first to measure the electric component of the electromagnetic field independently. The same is true of polarization effects. In general the electric field is measured by its effect on a stationary electric charge while the magnetic field is measured by the torque on a test magnet. In any actual physical set-up the electric and magnetic 'aspects' are clearly differentiated by reference to the materials, structure and mode of preparation of the equipment. To start with the simplest case. The rubbing of a glass rod with silk to produce a positive charge is a wholly different procedure from the magnetization of a bar of soft iron by stroking it with a loadstone. The difference between these procedures can be described without reference to electric or magnetic fields. In more sophisticated cases the differences in preparation remain robust. For instance a magnetic field always appears with a moving charge independent of the physical set-up, but a moving pole does not engender an electric field unless the 'lines of force' cut a conductor. Further, while electric charges seem able to exist without a complementary charge, the magnetic monopole remains to be discovered. If we restrict ourselves to the *physics* of H, E and G the decomposition of a resultant into component vectors is definitely non-arbitrary because, by the ontological argument above, the components are real. Philosophers tend to forget that physics is above all a material practice.

Cartwright's attack on a realist reading of the laws of physics

In her recent and very interesting work, *How the laws of physics lie*, Nancy Cartwright (1983) has launched a thoroughgoing assault on the idea that the laws of physics describe real natural tendencies. Cartwright begins with a flat denial of the rule of superposition. On p. 58 she says:

The [law of gravity] can explain only in very simple or ideal circumstances. It can account for why the force is as it is when just gravity is at work, but is of no help for cases in which gravity and electricity matter. Once the *ceteris paribus* modifier has been attached, the law of gravity is irrelevant to the more complex and interesting situations.

By the *ceteris paribus* modifier Cartwright means the usual qualification which physicists and indeed all scientists attach to tendency laws – that, other things being equal, they will manifest themselves directly in observable physical phenomena. This comment on superposition is just wrong.

The law of gravity is not irrelevant to the explanation of the motion of drops in a Millikan apparatus for instance. The equilibrium conditions on the drop are just the vector sum of the several independent influences of the electric, gravitational and hydrodynamic fields. Cartwright seems to have been led astray by a muddle between the case of velocity in which the resultant is real and the components notional, and the case of forces or causal influences when the opposite obtains. From the actual motion we infer the resultant (or notional force) and then with the help of our knowledge of the physical set up, say the Millikan apparatus, we resolve the notional force into its real components.

But by p. 62 the irrelevance argument against the joint use of the law of gravity and, say, Coulomb's Law has been dropped. Drawing on Creary, though many others have made the same point, Cartwright now says that the vector addition of real causes does yield a real resultant causal influence that produces the one actual motion. But that too is wrong. Though there is one and only one motion, there is no ontological ground for supposing that the independent causal influences 'add up' to one resultant force. But not to raise our hopes too high she asserts that this is just a very special case: 'First, in many cases there are no *general* laws of interaction [superposition rules]. Dynamics, with its vector addition law, is quite special in this respect.' Clearly this is overstated. The E of multiple charges is the vector sum of the Es of individual charges. And the list of cases in which there is some superposition rule with its associated algorithm could be indefinitely extended. Furthermore, if the issue is indeed the realist reading of laws of physics and the deepest of these ascribe tendencies to physical fields on the basis of assignments of quantitative measures of potential, then the argument that there are cases, higher in the hierarchy of physical processes, such as those described by some set of the laws of hydrodynamics, for which there are no clear superposition rules, proves nothing of interest. But, if the joint dynamics of gravitational and electromagnetic potentials (together with the dynamical variables of the weak and strong interactions) are indeed the basis of all physical processes, then the principles of superposition, which are operative among the real tendencies these laws describe, are instances of the most general vector addition law. And they permit (though they do not guarantee) a realist reading of the basic laws of physics.

All that is left to Cartwright is an attack on the ontology within which the fundamental laws of forces and fields are given a realist reading. She admits (p. 66) that 'in some concrete cases the strategy [of decomposing and recomposing components into resultants] will work' but she goes on to object: 'I see no reason to think that these intermediate influences can always be found', not because she objects to theoretical entities as such, 'but rather because every new theoretical entity which is admitted should be grounded in experimentation, which throws up its causal structure in detail.' But this is exactly what the basic project of physics has been since Faraday set this particular ball rolling. Dispositional theories, with their ontologies of forces and groundings in states of the world, are experimentally tested in particular by just those kinds of explorations of groundings that physicists have undertaken, in looking for ways of detecting the physical *sources* of the vector *components*. It is here that the most important of all physical properties, charge, finds its place. Cartwright does make a brief critical remark about the unsatisfactoriness of tendency theories in general, but fails to cite any specific examples of such theories, nor does she indicate how any one of them might be criticized. In the absence of any good reason to abandon the dispositionalist treatment of the basic laws of physics, I propose to continue my support for it.   Cartwright has another argument against the realist interpretation of the deeper laws of physics (see Cartwright, 1983, pp. 126–7). She notices that the laws of physics are not true of actual events. They do not hold exactly in Realm 1. *Ad hoc* adjustments must be made to introduce the necessary 'corrections'. Nor should anyone suppose that they hold exactly in Realms 2 and 3, to adapt my terminology to her argument. The laws of nature, then, cannot be about real, that is actual, events. But this is the fallacy of 'actualism'. It prejudges the way that the laws of nature engage physical reality. According to the arguments of this chapter, laws of nature do not describe sequences of actual events but rather the tendencies that produce them. Tendencies are almost never exactly realized because of countervailing tendencies. The best *we* can do is to try to construct apparatus that introduces yet other tendencies to block off those that obscure the pure realization of the tendency of interest. This point has been well made by Bhaskar, and is quite consonant with Popper's (1968) use of the concept of propensity. The *ceteris paribus* conditions which must accompany the statement of all laws of nature are not fudges against accusations of inaccuracy, but reflect the fact that each law singles out a tendency which is never independently activated in nature. Theory controls the mix of minor and countervailing tendencies which are rationally invoked to deal with the imperfect fit between laws and actual events. We have already seen that it is just this that provides the main dynamic of theory development for the theory-families typical of Realm 2 science.

Dispositions are properties. The most general question we can ask is whether there are any restrictions on the kind of subject to which they can be attributed. Events cannot have dispositions, since their manifestations are complete and categorical. Within a categorial framework that keeps its ties to the Kantian metaphysics of experience, extended substances and material particulars seem to be the only candidates. As Madden and I argued in our *Causal powers*, either could be adopted as a materialist meta-physics for science. But, once the choice was made, physics would develop within a distinctive categorial framework. General relativity has tended to spawn categorial frameworks in which the world system is an extended and continuous ur-substance, differentiated spatially and temporally by changing dispositions. These dispositions are grounded in the geometrical properties of the ur-substance, and manifest themselves in human experience as forces or the effects of forces.

Quantum field theory leads towards the individualist alternative and is in many ways reminiscent of the categorial framework proposed by Boscovich to remedy the contradictions in the Newtonian scheme. Dispositional properties as affordances are assigned to a menagerie of corpuscles, that is non-atomic particles basic only in interaction-defined categories. But there are no forces and all interactions are mediated by IVPs with their own characteristic affordances. The dispositional properties which high-energy physicists have provided for us are not the same kind of property as those with which I introduced the dispositionalist idea at the beginning of this chapter. Of these we can say that the manifestation is latent in the substance, as a general feature of its nature, and that feature can be described, albeit theoretically, in quite specific terms. Acidity is a specific disposition because acids have a quite characteristic composition, and so do the bases with which they traditionally react. 'Poisonous' is a target-relative disposition but poisons have quite definite chemical compositions. Affordances of which the dispositions of the particles of high-energy physics are a species, are yet another kind of disposition.

An affordance is the disposition of an unspecified substrate to manifest a definite interaction with a highly specified interactant. Usually the inter-actant and the manifestation it is built to encourage are matters of human choice and design. The properties of the corpuscles of quantum field theory are clearly affordances. There is not the ghost of an idea as to the theoretical basis of isospin, strangeness, colour, flavour, etc. These affordances chase each other down through the explanatory hierarchy to finish up as the properties of the quarks and gluons which are the current favourites for 'rock bottom'. Yet, in the complex but highly specific set-up created in the apparatus used in this branch of science, these properties are manifested in highly determinate ionization tracks and other reactions of detectors. Like Mach in the metaphysics of relativistic physics I shall try to show that Neils Bohr came very close to an adequate metaphysics for the physics of particles. To illustrate the complexity of the semantics of these 'new properties' I will look at three instances in some detail.

How three new physical properties have acquired their meanings

To trace out the complex semantic framework through which the concepts I shall be using to exemplify the semantics of physical predicates have acquired their working meanings, it will be useful to follow their etymology. Each passes through a sequence of meaning stages. The sequence begins with a literal meaning relative to a dispensable (often visualizable) *model* of the subatomic conditions that ground a disposition of the 'being in question' (whose status will be described below) to manifest a certain observable property. The sequence ends with a metaphorical meaning in which only the mathematical properties of the use of the concept in the context of the model (e.g. as a correlated vector-pair, one circulating and the other polar) survive together with the dispositional sense of the concept. The latter must be treated as an affordance, since the specific grounding in terms of the (visualizable) model has been left behind. Cartwright correctly notices that the material concepts of physical theory often literally describe models, but she fails to take account of the thinning out of those models into formal mathematical properties, together with dispositions. It seems to me that it is her unwillingness to admit the reality of dispositional properties that limits her vision in this regard. I present three illustrative cases. (For wonderfully clear accounts of these and other cases, see Dodd, 1984.)

1   *Spin*. The phenomenon to which the new property of 'spin' was germane was the splitting of some spectral lines. The literal semantic framework was the Bohr hydrogen atom in which the orbiting electron (as a moving charge) produced a magnetic field. If that electron was also spinning on an axis normal to the plane of its orbit, then if the spin was in an 'up' sense the magnetic field of the whole atom would be augmented, while if it was in the opposite sense the magnetic field of the whole atom would be slightly diminished. In this way the existence of a pair of slightly separated spectral lines, where on the simple model only one was expected, could be neatly explained. In the Bohr spirit there was quantization, 'in the Z direction', of spin up or spin down. In the second phase the concept of spin was generalized to all subatomic particles. This has the effect of dissolving the picture or model within which the original of the later concept was framed. To talk of 'intrinsic angular momentum' as a gloss on photon spin is surely semantically incoherent. It imports a concrete feature of the primary model into the second phase. All we need is the mathematical concept of the polar vector, and the relevant cluster of dispositions.

2   *Strangeness*. I have remarked already on the power of the general conservation principle in the 'design' of property concepts. The new property 'strangeness' was introduced to account for the anomalous behaviour of 'hyperons' and 'kaons'. The decay times of these particles, as manifested in the observable property of the length of their tracks, were appropriate to particles produced in the weak interaction process, though these processes were produced in processes involving the strong interaction, that is in which nucleons were implicated. A new quantized property, 'strangeness', was proposed by Gell-Mann and Nishijima, subject to overall conservation in any reaction. The primary model by which this concept acquires its first-phase meaning is clearly 'charge'. The measure of strangeness

$$Q = e \, (I^3 + (B + S)/2)$$

relates S (strangeness) to I (isospin), B (baryon number), e (the charge on the electron) and Q (electric charge). Since the values of I, B and S are just numbers, the concept of strangeness is intelligible within the same framework as, for example, baryon number, which is the factor by which the charge on a particle is related to its baryon composition.

Strangeness is so assigned to particles that in any subatomic interaction it is conserved overall. In the second phase it appears within that mathematical framework, and its content is the disposition which distinguishes hyperons from kaons, *inter alia*, with respect to their characteristic decay products. And the latter are manifested once again in the density, length, connectedness and curvature of *tracks*.

3   *Colour*. Once again we can trace an etymology through the same two stages. In the first phase the concept is given sense in the context of a rather visualizable model. Colour is clearly a species of charge. It is introduced via a quantum mechanical model of the three-quark architecture of hadrons. Within that framework it is constrained by the Pauli exclusion principle, since no two fermions, in the same system, can have identical quantum numbers. So somehow the three quarks invoked in the hadron constitution model must be differentiated. When 'colour' is included as an additional quantum property the three-quark model is made compatible with the Pauli principle. However, the primary model, charge, is now thinned out, since to differentiate the quarks three 'colours' are required.

For the second stage, a dispositional connection with some observable feature of an experimental set-up must be made. In this case the dispositional connection, unlike the two other cases, came last. The quark 'colours' were tied in to dispositions displayed in annihilation and interaction experiments. For example the disposition for some electron–positron annihilations to end in the production of hadron showers is thought to be mediated by a quark–antiquark pair, which later decay into the hadrons, and is accounted for in terms of quark 'colours'. Here 'colour', as an affordance, is linked by a quite complex conceptual structure to observational manifestation, in a certain sunburst of *tracks*. In principle the quark picture could be dissolved away almost completely while the 'colour' charge concept remained robust.

Ultra-groundings: the Mach principle

The rule that dispositions are ontologically respectable only when grounded has motivated a good deal of the discussion so far. But there are various possibilities for reaching a conceptual scheme for Realm 3, and the continued micro-decomposition of substances by the iteration of the use of this rule is only one. Perhaps the dispositions that are displayed in Realm 1 and Realm 2 are finally to be grounded not in some ultimate level of a micro-regress in Realm 3, but in the properties of the universe itself. This is the Machian way. A textbook example of the technique of ultragrounding is Mach's (1893) treatment of inertia, a disposition manifested in characteristic features of motion in Realm 1. In Boscovich's treatment the inertia of an observable material thing was the arithmetic sum of the inertias of the ultimate point-atoms of which it was composed. No further account of the inertia of the fundamental beings was offered. To get the flavour of the Machian way it is worth running over the famous thought experiment of the globes and a Machian analysis of it.

Newton proposed the thought experiment of the globes as part of an argument in support of the existence of absolute space as a unique frame of reference for at least some kinds of motion. The globes are isolated in an immense vacuum. We can imagine them connected by a spring balance. When they are set rotating, say (to update the story) by puffs of carbon dioxide of the kind used for orienting spacecraft, Newton presumed that there would be a force tending to separate them, which could be registered by the spring balance. The force would arise because of the acceleration due to rotation acting on the masses of the globes. The masses of the globes, being an intrinsic property, would be unaffected by the absence of all other matter. From the force as measured by the spring balance, the masses and the radius of the motion, the angular velocity could easily be calculated and this motion would be absolute. The essence of Mach's analysis is simple. How do we know that the globes would have a mass (inertia) in the absence of all other matter? Why should inertia, the disposition to resist acceleration, be an intrinsic property of each material body, when all other mechanical properties are relative to the rest of the system? The most conceptually coherent stance is to treat it as a disposition grounded in the properties of the universe as a whole.

Could this analysis provide the model for the final project of a physics conceived in the realist mode? The aim of science would be to ground the basic dispositions, the tendencies, propensities and powers of the simplest beings that theory requires and experiment sustains, in the properties of the whole universe. This move would solve the perennial problem that has beset attempts at creating a dispositionalist realism. It is the dilemma that confronts anyone who tries to universalize the dispositionalist account of properties. It seems as if one must choose between the inelegant alternative of grounding science on ungrounded dispositions, and the alarming prospect of an indefinite regress of groundings. Generalizing the Machian solution to all apparently intrinsic dispositions would eliminate both horns of the dilemma. The current finitist picture of the cosmos would leave physics with only a finite iteration of the dispositions/groundings move. The empirical foundations of science would be enormously strengthened. Ideally the dispositions which theoretical micro-regresses require physicists to ascribe to unobservable beings, like quarks and gluons, would be grounded, at least in principle, in observable properties of the universe. These properties would be occurrent rather than dispositional, embracing such matters as the quantity and distribution of energy fields. If unobservables are grounded in observables, the depth scepticism of Humean anti-realists is at least dented, since it would be irrational to doubt the existence of that which is to be grounded when we are in no doubt about the existence of that which is grounding.

Would there be any distinctive empirical consequences of adopting Mach's principle? Or is it just a 'conventionalist stratagem' ? There seem to be two contexts in which testable consequences might be possible.[1] If Mach's principle is accepted then Einstein's principle of separability (that if all action is local, widely separated physical systems must evolve independently of one another) must be abandonded, though it might survive as a practical maxim. Since the properties of all systems are influential *in* the properties of spatially (and perhaps temporally) separated systems, they could not be wholly independent of one another. For instance the general acceptance of a Machian point of view must surely alter our attitude to the Einstein-Podolsky–Rosen 'problem'.

The geometrization of charge

The Machian interpretation of inertia as a disposition grounded in the state of the universe at large is a relatively simple application of the idea of ultra-groundings, though the details of how a physical relation between grounding and disposition is to be explained remain, I understand, quite obscure. CPT conservation suggests a more subtle form of ultra-grounding for dealing with the important causal power we call 'charge'. The point I wish to make comes out if we take the component parameters of CPT separately to look at the possibility of defining 'good' symmetries.

Time reversal is not an ontologically interesting symmetry, since it does not satisfy the conditions of our mathematical epistemology. It does not lead to a conservation law. The argument, which I owe to Ian Aitchison, runs as follows. The time coordinate appears in the Schrodinger equation as $i\hbar(d\psi/dt)$. The Schrodinger equation will be covariant under the transformation t goes to $-t$, if ψ goes to ψ^*, its complex conjugate. Trouble arises because such transformations on ψ are represented by unitary operators. For such an operator the condition $U = e^{iA}$ must be satisfied where A is a Hermitian operator. Only Hermitian operators represent physical observables whose eigenvalues are conserved, corresponding to the symmetry implemented by U. In the case of the transformation t goes to $-t$ there is no such unitary operator, hence no corresponding Hermitian operator and hence no invariant set of eigenvalues. If there is no stable measure of a quantity then there can be no ground for hypothesizing a substance of the quantity of which such values would be the measure. So there is no conservation principle corresponding to 'time reversal'.

The second point germane to this discussion arises from the breakdown between 'geometrical indifference' and physical reality. If the spatio-temporal co-ordinate system is just a conventional referential grid laid over the world for our convenience in locating and tracking things and events, then we should not expect any of the properties of the grid itself to be ontologically significant. Though the laws of nature are covariant under some continuous geometrical transformations such as the translation and rotation symmetries, they do not seem to be covariant under at least one discrete spatial transformation, that from the left- to the right-handed sense of a circulating vector, the parity transformation. To bring out the ontological significance of the 'breakdown of parity' one can start with a schematic description of the original cobalt 60 experiment, which opened up a gap between geometry and the physical world. One can describe the set-up in purely physical terms. By imagining a mirror reflection of the entity type A we can create an 'image' which defines the anti-entity type B (see figure 15.2). In type A, B represents the polar vector, and the direction of the momentum vector, p, is opposite in sense to the polar vector and represents the direction along which any matter, for instance electrons, would be ejected from the system. In type B, mirror reflection reverses the circulating vector and so changes the direction of the correlated polar vector. If parity,

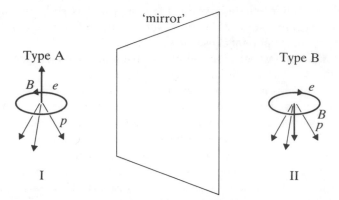

Figure 15.2   The parity transformation

the correlation between polar and circulating vectors, is conserved, mirror reflection leaves the matter vector p unchanged in magnitude and direction. To put this another way, the parity operation reverses the sign of only one of the x, y or z co-ordinates. The *geometrical realization* of this operation is mirror reflection, leaving the polar vector the same but reversing the sense of rotation in the x, y plane. Thus if in figure 15.2 e is a moving charge the field will obey a left-hand rule in I and a right-hand rule in II.

But when a field is applied to a mixture of entities and anti-entities defined by the above procedure the anti-entities of type B will line up with the field as in figure 15.3. Here the diagram is not a definition (as in figure 15.2) but a schematic representation of a possible experiment. The imposed field will line up the polar vectors B in the same direction for both type A and type B systems. But the matter vectors will now lie in opposite senses. If

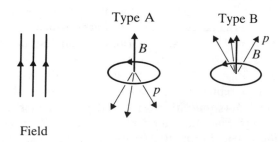

Figure 15.3   The parity experiment

parity is conserved we should expect matter (say electrons) to be discharged in roughly equal amounts in each sense. But in the real experiment electrons seem to be discharged preferentially in one direction. This is taken to show that type B entities do not exist. Parity, it is therefore concluded, is not conserved. The above 'definition' (figure 15.2) does not represent a good symmetry.

Theoretical physicists generalize the definition of parity to the general correlation between a circulating and a polar vector. If the 'screw sense' of any physical system was physically indifferent, then both the correlated and anti-correlated types of system should exist. In figure 15.4 I illustrate the general case. Any physical set-up in which an external coil is applied to a black box which emits some discharge, no matter what is in the box, represents this phenomenon. Experiment suggests that the universe is overwhelmingly composed of correlated rather than anti-correlated systems.

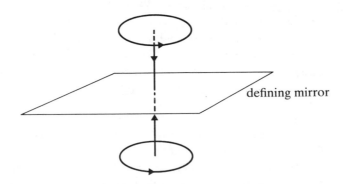

Figure 15.4   The general case

Only if we reverse the sign of 't', reverse the parity and change the sign of the additive of the quantum numbers that represent the difference between matter and antimatter (e. g. charge, baryon number, etc.) do we find a symmetry which has proved resistant to attempts at experimental violation. The laws of nature are covariant under these transformations. To a philosopher this result is of great ontological interest. Two leading features of the spatio-temporal structure of the universe are locked in with one another and with a third, charge, which seems to have nothing to do with spatio-temporal structure and to be a property of individual beings. How can this 'locking in' make any kind of sense unless the distinction between matter and antimatter is also interpreted as somehow a manifestation of a deep geometrical distinction? And since both the other features seem to have a cosmological reference should not the matter/antimatter distinction also have such a reference?

These reflections prompt another. Why is the universe asymmetrical? Why does it appear as if the systems of the real world are predominantly structured in such a way as to correlate polar and circulating vectors one way rather than the other? Contemporary cosmologists seem to take the view that this is not a manifestation of anything *deep*, but that the laws of nature reflected in the discrete symmetries are descendants of some accidental asymmetry in the conditions obtaining in the early history of the universe. As such they would have no ontological significance. Parity, time reversal and charge conservation would be good symmetries, and the laws of nature would be covariant under the discrete transformations just as they are under the continuous. One way of interpreting CPT conservation is as the current result of tipping the balance of nature towards matter rather than antimatter, left-handedness rather than righ-handedness, and increasing rather than decreasing entropy. In some way these three properties of gross physical systems are tied together in somewhat the way that the overt properties of molecules are tied together through their atomic constitution. Speculation can now run riot. Perhaps there is some global property of the universe which in Machian fashion manifests itself in the common grounding of those dispositions which are displayed in the kinds of the phenomena we experience as cobalt 60 decay, and like events.

Notice that this cluster of cases involves two quite distinctive epistemologies, illustrating the theme of part five in dramatic fashion. Time reversal turns out not to be a good symmetry because the mathematics of the Schrodinger equation and of the relevant operators forbids the derivation of *any* conservation law. Parity reversal turns out not to be a good symmetry because nature has spoken and forbidden us to conceive of the universe in terms of a balance between the geometrically possible structures of physical beings. However, though we talk of 'vectors', there is nothing mathematically objectionable that is marked by the breakdown of parity conservation. But both mathematical and experimental epistemologies *come together* in the reasoning that leads to the formulation of CPT conservation.

I draw the conclusion that the practice of physicists treats mathematical epistemology as on all fours with the experimental epistemology upon which philosophers of science have based their understanding of scientific method in the modern era. It is not that mathematical epistemology represents the principle that the logically impossible cannot be real, while experimental epistemology represents the principle that only nature can decide which among the logically possible worlds is this one. The Schrodinger equation is not a necessary truth. It is a law of nature. Nature might have been such that the equation whose covariance was at issue in the time reversal co-ordinate transformations in fact permitted them.

Infra-groundings

I have drawn attention in an earlier section to the kinds of difficulties that attend the attempt to carry through a programme of micro-explanation. After a finite number of steps the programme ends in a stratum of ungrounded dispositions, or an open regress of hypothetical natures seems to open out supporting each level of dispositions. The realization that Newtonian theory ran into this dilemma was widespread in the eighteenth century, and most philosophers of physics of that period, if they were of a scientific realist persuasion, opted for a stratum of basic physical powers (see Harré, 1983).

In this section I offer one more attempt to solve the difficulties of a dispositionalist analysis of the predicates of physical science, complementary to the idea of ultra-grounding, discussed in the last two sections. The basic idea is to exploit the Gibsonian notion of an affordance, a special kind of disposition whose main features have been introduced above. In the physical sciences well-constructed experimental set-ups permit manifestations and displays of dispositions to be sharply defined, but theory, at the frontier, so to say, leaves the ur-substance whose dispositions are thus revealed only vaguely delineated. This is the 'formula' for treating dispositions as affordances. I believe that in the philosophy of science of Neils Bohr we are presented with the one theory in meta-physics in which a coherent, unified account of all these matters can be achieved.

Bohr's argument has much of the character of the transcendental arguments used by Kant (Honner, 1986) Transcendental arguments work, if they work at all, by displaying some necessary condition for the possibility of some feature of the human condition, without which human life, as we know it, could not be carried on (see Bieri, Horstmann and Kroger, 1979). In short a transcendental argument displays a necessary condition for the possibility of some feature essential to our form of life. In particular a transcendental argument should show that the epistemological and metaphysical principles within which human knowledge must be framed are relative to a fundamental condition for the possibility of that knowledge. For Kant the principles were relative to the necessary conditions for the possibility of experience in general. For Bohr they are relative to the necessary conditions for the possibility of unambiguous and objective communication about the sorts of things a human being can experience. But, says Bohr (1958, p. 67), 'The main point to realize, is that all knowledge presents itself within a conceptual framework adapted to account for previous experience and that any such frame may prove too narrow to comprehend new experience.'

In the face of new experience for the comprehension of which our existing conceptual frameworks have proved too narrow, how can we go forward? There seem to be three possibilities.

1   We can conserve the existing general categorial framework and add new property concepts which obey the deep grammar of existing property concepts at some generic level. Classical physics seems to have been constructed almost wholly in accordance with this principle. The experiences which sustained the Galilean-Newtonian physical world-picture were selected from an existing repertoire, rather than forced on the scientific community by the irruption of kinds of things and events which were wholly new, and for which no concepts existed within the existing categorial framework. Even the greatest apparent novelty, inertia, is now known to have developed by easy stages out of a pre-existing bouquet of concepts (see Papineau, 1977). I have illustrated this in some detail in the discussion of the Galilean innovations in chapter 3.

2   At the other extreme is the possibility of trying to construct a purely formal science, whose mathematical operations express novel concepts which cannot be connected to existing conceptual systems, by any of the known semantic tropes, such as simile or metaphor. S-matrix theory in quantum mechanics is a textbook example of this approach. Hilbert space treatments of the same subject matter are something of a puzzle, though, as I have argued, they seem to be most comfortably treated as mere auxiliary mathematics.

3   The conditions of unambiguous communication seemed to Bohr to demand a conservative attitude to concepts. This intuition was expressed in the correspondence principle, which gave a special place to classical concepts. However, the exigencies of the 'new experiences' induced by experimenting with those beings we now call quantum mechanical objects required some pretty drastic changes in the deep grammar of this concep-tual system, notably the prohibitions expressed in principle of complemen-tarity. As Bohr said (1931, p. 19), 'experiences cannot be combined in their accustomed manner.' I believe that quantum logic is a partially correct response to this Bohrian intuition, but that it is aimed at a reform of the grammar of the classical system at the wrong point. If logic is part of the rhetoric of science, such principles as the distributive law must be conserved if the agonistic encounters of rival theoreticians are to be regu-lated in the customary way. But one could see the attempt to create quantum logics as a trial for a novel grammar. It should be aimed at the semantic rules

for combining predicates, the sub-categorial rules of deep grammar of the substantial concepts. That, I believe, is just the force of Bohr's principle of complementarity.

Bohr's philosophy of science can be seen as an attempt at a justification for the third approach. It is based on the concept of 'phenomenon' taken in a sense parallel to the Kantian sense of that term. It allows us to relax the conservative constraints on communication just enough to admit concepts for those properties which experience has forced upon physicists and which I have called, borrowing a term from Gibson, 'affordances'. The meaning of 'phenomenon' in Bohr's philosophy of science comes clearer through an explicit comparison with Kant's general philosophy.

I begin with the ontology of phenomena. In the Kantian account, phenomena, observable states of affairs of a physical world, are the result of the application of the schematisms to an unordered flux of sensation. This creates certain synthetic unities, and forms of order, such as individual substances and causal developments. The schematisms come from a finite set of categories, which reflect the totality of possible forms of judgement. The flux of sensation has an inexperienceable noumenal source. There are two sources of activity in this scheme, the noumenal world which is the source of the flux of sensation and the noumenal self which is the source of the activity manifested in the use of the schematisms to synthesize experience. Phenomena must display properties which can be thought about in terms of the concepts of the finite list of categories, expressible in the available forms of judgement. It is a cardinal error to try to apply the categories, by the work of pure reason alone, beyond experience. The fact that this move is an error shows up in the antinomies, paired sets of arguments which show that the attempt to apply concept pairs like 'finite/infinite' to matter, space and time leads to results in which no reasons can be found for preferring one attribution rather than its complement.

I believe we should interpret Bohr's philosophy of physics along the following lines. Phenomena, observable states of affairs, occur when pieces of material apparatus are physically applied to the ur-stuff of the world. (I prefer to nickname this stuff 'glub', to avoid any metaphysical temptations that arise from the connotations of the word 'stuff'.) The way an apparatus is built leads to the shaping up of the glub into this or that displayed phenomenon. If we choose to prod the glub with a bubble chamber and photographic apparatus we force the world in a particle mode, since it must display itself as *tracks*. Apparatus, like the Kantian schematisms, is itself constrained by the Newtonian (classical) properties of humanly manipulable and observable matter. All phenomena, then, must be describable in classical concepts. Though the concepts must be classical it may be that there are certain combinations of such concepts that are forbidden. The 'glub' does constrain phenomena in a general way, since there are only certain ways that it can be 'shaped up'. It is a cardinal error to attempt a noumenal application of the classical concepts, that is to try to describe the state of the glub by their use. It turns out that classical physics permits the realization in physical apparatus of two classes of concepts, particulate and distributed, particle concepts and wave concepts. The glub is such that the two classes of apparatus cannot be used together, and therefore a description of phenomena in which instances of concepts of each class are paired is unacceptable. Particles and waves are created out of the glub by the use of pieces of apparatus. We should not think of the glub as being either particulate or wave-like in the absence of such an interaction.

It seems to me that there is a genuine parallel between the Kantian ontology of phenomena and that proposed by Bohr. For both, phenomena are created by the application of something humanly created to something which, as far as human thought could go, must be taken to be un-differentiated. All we can say of it is that it has certain dispositions to permit shaping in this or that way, as apparatus would permit. New concepts realized in new equipment might reveal new dispositions of the glub. But the concepts of physics, as a descriptive science, are constrained to those by which observable, manipulable apparatus and its reactions can be described. Immediately certain epistemological conclusions follow. Since the apparatus must be visible, tangible, and so on, and since the phenomena are shaped up by it, the concepts of classical physics must provide the only recourse for unambiguous communication between people about pheno-mena. This is Bohr's correspondence principle. The route to it is exactly parallel to the Kantian transcendental deduction of the categories. All we can know of the glub are its affordances, dispositions of which only the consequent is well defined, and the compossibility conditions of the joint display of phenomenal categories in apparatus. This corresponds, perhaps less happily than the transcendental deduction, to the antinomies. This is Bohr's complementarity principle.

In the light of these considerations we should not call the activities of subatomic experimental physicists 'measurement'. Experiments, at this level, transform nature. They may not be assumed to mirror it. There is no 'measurement problem'. The form of *all* problems in subatomic physics is what sequence of transformation does the glub permit, given the apparatus which we are physically *and conceptually* capable of making. But, one might object, isn't the apparatus itself made ultimately of 'glub', so why make the 'cut' between apparatus and world where we currently make it? Just the other side of the photographic plate? Just the other side of the string of bubbles in the bubble chamber? The meaning of the correspondence principle, I believe, is that one must make a cut somewhere in the sequence of events that starts in the glub and finishes in a humanly observable place. This necessity follows from the manipulability condition on any apparatus that people could use. But it may turn out that making the cut at some particular place in the presumed sequence was a poor choice. It may require the neglect of small effects that turn out to matter for some purpose or other. For instance taking the lowest order of Feynman diagram to plan a search for an IVP may turn out to be a mistake. Why is a piece of apparatus relatively stable? The Machian spirit of this chapter suggests the following speculation. The principle of complementarity reflects the fact that we can make two kinds of glub-squeezing apparatus – so there are particle-like electron phenomena, and there are wave-like electron phenomena. Apparatus, like anything else, must be just glub, squeezed into some form or other. The universe at large is that which shapes up largish things like apparatus, just as apparatus shapes up particulate electron phenomena. But there is only one universe. The things which it shapes up out of glub have just one form, and so seem to us human observers to be quite stable.

To sum up the discussion: the notion of 'phenomenon' has two main features.

1   A phenomenon is an event or state that occurs within or qualifies an indissoluble blend of apparatus and 'glub'; 'no sharp distinction can be made between the behaviour of objects themselves and their interaction with the measuring instruments' (Bohr, 1958, p. 61). We cannot single out any aspect of the apparatus/glub meld and assign it to some hypothetical object as property of which the reaction of the apparatus might be a measure. The so-called 'measurement problem' in quantum mechanics is not a problem at all, but a metaphysical muddle. Any instrument reading is a property of a totality, the indissoluble union of equipment and just glub. Bohr's insistence that there is one wave-function describing, say, a pair production follows from this, and is a flat denial of Einstein's principle of separability. Only if we are willing to accept that principle does EPR seem to describe a paradox. Einstein's prejudice all along was to confuse *pheno-mena* with independently existing states of nature. Relative to any specified, humanly constructible apparatus the occurrent state of the glub cannot be specified. All we know is that when prodded with *this* kind of apparatus it can be shaped up *this* way. In short we can know only its affordances.

2   Phenomena are to be described by means of a language which draws only on predicates from classical physics. 'However far the phenomena transcend the scope of classical physical explanation the account of all evidence must be expressed in classical terms' (Bohr, 1958, p. 39). This

aspect of the theory of 'phenomena' needs careful qualification. While it is true that a track in an emulsion can be described only in terms of its length, curvature, thickness, and so on, novel concepts need to be introduced to create order among the results of such measurements. These are the quantum mechanically qualified properties of particle physics discussed in the last chapter. They have to be treated as affordances, but what the glub affords is relative to equipment actually switched on. The affordances are not simple dispositions of the glub itself, the ur-stuff. They represent what the glub affords *in the context of a particular physically specified, material apparatus*. We have no idea and could have no idea how they are ultimately grounded, that is what glub properties ground them. They are ur-stuff affordances, not occurrent properties of the glub.

Relative to human experience that totality of apparatus and glub whose states are Bohrian phenomena is quite objective. Bohr says (1963, p. 3), '[there are] the permanent marks ... left on the bodies which define experimental conditions. ... The description of atomic phenomena has in these respects a perfectly objective character.' We need no one to play Fichte to Bohr's Kant. Another helpful image can round off this brief exposition. One could look on physical apparatus as devices for forcing the ur-stuff to display itself in a certain 'shape'. A piece of apparatus designed to bring out the particle aspects of subatomic phenomena could be thought of as 'squeezing' the glub into particles. That the glub can be so squeezed is an interesting fact about it, but all we can say is that it has that affordance. For what physical reasons it can be so squeezed we have and can have no idea.

Phenomena are displays of joint affordances of apparatus and world. They are states of novel physical beings, half created by man, but indissolubly melded with glub. But the apparatus is a highly specified entity with quite determinate properties, while the "glub" is quite unspecified. The ur-stuff affords particle phenomena (punctiform scintillations) and wave-phenomena (interference patterns). It also affords those properties introduced to make a tidy tale about the tracks of particles, strangeness, isospin, colour, flavour, charm and various other novelties. It is not that the ur-stuff is not real. The physics of Realm 3 does not bring us that message; rather it can be described only in terms of the affordances it has in conjunction with well-defined pieces of apparatus. Those beings which the material terms of Realm 3 sciences denote are known to us through their affordances. But so are the beings of Realm 1. The infra-grounding of physical dispositions terminates in a world as real as that which grounds the world given to us in perception.

Natural-kinds in Realm 3

Throughout the discussions of part five my tactic has been to explore how far the world-winning features of Realm 2 science have analogues in the science of Realm 3. Any defence of a suitably modest form of referential realism for the discourses of Realm 3 science would be facilitated by a demonstration of the viability of the idea of treating type-concepts as referring to natural-kinds. The physical and biological sciences certainly appear to use kind terms as generously for Realm 3 beings as they are used elsewhere in the natural sciences. The use of real essences may be even more central to Realm 3 discourse than to other parts of science since, *a fortiori*, Realm 3 individuals could not present themselves for inspection.

In common with nearly all the concepts needed for a discussion of scientific practices, 'natural kind' is a dual-context notion. A natural kind is picked out by something like a nominal essence, a set of recognitive criteria fixed by human fiat and controlled largely by the exigencies of the practical contexts in which classifications of natural beings are made. But it is characteristic of scientific taxonomies to supplement quasi-nominal essences with theoretically grounded hypotheses about the real essences of the beings which are taken to fall into discrete (or nominally discrete) groups according to working classificatory criteria. These are hypotheses about the nature or constitution of the beings in question which are supposed to show why the practical criteria do actually sort things into distinctive groups. Locked into a complex but labile unity, nominal and real essences provide a relatively stable taxonomy of natural-kinds. It is only relatively stable because changes in practical interests and equipment may call for the adoption of new nominal essences, while changes in theory may either suggest new grounds for existing ways of classifying, or undermine the naturalness of some current taxonomy.

Realm 3 beings never appear in practical contexts as themselves, that is displaying the properties that theories with Realm 3 referents assign to them. Their affordances are invoked to explain the Realm 1 affordances of other beings. A water droplet can be seen by a physicist, but the ionization of which it is a manifestation is itself a manifestation of the charge on a subatomic particle. At this point we can invoke Ian Hacking's (1983) treatment of this issue. He shares the hierarchical idea but uses it in reverse, so to speak. Things are real, for him, in so far as we can *use* them to manipulate other things which are even more remote. But sometimes the final upshot of the manipulation of the remote by the near at hand is a visible track in Realm 1. To take a case in point, the actual manifestation hailed as 'the discovery of the W particle' was not a track which could have been made only by a particle having the properties that quantum field theory assigns to the W. Rather there were two other sets of tracks, and on the assumption that the second was a product of the same physical reality as had manifested itself in the first, the W was invoked as the only being which could have mediated the transition from the one to the other. It was the only possibility, *relative to this stage of physics*, that is relative to existing cognitive and material practices, that is the using of conservation principles and the recording of tracks. This point must be linked to the Bohrian proposals of the last section. The assumption involved in reading the evidence as confirming 'the discovery of the W particle' is a fragment of a corpuscularian metaphysics, of persisting individuals, the inspired 'misreading' of the Feynman diagrams discussed in chapter 14. If our apparatus is designed to display, at its 'human' end, *tracks*, then the viability of that apparatus/glub mix must depend on the glub having particulate affordances. *This does not mean that the glub really consists of particles*, but that if we build this kind of apparatus, and it works, if there are phenomena they will be corpuscularian, that is tracks. Study the world with Geiger counters, and if you get anything at all, you will get 'blips'. Apparatus which delivers blips shapes the world up into events.

Are Ws a natural-kind? Recall the problem that lay behind the cladistics controversy. Are taxonomic groups natural-kinds? In the biological case we have the entities in question, and a historically labile set of criteria for lumping and splitting groups of them into kinds. It was the status and necessity of a theoretical grounding of these practices that was at issue in the philosophical theorizing around transformed cladistics. There were nominal essences. Could or should they be grounded in hypothetical real essences delivered by theory? Positivism of course says 'No!', while realism says 'Yes!' The problem of whether there are natural-kinds among the denizens of Realm 3 is, so to speak, the complementary problem. There is no doubt that quantum field theory offers hypotheses as to the real essence of beings such as the W particle, that is it provides a bouquet of affordances characteristic of that *kind* of particle and no other. But the beings of Realm 3 can have no nominal essences, that is there is no descriptive vocabulary analytically adjusted to them as phenomenal presentations. They do not manifest themselves in phenomenal presentations, at least to human observers.

However, it seems to me that a sufficient surrogate for that phenomenal presentation is to be found in physics. For instance the tight relation of successive necessary conditions links the affordances of the W particle with the (track) manifestations of those particles which are the products of its decay. Following Hacking's line of argument again, it seems that the surrogacy can be almost as strong a contribution to the total nexus of concepts which make up a natural-kind as nominal essences themselves. The notion of natural-kind will be a little weaker, by reason of the string of (potentially revisable) disposition/manifestation steps intervening between an entity and the relevant Realm 1 appearances, but this is the kind of weakening that modest realism teaches us to expect.

An argument for a Realm 3 variety of realism

My defence of referential realism as a thoroughgoing alternative to truth realism depended heavily on the possibility of the translation of hypothetical acts of referring into material practices of searching and finding or failing to find an instance of the kind in question. The epistemological force of these practices depended on the creation of a physical link between the embodied experimenter and the being in question. The reasonableness of realism depended on establishing the possibility of that translation for theories in which, in a general way, the natural kinds of the world of common experience were conserved. This was a ground for realism because Gibsonian psychology provided a justification for the view that, analysed at the level of the Kantian categories, perception was 'direct'. The inductive argument by which policy realism, the variety of referential realism I am concerned to defend, was established as a reading of Realm 2 scientific practice depended on the possibility of Realm 2 beings becoming observable in just the same way as Realm 1 beings are observable. The category of 'possibly observable being' was based on the comparability of natural-kinds for Realm 1 and Realm 2 guaranteed by the constraints on theoretical concepts exerted by the source analogues of Realm 2 theories. At first sight it seems that a referential-realist account of the discourses appropriate to sciences concerned with beings inhabiting a realm beyond all possible experience could not be defended in this way. There can be no material practice of searching and finding or failing to find a specimen in Realm 3 in the sense in which this is meant for scientific practices in Realms 1 and 2. Yet physicists *talk* in policy realist ways about at least some of the denizens of Realm 3. Evaluating the force of such talk will go a long way towards bringing out the varieties of realism that Realm 3 science can bear.

The denizens of Realm 3, as conceived by scientists, are a heterogeneous lot. There are scientific discourses deploying concepts of beings, thought to be beyond all possible experience, which yet conform to the metaphysical principles of an ontology at least commensurate with the Kantian categories. The impossibility of observing the referents of such concepts, if indeed such beings do exist, is relative to the existing repertoire of laws of nature, particularly those embedded in the well-established theory-families of current physics. For instance galaxies whose relative velocity of recession exceeds the speed of light are Realm 3 beings, provided no influences propagated with supraluminal velocities are ever discovered. The boundary between Realms 1 and 2 was defined by technological constraints. This boundary is defined by theoretical constraints, but *neither is ontological*. In the light of this an extended form of the policy realist argument can be formulated as follows.

If it makes sense to take seriously hypotheses about the beings of Realm 2, the world as not yet experienced but as a possible object of experience, on the commonsense and historically supported grounds that experience of things and processes in that Realm may in time become possible for us through technical advances, we have a basis for accepting the general principle that theory can anticipate experience. In the arguments of Part Four we have legitimated the idea of theory anticipating experience, on the condition of the conservation of the metaphysical categories of Realm 1 natural kinds. For beings like the fleeing galaxies the metaphysical condition is satisfied, so we can have the idea of theory performing the same cognitive function relative to Realm 3 beings as it performs for those of Realm 2. If reference is to be understood in terms of a conjunction of cognitive and material practices, at least we have a model in the science of Realm 2 for reality-anticipating cognitive practices relevant to Realm 3. But could we extend the inductive argument that supported policy realism for Realm 2 science to the case of the theories that purport to describe events, individuals and processes in Realm 3? Again I argue by example, choosing a familiar case from the history of theories of disease.

In the seventeenth century theoreticians, working through diverse source analogues, had produced three rival theories of disease – the poisonous emanation theory, ancestor of the concept of 'malaria'; the bodily malfunction theory; and the alien *arche*, or micro-organic invasion theory of van Helmont. Optical microscopes existed and workers such as Hooke had shown the technical possibility of extending the realm of actual experience, in which bacteria could not be observed, to a realm of possible experience, in which they might reasonably be thought to be able to be examined, *in propria persona* so to speak. Improvements in the techniques of microscopy so altered the boundary between actual and possible experience that the bacteria almost certainly responsible for many diseases could be sought and were found. But theoretical physics had set a limit to the resolving power of optical microscopes, such that, if the remaining diseases did have microorganic causes, these beings would be for ever, it seemed, beyond the bounds of all possible experience. San Felice proposed a Realm 3 theory: that all diseases be deemed to have a micro-organic origin, the in principle unobservable micro-organisms to be distinguished by the old generic term 'virus'. Unexpectedly, and indeed within the framework of Newtonian science unexpectedly, it turned out that electrons could be diffracted, so that an apparatus for observing viruses became possible. The discovery of electron diffraction altered the boundary between Realm 2 and Realm 3. A similar story could be told about crystal structure, dislocation theory and the field-ion microscope; about optical, infra-red and radio telescopes, and so on. In the light of the above we picture science creeping forward across a heavily mined epistemic *kreigland*. In the schema outlined above empirical support runs through the double analogy of the theorizing typical of Realm 2 discourse, to intersect at judgements of relative plausibility for a Realm 3 theory, which are apportioned to the strength of the analogies, just as they are for Realm 2 theorizing.

A close examination of the structure of Realm 3 theory-families typified by special and general relativity and quantum field theory has shown that they are more similar than one might have expected to the theory-families typical of Realm 2 theorizing. There is a measure of metaphysical continuity in the conservative ontology to which theoretical physicists subscribe by virtue of the substantialist implications of the covariance constraint and corpuscularian implications of the preponderant practical restrictions of Bohrian phenomena to tracks and blips. The argument sketched above could be generalized into a sort of structuralist 'formula':

$$\frac{\text{Realm 1}}{\text{Realm 2}} = \frac{\text{Realm 1} + \text{Realm 2}}{\text{Realm 3}}$$

The above argument exploited the possibility of a revision of the physical theories that defined the boundary between Realms 2 and 3. But there is another argument that goes back at least to Locke ('microscopical eyes') and Kant ('magnetic sensibility') which would take us one further step into Realm 3. The natural-kind constraints which ensure the in principle observability of putative existents, and thus a strong ground for their physical linkage to the embodied persons who are experimenting, were tied, in the argument so far, to human sensibility. If we could imagine sentient beings equipped with different perceptual systems from ours, for whom the denizens of Realm 3, their properties and modes of behaviour would be perceptible in the Gibsonian way, that is through the detection of higher-order invariants in active exploration of that world, then we would have a watered-down but not neglible form of the policy realist argument for yet another layer of Realm 3. It would be good policy for Martians, say, to try to observe magnetic monopoles. The preponderance of iron in the soils of Mars has favoured the evolution of beings with magnetic sensibilities who can experience magnetic fields as graded sensory overlays, in the same sort of way we experience luminosity. An organ similar to our semicircular canals, but with iron rather than calcium in its platelets serves these tiny creatures. Other beings with even more exotic Realm 3 sensibilities have been imagined by science-fiction writers. This fable could not serve to ground any particular Realm 3 hypotheses as plausible or implausible. Rather these considerations give the idea of the material practices of policy realism some purchase on Realm 3 discourse. And so they support a mild confidence in the denotational robustness of the substantive terms of that moment in an evolving theory-family at which it seems to be plausible.

The joint use of the criteria of covariance and conservation, the latter needed as a supplement, since the former is weakened by mathematical generalization (e. g. from its role in special to general relativity, which step I have dubbed 'mathematical epistemology'), is clearly different from the extended iconic process exemplified in the history of the virus concept, or the extension of Gibsonian psychology to Martians. Energy, though conceived within the generic metaphysical category of substance, has none of the properties that would make it perceptible as such for any kind of being. The Kant–Bohr way of managing the cutting edge of infra-groundings leaves us only with affordances, dispositions whose grounding is quite unspecific. Is there any way in which a weakened version of the extended policy realist argument could reach these layers of Realm 3? At least energy 'stuff' falls under a substance concept, and the glub we know has both wave and particle affordances. (The matter seems to have been settled for the time being by the outcome of the Aspect experiment of 1985.)

It was the past success of policy realism in making possible readings of theories which provided the programme for experimental ruling in and ruling out of putative existents that provided the grounds for the inductive argument to the reasonableness of taking future Realm 2 theories in a policy realist way. Policy realism is made up of two root ideas. There is the idea of taking the referring implications of the grammatical form of a discourse seriously, and there is the idea of mounting a material search on the basis of those implications. Patently the kind of Realm 3 theory-families we have now reached do not sustain the second root idea. But do they preclude the first? Return for a moment to consider the role of source analogues in the theory-families devised for Realm 2. Policy realist readings of moments in the history of such theory-families depended on the constraints on the natural-kinds of the hypothesized beings of Realm 2 implicit in the content of the source analogue. The role of covariance and conservation in controlling the formulation of Realm 3 theory-families is, I claim, analogous to the role of source analogues in the formulation of Realm 2 theory-families. They determine the kind of being that a referential realist reading of the theory would require. In particular they constrain the conception of that being so that it falls within the generic category of substance, thus insuring that it is a *referable*. The fact that the glub can be shaped up into corpuscles by the two photon cascade in the first phase of the Aspect experiment at least makes some sense of progammes like 'the search for the W IVP'.

It seems that we could legitimately extend policy realism to the further reaches of Realm 3 only if both root ideas in the concept were able to be applied to the cases under discussion. We need to look more closely at the idea of searches. The characterization of what we seek has to be in terms of affordances to afford higher-order affordances, the strings of intermediate dispositions I drew attention to above. Looking for the W particle only makes sense if we can say clearly what it would be like to find it. If we could think of finding it as picking up its characteristic track in Realm 1 then indeed, while searching for it would differ greatly from hunting the okapi, it would closely resemble looking for the molecular basis of genetics. But unfortunately the traces which so excited the workers at CERN are the traces of other, familiar particles. It is only the particular configuration of those tracks that, via an application of the bookkeeping rules to the quantum numbers and the calculation of cross-sections, gives the W particle as their immediate precursor. But since the days of Christopher Clavius philosophers have been aware that existence claims based on this kind of consideration are weak. There are, at least in principle, indefinitely many alternative explanations for that particular configuration of tracks of which the existence of the W particle is only one. Belief in W particles is a complex epistemic state in the genesis of which the coherence of the whole state of physics plays a great part. In the end it seems that the referential realism which was intended to revive a plausible version of correspondence, by seeing the scientific enterprise as based on the welding together of cognitive and material practices, finally succumbs to considerations that force the community's assessment of the most basic theories in physics into the coherence mould.

The upshot of these discussions is the conclusion that reference for Realm 3 discourse, in general, cannot be fully explained in terms of the material practices of searching and finding or failing to find. The transformation of Roberts's IP format 'Whatever is (identical with/the cause of) Y is a triad of charmed quarks' into the DC form 'This is a charmed quark' is, in general, unachievable. Our best referential acts will perforce have to be just those which are expressible in the IP format. If in the end we have to admit that referring to the ultimate physical beings is not a material practice is it a myth, or worse a mistake, to suppose that Realm 3 discourse denotes anything? Perhaps the failure to sustain the IP to DC transformation just shows that the IP format ought not to be given a realist or referential reading? Perhaps IP formats are only 'about' the figments of the imagination of the speaker's community?

The argument of part five has been an attempt to justify the claim that there are clearly defined circumstances in which the IP format can be used referentially. The argument began with a reminder that the motivation for introducing into science a discourse apparently denoting beings which would, if real, be denizens of Realm 3, was the chronic incompleteness of causal accounts of phenomena using the disposition/nature format, a format already legitimized for the explanatory discourses of Realms 1 and 2. This step forward had its rationale in the Aronsonian view that explaining in the scientific style is the act of trying to reduce the number of independent phenomena, by mapping them token by token, and type by type, on to the appropriate elements of a common ontology. In many cases the beings which are those elements are in Realm 3. Both the causal and identity relations which realize the Aronsonian mappings in particular cases are fraught with heavy metaphysical assumptions. The identity relation requires that all three realms are ordered by *the same spatio-temporal grid*. The causal relation requires that there be at least some dispositional properties of Realm 3 beings that mediately, via intermediate dispositions, or immediately *are manifested as occurrent properties of beings of Realm 1 or 2*. These are very strong conditions. Why should they be accepted?

Space-time, so I have argued, is ontologically compound. It is a human creation out of certain properties of the material system, together with conceptual extensions of that system achieved by the invention of structured arrays of possibilities. In so far as it is a complex property of the material system, as we experience it in Realm 1, it is closely connected to the conceptual conditions for decomposing the world into mutually exclusive and enduring particulars and the changes that occur in and among them. The grid of locations is created to facilitate reference, that is the cognitive-material practice of finding and locating material beings among other beings of the same or similar kinds by establishing a physical link to the bodies of the embodied beings who make up the scientific community or its agents. Space-time represents one solution to the problem of how it is possible to apply a language to experience. Is it the only one?

This question surfaces at this point in the discussion because if it could be argued that it was a unique condition it would be easy to claim that the beings of Realm 3 could become objects of a descriptive and explanatory discourse only if Realm 3 were a spatio-temporal array. Unless we can find some necessity in this, what grounds have we for the assumption of an isomorphism of referential grids for Realms 1, 2 and 3? Aronson's 'identity mappings' from apparently independent phenomena to aspects of a common ontology seem to require that there be such an isomorphism. Even the rather weak 'identities' that would result from one-to-many or many-to-one mappings between levels of a hierarchical explanatory system seem to require some degree of similarity between the referential grids we use for locating phenomena and those we impose on their unobservable counterparts via the identity mappings. If a referential reading of the IP format is to be based on the isomorphism of phenomenal referents and deep ontological referential grids the case is weak, since we cannot claim to have established the isomorphism on the basis of the existence of the identities. These mappings are identities only if the referential isomorphism is granted.

Yet, as I have pointed out in discussing the metaphysics of quantum field theory and of particle physics in general, a universal and common space-time grid, under the restrictions of relativity, is assumed for all of physics. The clue to a resolution of the apparent difficulty lies in the very nature of space-time. It is not an empirical given. It is a construction to facilitate discourse, which draws upon certain local and immediate features of human experience. In so far as the world is capable of being apprehended scientifically it must be conformable to the transcendental conditions of human discourse. We could not discover that the beings of Realm 3 were not spatio-temporally ordered. At most we would find ourselves gradually abandoning the practice of referring to them as beings localizable by virtue of their spatio-temporal relations to the beings of Realms 1 and 2, and perhaps that part of Realm 3 whose denizens we had reason to believe did fall within the range of common natural kinds.

It follows from the above discussion that the IP format will not admit of an interpretation which would enable us to locate all categories of Realm 3 beings via their identity with beings in Realm 1 or Realm 2. Causal relations are another matter. While they would not allow us to locate Realm 3 causes by referring to their Realm 1 effects, we could at least infer the existence of the Realm 3 cause. Realm 3 is postulated just because a full causal story cannot (apparently) be filled out by reference only to beings, and their states and relations, of Realms 1 and 2. A textbook example of this kind of reasoning is the case of the neutrino. It was added as an unobservable, a Realm 3 being, to complete a causal story. (There is no place in science for claims to have isolated *the* cause of a phenomenon. That is a language game appropriate to casuistry and the law.) Reference does the work of individuating. In the case of the neutrino the overwhelming influence of corpuscularian concepts makes it natural to read the IP format in the DC mode as

Whatever is the cause of momentum disparity in beta decay is a particle of zero rest mass and no charge moving in such and such a trajectory.

Only if taken referentially does this statement license the undertaking of a spatio-temporal search for traces of the passage of a being of a kind defined by these parameters. But there is nothing in the IP format itself that would require that its referents be conceived as particulate. The logical grammar of the Realm 3 IP referential format is neutral. It is the conservative metaphysical predilections of physicists that push the ontology that way, and bring space-time with them as the basic referential grid which is to make location possible. Could there be a metaphysics for Realm 3 that was not particulate, and so did not smuggle in an isomorphism between the referential grids of the three epistemic realms? Few thoroughgoing alternatives have seriously been canvassed. David Bohm's (1975) 'implicate order' is a bold but so far isolated attempt.

Part Six

The Place of Logic in the Philosophy of Science

It seems to me [said Karenin] that the very process of studying the forms of a language has a beneficial effect on intellectual development.

Leo Tolstoy, *Anna Karenina*

Introduction

Throughout this study I have expressed some scepticism as to the usefulness of the search for logical forms of aspects of scientific discourse in illuminating the nature and value of science. In this final part I turn to some fairly detailed investigations of this issue. One must begin by distinguishing between the alleged role of logic in science, and the role it has actually played in the philosophy of science.

The role of logic in science, I have argued, is always secondary to the main thrust of scientific activity. In part one I identified a role for logic, as facilitating displays of deductive reasoning and the use of logical concepts such as contradiction, in scientific rhetoric. There is no doubt that written scientific discourses are presented in such a way as to conform, or at least seem to conform, to certain logical canons. But further investigation showed that this conformity is not in any obvious way essential to the knowledge-garnering process. It turned out that it is an important ingredient in success in the management of the competitive social relationships of scientific communities. A fumbling display of a shaky edifice of analogies, however true to the realities of scientific thought, will stand no chance of publication, nor would it get one very far in a conference hall.

At various points in the substantive discussion of parts three, four and five I showed logic in a heuristic role. In certain circumstances one can use fragments of deductive reasoning to draw out testable consequences of a slice of the cognitive object (theory-family) underlying particular discourses and practices. It has been clear, at least since the time of Hume, that one can apply the methods and concepts of logic, even in the restricted uses just mentioned, only under certain very stringent assumptions. One must assume that enough is known about the system under study and the conditions of its behaviour to be sure that what has gone in as premise material is adequate. One must suppose further that local conditions are stable, a point of great importance in the theory of the use of dispositional properties. And finally one must have that grand confidence in the universe itself, that it is not a capricious, disorderly shambles of spontaneous events. Notoriously none of this trio of assumptions can be supported empirically, and a priori, conceptual arguments for any of them have been hard to come by.

If logic has only a secondary role in the work of scientists it has assumed a very prominent position in the writings of philosophers of science, influenced by the prevailing logicism. Since the days of Russell it seems to have been taken for granted by many philosophers, not only those interested in the activities and products of the scientific community, that the task of philosophy is the discovery and display of the logical forms of the discourses of this or that field of human endeavour. But, if logic is to be the preeminent tool of philosophical analysis, there ought to be logical essences to be found with its help. Throughout this work I have questioned that assumption. I believe that it has become more and more evident that neither the cognitive activities of the scientific community, such as theorizing or classifying, nor the practical aspects of its work such as experimenting, have logical essences. Of course one might so trivialize what is meant by logic to include any form of canonical cognitive activity. But that would be to beg the question.

The logicist programme has been based on a very restricted repertoire of formal structures and concepts. The worst excesses of logicism have involved the bland assumption that the apparatus of the first-order predicate calculus will suffice to display all that is important in human discourse. It has often been suggested, and as frequently the suggestion has been ignored, that at least some of the famous 'problems' of the philosophy of science of the recent past should not be taken as puzzles to be solved, but as *reductiones ad absurdum* of the logicist programme. For instance, the difficulties that beset Hempel's D-N explanation format should not call forth yet more ingenious extensions of that idea, but should presage its demise. The proliferation of attempts to fit blite ravens and non-green non-emeralds into a coherent empirical discourse ought to suggest that putative logical essences based on the standard logical calculus are unilluminating because the analytical tools are inadequate.

What is the job in hand? Why would anyone have recourse to the formal concepts of logic as an analytical model for scientific discourse? As I see it logicism reflects a too narrow conception of the proper task of philosophy. If it is the project of displaying forms common to a variety of scientific discourses it is a mistake to try to carry out this task with inadequate tools. Instead of persisting in the face of difficulties with whatever analytical concepts are current we should be ever open to the possibility of adopting new formal tools. These will count as satisfacyory if the problems posed by logical essentialism no longer appear. Popper's early philosophy of science ran into trouble through his implicit reliance on *modus tollens* as the way we should understand the role of experiments. But if experiments are illustrative anecdotes, rather than the source of premises for some fragment of deductive reasoning, the difficulties that Lakatos convassed in creating his methodology of research programmes simply do not arise. I shall try to illustrate the power of an eclectic methodology in philosophy by comparing the results of using a quite different analytical system from first-order predicate calculus to display a content-free form which might be common to laws of nature in whatever scientific speciality they are formulated. By adopting an alternative method of analysis we shall be able to set aside as irrelevant the old chestnut of the white shoes that might be cited, contrary to our intuitions, as evidence for the blackness of ravens.

Not only have concepts like 'law of nature', 'explanation', and so on, been appropriated by logicists, but so have the modalities, 'possible', 'necessary' and 'probable'. In discussing them I shall have another target in view, namely extensionalism. The recent history of the study of modalities is rich with baroque metaphysics, which, I believe, can be put down to the unexamined extensionalist assumptions of many authors. The extensionalist position is based on a simple principle. Meanings are, in the end, reducible to the sets of objects denoted by a concept. As I have suggested in various places in the earlier parts of this work, many important scientific meta-concepts seem to require the adoption of a dual ontology. *Both* real-world beings *and* cognitive entities, the work of the human imagination, are required if we would understand how modal concepts are used in scientific thinking. There are intralinguistic ways of creating meanings, as well as those ways which depend on establishing a physical link between the user of words and the world to which they are used to refer.

16

Quantification and Generality: Alternatives to the First-Order Predicate Calculus

The first-order predicate calculus uses the particles of propositional logic as the building blocks for expressing the results of its syntactical analyses. The effect of this is to ensure that the logical form of those statements of scientific discourse we pick out as having significant generality, the laws of nature, are open sets of elementary propositional functions. The representation of sentences with which significant statements might be made is facilitated by two devices. Names can be substituted for variables, or open sentences can be closed by quantifiers. The closure of the open set of disjunctions of propositional functions is the achievement of the E-quantifier and of the conjunctive set that of the A-quantifier. It is against this background that I develop the critical commentary of this chapter.

Existence and the E-quantifier

The way in which quantifiers have been interpreted has been dominated by the famous slogan 'To be is to be the value of a variable.' As Quine (1953 p. 13) actually put it 'To be assumed as an entity is, purely and simply, to be reckoned as the value of a variable.' A moment earlier in that chapter he had tried saying *there is something* to the binding of a variable, that is to quantification, in particular to the insertion of the E-quantifier. And all of this, one may remember, comes from troubles about the ontological status of possibilities, troubles which recent work on the foundations of modal logic have revived with a vengeance. Quine is happy neither with an ontology of actualized possibles nor with possibilities as ideas in the mind.

Only in the first-order predicate calculus, and in formal systems which share its basic structure, with their restricted formal machinery, does this famous slogan have much force. I think it can be shown that, despite the authority of Quine's pronouncement, one is not committed to defend an ontological claim about the existence of that about which one is talking. We can and do conduct tightly rationalized discourses with the question of the existence of the referents of nominal terms in suspension. The practice of theoretical science requires the ability to reason about 'some' and 'all' the members of a kind without *prior* regard to the existence of referents for the substantive terms of theories. An existential reading of the E-quantifier makes this impossible. Extensionalism seems to have had a role in the background to the idea that the logic of the E-quantifier captures the 'grammar' of existence claims. But in theorizing, names and descriptions can be meaningful, without the question of the reality of that which they denote having been settled. I have tried to show how intralinguistic processes of meaning creation are at work in scientific discourses, prior to decisions about the existence of their putative referents. There must be a way of reasoning which is non-committal as to the existence of beings apparently denoted by the substantive terms of those discourses. This brings me to the unjustly neglected work of Lejewski (1954).

Lejewski argues that the problems that seem to beset our reasoning concerning beings about whose existence we are unsure reflect the particular way the quantifiers have been interpreted. In commenting on Quine's position, a position still largely unchallenged even today, he remarks (p. 108) that it follows from the Quinean viewpoint that 'we have to find out whether the noun-expressions we may like to employ, are empty or not' before we can safely use the standard laws of quantification, namely universal instantiation and existential generalization. But it is an empirical question whether this or that noun-expression denotes anything. And now comes the troubling consequence that ought to bother philosophers of science: 'all the restrictions which according to Quine must be observed when ever we reason with empty noun-expressions, will have to be observed also in the case of noun-expressions of which we do not know whether they are empty or not.'

Lejewski's solution is based on a distinction between unrestricted and restricted interpretation of quantifiers. While Quine (restricted) reserves existential quantification for cases where the ontology is, at least for the users of the logic, settled, Lejewski (unrestricted) interprets the E-quantifier as ranging over noun-expressions, that is as controlling the items which can be substituted for a variable. These items are not beings, but nouns or noun-expressions. On p. 110 we see the pay-off for the philosophy of science.

Under the unrestricted interpretation every component of an expansion [that is either an open disjunctive set of propositional functions or an open conjunctive set] contains a noun-expression of which we can say only that it is a meaningful noun-expression. It may designate only one of the objects belonging to the universe, it may designate more than one, it may designate nothing at all.

Within this interpretation of the E-quantifier fragments of practically useful deductive reasoning can go on without threat from ontology. To be is to have a place among the beings of a world, not to be the value of a variable. Lejewski's detailed recommendations for the analysis of existence claims need not detain us, except to remark that they draw on set theoretical notions of Lesniewski's 'ontology'.

If existence and quantification are not bound up in the way Quine supposes (and thirty-three years later, that supposition is still alive and well!) how are ontological matters tied in to the way we can reason? Again I turn to a proposal, of an even earlier vintage than that of Lejewski, namely Strawson's 'presupposition' relation. Lesniewski's treatment of substantive existence claims involves the construction of three predicates by means of which existence claims can be made to stand in truth-functional relationships with descriptive statements about the beings in question. But I find convincing the intuition that statements, known to be about non-existent entities (how dangerous that metaphor of 'aboutness' can be!), *within the framework of natural science*, are not to be taken seriously. But this must be qualified. There are serious and useful discourses about imagined beings, so idealized that we do not take their existence seriously. As I have argued in parts four and five, these discourses are worth attention only in a context in which the question of the representative power of the imagined beings, as resembling something in the real world, is useful. How can the above intuition be realized formally? Strawson's (1950) treatment of existence claims involves a relationship, namely presupposition that is not truth-functional in the usual sense. It works as follows:

P presupposes Q

means

If Q is true P is either true or false

and

If Q is false P is neither true nor false.

This relationship has a direct application in the reasoning typical of policy realism. Only if we can establish the existence of beings of some kind does it make sense to ask whether certain claims about their properties and behaviour are true or false. It should go without saying that throughout this part the words 'true' and 'false' are being used within the framework of the epistemology sketched in parts one and two, when they are not simply appearing in reports of logicist doctrines. Policy realism is the idea of mounting a search for exemplars of a hypothetical kind as the first step in their investigation. If we do find them then further refinement of our tentative beliefs about them is in point.

Strawson's presupposition relation needs some qualifications. I have described it in terms of the concepts of the strict system, namely truth and falsity. In real science we know we shall have to settle for something less. But whatever the strength of these assessments they will follow the same two principles. If we find the claim for existence plausible, then we can go on to consider whether we find the statements made about the beings in question plausible too. But if we do not then those claims lapse. It is not that some specific claim about the properties of beings we think do not exist are implausible. They are empty. This conclusion too needs to be qualified. I share with Cartwright the view that there are many discourses in the physical sciences that are about models of unknown real things and processes and other imagined beings. But we do not wish our claims about them to lapse. In Realm 2 science we assess our descriptions of these models by the degree of resemblance our models bear to the reality they represent. This assessment, as we have seen in part four, is a complicated matter. The ontological implications of the kinetic theory of gases, for instance, are assessed by reference both to the quality of the behavioural analogy and to the strength of the material analogy. In this way we have convinced ourselves as a community that whatever are the constituents of gases they closely resemble molecules. I shall take this point up in more detail in the chapter on modality, because what is at issue is how far a discourse about possibilities can be allowed to mimic a discourse about beings known to be real. To deal with that issue an account of what it is for a discourse to be *about* possibilities will need to be given.

Another residual problem concerns the way in which, within the framework of the presupposition relation, contrary-to-fact conditionals are to be dealt with. Intuitively we seem ready to say that some are true and others false. Even in our more overtly modest terminology of plausibility and implausiblity we seem to be entitled to make judgements of the epistemic quality of such statements. But don't we run into a classical problem of philosophical logic over just this point? A contrary-to-fact statement is surely about beings which do not exist. I hold this problem over to the chapter on modality.

The assessment of laws of nature

The favourite candidate for knowledge-bearer among those philosophers who confined themselves to the study of printed scientific texts was the 'law of nature'. We have already seen that such texts do not represent the cognitive aspects of science at all well, since they are 'drawn off' from only a very narrow section of the total relevant cognitive object. Laws of nature do indeed appear in the discourses of the scientific community, often shorn of the cognitive system in which they are actually embedded. How is their belief-worthiness assessed? There is a branch of the philosophy of science traditionally devoted to the study of this issue, lately called 'confirmation theory'. Characteristically it treats laws of nature as notionally independent hypotheses, represented by the isolated letter 'H'. It takes for granted that they are to be assessed by reference to something called 'evidence', represented by the letter 'e'. In classical confirmation theory 'e' is made up of a finite set of singular descriptive statements, supposedly unproblematically true or false. Logically considered they are instantiations of the propositional functions that appear in the laws, each of which is represented by a universal quantification of that propositional function. I am ashamed to confess I once took this idea seriously. I believe now that it is just a philosophers' fancy.

So far as I can see, laws of nature are *never* assessed by considering the logical relations that obtain between 'H' and 'e'. Members of the scientific community give or withhold credence on the basis of their attitudes to the current state of the whole cognitive object of which the laws form a partial description. Feyerabend has pointed out cases (Galileo's physics for instance) in which the instantial type of evidence was poor, even contrary, yet one set of laws was preferred over another, better-instantiated set. I believe these cases can be understood by reference to the total cognitive objects involved in the rival points of view. I shall call this the 'vicarious assessment account' of the belief worthiness of laws and theories. It could be expressed in the principle:

Laws of nature take the epistemic valuation of the state of the theory-family in which they are embedded at the moment of their assessment.

In short a law of nature is thought to be more or less plausible in so far as the theory-family from which it is drawn is thought to be more or less plausible.

Cartwright (1983) has argued that the laws of physics, when taken literally, describe the behaviour of idealized models of causal mechanisms, rather than the behaviour of those mechanisms themselves. This would have been correct and consistent with the theory-family approach if she had qualified her claim with 'in the first instance'. As practising realists, most members of the scientific community, if they have the technical resources, try to determine the degree of resemblance between the ideal model and the real mechanism. As we have seen, this is a complex matter, involving both behavioural and material comparisons. Working on the material comparison (epistemic access being required) is the most difficult, since it depends on establishing a more or less direct physical relationship with a representative instance of the kind of being in question. If the resemblance is good the associated law doubles its denotation, describing both the behaviour of the model and that of the real causal mechanism of which it is an iconic representation. We have also seen that this doubling of reference may involve a doubling of sense, in that a proper understanding of the whole range of use of the key terms in the discourse may involve the recognition of both a literal and a metaphorical meaning.

The only context in which isolated hypotheses are supported or undermined by strings of instances would be in scientific projects confined to the beings of Realm 1. But even in those cases, say classical kinematics, the instability of Realm 1 science is such that some schematic cognitive object is present in the resources of the community to provide the hypothesis with a context. I take *all* talk of the probability or otherwise of laws and hypotheses to be oblique references to the state of the explicit or tacit theory-family from which they are momentarily drawn. A policy realist would have no idea how to assess an isolated hypothesis.

The logical grammar of laws of nature

My argument, which relies heavily on some ideas of J. Aronson, is directed to showing that the classical 'problems' that emerge from traditional studies of the laws of nature are artefacts of the formal system chosen to express their structure. In particular, first-order predicate calculus will be indicted as the main culprit.

The demonstration of the inadequacy of that calculus to the task of expressing the formal structure of law statements further illustrates the defects of logicism. The calculi of logic are defective analytic tools not only by virtue of the problems they engender, but also because of their vagueness. The fact that the symbols of a formal system obey a small number of simple rules is no ground for claiming that the concepts they express are sharp and/or clear. For instance, though the universal quantifier expresses the thought that *somehow* the quantified variable ranges over all the objects in the universe, it does not distinguish between some very different ways in which that ranging might be accomplished. The precision of ordinary English is markedly greater than that of the standard predicate calculus. There are at least four quantifiers in English, the most important of which are 'each', 'any', 'every' and 'all'. Between them they neatly distinguish ways of ranging not differentiated by the A-quantifier of the predicate calculus.

But we can bracket the general deficiencies of the use of this logical machinery in analysis, in addressing the problem of finding the best way to display the formal syntax of law statements. There are two main features of the standard formula which lead to trouble.

1   By treating a law statement as a molecular statement, made up of two atomic propositional functions connected by the formal relation of material implication, we make possible the logical operation of contraposition. Thus

If anything is a raven then it is black

can be contraposed to give

If anything is non-black then it is a non-raven.

If by substitution or by quantification these propositional functions are made into propositions with truth values, it is clear that contraposition preserves truth value.

2   When the propositional functions above are universally quantified they yield forms like

For all x, if x is a raven, then x is black.

But that quantifier ranges over an unqualified and unrestricted universe of entities. Suppose now that we take the universal statement about the colour of ravens above to be a law. What do we expect it will apply to? Should it, for example, be taken to apply to white shoes? Our intuitions tell us that that law has nothing whatever to do with shoes, and at most it says something about birds. Why drag in shoes? Well, if we are permitted to perform the operation of contraposition on the unqualified law statement, whose quantifier ranges over all the universe, then everything in the universe except ravens falls under the category of non-ravens, including, of course, shoes.

Most readers will be only too familiar with the next step. If we take the discovery of a black raven as support for the law 'If anything is a raven then it is black' we are tacitly accepting a principle of instance confirmation. Laws are confirmed (or, if you are a fallibilist, disconfirmed) by the discovery of instances (or counter-instances) of the things they purport to describe. So long as we accept both the admissibility of contraposition and the universality of the quantifier we must admit that a white shoe would confirm, to some unspecified degree, the claim that everything which is non-black (e.g. white) is a non-raven (e.g. a shoe). But this last statement is the contrapositive of the law of ravens, and hence is logically equivalent to it. So we seem to be forced to admit that white shoes confirm a law about the blackness of ravens. The sources of the puzzle seem terribly obvious. Why should anyone accept that the contrapositive of a law of nature is also a law? And why should one accept that a law of nature purporting to be about a species of bird actually comprehends everything in the universe? Aronson has tried the raven paradox on working scientists, and one and all they reject the idea that the law of ravens applies to the complement class, non-ravens. No satisfactory solution has emerged within the framework of logicism. Can we step outside that framework to find another way of displaying the formal syntax of law statements? Perhaps adopting a different formal apparatus will reveal some other rather different structure, a structure which will not lead to this and other paradoxes that beset attempts at representing the assessment of laws of nature formally.

I have already developed arguments to defend the idea that quantifiers are not the best way of expressing the ontological commitments of a statement, despite their canonization in this role by W. V. Quine. From the point of view of the philosophy of science Strawson's presupposition relation fares much better. (It has been suggested to me that the Sneed-Stegmuller idea of 'intended applications' is yet another alternative to a quantifier account of ontological commitment.) The presupposition relation ties together assumptions about what we take to exist with the possibility of the statement to which it is tied being plausible *or* implausible, being assessable. Thus 'Ravens are black' is either a plausible or an implausible general assertion if there are ravens, but neither if there are not. But, the critic might reply, surely there is a quantifier buried in this reasoning, for we mean *all* ravens, not just a few or a lot, but all. True, but this is not a universal quantifier in the style of the standard first-order predicate calculus, since it quantifies only over ravens. And that restriction is ensured by the incorporation of the ontological clause 'and there are ravens' in the discourse. Presupposition (defined, for illustrative purposes, tidily in the strict system) is not a truth-functional relation, since the truth of a presupposition entails only the truth or falsity of what presupposes it, while its falsity entails that that which presupposes it is neither true nor false. A determined logicist might still argue that universal quantification has not been eliminated from the analysis, since the ontological clause contains an existential quantifier 'There are . . .' and this is equivalent to 'It is not the case that for all x, x is not . . .' And this quantifier comprehends the whole universe. But of course the rule which permits the above substitution is just another rule of the first-order predicate calculus. It is not uncontroversial to analyse the existence claim 'There are . . .' as that quantifier which is subject to the above rule. I have tried to show, following Lejewski, that the E-quantifier is not the best way to express material existence claims.

The move to presupposition instead of quantification provides a principled way of tying confirmation to natural kinds. It is because ravens are birds that it makes sense to contemplate the possibility of a lawful relation between their species and their colour, and even a naturally necessary relation. The mediator is the theory of natural selection. Another context where kinds and colours might be thought to be lawfully tied to one another is provided by the physical chemistry of gemstones. But despite the fact that green emeralds are undoubtedly correctly described as non-black non-ravens they have no role to play in assessing the plausibility of 'All ravens are black' because their existence is not among the existential presuppositions of that statement. The theory of natural selection does not apply to them, and so has no role to play in backing up the claim that the kind-to-colour relation is lawful. Aronson has developed a more or less identical argument, where he prefixes an ontological statement to the expression of the substantive content of the law. He would not express it in the form of the pre-supposition relation, but as the common ontology of the theory which has something to say about the colours of the plumage of birds. But this is a difference merely of rhetoric and not of substance. The power of this style of analysis shows up in the way that the generalizing function and the ontological function of discourse, elided in the traditional quantifier, are located in separate, functionally and formally distinct elements in the display of the formal syntax of law statements. Once again first-order predicate calculus is convicted of intolerable vagueness, since the functional distinction between displaying the scope of generalization and expressing its ontological commitment is not adequately marked.

There still remains the question of the propriety of the expression of the substantive content of the law statement as a relation of material implication between propositional functions. The next phase in this argument I owe wholly to Aronson. Take a simpler example than that of the colour of ravens, say the Newtonian Second Law, that $F = ma$. Following the tradition, one would try to express it as

> If anything is subject to a constant Force then it will accelerate at a rate proportional to the quotient of the Force exerted upon it and its Mass.

In this form the law can be contraposed.

> If anything does not accelerate at a rate proportional to the quotient of the Force exerted on it and its Mass then it has not been acted by a constant Force.

The extension of the first substantive term of this formulation includes not only stationary things, but singing things, glowing things, and so on. Finding a glowing thing, which is a non-accelerating thing which has not been acted on by a force, should support Newton's Second Law.

However, there is an alternative way of formally presenting the logical syntax of the Newtonian Second Law. It can be set out as a function, that is as a mapping from one *set* to another. These sets could be values of variables representing phenomena, or, perhaps better, one could treat a law as a mapping relation between the states themselves. Whichever way the law is taken, $F = ma$ is not a molecular proposition expressing a conditional relation between atomic propositions. It is the succinct expression of a mapping relation between sets. Aronson has pointed out that *as a mapping relation it has no contrapositive*. The case of a body which is not accelerating and is not acted on by a force is already included in the law as the mapping from the first member of the 'F' set onto the first member of the 'a' set. Thus 'non-accelerating' means '$a = 0$', that is either stationary or moving uniformly relative to the relevant inertial frame, and so cannot mean, *inter alia*, 'glowing'. As a mapping from one set to another the law applies only to those beings which are accelerating because acted on by forces, and tells how they perform. That the law is about them and no other beings is determined by its existential presuppositions.

We now have an alternative formal analysis of the logical syntax of a law statement. There is no universal quantifier prefixed to the sentence form, but instead there is an ontological clause standing in a presupposition relation to the rest of the law statement. The core of the law statement is not a molecular conditional proposition formed by material implication from atomic propositional functions, but a mapping from one set to another. This analysis displays a formal structure from which the raven paradox cannot be generated. The ontological clause ensures that any quantifiers are restricted in range to relevant entities, while the mapping relation precludes the operation of contraposition. It should now be entirely clear why the raven paradox is an artefact of the choice of formal apparatus. And the actual exposition of a formal apparatus, alternative to the first-order predicate calculus, shows that the traditional formalism is not the only possible formal apparatus. We can also now see why laws of nature can be assessed only relative to the theory-families in which they are embedded. It is only by virtue of the theory-family that the content of ontological presuppositions can be filled out, and the range of beings relative to the assessment of the plausibility of the statement of a law assessed.

Metaphysical consequences of the shift in syntax

What are laws of nature about? The Machean view that they are convenient summaries of experience ties in well with the extensionalism implicit in the standard representation. If universal quantification represents a conjunction of instantiations it is not hard to interpret these as representing actual or possible experiential moments. Some years ago now Dretske (1977) published an interesting paper, scarcely noticed, which used problems with the results of the use of the traditional analytical formalism to make a quite radical suggestion about the denotation of law statements. (See also Armstrong, 1983.) He pointed out (p. 250) that universal truths of the form $(Ax)(Fx \rightarrow Gx)$ are 'transparent' at their predicate positions, that is any extensionally equivalent predicate letter can be substituted, *salva veritate*. But, if one tries the same move with a statement which is taken to express a law of nature, the predicate positions are 'opaque'. The result of the substitution is not, in general, a law of nature. Dretske's explanation of this phenomenon is that a law of nature, say the law that relates gravitational potential to the masses of gravitating bodies, 'is not a statement about the extensions of the predicates "F" and "G", but is a singular statement describing a relationship between the universal properties F-ness and G-ness' (p. 252). It may be that, as a matter of fact, all bodies with mass have some electrical charge, but it does not follow that there is any relationship between the property of engendering a gravitational potential and being electrically charged.

His second line of argument is familiar enough, that producing instances in which the properties referred to by the predicates of the law are coinstantiated is worthless as inductive support. But instances are very good grounds for accepting laws of nature, though, importantly, 'laws of nature are the *sort* of thing that can become well established prior to an exhaustive enumeration of the instances to which they apply' (p. 252).

The properties to which laws make reference are generally dispositions, according to the analyses of earlier parts of this work, and some of the dispositions that are prominent in natural sciences are affordances. Dispositions are part of the scientific conception of nature just in so far as they can be actually or theoretically grounded in the constitutions of kinds or the generative mechanisms of processes. I have dealt in some detail with the regress of properties that this account of first-level properties opens up. There are principled ways of ordering the hierarchies of properties recognized by a science to sustain the general application of the 'double-level' account of every metascientific concept. Dretske simply takes this hierarchical organization of theory and reality as unproblematic. He says: 'the modality [of law statements] at level n is generated by the set of relationships existing between the entities at level $n + 1$.' A material individual has the property 'redness' just in so far as it has the electronic and molecular constitution which, in the appropriate circumstances, will differentially reflect light in such and such a way. 'Redness' is a universal just in so far as it is possible for the molecular constitutions of things to resemble one another. And the same step is taken to defend the claim to be a universal for the properties of each level of the natural hierarchies. No mysterious platonic realm is invoked in this account of universals. I take for granted that the concept of resemblance can be explicated in a common-sense way too.

The account of the formal syntax of laws of nature which I drew from Aronson's ideas is well fitted to express Dretske's metaphysical intuitions. The mappings that create the first-level correlations in Aronson's account of laws are significant only if they are grounded in a deeper mapping of those correlations on to a common ontology. So laws appear only relative to a theory. But the double-level account is just what is needed to sustain a defence of the practical utility of treating classifications made on the basis of the regular copresence of certain disjunctive clusters of properties as reflecting, if possible, natural-kinds. In the end, then, we come to another welcome conclusion, that the use of evidence from instances to provide reasons for accepting putative laws of nature must be considered relative to natural-kinds.

17

Modality in Scientific Discourses

The problems of modality

The philosophical study of modality presents several problems. On the one hand one must try to give an account of the meaning of expressions like 'must', 'may', 'could', and so on, appropriate to the context and subject matter of a certain kind of discourse. I shall follow the usual practice of simplifying the task, though with some reservations, by carrying on the greater part of the discussion with respect to the rather gross concepts, 'necessity' and 'possibility'. At the same time, and consonant with that account, a reasonable theory of the conditions under which these concepts would be used is required. The final step will be to see whether my humdrum accounts of the meanings and conditions of use of modal concepts can reproduce the main structure of 'possible-worlds semantics'. By adding this desideratum I hope to establish suitable fragments of formal syntax for the expression of modality in the three discourses of science. Modal concepts are adverbial qualifiers. The rules for their use can, I believe, be fruitfully examined in relation to the structure of systems proposed by modal logicians, without committing oneself to any particular view of the logical syntax appropriate to express the inner structure of modally qualified statements. I shall be making use of Kripke's (1963) ingenious application of the Leibnizean 'possible worlds' metaphor with the help of which he (and others; cf. Hintikka, 1969) have developed a way of interpreting the various modal logics as if the main modal concepts, 'necessity' and 'possibility', behaved something like quantifiers.

A statement is necessary if it is true in all possible worlds and possible if it is true in at least one possible world. This world is a possible world. Both Kripke and Hintikka added an ingenious refinement to this simple specification, by the help of which the main systems of modal logic were able to be differentiated. The idea again is very simple. (I shall not concern myself with expounding the algebraic realization of these ideas, since they are readily available in the literature; cf. Linsky, 1971.) As Hintikka puts it, 'Not every possible world (say P) is really an alternative to a given possible world (say Q), in the sense that P could have been realized instead of Q.' Thus imaginary (though not of course 'imagined', since it is contingent whether or not I can actually imagine any given 'world') worlds are ordered by their possibility relative to some given world. Kripke calls this 'accessibility'. This ties in nicely with the general account above of what modalities are to mean. If 'necessity' expresses the thought that there are no alternatives to what has been expressed, described etc., then in all worlds accessible from this world whatever is necessary must obtain, *pace* the metaphor. The Kripke test is based on the properties of the accessibility relation. There are various possibilities. It could be (1) reflexive, (2) reflexive and transitive, or (3) reflexive, transitive and symmetrical. If (1) then it conforms to the basic modal system, usually called 'T'. In T the principle 'Necessarily p entails necessarily necessarily p' does not hold. The modal parts of T are the principle 'If necessarily p implies q, then necessarily p implies necessarily q' and the principle 'Necessarily p implies p'. In the axiomatic reading of T any schema which is derived from the axioms in accordance with rule can be qualified by 'necessarily'. A different theory of modality will emerge for the distinctive discourses appropriate to the sciences of each of Realms 1, 2 and 3.

I hope to reproduce the main results of these workers without slipping into the bizarre ontologies that have beguiled some of their followers. (See Loux, 1979, for an excellent critical summary of the more important aspects of these odd developments.) By making selective comparisons between different modal logics I shall allocate modal grammars to each of the three kinds of discourses. These comparisons will be based on the Kripke test. By that I mean a comparison of the properties of the accessibility relation between possible worlds, for each referential realm. Roughly the idea is this: taking, say, this world as actual, is some other world, specified in a certain way, possible? If it is then it is a world accessible from this one. Since 'accessibility' is a two-term relation it could be reflexive or irreflexive, symmetrical or asymmetrical and transitive or intransitive, and as described above the form the accessibility relation takes is a test for the proper modal grammar. We shall find that discourses in the three epistemic realms significant for science differ in ways expressible in this conceit.

The question remains as to whether the modalities which appear in scientific discourse reflect features of the real world or merely conceptual relations created by human convention. We have seen already, in considering the notion of natural kind, a genus of important organizing concepts for scientific thought and practice, that it may be necessary to admit that kind concepts require grounding in features of physical reality and in conventions of discourse. Each kind concept is stabilized, at least temporarily, by its place relative to two networks of relations. One of these is conceptual, by which the kind concept is adjusted to certain human practices. Here there is an element of convention. The other is empirical, by which the kind concept is adjusted through the growth of theory to the unobservable but real constitutive properties of beings of that kind. It will emerge that modal concepts have a similar duality.

The role of the modalities is, I believe, to indicate whether whatever they qualify admits or does not admit of alternatives. This generic property of modalities has to be realized in particular contexts. Whether 'something' is to be thought to have or not to have alternatives can be judged only *relative to a certain bouquet of assumptions*. For example how much of our scientific beliefs admit of alternatives is relative to the degree of contingency we assign to the assumption of the uniformity of nature. Those who hold that nature might behave in new ways, different from those it has manifested in the past, will be ready to admit a larger scope for the imagination of alternative worlds than those who assume that our confidence in the persistence of natural laws is well founded.[1]

The meaning of modal concepts

To begin with the concept of 'necessity': what thought do apodeictic qualifications of assertions express? I believe they are used to indicate that the state, event, proposition, conclusion, etc., given the sometimes unstated conditions of its existence, admits of no alternative. But there are many different kinds of grounds for qualifying a judgement in this way. So, though the meaning is constant, uses of the apodeictic modality are context-dependent. To establish a necessity we must produce a ground for the elimination of (nearly) all logically possible alternatives. An 'alternative' is a more sharply restricted 'other' than merely a disjunct which does not logically contradict the conditions of existence of the realm in question. A good model for alternatives relevant to the philosophy of science is the relation of determinates under a determinable, say hues under colour. Red is an alternative to blue, but it makes no sense to set off yellow as an alternative to square. Possibilities are not coextensive with alternatives. There are real possibilities in so far as there are alternatives *conceivable* by reference to the variable conditions under which certain fixed concept-clusters, say those expressed in laws of nature, can be applied to experience. Again we have the mix of *de re* and *de dicto* considerations. Concept-clusters are grounded in the real natures and constitutions of material beings, but the variations in the conditions of their application are imagined by a human scientist in the light of the variations in conditions he or she has already observed. On this view the meaning of modal concepts is the same in all contexts. The apodeictic modality indicates that there are no context-relative alternatives to that which it qualifies, while the possibility modality indicates that there are alternatives conceivable within the local context. It is the grounds and assumptions of the use of the modalities that vary with context. This fits in well with the general Kripkean line to be adopted in the next section. I shall be arguing that the contexts provided by the three epistemic realms require somewhat different principles of logical syntax to govern the way the modalities are used. But the generic sense of a modal qualification is the same in each, based on the difference between exclusion or inclusion of alternatives within the conceptual possibilities defined by the context.

Modal qualifiers in Realm 1 discourse

How could there be modalities in the discourse of a scientist devoting his or her attention just to the world of common experience? We might imagine an ethologist observing a new species of monkey and marking a card to produce an ethogram of the behaviour of the members of a monkey family. After some time the ethologist might be able to announce certain behavioural regularities appropriate to this species of monkey. For instance something like this is expressed in Chance's hedonic and agonic attention structures (Chance and Larsen, 1976). One would hardly call a cluster of such 'laws' a theory. They have no explanatory power, and we should be reluctant to qualify them as necessary. But there are Realm 1 discourses where the concept of necessity seems a natural qualification of the statements of empirical regularity. It will be illuminating to ask why. Kinematics is of particular interest. We could say that kinematics was a reticular theory, a set of *interconnected* laws, with the help of which the motions of material things under certain conditions could be described within the same system of conceptual resources and indeed predicted. We are liberally supplied with laws like $s = vt$ and $v = u + at$. How are these laws to be understood? Both Koyré and Feyerabend have pointed out, forcefully, that the idea that these are inductive generalizations supported by favourable evidence and not contradicted by experience is nonsense. These laws turn up as ways of applying a certain system of definitions, which set up clusters of concepts useful for classifying motions. An expression like $dx/dt = v$ is a way of relating distance and time so that motion at uniform velocity and accelerated motion can be distinguished. It creates two taxa. By adding the definition of acceleration as the second derivative of space and time, one is provided with a further classificatory possibility, in that motion under uniform acceleration and other kinds of accelerated motion will fall into different taxa. One fruitful way of looking at kinematics is as a system of classification. It has no resources for addressing the question of why in this or that physical set-up uniform or non-uniform motion occurs. Reticular theories engender no explanations. What, then, are we to make of a claim such as the following: 'If released from rest under a uniform acceleration of 980 cpsps, a body must fall 3. 92 m in 2 secs *ceteris paribus*'?

Since there is no second level, no recourse to causes, kinematic statements must partake of the logic of nominal essences. They are overt or covert definitions of concept-clusters shown to be useful for managing a practice, the practice of anticipating and planning movements. Extended by Galileo to the management of gunnery, kinematics provided the conceptual resources for decomposing the opaque and hence unclassifiable motion of a projectile into a uniform velocity parallel to the surface of the earth and another motion, under uniform acceleration in the vertical plane. It would be proper, I believe, to see this as an achievement in classification. I prefer to reserve the word 'taxonomy' for a classification system the demarcations of which can be grounded in real essence distinctions. There is no question whether s = vt is or is not true, only whether there are any actual motions which it clearly picks out. Such a law is not falsified by failure to find a use; rather it may turn out not to apply to anything. In trying to find a right way to describe falling bodies Galileo first considered a motion in which the rate of descent was proportional to the distance rather than the time during which a body had fallen. There is no such motion on earth, that is within a gravitational field which is approximately uniform for short descents.

If kinematics is a classification scheme (and it is certainly not a causal or explanatory theory) it must have a strategy for managing borderline cases. Indeed it seems to operate with the usual devices of schemes in which nominal essence is dominant. One can preserve the conceptual structure and exclude the borderline case. We simply ignore, for most purposes, the effect of the rotations of falling bodies about their own axes. Alternatively, if the case is important, the conceptual cluster which picks out the general class to which it might belong is accommodated in such a way that it does belong. For instance Stoke's Law permits viscous motion to be treated kinematically. We have a new kind of uniform motion, viscous motion. Either way *de dicto* modality is maintained, and the necessity that a falling body must be at a certain place at a certain time is still maintained within the new framework. If it didn't get there the law isn't falsified; rather, barring an odd accident, we know it is *not that kind of motion after all*. If it is that kind of motion there is no alternative, *conceivable* within that framework, to the body being anywhere else. The apodeictic modality appears *de dicto*. But one must remember that we have just those conceptual clusters which form our kinematics because around here the gravitational fields are the way they are, and locally the space is nearly Euclidean. The apodeictic modality now appears somewhat *de re*. But that is to slip into another scientific context, since gravitational fields, the forces they engender, and so on, are Realm 3 entities, the description of which requires theoretical concepts and takes us towards real essences. Dynamics is not a Realm 1 science.

To apply the Kripke test to decide which principles should be admitted to the logical syntax governing the modalities whose concrete conditions of use have been sketched above, we turn to an examination of the properties of the accessibility relation. Anticipating the metaphysical discussion of modalities I shall take 'possible worlds' to be the alternative states of affairs imaginable by an idealized thinker relative to the kinds of differences he or she (or it) can imagine from the world already known. The Kripke test is to ask whether in an ensemble of imagined alternative worlds we would expect whatever was necessary (possible) in our world to be subject to the same modal qualification imagined to hold in an ensemble of imagined worlds thought up according to some principle.

There are two steps by which a thinker might imagine alternative worlds to ours, apropos of applying the Kripke test to the modalities of Realm 1 discourse.

1   The same concept-clusters are found useful for us in classifying events and things, but the initial conditions of at least some of the processes they help us to follow are different.

2   It might be that a different selection of concept-clusters from all logically possible concept-clusters is required to manage the alternative world. But our old concept-clusters with which we manage this world are still conceptually necessary, the only difference being that there are no events or things to which they apply.

According to the Kripke test this calls for an S-5 grammar. Accessibility is an equivalence relation, in that what is apodeictic in any fantasy world imaginable in either of these ways is necessary in any other. The relation of relative possibility between any fantasy world and this world, or between any two fantasy worlds, is reflexive, symmetrical and transitive. No particular events or things are necessary, but conceptual relations, whether having application or not are. To say that this kind of discourse needs an S-5 grammar means that, by whatever modality a statement is qualified, it takes that qualification of necessity. So the two main syntactic principles of this grammar are CpLMp and CLpLLp. For instance phlogiston necessarily has negative weight in whatever world we may choose to imagine, because that statement is grounded in the internal structure of the concepts involved. It is necessarily true in this world, though there is, in fact, no substance to apply it to, that is there is no phlogiston. This ties in with the discussion of the role of existence presuppositions in chapter 16. Though 'Phlogiston has negative weight' is a necessary *truth* it is neither plausible nor implausible as a scientific statement relative to our real world. The logical syntax of scientific discourse does not include the rule CLp'Plausible'p. One might imagine an objection to this argument along the following lines: if the laws of this world are really a practical format for certain concept-clusters given a priori – such as that which expresses the quotient of displacement to elapsed time, or the relation between mass and gravitational potential – and these clusters have no application in some imagined world, where, say, there are no diamonds, so that the concept-cluster by which diamond is crystalline carbon is an apodeictic taxonomic principle but does not have a use, should we call these 'laws' at all? A model for this case would be the phlogiston story, in which the laws governing the behaviour of phlogiston have no application in our world. To answer this objection one simply picks up the central feature of the philosophy of science for Realm 1 studies. What counts as a law in Realm 1 discourse is not an inductively supported empirical generalization but a concept-cluster as applied to this or that experienced situation. The concept-cluster maintains its necessary internal structure, but we would not want to *call* it a law in circumstances where it is, though necessarily true, of no conceivable use. Laws are plausible or implausible, concept-clusters are internally structured or they are not.

Modal qualifiers in Realm 2 discourse

Realm 2 discourse includes that of Realm 1, since the use of analytical models is selective and refines descriptions of the world as it is manifested in perception. But Realm 2 discourse also describes models of the internal constitutions of substances and individuals explanatory of their manifest appearances, and of the persisting generative mechanisms that ground our picking out of some event sequences as causal. As I have argued, the use of such descriptions to control searches of the real world is well supported by example. The situation for modalities is greatly changed. Modal qualifications of causal and taxonomic generalizations can be backed up with revisable claims about real essences. What is going on? As I argued in part two the role of theory is to provide empirical, and hence revisable, hypotheses about real essences. These justify claims about the correctness of the use of this or that concept-cluster in the science of this world. Since Realm 2 discourse refers to beings which, given developments in technology, might be observable, Realm 2 discourse invokes the imagination to create anticipations of experience of thinkable, in short possible, worlds. Thus while Realm 2 discourses do not affect the modalities of Realm 1 that reflect conceptual matters, the modality of that part of the Realm 2 discourse that refers to unobserved but in principle observable beings is dependent for its grounding on matters of fact, in the etiolated sense of 'fact' defended in earlier parts. Now to apply the Kripke test. What changes when we consider the status of a concept-cluster in a world now more richly imagined through the possibility of adding the real-essence component to our fantasies is not its necessity but the propriety of its selection as the *law* for that world. If molecules have significant volumes, $PV = K$ is not a good law. We had better pick $P(V - b) = L$. But in a world in which the Realm 2 discourse was about point particles the former relation would be (indeed, was) a good choice.

Yet intuition suggests that if we are satisfied that molecules do have significant volume, in this world, by the alternatives principle, that view rules out any alternative other than some further refinement of $P(V - b) = L$. This opens up the possibility of introducing another pair of modalities, natural necessity and possibility. Since natural necessity relies on the groundings of Realm 2 discourses, and these describe different imaginable worlds, the natural necessities of this world (or any of its imagined alternatives) are not exportable one to another. The Kripke test would show that the accessibility relation is neither symmetrical nor transitive. Thus, while a world of point molecules is possible relative to our world, $P(V - b) = L$ is naturally necessary in our world of lumpish molecules but has no application in a world where the general gas law *must* be $PV = K$. Nor would the latter, naturally necessary in a Boscovichian world, be acceptably qualified with that modality in ours. The logical grammar of natural necessity is not S-5, but only system T. The rule CLpLLp clearly does not hold if 'L' is read as 'naturally necessary'.

The model for an analysis of the empirical generalizations of Realm 1 discourse was the applicable or inapplicable conceptual truth. A plausible law was a useful necessary truth, an implausible law a useless one. This model highlighted the nominal essences of taxonomy and the a priori conceptual definitions of kinematics. Statements expressing these were transworldly because they were necessarily necessary. To complete a defence of the above account of a dual modality for Realm 2 discourse it will be necessary to argue for a similar analysis for a statement like the general gas law. In what way is '$PV = RT$' a conceptual relation? To see that there is this aspect to the law one can turn to a dimensional analysis. P has the dimensions of rate of change of momentum, that is $MS/T/T$. V has dimensions S^3. If we divide through by T we have R = PV/T giving us the dimensional expression for R as MS^3/T^3. R is not a number, it is a physical concept, defined by the above relation. Looked at this way the general gas law expresses a conceptual relationship, having that breed of necessity which is picked up by the logical grammar of modal qualifiers in Realm 1 discourse. But located in the discourse of Realm 2 it is naturally necessary only in this and imagined worlds which differ from this one only in initial conditions, since it is grounded in what happens to be the real molecular structure of gases. Conceptual necessities brook of no alternatives – they are necessarily necessary – but natural necessities do admit of alternatives so they are only contingently necessary. By the Kripke test the logical grammars of these concepts differ. The lesson to be draw at this point is only too obvious. Careful qualifications of apodeictic qualifiers are needed to avoid mistakes in reasoning. The concept of 'possibility' must split along the same lines. The real-essence style talk of Realm 2 discourse constrains the imaginability of alternatives in ways that Realm 1 discourse does not. Alternatives can be imagined by dreaming up not only a fantasy in which the initial conditions of the universe are different, but also one in which the underlying 'hidden' processes too are not as they are suspected to be in our world.

Modality in Realm 3 discourse

The hierarchical structure of Realm 2 discourse continues into discourses whose putative referents are in Realm 3, the realm of beings beyond all possible experience. The boundary between these realms turned out on reflection to be rather more historically conditioned and permeable than it might have seemed at first sight. However, the interesting and important reaches of this level of science, despite the metaphysically conservative effects of the principles of mathematical epistemology, turned out to be Bohrian in character. Dispositions were the affordances of an undifferentiated grounding reality. The move to ground the natural necessity of observably instantiated conceptual relations in the natures of substances and processes, which characterized the methodology of theory construction for Realm 2 science, is repeated for Realm 3. However, it depended, we saw, on rather tentative analogies between the natural-kind constraints of Realm 2 theorizing and the mathematical constraints of theorizing for Realm 3.

In terms of the Kripke test this means that, while conceptual relations would be maintained in whatever world we imagined, the powerful control exercised over natural necessities by the existential testing of putative referents of Realm 2 theories, within the framework of policy realism, cannot be relied upon, even in principle, for Realm 3 discourse. So for those relations which are thought to be naturally necessary by virtue of groundings in Realm 3 causally productive processes or constitutions of kind, the modal claim is only weakly supported by theory. The Clavius paradox tells us that, without the constraint of existence tests, coherence is not enough to base reality claims on. It was the strength of Realm 2 considerations that made possible the restriction of modal qualifications of natural necessity to each world, our real one as we think it to be, and others which we can imagine by varying the hypotheses about how natural relations are grounded. Of course we can still do this, in thought. But in the end we have had to admit that we know and probably can know nothing about the glub except what it affords. That is we can never know why the glub has the affordances it has in the same way as we can know (scientifically) why vinegar, dynamite, strychnine or acorns have the affordances they display as behaviour, effects or developments under suitable conditions. Claims to have picked out naturally necessary relationships in this world are thereby weakened. The position with respect to the Kripke test is, then, indeterminate. The unimaginability of the state of the glub, or even whether it is proper to think of the glub as having states, means that the very idea of promiscuously just thinking up alternative foundations for the world has to be dropped. Different mathematical constructions may be possible but their metaphysical commitments would have to be studied case by case. It is clear, even to the amateur onlooker, that the ontology of Penrose's twistor theory, if it could be worked out, would be nothing like the implicit ontologies of substances and corpuscles that the mathematical constraints of covariance and gauge invariance have severally imposed on contemporary physics. In the light of these considerations the minimalist logical grammar of system T had better be adopted for the control of reasoning with natural necessity in the context of discourses about the putative beings of Realm 3.

Some ontological observations

Until recently the question of how possibility and necessity were to be understood seemed simple. They were ideas applicable only to discourses, or perhaps thoughts. It had seemed to many that Hume had put paid to the idea that the 'necessary' in 'necessary connection' qualified relationships by virtue of denoting something in the same real world as events, things and so on. But the arguments I have sketched in this work seem to give (qualified) support to the idea that in at least one use the concept of necessity denotes something in the real world: the real grounding of what appears in an orderly fashion in experience, namely the stable collocation of properties of substances, and the regularity of causal sequences of events, *ceteris paribus*. Substances have inner constitutions and constitutively potent locations in larger structures. Causal sequences are produced by persistent generative mechanisms. And in certain favourable circumstances these necessity-grounding beings can be demonstrated to exist alongside the other furnishings of the world. However, a realist ontology of the possibility modality does not fit so comfortably with scientific realism. Lewis's (1973 and later) insistence on the existence of possible worlds has seemed both perverse and important. It is perverse because the claim that possible worlds exist in just the way that the real world does, only they are not actual, seems daft. 'We call it alone actual', he says (p. 87), 'not because it differs in kind from all the rest but because it is the world that we inhabit.' It is important because it has brought forth an interesting literature aimed at getting the status of possibilities right. Throughout this chapter I have been arguing for the status of this or that modal usage with some kind of conceptualist account of possibility in mind.

The idea that possible worlds are works of the imagination runs into one obvious difficulty. Surely one might say there are more possibilities than anyone has actually thought of. The cognitive concept needed here must be imaginable rather than imagined. A preliminary reply might be that we are talking about dispositions of the mind (implicit contents of propositional systems) though this thought will need to be made good. The basis of a non-inflationary treatment can be found in an extended remark of Rescher (1973b).

Unrealized possibilities do not exist as such. What exist are minds and their capabilities, and consequently languages and their rules. Unrealized possibilities are *generated* by minds, and so they can be said to exist only in a secondary and dependent sense, as actual or potential objects of thought. Such possibilities are the products of an *intellectual construction*. The ontological status of the possible is thus fundamentally mind-dependent, the domain of the possible being a mental construct.

Adams (1974) has taken something like this idea a stage further to lay out in some detail a theory of 'world-stories', propositional ensembles which have some of the coherence that such stories, *qua world*-stories, must have. This development of the conceptualist ontology reserves actuality for this world in a very robust sense, but also allows these stories to be among the furnishings of this world. Further pursuit of these issues is beyond the scope of this work. Enough has been said to show how a consistent treatment of the possibilities upon which the Kripke test so heavily depended can be worked up within a non-inflationary ontology. There is only this world.

Some of its creatures can add certain stories to the furnishing of this world, with which they perform some amazing conceptual feats. In part two I suggested that among those feats is the creating in thought of the past and the future, and in this part I have suggested that the complementary conceptual trick of considering and ruling out alternatives is not beyond them either. There at least for the moment I must let the matter rest.

Nevertheless there is one residual use of expressions like 'there is a real possibility that . . . ' that is grounded in the physical reality of this world. Mostly I think we mean by such expressions that the beings actually present or likely to be present in a situation already possess such dispositions as would, if activated or stimulated, lead to the result in question. The conditional clause about activation can be read as an ignorance qualification, apropos of what are likely to be the totality of conditions in that situation. So the use of the concept of possibility here is quasi-ontological, in that it implicitly invokes constitutive properties upon which the existence of the dispositions depends. But it is also quasi-conceptualist, in that it involves the contemplation of some future states of affairs when certain currently non-existent states of affairs might obtain. This residual use fits neatly into the general treatment.

18

Probability Concepts in Science

Occasions for the use of probability concepts

Carnap (1950) noted that probability concepts were used in two main contexts. There were empirical contexts, in which an empirical concept of probability was used for economically describing observed statistical regularities. A concept of probability also appeared among the concepts used to express epistemic assessments of hypotheses. Carnap regarded these contexts as sufficiently different to justify the idea that there were at least two different concepts of probability at work.

Before I comment on whether the difference in contexts justifies the marking off of two concepts, there is another dimension of distinction in occasions of use that is noteworthy. I shall assume, without further argument, that *pace* Lucas (1978) 'probable' as an epistemic qualifier, belongs in a continuum with 'uncertain' and 'certain' rather than between 'false' and 'true'. In science we are driven towards the uncertainty pole for two main reasons. We may be ignorant of the causes of a statistical spread in the outcomes of repeatedly applying some apparently similar treatment to a physical system (say tossing a coin on earth in still air). Or we may have some reason to think that the treatment we are using actually under-determines the nature of the events or states it produces. Persistent failure to find an inclining cause could be such a reason. In the former case the remedy lies in more careful observation and control, but as reflecting a condition of the world the latter is without human remedy. Until recently the practitioners of natural science took it for granted that the latter case was not genuine. All cases of statistical distributions among the results of apparently similar treatments were thought to be of the former kind, differing only in their degree of intractability.

I shall try to show that along both dimensions the concept of probability is best taken as univocal, as always *meaning* the same. Nevertheless our grounds for using it and for evaluating probabilities in different degrees are very different in different contexts. I own to having been strongly influenced in this opinion by the writings of de Finetti (1964) and Mellor (1974). I take it that the univocal meaning of a probability qualification of an assertion, whether qualitative or quantitative, is the expression of a certain degree of belief in 'something'. I take the traditional 'theories' of probability to be descriptions of different kinds of grounds for the relative strengths of beliefs, each of which has its own proper context of application.

Carnap's original suggestion leads straight to a dual ontology. Statistics is a technique for describing events or ensembles of events, and confirmation theory, the technical approach to epistemology, is a way of talking about propositions or clusters of propositions. But if the univocal meaning of probability qualifications is an expression of degree of belief is there some one category of beings about which our beliefs are thus qualified? I believe that there is. I believe our probabilistically qualified beliefs are about whether a forthcoming (expected) *event* will be of one *kind* or another. Will the outcome of this horse-race be of the Red-Rum-winning kind? Will the outcome of work directed towards testing this hypothesis or theory be of the turning-out-to-be-true kind? Red Rum could lose, and the theory could turn out to be false. So, as long as these are deemed possible, there is a role for probabilified beliefs about the alternatives. Probability could be thought of as a second-order modality imposed on modally qualified contexts of the first order.

Some people may want to say that what is probable is that the hypothesis *is* true. And that it is true or false (plausible or implausible) before anyone has investigated it, if it is not built around a time indexical. If one believes that what is true is always true, then the retrospective truth follows immediately from the turning-out-true of the belief. It was true all along. Indeed some have made out cases for even temporally indexical propositions being true all along. Even though the two beliefs are different that difference in the end seems to make no practical difference. Yet it is a difference in ontology. In the same way few seem to have bothered with the difference between 'Gold is yellow is necessarily true', and 'Gold is necessarily yellow is true' even though in the former the modal adverb qualifies a statement about a proposition and in the latter it qualifies a statement about a metal.

Adopting a uniformitarian ontology permits a tidy treatment of the quantitative concept of probability as a derivative from betting odds. According to de Finetti a person must show their degree of belief in some action before it can be taken seriously. The action most clearly indicative of degree of belief is the acceptance of odds. And via the simple formula that transforms betting quotients into probabilities a numerical value for degree of belief is easily obtained. But how should a rational person assess the odds on some expected event turning out to belong to this or that type? Take into account whatever objective evidence can be found. In this way I open up the topic of the ways we might ground our beliefs. The groundings can be ordered in respect of the depth of knowledge of the system producing the events in question, be it a physical device like a roulette wheel or a knowledge-garnering technique like experimenting on samples. Will it turn out to land on the red? Will it turn out to be methylethylsulphonate (a rather nasty mutagen)?

The minimal grounding condition would be that in which I know what the alternatives are likely to be (heads or tails? boy or girl? true or false?) but that is all. By adopting the only principle I can clutch at in this case – that what is equally possible is equally probable, for instance alternatives which are determinables under the same determinable, and various other assumptions that at most one alternative will occur and that that is all the alternatives there are – I can assess a probability at level 1.

But, if I go on to collect statistics of how the operation of this system turns out time after time, those first naïve assessments will surely be modified. I believed that there were only two sexes, but as I collect statistics my first naïve idea of the odds on any next birth being a boy will be modified (level 2).

However, a few days in Reno hanging about Harold's Club and other such venues on Virginia Street are likely to draw one's attention away from the statistics to the construction of the event-producing system. In Reno the roulette wheels have two green slots and a zero and double zero. Yet the odds offered on 'Rouge ou noir' are the familiar evens. One does not need to be Laplace to decide to refrain from playing. There is a mapping relation between the structural properties of the wheel and the structure of the long-run event sequence. Only the latter is available at the previous level. When we know about the system of X and Y chromosomes the fact that more boys than girls are conceived needs some further explanation. So knowledge at levels 2 and 3 can interact, each critically assessing the other. To use level 3 knowledge involves some of the same assumptions that were needed at level 1. That is we need to assume that the apparently equipossible slots are equi-probable. Fair gambling is possible only *ceteris paribus*, and the use of magnetic devices to alter the probabilities of the apparently equipossible outcomes is looked on with disfavour. Kneale pushed this argument through to its end by setting up his range theory of probability on the basis of ultimate subclasses of kinds, numerical disparities being dealt with by the decomposition of qualitative kinds into quantitatively identical sets.

This brief analysis has ordered our knowledge of the set-up in which statistical descriptions are required in such a way that each level represents a classical probability theory. By treating the classical theories as theories of groundings for probability judgements rather than as analyses of those judgements, one can accommodate all three classical theories within the same framework, a framework which is based on the original intuitions of Laplace. In the next section I want to apply this treatment to probability as a substantive concept in scientific discourse.

Probabilities in the sciences of the three realms

The proto-scientific discourse of Realm 1 is shot through with probabilistic qualifications. The positivistic restriction of the subject matter of science to the deliverances of sense is just the restriction of science to an account of Realm 1. It is not surprising, then, to find that in von Mises's (1939) treatment within the framework of empiricism probability is identified with the relative frequency of a subclass of events within a reference class. The step to identifying the meaning of a probability with a relative frequency is accomplished through the positivistic meaning theory that generally identifies the meaning of a judgement with the grounds for it. Deleting the verificationist theory of meaning from the favoured philosophy of science allows me to treat the frequency theory as an account of the only objective grounds for probability assessments, taken as expressions of degrees of belief, that would be open to an investigator who was, for whatever reason, practical or metaphysical, confined to the beings of Realm 1.

The more sophisticated way of theorizing, which is based on tentative and controlled reference to beings that are of such a natural-kind that technical advances might make them perceptible, opens up a science of Realm 2. Our rational expectations of how things are going to turn out, particularly when we are following a patterned sequence of like events, were strengthened by knowledge of the structure of the mechanisms which produced them. For many cases this knowledge is provided by Realm 2 theorizing. The microscopic observation of the sexual dimorphism of human genetic material grounds the statistics of births (roughly) in the mechanism of meiosis. At one time this mechanism was a Realm 2 referent, happily made available to the human eye through technical advances in staining and microscopy. The structure of the mechanism is reproduced in the structure of the event sequence that mechanism produces. There are some fascinating philosophical problems that arise in this matter. One and the same roulette wheel, used over and over again, produces the statistically patterned sets of events that are the subject matter of the probability assessments grounded in the structure of *that* mechanism. But the birth statistics of human babies are the result of the operation of many distinct individual realizations of the same pattern of mechanism. I pass these problems by for another occasion. We can connect this analysis to Popper's (1967) 'propensity' story. In the circumstances outlined, when there is a structural isomorphism between the generator and the pattern of the event sequence we can say that the generator, in that physical environment, has a propensity to produce that kind of event sequence. Probability assessments are made, in this context, on the joint basis of statistics of events and the structures of their generators, *ceteris paribus*. Hypotheses about those structures, provided they are within the range of the Realm 2 ontology, are, in principle, testable and fit in nicely with policy realism, calling as they would for an exploration of nature to verify the claims about structure.

It would seem natural to try to extend this account to discourse about statistical regularities grounded in Realm 3 generators. But the really interesting case, quantum mechanics, raises severe difficulties for this rather domestic account of the probability concept. The issue is only too simple to state. A system, prepared on each occasion in an identical initial state, so far as we can tell, issues in different events, for example the location of electron strikes on a detector. This 'dispersion' is systematic and mathematically calculable. The statistical form of this dispersion is surprising, since the observable patterns of those dispersions approximate those of advancing wavefronts. If the traditional methodology of science were to be workable for these phenomena, a model of the real mechanism, that is a hypothetical generative mechanism, would be thought up, based on some suitable source analogue, guaranteeing the robustness of the natural-kinds invoked in the model, and their comparability with real-world things and processes. It would be so constructed that its behaviour would be analogous to the real-world mechanisms, the details of whose properties we would then be in a position to seek. Something like Popper's propensity theory could be invoked, or the more transparent structural isomorphism methodological principle, to tie the structure of the generator to that of the produced sequence of events. But after seventy years the best we can do is ascribe affordances, defined in terms of the observable frequencies, via the standard interpretation of the wave function, to the glub.

I want to conclude this work by taking this discussion one step further. The barrier to the use of the standard method of science is not only the inaccessibility of the deeper structures or their unobservability in principle, issues addressed in part five. The story of hidden variable theories in quantum mechanics has involved mathematical as well as ontological and epistemological arguments. It is not just that Bohrian philosophy of science leaves us only the affordances of an undifferentiated ur-stuff to play around with. There has been a sequence of attempts to show that no mathematical formulation of an HVT (hidden variable theory) that accommodated the existing quantum mechanics, admired on (almost) all hands, was possible. The arguments around these attempts have been instructive because they have brought out more and more clearly certain hidden assumptions in the physics which spawned them. I want, very briefly, to describe the recent work of Pitowski (1982, 1984). So far as I can follow his treatment, Pitowski has shown that there is a mathematical model which will reproduce one fragment of the troublesome statistics of quantum mechanically described systems. In Pitowski's analysis the physical system, a spherical electron, has all its properties at all times. But probabilities are contextual (cf. Shimony 1985), that is depend on methods of measurement. Taken together, the methods of measurement and the properties of the imagined 'electron', are mathematically adequate to reproduce the spin statistics. (I owe such tenuous grasp as I have of this matter to Michael Redhead and Jeffrey Bub, both of whose lectures on this topic have been models of expository clarity.)

Contextuality strikes me as a mathematical version of Bohr's basic idea, that variables (and *a fortiori* their values) could exist only in contexts defined by the nature of the physical system built by a physicist, or some natural system which interacted with the glub in a similar fashion. On this view, probabilities are contextual, that is related to some method of measurement. Pitowski bases his analysis on a spherical electron model. He shows that a property with the 'logic' of 'spin' can be distributed over the surface of the sphere so that, relative to different ways of counting, the peculiar probabilistic rules for 'spin' are reproduced. Essentially he proves a theorem to show that there exists a decomposition of the surface of a unit sphere $S(2)$, into two sets A^+ and A^-, such that

1 $w \in A^+$ if and only if not-$w \in A^-$
2 For all $z \in S(2)$ and all $\theta < \pi$ $P_{z\theta}(A \cap C_{z\theta}) = \cos^2\theta/2$ if $z \in A$ and $-\sin^2\theta/2$ if z not $\in A$.

By integrating over the surface according to one rule one gets a certain answer, and by integrating according to the complementary rule one gets a different answer. These are the contexually distinct values of the observable 'spin'.

This result seems to show, admittedly for a rather special case, that a mathematically acceptable HVT can be constructed. But as Bub has pointed out (personal communication), this is not enough to recommend it. It does not look very physically plausible. The theoretical 'picture' of how an electron 'looks', so to speak, seems unlikely to be right.

There are two questions whose answers are germane to the propriety of extending policy realism to theories which seem to denote beings of Realm 3, and with the 'degree of belief/objective grounding' account of probability.

1 Are HVTs logically possible?
2 Is any actual HVT physically plausible?

Pitowski's success in constructing an HVT for spin shows that while the answer to question 1 is a qualified 'Yes' so far the answer to question 2 remains 'No'. But the simple negative answer hides a complex issue. Physical plausibility is, as has been demonstrated for Realm 2 theorizing, actually a matter of metaphysical plausibility, since it refers back finally to the metaphysical foundations of the source analogues that control the evolution of theory-families. The situation is the same for Realm 3 theorizing. This was evident in the case of quantum field theory, where the implicit adherence to corpuscularianism dominated the way theories were interpreted as guides to experimenters, that is in a policy-realist way. . But adherence to this or that metaphysical foundation is influenced by work such as that of Pitowski. The negative answer to question 2 apropos Pitowski's model, if based on the physical implausibility of the electron model, stands only in so far as the metaphysical foundation remains stable. (Incidentally the same argument could be constructed for caution in dismissing HVTs on the grounds of non-locality assumptions or the invocation of supraluminal influences.) Here we have an interesting case of the kind of issue Redhead has remarked on as one of the charms of the philosophy of physics and one of the important reasons for studying it. The answer to a philosophical question about the proper uses of the concept of probability seems to be intimately bound up with an issue in physics. Should probability talk, forced on us by the statistical character of experimental results, be grounded in a deep structural hypothesis about the nature of certain causal mechanisms? Or must we rest content with real propensities, assigning tendencies to those combinations of apparatus and ur-stuff that we find in the laboratories of physicists? Pitowski's result, whatever its ultimate fate, has contributed to the ways in which we can answer these questions. His work seems to be a pretty conclusive demonstration that it is not the threat of a demonstrable and absolute mathematical incoherence that lies in the path of grounding quantum mechanical probabilities, but a subtle combination of metaphysics and physical theory. But science, as I have tried to show, is realist just because in that blend of mathematical ingenuity, metaphysical assumptions and material practices is its very nature.

Notes

Part One   Locating realism

1 My rejection of logic as an exclusive resource for philosophical analysis of cognitive practices is not meant to lead to a rejection of logic as a heuristic tool. But the most tantalizing issue that comes up when logical essentialism is criticized is whether there are any structural principles of scientific discourse, drawn from that resource, that must be retained. It would seem that at least the principle of non-contradiction ought to be embedded in any discourse whatever. The ground for this intuition ought to be more deeply lying than just the customary practices of scientific debate. For instance the formal commonplace that from a contradictory premise any conclusion whatever can be drawn seems to tie the ban on contradiction to the conditions for the very intelligibility of science.

However, the matter is not so simple. It is worth remarking that formal contradictions do not always disappear from a scientific discourse once they have been identified. Rather specific contradictions are embedded in larger conceptual structures in which they are remedied. For example, unlike the transformations of the formally contradictory Newtonian physics of Newton himself, first clearly revealed in Maclaurin's paradox, which led to several alternative non-contradictory discourses, the wave–particle dualism is merely remedied by proposals like the vacuum oscillator plenum. The discourse still retains, at different locations, statements to the effect that subatomic particles are particulate and that 'they' are spread out through space. The aim of the remedy is, of course, to provide a common ontology in terms of which the physical phenomena which are describable in the overtly contradictory statements are presented as contextually distinct manifestations of one and only one underlying kind of state. And so it remains conceivable that the remedy should remain forever conjectural.

There are other kinds of remedies. As I shall argue in chapter 6, contradictory predications to an individual subject can be remedied by the twin devices of temporal and spatial interval. The fact that the contradiction is remedied rather than removed is obscured by the fact that a tensed verb, say 'was', involves both the tenseless 'is' of predication and a time relation. To say something was hot and is cold involves the contradictory predications 'is hot' and 'is cold' which are remedied by combining them with distinctive time relations to the temporal present. This amounts too to a contextualist solution.

Chapter 1   Science as a communal practice

1 An interesting proposal of this sort is Mario Bunge's way of treating 'classical' and 'romantic' causation concepts as species of a generic concept of determination cf. his *Causality*, 1959.

Chapter 3   Realism revised

1 I am well aware how schematic is this exposition of the uses of the ordinary language words 'true' and 'false' and the implications this treatment has for the rest of the alethic vocabulary of everyday discourse. A great deal more detailed analysis and supplementary argument would be needed to sustain it fully. All I intend to show is that there is a defensible distinction between the idea of the truth of everyday as a defeasible pragmatic consensus, and the rigid relation of words and world that is implicit in the concepts of truth and falsity that figure in the bivalence formulation of scientific realism. It is my contention that the colloquial uses of 'true', 'false', etc. express relations of consensus between the makers of discourses and of trust between them as persons. I shall often use 'true' and 'false' in just this way.

Chapter 6 Referential grids

1 The most economical explanation of the epistemological priority of 'now' is that past and present events do not exist. If 'being present' and 'existing' are not just coextensive but cointensional expression, 'now' is not only epistemologically but ontologically basic. It is both the indexical of contemporaneity and of being. So the B-theorist's claim that all events are timelessly real is not just question-begging but self-contradictory. If the block theorist tries to remedy the 'up-front' contradiction by claiming that only some real events exist, that is those that happen to occur now, we need an account of how a non-existent event can be real. Citation of tensed predications is not available to the B-theorist. I owe to Malcom Musa the further objection that if each 'now' is tied to a psychological event of event/awareness we would need a further account of how, from the timeless sequence of psychological events, the successive psychological presents were picked out as 'nows'. This seems to land the B-theorist, who has a psychological account of the present in terms of consciousness, in a vicious regress. Furthermore, the co-occurrence of my awareness of public event and your awareness of 'it' must be problematic for the B-theorist, since there is no place for meta-awareness to provide a simultaneity class for moments of our mental lives taken together. In short B-theorists must accept some form of pre-established harmony.

2 In brief summary the situation seems to be as follows. Time discourse: indexical statements form an epistemological conjunction, but an ontological disjunction. No block universe is conceivable.

Spatial discourse: indexical statements form an epistemological disjunction, but an ontological conjunction. In short we can infer that there is a contemporaneous state of the whole universe, though we can never know what that state is.

If world lines are histories and not spatio-temporal trajectories, the theorem that there is no unique hypersurface orthogonal to all world lines expresses an epistemic fact, and this is perfectly consonant with the conclusions laid out in Figure 6.3.

Grunbaum claims somewhere that there is no representation of 'now' in physics, but this is clearly mistaken. It falls to the simplest 'dead pan' argument. The mass of the universe in general relativity is the 'now' mass of its contemporaneous parts, not the totality of the masses of its successive parts. One can make the same kind of point in terms of the concept of change. The properties of substances change not the substances. At any moment there is the same old substance differently distributed (to a crude approximation).

Chapter 12   The reasonableness of policy realism

1 The case against logical essentialism should not be overstated. The rejection of that doctrine as a methodology for philosophy does not entail the equally extravagant thesis that there are no logical constraints on thought. As I have argued, the principle of non-contradiction must have a special place in the construction of scientific discourses. This is not just because failure to observe it is fatal in scientific controversy, but also because a discourse in which overt contradictions are not remedied is weakened. But as Waismann has argued (1968) the weakness is not simply a matter of failing to conform to some deep ontological principle–that forbids a natural *being* both to have and not have a certain determinate property at the same time, and there are cases where that is just what we do want to say. But a *discourse* in which that kind of talk is not remedied is at odds with the usual way in which the grammar of descriptive predicates operates. We do not know how to understand it.

Chapter 14   Deeper into Realm 3: quantum field theory

1 The problem for a philosopher is at bottom how to understand the motivation for a certain kind of talk: photonic talk. The conditions for the mathematical forms of description typical of the physical sciences do not always fully determine how every aspect of a mathematical formalism is to be taken. A parallel example to the problem of understanding how the photon propagator comes to take that title, with all it implies for the origins of photonic talk in QFT, is Maxwell's 'displacement current' (cf. Whittaker, 1951). There was a feature of his mathematical

description which did not have a direct interpretation within the framework of the existing conceptual structure, tied in as that was to the phenomena of electro-magnetism. But by applying the ether *models* the displacement current interpretation falls out. Something similar is going on in QFT. I have called this 'parsing the amplitude'. I shall try to show that the real force of Feynman diagrams lies in their being iconic devices for that act of parsing.

2 A defence of a shadowy reality for IVPs as phenomenal 'would be's' is attractive– the counterfactual might be explicated through an ontology based on vacuum physics. Dispositions, in general, can be grounded in some state, structure or condition of the substance to which they are ascribed. Photons can be treated as non-fundamental beings when they are taken as elementary quanta of excitation of the oscillator plenum of which the ground state is the vacuum. In the vacuum state only the average energy of the plenum is zero. Has the oscillator plenum any claim to be a representational model of reality? Can both 'real' and 'virtual' photons be interpreted within a common ontology based on the idea of the oscillator plenum? The metaphysics of the oscillator story is tricky, since the oscillators so invoked are mathematical abstractions of 'something else' (cf. Aitchison, 1985, 335–6).

Nevertheless the idea deserves exploration. The Lamb shift can be described in photonic talk, in terms of the emission and reabsorption of a virtual photon. It can also be thought of as the effect of an interaction between an electron and a random fluctuation in the vacuum field. Perhaps virtual photon talk is a photonic way of describing fluctuations in the vacuum field, while real photon talk describes the behaviour of quanta when the average energy is non-zero. Approached in this way the apparently naïve claim 'Virtual particles might be real' is a photonic way of claiming that the dispositions (affordances) of the basic stuff (the glub) can be notionally grounded in the oscillator picture. Since oscillator talk is also meta-phorical the oscillator plenum is another icon, a Cartwright model of the glub.

3 In the reasoning that leads to a policy-realist interpretation of the W-particle there are two analogies. The photonic concept is first legitimated in the electro-magnetic case through its traditional application to luminiferous phenomena (in Bohr's sense). Its success through explanatory power in 'parsing the amplitude' justifies the concept of the 'virtual' species. The whole scheme is applied by analogy to the weak interaction. But the analogy between real and virtual species is reversed. It is the concept of the virtual species that is legitimated via explana-tory power in the tidy accounting of the weak interaction, and the search for the real species is dependent on an analogy in which the virtual species is the source, and the real species the subject.

4 For a very clear account of the inner 'logic' of renormalization see P. Teller (1987).

Chapter 15 Dispositions and their groundings

1 I have taken for granted, and for the sake of argument, that there is a prior presumption in favour of a generally Machian treatment of the mechanical parameters. Harvey Brown has drawn my attention to an excellent discussion of

the scientific viability of a generally Machian approach by L. Sklar (1963, particularly pp. 216–21). Sklar considers five basic tenets of Machian mechanics and checks out each against contemporary views, particularly general relativity. His conclusion is temperate. While on no one issue is a Machian approach totally discredited the present weight of evidence must tell against that kind of cosmic holism. It seems to me that there is just sufficient toehold to make the Machian position still worth defending in a general way. (Cf. also P. Teller, 1986.)

Chapter 17   Modality in scientific discourses

1 This distinction could be greatly elaborated. Taken *de re*, as applied to things, it marks the contrast between the dispositions of beings of such a nature that, whatever the circumstances, these dispositions are manifested in only one way; and dispositions whose groundigns in natures are such that in one set of circumstances the beings which have them behave in one way, and in another set behave in another. This is a real difference between natures. Taking the distinction *de dicto*, or conceptually, the two modalities differ in the range of contextually permitted predicates that are available for discourses about beings of this or that kind. These structures should match neatly. Natural necessity and natural possibility thus become the empirical grounds for claims of conceptual necessity and possibility.

References

Adams, R. M. 1974 'Theories of actuality'. *Nous*, 8, 211–31.

Angel, R. B. 1980 *Relativity: the theory and its philosophy*. Oxford: Pergamon.

Aitchison, I. J. R. 1985 'Nothing's plenty: the vacuum in modern quantum theory'. *Contemporary physics*, 26, 333–91.

Aitchison, I. J. R. and Huy, A. J. C. 1982 *Gauge theories in particle physics*. Bristol: Adam Hilger, 29, 171 ff.

Annis, D. 1982 'Epistemology naturalized'. *Metaphilosophy*, 5, 205 ff.

Armstrong, D. M. 1983 *What is a law of nature?* Cambridge: Cambridge University Press.

Aronson, J. R. 1982 'Untangling ontology from epistemology in causation'. *Erkenntnis*, 18, 293–305.

Aronson, J. R. 1984 *A realist philosophy of science*. London: Macmillan.

Austin, J. L. 1961 'How to talk – some simple ways'. In *Philosophical papers*. Oxford: Clarendon Press. Chapter 8.

Austin, J. L. 1962 *Sense and sensibilia*. Oxford: Clarendon Press.

Baker, G. P. and Hacker, P. M. S. 1983 'The concept of truth-condition'. *Conceptus*, 17, 11–18.

Baker, J. 1985 'An analysis of the concept of "trust"'. Paper read at the International University Centre, Dubrovnik.

Barnes, S. B. 1977 *Interest and the growth of knowledge*. London: Routledge and Kegan Paul.

Ben-Zeev, A. 1981 'J. J. Gibson and the ecological approach to perception'. *Studies in history and philosophy of science*, 12, 107–39.

Ben-Zeev, A. 1984 'The Kantian revolution in perception'. *Journal for the theory of social behaviour*, 14, 69–84.

Bhaskar, R. 1978 *A realist theory of science*. 2nd edn. Brighton: Harvester.

Bieri, P., Horstmann, R. P. and Kruger, C. 1979 *Transcendental arguments in science*. Dordrecht: Reidel.

Black, M. 1949 *Language and philosophy*. Ithaca, NY: Cornell University Press.

Black, M. 1962 *Models and metaphors*. Ithaca, NY: Cornell University Press, 25–47.

Bloor, D. 1976 *Knowledge and social imagery*. London: Routledge and Kegan Paul.

Bohm, D. 1980 *Wholeness and the implicate order*. London: Routledge and Kegan Paul.

Bohr, N. 1931–4 *Atomic theory and the description of nature*. Cambridge: Cambridge University Press.

Bohr, N. 1958 *Atomic physics and human knowledge*. New York: Wiley.

Bohr, N. 1963 *Essays (1958–1964) of atomic physics and human knowledge*. New York: Wiley.

Boscovich, R. J. 1763 *A theory of natural philosophy*. Venice. Boston, Mass.: MIT Press, 1966.

Bostock, D. 1978 'Problems of the theory of reference'. Paper read to the Philosophical Society, Oxford.

Boyd, R. 1979 'Metaphor and theory change: what is "metaphor" a metaphor for?' In A. Ortony (ed.), *Metaphor and thought*. Cambridge: Cambridge University Press, 365–408.

Bunge, M. 1959 *Causality*. Cambridge, Mass.: Harvard University Press.

Bunge, M. 1973 *Method, model and matter*. Dordrecht: Reidel.

Campbell, N. R. 1957 *The foundations of science*. New York: Dover. (Reprint of *Physics: the elements*, 1920.)

Carello, C., Turvey, M. T., Kugler, P. H. and Shaw, E. E. 1984 'Inadequacies of the computer metaphor'. In M. Gazzaniga (ed.), *Handbook of cognitive neuroscience*. New York: Plenum, 234–6.

Carnap, R, 1950 *Logical foundations of probability*. Chicago: Chicago University Press.

Cartwright, N. 1983 *How the laws of physics lie*. Oxford: Clarendon Press.

Chance, M. and Larsen, R. R. 1976 *The social structure of attention*. London: Wiley.

Charig, A. 1981 'Cladistics: a different point of view'. *Biologist*, 28, 19–20.

Clavius, C. 1602 *In sphaeram Ionnis de Sacro Bosco*. Lyon. 518–20.

Cohen, L. J. 1974 *Implications of induction*. London: Methuen.

Cohen, L. J. 1974 'Professor Hull and the evolution of science'. *British journal for the philosophy of science*, 25, 334–6.

Cohen, L. J. 1977 *The probable and the provable*. Oxford: Clarendon Press.

Cohen, L. J. 1985 'Third world epistemology'. In G. Currie and A. Musgrave (eds), *Popper and the human sciences*, Dordrecht: Reidel.

Collins, H. M. 1981 'Son of seven sexes: the social destruction of a physical phenomenon'. *Social studies of science*, 11, 33–62.

Costall, A. 1981 'How so much information can control so much behaviour'. In G. Butterworth (ed.), *Infancy and epistemology, Brighton: Harvester Press*.

Cutting, J. E. 1982 'Two ecological perspectives: Gibson *v.* Shaw and Turvey'. *American journal of psychology*, 95, 199–222.

Dodd, J. E. 1984 *The ideas of particle physics*. Cambridge: Cambridge University Press.

Donellan, K. 1966 'Reference and definite descriptions'. *Philosophical review*, 75, 281–304.

Dretske, F. I. 1977 'Laws of nature'. *Philosophy of science*, 44, 248–68.

Duhem, P. 1914 *The aim and structure of physical theory*. Paris: Rivière. Trans. P. P. Weiner. Princeton, NJ: Princeton University Press, 1954.

Dummett, M. A. 1978 *Truth and other enigmas*. London: Duckworth.

Einstein, A. 1948 'Quanten-mechanik und Wirklichkeit'. *Dialectica*, 2, 320–4.

Einstein, A., Podolsky, B. and Rosen, N. 1935 'Can quantum mechanical description of physical reality be considered complete?'. *Physical review*, 47, 777.

Ellis, B. 1979 *Rational belief systems*. Oxford: Blackwell. Further related papers forthcoming.

Ellis, B. 1982 'Lectures of truth and reality'. Delivered at Oxford.

Evans, G. 1982 *The varieties of reference*. Oxford: Oxford University Press.

Fales, E. 1979 'Relative essentialism'. *British journal for the philosophy of science*, 30, 349–70.

Feher, M. 1985 'The rise and fall of crucial experiments'. Paper read at the International University Centre, Dubrovnik.

Feyerabend, P. K. 1978 *Science in a free society*. London: New Left Books.

Feyerabend, P. K. 1984 'The Lessing effect in the philosophy of science'. *New ideas in psychology*, 2, 1–10.

Feynman, R. P., Leighton, R. B. and Sands, M. 1974 *The Feynman lectures on physics*. Reading, Mass.: Robert Benjamin.

Field, H. 1972 'Tarski's theory of truth'. *Journal of philosophy*, 69, 347–75.

Field, H. 1980 *Science without numbers*. Princeton, N. J: Princeton University Press.

Finetti, M. de 1964 'A personalist theory of probability'. In H. E. Smokler and H. F. Kyberg (eds), *Studies in subjective probability*. New York: Wiley.

Fleck, L. 1935 *Genesis and development of a scientific fact*. Trans. F. Bradley and T. J. Trenn. Chicago and London: Chicago University Press. Chapters 3 and 4.

Fodor, J. A. 1980 'Methodological solipsism'. *Behavioural and brain sciences*, 3, 63–109.

Fraasen, B. C. van 1980 *The scientific image*. Oxford: Clarendon Press.

Freeman, D. 1983 *Margaret Mead and Samoa*. Cambridge, Mass.: Harvard University Press.

Friedman, M. 1974 'Explanation and scientific understanding'. *Journal of philosophy*, 71, 5–14.

Gale, R. 1968 *The language of time*. London: Routledge and Kegan Paul.

Gergen, K. J. 1983 *Social knowledge as transformation*. New York: Springer-Verlag.

Gibson, J. J. 1964 *The senses considered as perceptual systems*. London: Allen and Unwin.

Gibson, J. J. 1979 *The ecological approach to visual perception*. Boston: Howard Miflin.

Gilbert, G. N. and Mulkay, N. 1982 'Warranting scientific beliefs'. *Social studies of science*, 12, 383–408.

Goffman, E. 1969 *The presentation of self in everyday life*. London: Penguin.

Goodman, N. 1954 *Fact, fiction and forecast*. London: Athlone Press. 73–80

Gregory, R. L. 1974 *Concepts and mechanisms of perception*. London: Duckworth.

Grene, M. 1983 'N dogmas of empiricism'. In R. S. Cohen and M. W. Wartofsky (eds), *Epistemology, methodology and the social sciences*. Dordrecht: Reidel, 89–106.

Grunbaum, A. 1964 'Time, irreversible process and the status of becoming'. In J. J. C. Smart (ed.), *Problems of space and time*. New York: Macmillan.

Hacking, I. 1983 *Representing and intervening*. Cambridge University Press.

Hallam, A. 1973 *A revolution in the earth sciences*. Oxford: Clarendon Press.

Hanson, N. R. 1958 *Patterns of discovery*. Cambridge: Cambridge University Press.

Hanson, N. R. 1963 *The discovery of the positron*. Cambridge: Cambridge University Press.

Harré, R. 1961 *Theories and things*. London: Sheed and Ward.

Harré, R. 1983 *Personal being*. Oxford: Blackwell.

Harré, R. 1984 *Great scientific experiments*. Oxford: Oxford University Press.

Harré, R. and Madden, E. H. 1977 *Casual powers*. Oxford: Blackwell.

Harvey, W. 1649 *An anctoral disquisition on the circulation of the blood*. London.

Hempel, C. G. 1965 *Aspects of scientific explanation and other essays in the philosophy of science*. New York: Free Press.

Hennig, W. 1966 *Phylogenetic systematics*. Chicago and London: University of Illinois Press.

Hesse, M. B. 1963 *Models and analogies in science*. London: Sheed and Ward.

Hesse, M. B. 1974 *The structure of scientific inference*. London: Macmillan. Chapter I, section III.

Hesse, M. B. 1980 *Revolutions and reconstructions in the philosophy of science*. Brighton: Harvester.

Hinckfuss, I, 1975 *The existence of space and time*. Oxford: Clarendon Press.

Hintikka, J. 1963 'The modes of modality'. Reprinted in M. J. Loux (ed.), *The possible and the actual*. Ithaca, NY, and London: Cornell University Press, 1979 70–7.

Hintikka, J. 1969 *Models for modalities*. Dordrecht: Reidel.

Holton, G. 1981 'Thematic presuppositions and the direction of scientific advance'. In A. Heath (ed.), *Scientific explanation*. Oxford: Oxford University Press.

Honner, J. 1986 *Bohr's transcendental philosophy*. Oxford: Clarendon Press.

Hull, D. 1974 'Are the "members" of a biological species similar to one another?' *British journal for the philosophy of science*, 25, 332–4.

Hull, D. 1984 'Units of evolution'. In R. N. Brandon and R. M. Burian (eds), *Genes, organisms, populations*. Cambridge, Mass., and London: MIT Press, chapter 10.

Hume, D. 1739 *A treatise of human nature*. London. Book I, parts II and III.

Kant, I. 1781 *Critique of pure reason*. Riga.

Katz, J. J. 1979 'The neo-classical theory of reference'. In P. A. French, T. E. Uehling and H. K. Wettstein (eds), *Contemporary perspectives in the philosophy of language*. Minneapolis: University of Minnesota Press.

Kelly, J. 1984 *Non-propositional justification*. Forthcoming.

Kemp, T. S. 1986 'Models of diversity and phylogenetic reconstruction'. *Oxford surveys in biology*. Oxford: Oxford University Press.

Kekes, J. 1985 'The fate of the enlightenment program'. *Inquiry*, 28, 388–98.

Klein, P. D. 1981 *Certainty: a refutation of scepticism*. Minneapolis: Minnesota University Press.

Kneale, W. 1949 *Probability and induction*. Oxford: Clarendon Press.

Knorr-Cetina, K. 1981 *The manufacture of knowledge*. Oxford: Pergamon Press.

Korner, S. 1974 *Categorial frameworks*. Oxford: Blackwell.

Koyré, A. 1967 *Metaphysics and measurement*. London: Chapman and Hall, 13.

Kripke, S. A. 1963 'Semantical analysis of modal logic I'. *Zeitschrift für mathematische Logik und Grundlagen der Mathematik*, 9, 67–93.

Kripke, S. A. 1980 *Naming and necessity*. Oxford: Blackwell. 122–39.

Kuhn, T. S. 1962 *The stucture of scientific revolutions*. Chicago: Chicago University Press.

Lakatos, I. 1970 'Falsification and the methodology of scientific research programmes'. In I. Lakatos and A. Musgrave (eds), *Criticism and the growth of knowledge*. Cambridge: Cambridge University Press.

Latour, B. and Woolgar, S. 1979 *Laboratory life*. Los Angeles: Sage.

Laudan, L. 1977 *Progress and its problems*. Berkeley: University of California Press.

Leibniz, G. 1717 *The Leibniz—Clarke correspondence*. Ed. H. G. Alexander. Manchester: Manchester University Press, 1956.

Lejewski, C. 1954 'Logic and existence'. *British journal for the philosophy of science*, 5, 104–19.

Lenin, V. I. 1908 *Materialism and empirio-criticism*. Moscow: Progress Publishers, 1970.

Leplin, J. 1979 'Reference and scientific realism'. *Studies in history and philosophy of science*, 10, 265–84.

Lewis, D. 1973 *Counterfactuals*. Cambridge, Mass.: Harvard University Press.

Linsky, L. 1971 *Reference and modality*. Oxford: Clarendon Press.

Lipton, P. 1985 *Explanation and evidence*. Oxford: Doctoral dissertation.

Loux, M. J. (ed.) 1979 *The possible and the actual*. Ithaca, NY, and London: Cornell University Press. Introduction.

Lucas, J. R. 1973 *A treatise on time and space*. London: Methuen. 202–3.

Lucas, J. R. 1974 *The concept of probability*. Oxford: Clarendon Press.

Luntley, M. 1982 'Verification, perception and theoretical entities'. *The philosophical quarterly*, 32, 245–61.

Luntley, M. 1986 *Language, logic and experience*. London: Duckworth.

McMullin, E. 1979 'Laudan's progress and its problems'. *Philosophy of science*, 46, 623–44.

Mach, E. 1893 *The science of machanics*. New edition. La Salle, Ill.: Open Court, 1961.

Manicus, P. T. and Rosenberg, A. 1985 'Naturalism, epistemological individualism and the "strong programme" in the theory of knowledge'. *Journal for the theory of social behaviour*, 15, 78–101.

Mannheim, K. 1960 *Ideology and utopia*. London: Routledge and Kegan Paul.

Martin, B. 1981 'Phylogenetic reconstruction versus classification: the case for clear demarcation'. *Biologist*, 28, 127–32.

Martin Soskice, J. 1985 *Metaphor and religious language*. Oxford: Clarendon Press. Chapter 2 and 6.

Maull, N. L. 1978 'Cartesian optics and the geometrization of nature'. *Review of metaphysics*, 32, 253–73.

Maxwell, J. C. 1890 *The scientific papers of J. C. Maxwell*. Ed. W. D. Niven. Cambridge: Cambridge University Press.

Maxwell, N. 1984 *From knowledge to wisdom*. Oxford: Blackwell.

Maxwell, N. 1986 'The fate of the enlightenment: reply to Kerkes'. *Inquiry*, forthcoming.

Mellor, D. H. 1977 'Natural kinds'. *British journal for the philosophy of science*, 28, 299–312.

Mellor, D. H. 1978 *The matter of chance*. Cambridge: Cambridge University Press.

Meyerson, E. 1930 *Identity and reality*. London: Allen and Unwin.

Michaels, C. F. and Carello, C. 1981 *Direct perception*. Englewood Cliffs: Prentice-Hall.

Miller, A. I. 1984 *Imagery in scientific thought*. Boston, Mass.: Birkhauser. Chapter 4 and 6

Miller, D. 1985 'A critique of good reasons'. In C. Wade Savage and Mary Lou Maxwell (eds), *Science, mind and psychology*. Dordrecht: Reidel.

Misak, C. 1986 'Peirce, Levi and the aims of inquiry'. Paper presented at the philosophy of science section, the International University Centre, Dubrovnik.

Mises, R. von 1939 *Probability, statistics and truth*. London: Hodge.

Moked, G. 1971 'A note on Berkeley's corpuscularian theories in *Siris*'. *Studies in history and philosophy of science*, 2, 257–71.

Musgrave, A. 1983. 'Constructive empiricism and the theory–observation dichotomy'. *Proceedings of the 7th international congress of logic, methodology and philosophy of science*, section 13.

Nagel, E. 1961 *The structure of science*. London: Routledge and Kegan Paul.

Nerlich, G. C. 1976 *The shape of space*. Cambridge: Cambridge University Press.

Newton-Smith, W. 1981a *The rationality of science*. London: Routledge and Kegan Paul.

Newton-Smith, W. 1981b 'In defence of truth'. In R. Harré and U. J. Jensen (eds), *The philosophy of evolution*. Brighton: Harvester Press.

Norris, S. P. 1981 'A concept of observation statements'. *Philosophy of education*, 12, 132–42.

Norris, S. P. 1982 'A speech-act conception of observation statements'. In J. Clarke and R. King (eds), *Papers from the 6th annual meeting of the Atlantic Provinces Linguistic Association*. St Johns, Newfoundland: Memorial University.

Overington, M. 1979 'Doing the what comes rationally: some developments in metatheory'. *The American sociologist*, 14, 2–12.

Pais, A. 1982 '*Subtle is the Lord . . .*' Oxford: Oxford University Press.

Papineau, D. 1977 'The *vis viva* controversy: do meanings matter?' *Studies in history and philosophy of science*, 6, 111–42.

Patterson, C. 1980 'Cladistics'. *Biologist*, 27, 234–40.

Peirce, C. S. 1931–66 *Collected papers*. Ed. C. Harteshorn and P. Weiss. Cambridge, Mass.; Harvard University Press, vols 1–8.

Pickering, A. 1981 'Constraints and controversy: the case of the magnetic monopole'. *Social studies of science*, 11, 63–93.

Pitowski, I 1982 'A resolution of the EPR and Bell paradoxes'. *Physical review letter*, 48, 1299.

Pitowski, I 1984 'A deterministic model of spin statistics'. *Physical review*, 27, 2316.

Polanyi, M. 1962 *Personal knowledge: towards a post-critical philosophy*. London: Routledge and Kegan Paul.

Popper, K. R. 1957 'Propensities, probabilities and the quantum theory'. In S. Korner (ed.), *Observation and interpretation*. London: Butterworth.

Popper, K. R. 1959 *The logic of scientific discovery*. London: Hutchinson.

Popper, K. R. 1963 *Conjectures and refutations*. London: Routledge and Kegan Paul. Appendix 3.

Popper, K. R. 1972 *Objective knowledge*. Oxford: Clarendon Press. Chapter 9.

Putnam, H. 1975 *Mind, language and reality*. Cambridge: Cambridge University Press.

Putnam, H. 1978 *Mathematics, matter and method*. Cambridge: Cambridge University Press. 146, 358–61.

Quine, W. V. O. 1953 *From a logical point of view*. Cambridge, Mass.: Harvard University Press. Chapter 2, section 6.

Quine, W. V. O. 1969 *Ontological relativity and other essays*. New York: Columbia University Press. 82.

Ramsay, F. P. 1931 *The foundations of mathematics*. Ed. R. B. Braithwaite. London: Routledge and Kegan Paul. Chapter 6.

Redhead, M. 1975 'Symmetry and intertheory relations'. *Synthese*, 32, 77–112.

Reed, E. 1983 'Gibson's ecological approach to perception'. *Synthese*, 54, 85–94.

Reid, T. 1787 *An inquiry into the human mind*. T. Duggan (ed.), Chicago: University of Chicago Press (1970).

Rescher, N. 1973a *The coherence theory of truth*. Oxford: Clarendon Press.

Rescher, N. 1973b 'The ontology of the possible'. In M. K. Munitz (ed.), *Logic and ontology*. New York: New York University Press.

Richards, A. I. 1936 *The philosophy of rhetoric*. Oxford: Oxford University Press.

Roberts, L. 1985 *Synthese*, In press.

Roche, J. *An essay in critical physics: the intensity vectors of electromagnetism*. Forthcoming.

Rorty, R. 1980 *Philosophy and the mirror of nature*. Oxford: Blackwell.

Rousseau, G. S. and Porter, R. 1980 *The ferment of knowledge*. Cambridge: Cambridge University Press. Chapter 1.

Scheibe, E. 1981 'Invariance and covariance'. In J. Agassi and R. S. Cohen (eds), *Scientific philosophy today*. Dordrecht: Reidel. 311–31.

Schilpp, P. 1949–51 *Albert Einstein: philosopher-scientist*. New York: Adacemic Press.

Schlesinger, G. 1980 *Aspects of time*. Indianapolis: Hackett.

Schon, D. 1968 *Displacement of concepts*. London: Tavistock.

Searle, J. R. 1979 *Expression and meaning*. Cambridge: Cambridge University Press.

Sellars, W. 1968 *Science and metaphysics*. London: Routledge and Kegan Paul. Chapter 3, section 10.

Shimony, A. 1985 'Contextual hidden variable theory'. *British journal for the philosophy of science*, 35, 24–36.

Shotter, J. 1985 *Social accountability and selfhood*. Oxford: Blackwell.

Siegel, H. 1983 'Truth, problem solving and the rationality of science'. *Studies in history and philosophy of science*, 14, 89–112.

Sklar, L. 1974 *Space, time and spacetime*. Berkeley: California University Press.

Smart, J. J. C. 1963 *Philosophy and scientific realism*. London: Routledge and Kegan Paul.

Sneed, T. 1971 *The logical structure of mathematical physics*. Dordrecht: Reidel.

Stegmuller, W. 1979 *The structural view of theories*. Berlin and New York: Springer-Verlag, 27–8.

Stein, H. 1968 'On Einstein-Minkowski space-time'. *Journal of philosophy*, 65, 5–23.

Stone, M. and Stone, M. 1985 'Natural selection and naturalized epistemology'. *Proceedings of the Crichton Club of New York*, Fall.

Stove, D. 1982 *Popper and after: four moden irrationalists*. Oxford: Pergamon Press.

Strawson, P. F. 1950 'On referring'. *Mind*, 59, 320–44.

Strawson, P. F. 1956 'Truth'. In G. Pitcher (ed.), *Truth*. Englewood Cliffs, NJ: Prentice Hall, 1964.

Strawson, P. F. 1959 *Individuals*. London: Methuen.

Tayler, R. J. 1980 'The origin of the elements'. In G. Bath (ed.) *The state of the universe*. Oxford: Clarendon Press.

Teller, P. 1986 'Relational holism and quantum mechanics' *British journal for the philosophy of science*, 37, 71–81.

Teller, P. 1987 'Three problems of renormalization'. In H. R. Brown and R. Harré (eds), *Philosophical foundations of quantum field theory*, forthcoming.

Toulmin, S. E. 1959 *Philosophy of science*. London: Methuen.

Waismann, F. 1968 *How I see philosophy*. London: Macmillan. Chapter 5.

Walters, G. 1985 'Mach's attitude to relativity: a case of fraud?' Paper presented at the International University Centre, Dubrovnik.

Weingard, R. 1972 'Relativity and the reality of past and future events'. *British journal for the philosophy of science*, 23, 119–21.

Weisburd, S. 1985 'A fault of youth'. *Science news*, 127 (23), 363–5.

Weissman, D. 1978 'Dispositions as geometrico-structural properties'. *The review of metaphysics*, 32, 275–97.

Whewell, W. 1847 *The philosophy of the inductive sciences*. London. New York: Johnson, 1967. Book I.

Whittaker, E. 1951 *A history of theories of aether and electricity*. New York: Harper (1960). 250–1.

Wigner, E. P. 1967 *Symmetries and reflections*. Ed. W. J. Moore and M. Scriven. 2nd edn. Cambridge, Mass.: MIT Press, 1970.

Wonsor, M. P. 1976 *Starfish, jellyfish and the order of life*. New Haven: Yale University Press.

Worral, J. 1984 'An unreal image'. *British journal for the philosophy of science*, 35, 65–80.

Zahar, E. 1973 'Why did the research programme of Einstein replace that of Lorentz?' *British journal for the philosophy of science*, 24, 223–43.

Zahar, E. 1980 'Einstein, Meyerson and the role of mathematics in physical discovery'. *British journal for the philosophy of science*, 31, 1–44.

Zemach, E. M. 1976 'Putnam's theory on the reference of substantive terms'. *Journal of philosophy*, 73, 116–27.

Additional References

Agassi, J. 1985 'The cheapening of science'. *Inquiry*, 28, 166–71.

Deritt, M. 1984 *Realism and truth*. Oxford: Blackwell.

McMullin, E. 1974 'Models and analogies in science'. *New Catholic encyclopaedia*, 16 (suppl. vol.).

Margolis, J. 1986 *Pragmatism without foundations*. Oxford: Blackwell.

Naletor, I. 1984 *Alternatives to positivism*. Moscow: Progress Publishers.

Rescher, N. 1973 *The primacy of practice*. Oxford: Blackwell.

Sheldon, N. A. 1985 'One wave or three?' *British journal for the philosophy of science*, 36, 431–6.

Smith, P. 1981 *Realism and the progress of science*. Cambridge: Cambridge University Press.

Name Index

Subject Index